Praise for Put Your Money Where Your Soul Is

This book is a model example of how to think through the deepest problems of our time—it proceeds from a coherent ethical code to strong but plausible action, and it combines the necessary analytical calm with the even more necessary conviction that we are in a difficult place where much is demanded from those of us who can give it. A tour de force that will make a serious difference in the world!
Bill McKibben
Founder, 350.org and Third Act

This is a truly remarkable book. I recommend it as a must-read to people who would like to invest more ethically...This book is an intellectual delight. It offers a cornucopia of good ideas, institutions, and advisers. These can ease the transition for institutions and individuals from pure profit nature investing to deploying one's capital to repair the world, lift up the poor, and aid the needy and vulnerable. The sources alone—ranging from the Bible, Talmud, and codes to contemporary economics and sophisticated financial reporting—are worth the price of admission.
Rabbi Yitz Greenberg
Founding President, CLAL and author, *The Jewish Way*

A powerful argument grounded in Jewish sources for why our ethics and values must inform our financial and business decisions. A joy to read! Timely and provocative.
Moses Pava
Former Dean, Sy Syms School of Business
Alvin Einbender Professor of Business Ethics, Yeshiva University

As the CEO of a Jewish institution with over $700 million in investment capital, I highly recommend Put Your Money Where Your Soul Is. It is vital that we take the next step to align our investments with our values, and Rabbi Siegel has provided an invaluable resource to guide us in doing so. Rabbi Siegel guides us on a journey through Jewish texts and the modern investment arena, making Jewish wisdom accessible and relevant to our investment decisions. Whether you are an individual investor or chair of an investment committee, I hope you will pick up this book and seriously consider the implications it has for how we invest.
Beth Sirull
President and CEO, Jewish Community Foundation of San Diego

Faith-based investors were pioneers in using their investments as a way to hold the world's most powerful companies accountable for their impacts on our planet and on all people who live on earth. This book helps translate that message—that we must do justice, *tzedek*, with our money, not just give *tzedakah*—to Jewish audiences, both individuals and Jewish institutions trying to live out their most sacred values. Interwoven are models for action, the people and organizations whose stories of financial protest will inspire each one of us on our journeys to repair the world.
Rabbi Rachel Kahn-Troster
Executive Vice President, Interfaith Center on Corporate Responsibility

This significant book is both erudite and very readable—the perfect combination to convey the many important messages that the author is invoking. Rabbi Jacob Siegel mixes deep rabbinic scholarship, historical context, and extensive financial data, dissecting the issues surrounding endowments, asset management, corporate action, and personal investing, all while drawing on source material from ancient to modern times. He is a knowledgeable and helpful guide in applying our values while making investment choices, utilizing contemporary/real-world examples to bring the commentaries/approaches of our sages into modern applications. This book will prove invaluable to the Jewish impact investor seeking to understand the underpinnings of their investment philosophy, and it stands as a universal roadmap for anyone who is considering an ethical approach to investing.
Michael P. Lustig
Impact Investor, Adjunct Professor of Finance at NYU|Stern School of Business, and author of the Jewish Funders Network's "Greenbook: A Guide to Jewish Impact Investing"

This book is like the Hebrew Bible, rooted in Jewish wisdom but a vital text for all who care for this world and its people and all life on earth. It takes us on a journey into insights deep within the Hebrew Bible, but which have such immediate pertinence for the world of today. It shares teachings, stories, and lessons learned the hard way through the centuries but always told with a sense of fun, delight, or depth which is rare to find anywhere else.

This is a book of spiritual and practical wisdom for the modern perplexed, like the famous Guide by Maimonides in another time of financial, social, and political turmoil. If you want to know how to put your money where your soul is, this is the book and here is the Guide.
Martin Palmer
Founder and CEO, FaithInvest

This is a book for right now, rooted in Jewish values from historical antiquity and the great stories of the mythic past. In PUT YOUR MONEY WHERE YOUR SOUL IS, Rabbi Siegel shows us a new paradigm of being smart about money, wherein Judaism as "a religion of protest" guides us morally to counter "disaster capitalism" through impact investing. Whether we are seasoned investors or have never bought a single share, we all need to learn the lessons Rabbi Siegel teaches and work through the practical exercises he provides. Rabbi Siegel does what a rabbi should do: he makes the serious discussion of challenging topics both safe and accessible. He demonstrates compassion and inspires hope. Smoothly interweaving ancient ethical teaching with contemporary economic theory and relatable personal anecdotes, Rabbi Siegel is a trustworthy expert and an appealing storyteller. Invest in this book!
Rabbi Sharon Kleinbaum
Commissioner, United States Commission on International Religious Freedom
Rabbi, Congregation Beit Simchat Torah

In PUT YOUR MONEY WHERE YOUR SOUL IS, Rabbi Siegel masterfully interfaces Jewish texts with our responsibility to the larger world...a refreshing original thinker...an important, important read.
Rabbi Avi Weiss
Rabbi emeritus, Hebrew Institute of Riverdale and author, *Spiritual Activism*

Put Your Money Where Your Soul Is

Jewish Wisdom to Transform Your Investments for Good

Rabbi Jacob Siegel

Ben Yehuda Press
Teaneck, New Jersey

PUT YOUR MONEY WHERE YOUR SOUL IS ©2023 Jacob Siegel. All rights reserved. No part of this book may be used or reproduced in any manner whatsoever without written permission except in the case of brief quotations embodied in critical articles and reviews.

Published by Ben Yehuda Press
122 Ayers Court #1B
Teaneck, NJ 07666
BenYehudaPress.com

To subscribe to our monthly book club and support independent Jewish publishing, visit Patreon.com/BenYehudaPress

Ben Yehuda Press books may be purchased at a discount by synagogues, book clubs, and other institutions buying in bulk.
For information, please email markets@BenYehudaPress.com

ISBN13 978-1-953829-43-6

Parts of Chapter 4 were originally published in Tablet Magazine on February 3, 2022.

About the cover: Artwork is by Rabbi Linda Motzkin. The text reads *"bishvil shetit'asher,"* translated as "that you may become wealthy." The quote is from the Talmud, where the Sages teach that wealth comes from being generous with one's money to those in need.

Disclaimer: This book is for educational purposes only and is not to be construed as legal, tax, or investment advice.

23 24 25 / 10 9 8 7 6 5 4 3b   20240102

To Ruhi Sophia

Contents

Introduction 1

1. The Story of Impact Investing 7
2. Jewish Money Ethics 17
3. Financial Return 39
4. Institutional Capital and Social Change 59
5. Negative Screens and Stumbling Blocks 77

Asset Classes

6. Getting Started: Asset Classes and Investment Advisors 103
7. Public Equities 113
8. Debt: Free Loans and Shared Risk 135
9. Private Equity and Debt: Local Investing 155

Issue Areas

10. Changing Climates 171
11. Centering Racial Justice 193
12. Investing in Israel 215
13. Investing in Peacebuilding 223

Epilogue 233

Acknowledgments 235
Glossary of Jewish Terms 237
Glossary of Investing Terms 241
References 247
Notes 251
Index 289

Introduction

Inside Vatican City, past the Swiss Guard dressed in bright primary colors and to the left of the basilica, Pope Francis has convened a conference. It sounds like the start of a lengthy joke: a nun from the Philippines, a Hindu land activist from India, a Buddhist monk, an Inuit elder from Canada, and an Indigenous leader from Morocco all walk into a conference room and sit together around tables. Even those who in other contexts might be enemies, like a rabbi from Israel and a Muslim judge from Southern Lebanon, join together in dialogue.

But the punchline is serious, even dire. In 2015, the United Nations had released a set of ambitious goals, the Sustainable Development Goals, encompassing aspirations like an end to world hunger and poverty and a healthy relationship with the planet. Yet, by the Vatican conference four years later, the world seems headed on the opposite path. A speaker from one of the conference's environmental nonprofit partners confesses, "we have twelve years left to avert climate catastrophe, and I am terrified."

I joined the conference at the Vatican representing Jewish communal investment capital. Professionally, I served as rabbi at a Jewish socially responsible investing organization. I had spent years working directly with Jewish institutions and individuals to bring Jewish values into investment portfolios.

Faith groups are hidden powerhouses when it comes to sustainability, and this conference is the Catholic Church's way of organizing them together. Faith groups represent a majority of the world's population and are significant holders both of land and of pools of capital.[1] But beyond acres and investment dollars, faith groups bring a far more important, if less tangible, asset: traditions, practices, and beliefs, the raw spiritual resources to transform a system that is deeply in trouble.

Like fish swimming in water, when we are living and breathing a reality constantly, it is hard to imagine any possibility for change. Even the alternatives we generate are often just other ways of managing within our current system. But our current economic way of doing things is on a devastating trajectory.

Take economic suffering. According to Michael McAfee, president and CEO of the national research institute PolicyLink, one-third of all people in the United States live under 200 percent of the poverty line.[2] Even before the coronavirus pandemic, four in ten Americans didn't have $400 in their bank account to cover an unexpected necessary expenditure (like a medical bill).[3] According to the international nonprofit Oxfam, economic, gender, and racial inequality now contribute to the death of at least one person every four seconds.[4] Circumstances like these leave people desperate. As McAfee puts it, the current economy is no longer just a moral issue, but a national security issue that threatens our democracy.[5]

This economic suffering is not inevitable, and it comes hand-in-hand with rising inequality. Take investing, for example. While nearly half of Americans don't own any stock,[6] the wealthiest 10 percent own 84 percent of the entire market. The top one percent alone hold 38 percent of financial assets.[7]

Globally, the numbers are even more striking. A person with $1 million in net worth (a common retirement goal in the US) as of 2019 had made it not only into the global one percent, but into the top 0.3 percent. And by the way, those individuals control a whopping 40 percent of global financial assets.[8]

The status quo is devastating, unless one is wealthy, in which case things seem on the surface to be rosy. According to the Institute for Policy Studies, the pandemic failed to prevent a windfall of over $1.06 trillion for the country's billionaires, and in some cases even contributed to their increase in wealth.[9] High net worth families, with more than $1 million, saw their wealth double over the past 15 years.[10]

But the devastation extends to the natural world around us. Take climate change. Even those of us who thought of ourselves as privileged and safe are already feeling its impacts. On the West Coast of the United States, where I live, the wildfire season in 2020 gave the region the worst air quality in the world for a stretch of days, all in the midst of the COVID-19 pandemic. Three years later, in 2023, New York's air quality earned the same unfortunate distinction, with over 100 million people in the Northeast affected by wildfire smoke streaming in from Canada.[11] It is sometimes difficult to define precisely to what extent climate change is contributing to a catastrophic weather event, but the global consensus of climate scientists is clear. Human-induced climate change, mostly caused by extracting and burning fossil fuels, is causing wildfires, hurricanes, floods, heat waves, and other (formerly) 100-year weather events to occur with increasing frequency and damage.[12]

It is not just that our current economic practices are out of alignment with Jewish values. Our economy actively resists attempts to bring it more into alignment with those values.

For example, Judaism teaches that profit should not be the absolute motive in life, but rather may be sought in service of living a righteous life. Profit is not evil. In fact, Jewish tradition teaches that treating workers well leads over the long term to better and more sustainable financial performance. The CEO of Danone Corporation, which produces well-known brands like Dannon yogurt and Silk soymilk, steered the company in recent years to become a public benefit corporation, a new legal status that allows the corporation to do things like treat workers well even if it means a temporary drop in profits. But our economy focuses our attention on short-term gains, and nowhere is this truer than hedge funds.[13] In March of 2021, the CEO was ousted by two hedge funds disappointed in the company's financial performance.[14]

Jewish wisdom teaches that a socially responsible business is a more sustainable business. This position is increasingly stigmatized by a wave of pushback against "ESG investing" (which we will discuss in depth later). For example, Florida's governor managed to secure a rule directing the state pension fund to seek "the highest return on investment for beneficiaries, without consideration" for "social" concerns or anything else. Nearly two dozen state treasurers in the US are seeking similar measures, some extending to private investors as well.[15] And in early 2023, the US House and Senate both passed a bill (vetoed by the president)[16] seeking to overturn a Department of Labor rule that allowed pensions and other investors to consider environmental, social, and governance (ESG) factors if they thought those might be relevant to an investment's performance.[17] To be fair, state pension funds have a primary duty to steward their pensioners' assets responsibly over the long term—which is why pensions ought to consider issues that impact their portfolio companies' long-term sustainability. But a growing number of politicians feel threatened even by the idea that whether a business operates ethically and sustainably might affect its profits over the long term. Overall, these efforts represent a significant political win bolstering those who think that morality and values should have nothing to do with investment decisions.[18]

※ ※ ※

The fact that the system is deeply in trouble is not news to many frontline communities whose suffering has been the first casualty. Anne Price, a Black woman who serves as the first female president of the Insight Center for Community Economic Development, notes: "Black women over 50 years ago were saying we need a new way of thinking about the structure of our economy. These are women who came out of sharecropping, and they could see not just what was happening around their lives and our community, but our nation, and the moral compass of our nation."[19] The difference, fifty years later, is that suffering has grown to affect not just frontline and marginalized communities but all of us. Similarly, the environmentalist at the Vatican who expressed fear at facing twelve years to avert climate catastrophe missed the fact that climate catastrophe had already arrived for millions of people globally facing increasing droughts, fires, and agricultural devastation. These catastrophic weather events are already leading to civil unrest that eventually affects all of us.[20]

COVID-19 exposed the system's effects further. During the pandemic, when some were claiming a need to get back to where we were prior to the pandemic, Anne Price retorted: "No, we don't. Where we were wasn't working." That is a key message of the pandemic for Price: "Some of our systems and structures were doing what they were designed to do—they weren't broken, they were designed that way—they were designed in ways that excluded, that made it harder for people to get access, that made it unsafe for some people to work."[21]

It has become ever clearer that whether you call it "disaster capitalism," or "extractive capitalism," or even "Capitalism 1.0," the tools of our current version of capitalism are failing. We need a new vision. As author Naomi Klein puts it, "saying no is not enough. If opposition movements are to do more than burn bright and then burn out, they will need a comprehensive vision for what should emerge in place of our failing system."[22] The Pope thought so, too.

A Faith-Based Call for A New Kind of Capitalism

Standing at the front of a narrow, cavernous hall, framed by a row of cardinals, imams, and other religious leaders, Pope Francis dons his glasses and begins to speak. He invites the representatives of world religious traditions to unleash all the tools in our spiritual toolkits to help the world change course. He begins with a call to include and listen to all types of voices, "especially those usually excluded from this type of discussion, such as the voices of the poor, migrants, Indigenous people, and the young." He decries "the myth of unlimited growth and consumption," noting that we are on a dangerous path where progress is assessed only in terms of material growth. This has led, among other problems, to immense debt burdens placed on the shoulders of the poor, widespread unemployment, and environmental destruction of what he calls "our common home." Pope Francis argues instead that "economic and political objectives must be sustained by ethical objectives." He highlights the role that religions can and must play: "Those of us who are religious need to open up the treasures of our best traditions."

Our economy has embraced growth and profit as its primary motive, even at the expense of human dignity. A growing chorus of voices is shouting "no!" Yet coming up with an alternative, a truly sustainable approach to development, can be incredibly difficult. Faith groups can offer the "yes!"—a set of ancient, creative, resilient approaches to lead our civilization out of the dire place it finds itself.

Judaism has a unique gift to offer the world in this regard. Judaism embodies sustainability. It is one of the world's oldest religions, the parent religion of the majority of the world's faithful, and a religion that maintained its core teachings despite the destruction of our ancestral Temple and thousands of years of diaspora. Judaism is a "religion of protest," a radical ethical monotheism formed amid unjust societies and living proof that a small group of people making ethical choices can transform the world.

Judaism contains a richly textured set of traditions, grounded in human dignity, focused on an ideal of a redeemed world but informed by the reality of human urges and behaviors, to guide our economic decisions. In response to the call from faith communities around the world to unleash our treasure troves, I felt a need to highlight the brilliant countercultural guidance that Judaism offers for our moment—in other words, to write this book.

How to Use This Book

The other reason I wrote this book is that I wish I'd had something like it when I first began learning about investing. I want this book to be a practical resource. To that end, every chapter closes with a summary and a list of practical next steps individuals and organizations can take.

I hope you will find the book inspiring enough to read it through in its entirety. For those who don't tend to read books in order, here are some hacks. The book is broken into three broad sections. I encourage you to make your way through the first section to get important grounding in the topic.

The first section explores the theory underpinning a sustainable Jewish approach to capital. Chapter 1 looks at the landscape of impact investing, a popular and growing movement, and probes its origins and its meaning. Chapter 2 outlines a broad approach to Jewish money ethics, focused on the importance of "enough." Chapter 3 explores financial return—what should one expect to earn from an investment portfolio, from a Jewish perspective? Chapter 4 focuses on the role of institutions and institutional capital, which have received special treatment in Jewish tradition. Chapter 5 explores ancient Jewish wisdom on living an ethical life while surrounded by a society making immoral choices and introduces the idea of negative screens.

The second section begins with Chapter 6 introducing asset classes and diving deeper into cash. Chapter 7 delves into public equities and corporations, a dominant and relatively recent force in our economic system. Chapter 8 explores debt—in particular, how to lend responsibly and equitably from a Jewish perspective. Chapter 9 focuses on private equity through the lens of local investing, grounded in the Jewish value of supporting local community.

The third section addresses issue areas. Chapter 10 focuses on climate change; Chapter 11 focuses on racial justice; Chapter 12 explores the Jewish value of investing in Israel; and Chapter 13 discusses investing in peacebuilding and coexistence.

Again, this book is for educational purposes and is not to be construed as financial advice: please consult your financial advisor for official guidance. On the other hand, this book is very much intended as spiritual advice to help investors along the journey.

So let's dive into the story of impact investing.

Chapter 1

The Story of Impact Investing

I opened my first retirement account around the time I started rabbinical school. Since I was going to become a rabbi and community leader, I wanted to be sure that Jewish values were guiding me in all my life decisions, including how to invest. I didn't find any investment funds designed for rabbis, but as I began to research, I did discover hundreds of funds claiming to approach investing from a more socially responsible perspective. I didn't have the word for it at the time, but what I was trying to do in my early twenties is called impact investing.

Impact investing means using investment capital to achieve positive impact for the world alongside financial return. Broadly speaking, it involves aligning one's investment decisions with one's values and ethics.

The modern field of impact investing has grown immensely in popularity in the past decade. By some counts, a third of all investment capital worldwide is invested in funds labelled responsible or sustainable (and the number is even higher in Europe).[1] The amount of money invested with some sort of responsible approach has multiplied more than tenfold in the past 25 years.[2] Let's begin by understanding the basics of this field and its popularity. Then we will explore a deeper narrative behind it and what Judaism has to say about it.

The Story of Impact Investing—Version 1

The typical tidy version of the story of modern impact investing usually begins in the year 1970.[3] Prior to that year, there were sporadic examples of values-based investing activity, especially from faith groups. For example, some Quakers from the 17th century onward specifically divested from slavery and other sectors. In 1928, a Christian religious fund established rules to avoid investments in companies involved in alcohol or tobacco.[4]

The modern responsible investing movement really began in 1970, when the issue of South African apartheid had gripped the conscience of a group of religiously minded investors in the US. The Episcopal Church used its power as an investor in

7

General Motors to attend the company's annual meeting and called on the company to cease business with the apartheid regime. To give a sense of the uphill battle they were fighting, consider that Milton Friedman, the famous economist at the University of Chicago Business School, published an iconic essay in *The New York Times* the same year entitled "The Social Responsibility of Business Is to Increase Its Profits" in which he explicitly critiqued the General Motors campaign.[5]

Despite being sidelined by mainstream economists, the movement grew. In 1971, the United Methodist Church established the Pax World Fund, which avoided investments in businesses involved in armaments, alcohol, and gambling.[6] At the same time, religious investors began offering loans and investment capital directly to small business owners in communities (especially communities of color) who were being turned away from the traditional banking system. This developed into the field of **community development finance**.[7]

Interest in **socially responsible investing (SRI)** grew as more investors sought to bring their values into their investment portfolios. A major concern in the early years was financial return. Mainstream investors and their financial advisors assumed that SRI investing would require sacrificing financial return, something that few were willing to do. As socially responsible investment portfolios developed a longer track record, proponents were able to demonstrate that it was possible to earn just as much money investing responsibly as through traditional investing.

The field has grown exponentially in popularity in the past ten years, thanks to the significant transfer of wealth to the hands of younger generations, growth in parallel social movements like ethical purchasing of fair trade and organic goods, and increased awareness of the fact that all investments have an impact whether they align with our values or not.

In 2012, a group of investment practitioners at the Rockefeller Foundation developed the term **"impact investing."** Some used it narrowly to refer to direct investments that achieve a specific positive impact, generally not traded on the stock market. This category includes some of the splashiest examples of socially responsible investing, such as an investment in a small private company that builds decentralized solar energy systems or a loan to a cooperative of women fair trade coffee farmers in Rwanda. (Please see the Glossary for more definitions of these and other terms).

Others use the term "impact investing" more broadly, as a synonym for socially responsible investing. All investments have an impact, and impact investing is the practice of intentionally managing that impact in alignment with one's values.

It is often said that young people are one of the driving forces behind the growth of impact investing. 87 percent of millennial investors believe that environmental and social concerns should play a role in investment decisions. 77 percent of affluent millennials have made an impact investment.[8] The other group that has demonstrated tremendous leadership in driving the field of impact investing forward is women. But, as many elders in the Jewish community have reminded me, impact investing is popular across all ages and genders.

Holes in the Story

The problem with the story of impact investing as it is normally told (and as I just told it) is that it doesn't make sense. The idea that, with a few scattered exceptions, investors began considering their ethical values in their financial decisions only in the 1970s, disregards the reality that faith communities have been incorporating values into investment and business decisions for thousands of years.

Ethical business behavior is central to the Jewish spiritual path. Dr. Meir Tamari, of the Jerusalem Center of Business Ethics, notes that of the 613 commandments listed in the Torah, over 100 concern business ethics, compared to 28 for kosher food, for example.[9]

Throughout Jewish history, ethical considerations have pervaded business decisions. Jewish law and tradition addressed questions of financial return, of institutional capital and social change, of debt and shared risk, of local investing, and much more. Impact investing is not something new and radical, but something old and radical. And I mean that literally: radical, returning to roots. Judaism and other faith traditions are in the best position to know this.

Normally, the story of impact investing starts with a default assumption that impact investing is a new variation on "traditional" investing, as it was practiced prior to the 1970s. We would be better served not by asking how values-based investing came to be so popular, but rather how and when mainstream investing stopped being driven by values and ethics in the first place.

Profit at all Costs: The Origins of Business as Usual

A number of books and articles have come out in recent years identifying problems of our current economic system. Some call it **disaster capitalism**, or **extractive capitalism**, or **Capitalism 1.0**, and contrast it with potential alternatives: **regenerative capitalism**, **sustainable capitalism**, or the anticipatory **Capitalism 2.0**. The Vatican, following the conference I described in the introduction, launched the Center for Inclusive Capitalism, seeking to transform our current system into something more sustainable. These terms are helpful to the discourse because they point out that what we have now is not inevitable (and in fact is a historical anomaly).

But we need to make the discussion more explicit. Our current iteration of economy-as-usual, in a significant shift from earlier economic approaches, centered on growth at all costs. It grew directly from imperialism and slavery to become the dominant economic system in the world. It underpins the investment arena today.

This is a vital frame for thinking about the guidance Judaism has to offer our investment choices, so let's go on a bit of a journey by exploring what other experts have already written about the bloody origins of our current approach to capitalism. To tell this version of the story, we need to rewind well before 1970, to the 17th and 18th centuries.

In Europe, our current version of "business as usual" grew out of and was a crucial tool of imperialism. When European monarchs pursued imperial expansion, they did so by chartering state-sponsored companies. These companies are the direct predecessors to our modern corporations.[10] For example, John Micklethwait and Adrian Wooldridge from *The Economist* wrote a book on the history of companies. They chronicle the rise and fall of Britain's East India Trading Company. The company, chartered by Queen Elizabeth in 1600, accounted at its peak in the 19th century for nearly half of all Britain's trade. (Britain itself was the dominant global economy until late in the 19th century).[11] The East India Company colonized and ruled India with a private army of 260,000 troops. Britain's own army was only half the size.[12] The British government granted the company the right to declare war. It did so by conquering India in the 1700s.[13]

While especially significant for its historical role, the British East India Company was only one of multiple "chartered companies" from different European powers. The Dutch chartered their own East India company in 1602, for example. As Micklethwait and Wooldridge write, "chartered companies represented a combined effort by governments and merchants to grab the riches of the new worlds," with exclusive royal charters that leveraged private investment capital to further imperialist ambitions.[14]

The economics and "morality" of early corporations were often intertwined and sometimes relied on explicitly Christian justifications for conquering heathens and taxing them. Edgar Villanueva, an expert in race, wealth, and philanthropy and member of the Lumbee Nation of Native Americans, writes: "As far back as the 1400s, white supremacy, often in the name of Christianity, was employed to justify colonization—the conquest and exploitation of non-European lands—by claiming the inferiority of Africans and Indigenous people.... Violence and exploitation are always part of the process."[15]

Some of these early companies make contemporary corporate offenses look humane and genteel by comparison.[16] In modern times, we are confronted by corporate abuses like Amazon's horrendous treatment of workers,[17] Enron's and WorldCom's untrammeled greed, and Meta's (formerly Facebook's) undermining of democratic institutions through rampant disinformation.[18] But the investment vehicles shaping early capitalism engaged in imperialism, wars, massacres, and slavery, not to mention cheating and taking extensive advantage of monopoly power. The British East India Trading Company's monopoly over tea in America helped provoke the Boston Tea Party and the American Revolution. Even British public opinion in the 19th century, which seemed comfortable enough with the company's colonization of India, could not stomach its use of slave labor to extract sugar from the West Indies, leading to the first consumer boycott of a company in modern history.[19]

The early rise of the corporation is the paradigmatic story of Capitalism 1.0. Most public corporations are designed to prioritize profit above all else. The late David Graeber, professor of anthropology at the London School of Economics, notes in his book *Debt: The First Five Thousand Years*: "It is a peculiar feature of modern capitalism to create social arrangements that essentially force us to think this way. The structure of the corporation is a telling case in point—and it is no coincidence that the first major joint-stock corporations in the world were the English and Dutch East India companies, ones that pursued that very same combination of exploration, conquest, and extraction as did the conquistadors. It is a structure designed to eliminate all moral imperatives but profit."[20] Graeber notes that early corporations' focus on profit was such a departure from previous norms that pre-capitalist societal institutions, including the medieval church, explicitly opposed this growth as it was happening. (We will discuss Judaism's perspective on modern corporations more in Chapter 7.)

In the United States, the world's largest economy, the major pillar of Capitalism 1.0 and the foundation for our modern investment portfolios has been slavery: specifically, the forced enslavement of Africans and their descendants in the US South to produce cash crops, especially cotton.

Popular mythology, and indeed many historians, like to claim that slavery was never profitable, and that it surely would have ended sooner or later on its own without bloody civil war.[21] The economic reality, however, is that slavery in the American South was immensely profitable. In fact, it is not an exaggeration to say that the United States system of slavery was the economic engine of growth for modern capitalism. Edward Baptist, professor of history at Cornell University and author of *The Half Has Never Been Told: Slavery and the Making of American Capitalism*, describes the centrality of slavery in the growth of the cotton industry in the American South. "Cotton, like oil later on, was the world's most traded commodity, but that analogy doesn't even begin to explain how crucial the ever-growing efficiency of cotton-picking was to the modernizing world economy. Neither Britain nor any other country that followed it down the path of textile-based industrialization could have accomplished an economic transformation without the millions of acres of cotton fields of the expanding American South."[22]

Baptist goes on: "Cotton was the most important raw material of the industrial revolution that created our modern world economy. By 1820, the ability of enslaved people in the southwestern frontier fields to produce more cotton of a higher quality for less drove most other producing regions out of the world market. Enslaved African Americans were the world's most efficient producers of cotton... between the 1790s and 1820, the United States acquired a near-monopoly on the world's most widely traded commodity, and after 1820, cotton accounted for a majority of all US exports."[23]

In numbers, by 1860, cotton represented more than 60 percent of all US exports. 80 percent of cotton grown in the United States was exported, almost all of it to Britain, the world's most powerful economy at the time. The US share of cotton imported to Britain was 88 percent; the US share of world production was 61 percent.[24]

Beyond their uncompensated labor that built the country's most significant industry in the 1800s, enslaved humans themselves made up nearly one fifth of the total assets of the United States. This number held steady for decades, beginning in the 1830s and continuing until the Civil War. Enslaved humans comprised not only investors' "real" assets but also their investment portfolios. Slaves were mortgaged like houses are today, and the mortgages were combined into investment vehicles called securities (like the mortgage-backed securities that caused the 2008 financial recession) that were sold in all the major financial centers of the Western world, even in areas where slavery itself was outlawed: Paris, London, New York, and more.[25]

While slavery was outlawed in the US in 1865, racial discrimination in other forms continued to build on its foundation, with a compounding effect on the investment arena today. One way this has manifested is through an increasing gap in wealth between white people and people of color. The research institute Center for American Progress draws the clear line from past to present: "The persistent Black-white wealth gap is not an accident but rather the result of centuries of federal and state policies that have systematically facilitated the deprivation of Black Americans, from the brutal exploitation of Africans during slavery, to systematic oppression in the Jim Crow South, to today's institutionalized racism."[26] As the author Ta-Nehisi Coates puts it, "The wealth gap merely puts a number on something we feel but cannot say—that American prosperity was ill-gotten and selective in its distribution."[27]

Some people, and especially people of color, have been stating this for years. Isabel Wilkerson puts it bluntly in her book *Caste*: "The country cannot become whole until it confronts what was not a chapter in its history, but the basis of its economic and social order. For a quarter millennium, slavery *was* the country."[28]

While contemporary investors are not to blame for American slavery, we must reckon with the fact that American slavery has directly influenced the contemporary investment arena. Here is one powerful rendition from Ed Whitfield, a consultant on community economic development and board member at Seed Commons:

> Even people who were not directly involved in the early accumulation of that [wealth from slavery] ended up coming to this country and being here at a time when they could engage in what I call gambling on a table that is loaded down with stolen money. While you can make a legitimate claim that you yourself did not steal any of the money that was put on the table, and that you are indeed a good gambler, and that you brought your own ante to get into the game—still, you are playing at a table loaded down with stolen money, and it creates for you opportunities that would not otherwise be there, and those opportunities are historically rooted in the system that piled that money up on that table.... The genocide—the unfinished, incomplete genocide, against the Native population is part of it. The entire slave system, which is another part of it, has helped create this pile of money on the table that folk are gambling at.[29]

In the past six decades, the cultural underpinnings of our current way of practicing capitalism have only become more extreme. When she became prime minister of Britain, Margaret Thatcher appointed Milton Friedman as her macro-economic advisor. But unlike Friedman, Thatcher freely admitted a "social" objective, stating that "economics are the method—the object is to change the heart and soul." Indeed, an accelerating emphasis on profit at all costs has shifted the priorities of vast numbers of people in our society. In 1966, a survey of US college freshmen found that only about 44 percent thought that making a lot of money was "very important" or "essential," a number that had climbed to over 80 percent by 2013.[30]

In critiquing our current trajectory, I do not mean to naïvely romanticize pre-capitalist societies. For as long as there have been faiths and other social structures guiding people to make economically just decisions, there have been greedy businessmen, unscrupulous predators, and those willing to turn a blind eye for a share of the profits.

I also do not mean to ignore the environmental and social harms perpetrated over the past several hundred years by planned or centralized economies. There is plenty to say, but I do not focus on them here, as those economies are not the driving forces influencing the investment arena relevant to most readers of this book.

Indeed, economic growth has brought tremendous benefits, at least to many of us. Entire global economic growth per person prior to the mid-18th century averaged around 0.01 percent per year.[31] Since 1750, growth has multiplied more than a factor of 37.[32] That growth has brought with it a rising standard of living for millions, even billions of people. Yet it has also brought side effects of terrible and widespread human suffering and environmental devastation. Our society's growth has been spurred by a societal focus on growth and profit, not as tools for human happiness, but as an ultimate value in and of themselves.

Attempting to move ahead with change without acknowledging the full cost of the current approach will ultimately fail, according to Anne Price, president of the Insight Center for Community Economic Development.[33] What is truly unique about our current "business as usual" is the extent to which a focus on profit and growth has overtaken any other value, leading to an ever more intense exploitation of people and the natural world in pursuit of that goal.

※ ※ ※

In this version of the story, values-based investing is a movement of resistance. It is a protest against a narrative that has grown increasingly dominant over the past several centuries, and accelerated over the past several decades, that puts profit at the center of the human story. It is actively building the "yes!," the Capitalism 2.0, the alternatives to our current situation.

Indeed, since the beginning of our current version of capitalism, there have been some investors and capital owners willing to stand in resistance. Ensconced in a United States economy built on slavery, some (though not many) religious and faith leaders agitated against it, prohibiting investment in slavery and calling for its abolition at a time when such a stance was wildly unpopular. The Episcopal Church demonstrated that same moral determination when it stood up and demanded that General Motors stop profiting from apartheid. The similarity of these two battles belies the myth many of us were taught that the fight is long over and business as usual is fine.

When we tell the story this way, impact investing becomes less of a new, fringe idea. Instead, it is the latest manifestation of protest, of ongoing efforts to mobilize society away from the extremes of our current approach to capitalism and the primacy of profit to a more sustainable and ethical relationship with the world around us.

Judaism is a religion of protest, according to Rabbi Lord Jonathan Sacks, the late Chief Rabbi of the United Hebrew Congregations of Great Britain and the Commonwealth, and it excels at the task. In a world that pressures us to run 24/7, Judaism offers us the radical practice of Shabbat, a day to rest and step out of the grind. In a society defined by its consumption, Judaism offers us kashrut, the countercultural spiritual discipline of refraining from eating certain foods. In an era where the primary value is profit at all costs, Jewish impact investing is an act of resistance against decades and centuries of exploitation for the sake of profit. It is a defiant statement that there are alternatives and Judaism can guide us to them. It is a choice to overcome the pressures of the modern world and deeply live the wisdom of Jewish tradition about how to relate to money and investment.

This book is focused on the questions facing investors today—how to think about mutual funds, bonds, savings accounts, and more. But before we can explore what Judaism has to say about the modern choices facing investors, we need to explore what Judaism has to say about money in general and our relationship to it. We need to understand Jewish money ethics.

Next Steps—Chapter 1

This chapter outlined the origins of "business as usual" and the increasing devastation it is causing. Jewish tradition has always held our values as relevant to our investments. But over the last several centuries, and accelerating in the 20th century, "business as usual" came to mean centering only profit.

- **Step 1: Journal about the following prompts.** They are meant to spark your imagination and motivate you to action. If journaling or writing isn't your thing, feel free to use these as prompts for a meditative walk. Or, if you are reading this book with a group, you can discuss your answers to these questions together. The point is to use them to catapult your journey.
    - In what ways does my current approach to investing default to "business as usual"?
    - What are the challenges that arise when I start thinking about shifting away from a "business as usual" approach?
- **Step 2: Find support for your journey on impact investing.** Consider reading this book in a book club. As a group, discuss both the content of the book and your personal relationship to your investment assets.

Chapter 2

Jewish Money Ethics

It was a shame, thought the students of Shimon ben Shetach (Jerusalem, 140-60 BCE), that their teacher worked so hard combing flax to make a cheap product like linen to earn a living. They offered to buy him a donkey, so he could switch to a more lucrative trade and have more time to study. To the students' surprise and delight, the donkey they bought for him had a valuable jewel strung around its neck. Shimon asked them, "did the owner know he sold the jewel too?" They said no. He insisted they return it.[1]

Judaism has always held a high ethical standard concerning money. The Talmudic Sage Rava, head of the most prominent Babylonian academy of his era (280-352CE), taught that, when a person dies and is brought to judgment for the life they have lived, the first question they will be asked is, "did you conduct business faithfully?"[2]

Capitalism 1.0 has led to enormous growth in humans seizing power, leading to amazing technological advances and the creation of wealth, raising living standards worldwide. At the same time, it has imprinted in us a new and unsustainable mindset: growth at all costs, profit by any legal means, ostentatious consumption, harmful exploitation, and growing societal inequality. This mindset has led to accelerating disasters both natural and human. Jewish thought can help us return to a more sustainable mindset around money that can ground us as we approach the technical questions of what ethical investing looks like and how to do it.

In response to our current version of capitalism's focus on profit at all costs, the first principle of Jewish money ethics we will examine is the "economics of enough." This is the countercultural idea that our economic aspirations should be bounded by and balanced with other values, like supporting the needy, visiting the sick, and our own spiritual learning and growth.

Judaism offers numerous values that can help guide our mindset around money. There are too many to name here, so this chapter will focus on those that most directly respond to the imbalance created by our current approach to capitalism and steer us on a more sustainable path.

To ground us in our study, it will be helpful to have a brief overview of the Jewish canon. (You can also see the Glossary for more Hebrew terms).

Introduction to Jewish Sources

At the Vatican's multi-faith conference I attended as a representative of the Jewish community's investment capital, religious leaders spoke about bringing forth the best treasures of their religions. One of Judaism's treasures is an ancient approach to economics and social justice that has proven sustainable for thousands of years. This approach is first articulated in the **Torah**, the sacred foundational text of Judaism. The Torah dates from the time of the ancient **Israelites**, who left Egypt and received it from God on Mount Sinai more than 3,000 years ago. After the death of **Moses**, leader of the Jewish people, came the era of the **Prophets**, whose teachings are recorded in later books. The Israelites built the **Temple** in **Jerusalem**, which stood for more than 400 years. The first Temple was destroyed and the Jews were exiled, but they returned 70 years later to build the **Second Temple**. Additional writings span this era, which together with the Torah and the Prophets make up the **Tanakh**—the sacred canon, also known as the Hebrew Bible.

When the Second Temple was destroyed in 70 CE, Judaism had to adapt to the reality of spiritual life without a physical center. The teachings of the rabbinic **Sages** at the end of the Second Temple period and shortly after its destruction gained primacy (I refer to these as "the Sages," to distinguish from later rabbinic authorities). They were compiled first in the work known as the **Mishnah**, around 200CE. The Mishnah is full of debate and disagreement. Over the next several hundred years, the Sages added commentary, known as the **Gemara**, and compiled in the **Talmud**. (There were really two Talmuds, the primary one compiled in Babylon and another compiled in Jerusalem; in this book, "the Talmud" refers to the Babylonian Talmud unless indicated differently).

Judaism is a law-based religion, and a legal or ethical precept is known as a *mitzvah* (*mitzvot* in plural). The full body of Jewish law is known as **halakha**, which translates as "the path." But the Talmud is more than a book of Jewish law and practice. It encompasses the Sages' perspective on every single aspect of life, from when we wake up until we go to sleep, from when we are born until we die, and beyond. It is full of rabbinic parables, jokes, occasional bawdy stories, heated debates, and precepts for social justice.

Later generations compiled **commentaries** on the Talmud, as well as a series of legal codes, accessible to the layperson, which summarized the positions in the

Talmud. These legal **codes** and commentaries, and later **responsa** that followed, continue to provide the foundation for Jewish practice today.[3]

Jewish life until the middle of the 19th century was characterized by communal rule, with independent legislative and fiscal authority.[4] In the past 200 years, the increasing freedom of Jewish communities in Europe and the Industrial Revolution have transformed Jewish community yet again. As Jews and Jewish communities reacted in different ways to gaining political freedom through emancipation, the modern Jewish **denominations** arose. They offer diverse approaches to interpreting accumulated Jewish tradition. These range from a continuation of the law handed down to Moses at Sinai (the Orthodox movement), to a variably nonbinding but culturally meaningful body of text and narrative that inspire Jews to ethical action in the world (the Reform, Conservative, and Reconstructionist movements). (See the Glossary for these and more terms.)

※ ※ ※

Learning is as central to Judaism as breathing is to the human body. The word Torah literally means Teaching. Importantly, Jewish learning is not organized according to modern Western models. In the Talmud, the text flows freely, meandering from topic to topic without a clear logical structure. Imagine yourself scrolling the internet, clicking on hyperlink after hyperlink, as subjects are refracted through a prism of relationship to each other, and you begin to have a feel for what it is like to learn Talmud.

Edgar Villanueva, Native American and expert on racism, wealth, and philanthropy, notes that there are many ways racist systems pervade our lives—even the way we structure our thinking. "Colonial white supremacist organizational practices seem inevitable because they were so universally adopted, and they still govern the great majority of our institutions, but they were *design choices*. This means that other choices are available, even when they seem far-fetched."[5] The ancient Jewish texts and debates were not structured according to linear Western models, with thesis and supporting paragraphs. Meir Tamari, director of the Jerusalem Center for Business Ethics, notes that "for many trained in the Greek thought process, the Gemara remains a difficult book to master."[6]

Inspired by Jewish tradition, I have deliberately chosen to quote in this book Jewish texts that, at times, unfold in a non-linear way. Some quotes reflect wisdom and practical advice, others reflect technical debates, all blended together with stories about real people and the decisions they faced. I will make frequent reference to the Talmud and do my best to frame the Talmudic learning so that it is accessible to those who have not engaged in its study before. I strongly recommend reading each of the Talmudic excerpts a few times before moving on, to help grasp the flow of the text.

One additional note: Judaism is a law-based religion (similar to Islam, but different from many denominations of Christianity). Often the debate about values and ethical living takes the form of a legal discussion. Yet there are also Jewish values, customs, and stories that guide a Jewish perspective on the issues we will discuss. I am an Orthodox rabbi, meaning I ascribe to the law-based aspects of Judaism, and I find them a rich place to start our discussion. But we will also move beyond them to talk about Judaism's ideals for money ethics.

The Economics of Enough

After my grandmother passed away in 2016, her grandchildren were invited to explore her condo for keepsakes we might want to take with us: musical instruments, files, silverware. The most valuable item I found was a trove of additional copies of three books my grandfather had written in the final years of his life, compilations of his short stories.

There was the story about how he and my grandmother, the first to leave Brooklyn since their families arrived from Eastern Europe in the early 1900s, responded to an aunt who asked which ocean they would cross to get to Iowa. Stories of how my grandfather, a professor, kept his clothes until they were truly worn out, and replaced them through a careful (and sometimes belabored) shopping process. Stories of how they dealt with small-town Jewish life in the Midwest, including purchasing their first bedroom furniture set from a local Jewish business owner. Rereading his books recently, I was struck by the reminder that they kept that furniture set for over 55 years, until the day they died.

Jewish tradition is grounded in what Meir Tamari of the Jerusalem Center for Business Ethics calls "the economics of enough." My grandparents lived by the economics of enough—they needed a set of bedroom furniture, so they bought it, but one was enough for a lifetime.

On the one hand, Judaism sees no merit in ascetic poverty.[7] The poet-philosopher Yehuda Halevi (Spain, 1075-1141) wrote: "Decreasing wealth is not a valued spiritual act, when wealth is gained in a lawful way and earning it does not distract from learning and from doing righteous deeds, especially for one who has children and intends to spend that wealth for the sake of Heaven."[8]

On the other hand, pursuit of profit, even when scrupulously earned, cannot be the ultimate goal. The book of Ecclesiastes describes how "those who love money will never be satisfied with money. One who loves abundance will never be sated."[9] Rather, the goal is to achieve enough financial success to secure one's needs, and then prioritize one's time on the more important things in life.

To support that goal, Judaism expressly limits the amount of time available to spend on making money. The rhythm of Jewish life imposes a break from all economic activity once every seven days, to observe Shabbat, a day of rest. Judaism also calls for a pause from economic activity on all major holidays and when an individual goes through a period of mourning. Reflecting Judaism's origins in an agrarian society, the Torah calls for one in every seven years to be a year of complete rest for the land, known as the *shmita* (Sabbatical) year, which we will discuss more later in the chapter.

Judaism also limits economic activity by prioritizing a whole set of other obligations—caring for the vulnerable, acts of kindness, and above all study of Torah. In the traditional Jewish framework, Torah study is unbounded. Every second of every day, from one's youth to one's dying day, is a potential opportunity to study Torah. Some reading this book may not relate to Torah study in the traditional way, but the point is still relevant: regular practices that help you find meaning, moral direction, and spiritual grounding in life are a useful tool to place an upper limit on economic activity.

The medieval scholar Rambam (Egypt, 1135-1204) called Judaism a "middle way," where one devotes time both to earning a living and to studying Torah—but he posited Torah study should be dominant.[10] Rambam even offered a paradigm: a third of the day spent in sleep, a third in gainful employment, and a third in Torah study.[11] As Meir Tamari puts it, "the obligation to study Torah will always place a brake on the economic development of the individual."[12]

* * *

The economics of enough begin with gratitude. Traditionally, the first words out of a Jewish person's mouth every morning are the prayer "I am grateful." The Hebrew word for Jewish (*yehudi*) stems from the same root as the Hebrew word for gratitude. When the Biblical patriarch Jacob reunited with his brother Esau after decades, he offered Esau a series of gifts. Esau tried to decline, saying, "I have a lot," but Jacob went one step further, saying, "I have everything."[13]

Gratitude helps us frame our money-making in spiritual terms. Tamari notes that from a Jewish perspective, "all wealth originates with God who grants it to human beings to satisfy their needs in a normal manner, thus making economic activity legitimate.... The divine source of wealth makes any fraud or theft a religious sin both against man and God."[14] Tamari emphasizes: "Judaism has no concept of unlimited private property; rather part of our wealth is granted to us by God to assist others, to execute justice and to protect the environment ... society has rights in the private wealth of the individual."[15]

The economics of enough are a crucial tool to transition from our current approach to capitalism to a more sustainable alternative. A study on climate change published in May 2021 in the scientific journal *Nature Communications* argued that only a scenario in which the economies of the world's rich nations stop growing and start contracting can limit the most catastrophic impacts of climate change, at least without unrealistic reliance on rapid technological development and carbon capture. This is a politically difficult position, the authors note. But they point out that, "on wellbeing, research shows that high-income countries could scale back their biophysical impact (and GDP), while maintaining or even increasing social performance and achieving higher equity among countries."[16] In other words, the wealthiest nations currently have too much, and having less will actually help us increase our happiness and well-being. The only way to avoid further global crisis is for us to right-size our lives to "enough."

Done well, right-sizing our lives to enough is not an act of sacrifice. As contemporary rabbi Jeremy Benstein writes, the *shmita* year "is a stirring example of an entire society choosing to live at a significantly lower material standard of living for a year in order to devote itself to more spiritual pursuits than the daily grind."[17] More pointedly, author and activist Rebecca Solnit writes about the climate crisis, "what if we recognized that what is demanded of us is not austerity and sacrifice but giving up poison?"[18]

Judaism's economics of enough are important not only in the fight against climate change, but also in all interlinked struggles for social justice. For those of us with any access to wealth, Judaism expects that our gratitude to God will help us reflect on the origins of that wealth and pay it forward. Three generations ago, my family on both sides were relatively poor immigrants from Eastern Europe who settled in Brooklyn. The men of my great-grandfathers' generation were house painters, post office employees, and convenience store operators. My grandfather was the first in his family to go to college. He never stopped, eventually earning his Ph. D. Our family was set on the path to financial comfort when he accepted a professorship at the University of Minnesota in 1961, in a city that in 1946 had been termed the "capital of anti-Semitism in the United States,"[19] at a university that until a few years prior maintained strict quotas for Jewish students and continued to discriminate against Black students.[20] What I have now is the result of generations of hard work and overcoming obstacles—but ultimately, it came from a Divine blessing.

The economics of enough, grounded in gratitude, provide both a spiritual practice and a framework for action. My family has been blessed with enough and often more than enough. I have a spiritual responsibility to share the abundance of what

Jewish Money Ethics

I already have. There is no more powerful spiritual brake on the engine of profit at all costs than that of a commitment to "enough" over excess, spiritual awareness and gratitude for what we already have, and the responsibility we have to God and other humans because of it.

Living in Balance

If anyone knows how to live in tension between two extremes, it is Rabbi Yitz Greenberg, a Modern Orthodox rabbi, Harvard Ph. D., and scholar. Rav Yitz, as he is known to his students, was born in 1933. He lived through a tumultuous era that saw the rise and fall of the right-wing fascism of Nazi Germany and the rise and fall of the communist authoritarianism of the USSR. Rabbi Greenberg cuts a strikingly tall and handsome figure (he's been compared in appearance to British actor Sir Patrick Stewart). His theology is even more striking, centered on the human covenant with God and a profound approach to human dignity. His theology frames everything from how Shabbat is observed every week, to Jewish-Gentile relations, to how we think about death.[21]

We are living in a moment when society is pulled between two opposites. At one pole is the ideology of business as usual, despite the mounting evidence of the harm it is causing to fellow humans and to our planet. At the other pole is an ideology of burning it all down and starting anew, without acknowledging the devastation such an approach could cause.

There is a phrase for living between two opposites: dialectic tension. Judaism teaches us how to live in the balance. Jewish wisdom (and Rabbi Greenberg's theology) become especially relevant at moments of dialectic tension.

On an individual level, Jewish thought and tradition accept pursuit of wealth as a legitimate human activity, one that helps build a functioning society. According to the Talmud, all the prophets were wealthy, though they achieved that wealth through scrupulous means, sometimes Divinely so.[22] The Psalms say, "The heavens are heavens for God, and the earth God gave to humans," meaning self-centered human activity on earth is fine from God's perspective.[23] On the most solemn day of the Jewish calendar, Yom Kippur, we pray to be inscribed in the Divine Book of Life—but also the book of financial success. Indeed, the High Priest in ancient times, after finishing the most holy service on that most holy day of the year in the Holy Temple, offered a special prayer full of references to material success, asking for a bountiful year when the community will be able to sustain itself without dependence on others for charity.[24]

Judaism ascribes to humans two primal urges: a selfless, noble urge, the *yetzer tov* (literally, the "good urge"), and a self-centered urge, the *yetzer hara* (literally, the "evil urge.") Jewish tradition teaches that the *yetzer hara* is just as holy and necessary an urge as the *yetzer tov*.

A rabbinic interpretation of the beginning of the world notes that, while each of the six days of creation was called "good," the day humans were created was "very good." The extra praise, according to the Talmud, is for the self-centered urge. "Without the *yetzer hara*, no man would build a house, take a wife, beget children, or engage in business."[25] Doing business is an essential part of human experience, as fundamental to our society as romantic relationships, children, and a home to live in. And the self-centered urge is praiseworthy for motivating us toward those actions.

In another variation on the same theme, the Talmud recounts a story when the Sages prayed to capture the *yetzer hara*, the self-centered urge, and succeeded. They imprisoned the *yetzer hara* for three days. During that time, they couldn't find a single fresh egg in the entire land of Israel, as the urge to create and reproduce had vanished even from chickens.[26]

On the other hand, in Judaism, profit cannot be an individual's ultimate goal. It is bounded by an entire structure of ethics, laws, and cultural guidelines. All of this leads investors away from a paradigm of "more is better than less" to what Tamari of the Jerusalem Center for Business Ethics terms "the economics of 'enough.'"[27] Dr. Erica Brown describes "financial moderation" as key to the Jewish attitude toward money. She even quotes the lyrics of "If I Were a Rich Man" from the musical *Fiddler on the Roof*, which culminates in the main character dreaming of being rich enough to have the freedom to study hours every day, the "sweetest thing of all."[28]

Our economy has excelled at the self-centered urge. Adam Smith taught that "It is not from the benevolence of the butcher, the brewer, or the baker, that we expect our dinner, but from their regard to their own interest." But Judaism insists that the self-centered urge represents only half of the picture of a human soul. When we focus solely on the self-centered urge, we tip ourselves and society out of balance, which can lead to increased suffering.

That same internal tension between the selfless and self-centered urges, expanded outward, manifests itself in our investment portfolios. Impact investing can sometimes feel like it is bridging two different worlds. The world of financial professionals has been generally skeptical about the idea of ethics and values informing investment decisions. Financial professionals have often feared values-based investing, operating under the (false) assumption that it requires sacrificing financial return. They have found it too messy to try to define values and bring them into financial decisions. It is also a lot of work to customize typically mass-produced financial advice to each individual client based on their values. On the other side, the world of community activists engaged in social justice work, and mission-driven nonprofit professionals, have sometimes been skeptical of capitalism in the first place. They have wondered whether profit-driven business and finance have any moral value at all.[29]

In 2017, Rabbi Greenberg presented on a panel I moderated at the Jewish Impact Investing Summit (incidentally, the first investment conference ever to open with a panel of rabbis and a Jewish text study). Rabbi Greenberg described impact investing as a quintessentially Jewish act: balancing between two opposite poles. "This is what I feel is the heart of being Jewish…you marry a kind of an ideal, socialist if you will, utopian vision with a very pragmatic, self-interested, very human, incremental direction which we call, in brief, covenant, and expresses itself in Jewish law and Jewish traditions."[30]

That same tension expands beyond our investment portfolios to society at large. In Rabbi Greenberg's words: "In the Torah—on the one hand, it's clear its vision is socialist. On *shmita*, the Sabbatical year, all private property is suspended, and anybody can come in and take the food of the land. On *yovel*, the Jubilee, every fifty years, you redistribute all the land equally to every family, so that in fact you will have an economic equality structure." We will explore more about the messages of the *shmita*/Sabbatical year later in this chapter. Rabbi Greenberg continues: "having said that, the Torah turns right around, accepts private property, recognizes it." The Torah's commandment to give to those in need, according to Rabbi Greenberg, is itself a balance to the inequality that inevitably arises from private property.[31]

We need to hold in our imaginations an explicit redemptive vision of equitable and just access to land and other resources. That could look like regular cancellation of debt and suspension of private property, where all is shared and each person takes what they need. Without that guiding redemptive vision, those stuck in poverty will face ever more dire struggles to meet basic human needs. Meanwhile, the wealthy will face an ever-growing spiritual weight borne of the harm caused to so many in the very system that enabled their acquisition of wealth.

On the other hand, we cannot always, or even often, live on sabbatical in the *shmita* year. It might be environmentally sustainable, but it would not be sustainable from a perspective of human society. The Torah expects us to hold private property and engage in productive work six out of seven years because it recognizes the importance of private property and economic incentives to build a thriving society. Indeed, even living on sabbatical one year every seven is a psychological challenge, which the Torah acknowledges by reassuring the people with a Divine promise of enough to eat during the *shmita* year.

Our current version of capitalism evinces a problem of forces out of balance. Judaism is a religion of dialectics, living in balance between extremes. We as humans thrive in balance. Instead, we have wound up at an extreme, where the self-centered urge, the *yetzer hara*, has overwhelmed everything else. This has led to tremendous human productivity at tremendous moral cost.

Jewish wisdom can guide us as we transform our current approach to capitalism into a new system that works for everyone. Rabbi Greenberg explains:

> It seems to me we have seen, in the last hundred years particularly, that the self-interested, the self-driven—if you will, selfish—private property structure is far more productive, far more creative of wealth, far more powerful in overcoming poverty than any other system. And that we affirm; that we accept. …This is one of the great civilizations of all time in terms of humans taking power … humans creating wealth on a staggering scale—on a staggering scale. And the truth is, living standards worldwide have been transformed and raised. …
>
> But—and here's the catch—we're living in a time where that power has become so staggering, so powerful, that we're beginning to get the side effect question of collateral damage.… The affirmation of the profit margin now has to be matched by the challenge that it's not absolute and it's not self-validating. And when it has negative consequences, then it must be corrected and taken under control. And of course, that's what we're seeing now in terms of the reckless investment forms that created mineral developments that pollute and toxify. We've seen what happened in South America, or Indonesia, and so on, where the forests are totally being wiped out, endangering the local population and its ability to function, but also the planet itself.
>
> So this is where I think the Jewish people have a contribution to make to the whole world.[32]

Beyond the Letter of the Law

In September of 2021, the International Consortium of Investigative Journalists published the Pandora Papers, a revelatory analysis of the techniques of wealthy individuals and corporations to shift profits to tax havens, based on a data leak of millions of documents. The papers exposed many wealthy companies and individuals seeking to avoid tax burdens in a way that "benefits the wealthy at the expense of nations' treasuries and ordinary citizens' wallets." For example, the Pandora Papers describe how sportswear company Nike contracted with the country's biggest law firm, Baker

McKenzie, to set up a Dutch tax shelter and minimize its tax burden.[33] When contacted by the journalists behind the investigation, Nike stated that it complies with all local regulations.

Many companies defend their actions by noting they adhere to the letter of the law. But most of us, when asked to set a moral threshold for behavior, would agree that "legal" is too low a bar. Even Milton Friedman, the famous economist from the Chicago Business School, thought companies should make money "while conforming to the basic rules of society, both those embodied in law and those embodied in ethical custom."[34] In every legal system, there are loopholes that cheaters seek to exploit. This is especially true when the law is written in ways that benefit those seeking the loopholes, like the political lobbying that Baker McKenzie does across the globe to ease the regulatory burdens on itself and its clients.[35]

It is important to acknowledge that corporate management has a **fiduciary duty**. Fiduciary duty requires a company's leadership to prioritize what's best for the company's owners (its shareholders). By the way, boards of Jewish organizations are also bound by fiduciary duty, with an obligation to put the organization's interests first. We will talk more about fiduciary duty in the next chapter. Fiduciary duty is usually understood to mean corporate management has a responsibility to make as much money as possible on behalf of the shareholders, regardless of how. But Judaism would see it as an integral part of fiduciary duty for a company's leadership to steer the company to make money while meeting ethical standards, beyond the mere letter of the law.

Tax avoidance is not the only way companies aim no higher than the letter of the law. In July 2021, the Clean Clothes Campaign released a report asserting pervasive "wage theft" in the garment supply chains of major corporations. According to UK newspaper *The Guardian*, the report found that while none of the companies analyzed had broken any laws, they failed to ensure their workers were properly paid during the pandemic. At the same time, all of the companies mentioned in the report have rebounded to substantial profits.[36]

Profit by any (legal) means is a key pillar of our current approach to capitalism. It is also the logical conclusion of the Milton Friedman doctrine. Remember, Friedman's seminal article in The New York Times in 1970 was titled, "The Social Responsibility of Business Is to Increase Its Profits." The Friedman doctrine of profit maximization helped shape mainstream economic thinking for decades,[37] and alongside British Prime Minister Margaret Thatcher, he also advised US President Ronald Reagan (influencing Reaganomics).

Friedman claimed it was a major error "to believe that it is possible to do good with other people's money,"[38] a position so diametrically opposed to Jewish teachings that all the major Jewish business scholars since Friedman's article in 1970 have declared their opposition. In the words of Tamari of the Jerusalem Center for Business Ethics and his colleague Walter Wurzburger in 1980: "Judaism has never endorsed an unadulterated capitalism nor favored a radical laissez faire policy."[39] From the late Rabbi Dr. Aaron Levine, author of *Free Enterprise and Jewish Law*: "A Jewish business ethic is incompatible with Milton Friedman's view that the 'social responsibility of business is to increase its profits.'"[40] From Dr. Moses Pava, former dean of the business school at Yeshiva University: "The more traditional views of the corporation which emphasize profit maximization, to the extent that they are founded solely in a self-serving view of decision making, are at odds with the vast majority of Jewish sources."[41]

Friedman's doctrine takes a beating throughout this book, so to be fair, I concede that Friedman himself thought there were limits to acceptable behavior. As we just saw, he recognized the importance of following both law and "ethical custom."[42] Friedman also saw a vital place for government and thought business executives should avoid assuming a political role without going through the political process, an idea he found "intolerable."[43] Yet since Friedman wrote those words fifty years ago, the idea of "ethical custom" has lost its power, and much of business seems quite happy to spend millions lobbying Congress and taking over the legislative role in ways that benefit companies' bottom line.

Judaism would have a powerful response: the law itself requires that we go beyond the minimum standards enshrined in law. This beautiful concept is known in Hebrew as *lifnim mishurat hadin* ("beyond the letter of the law"). Going above and beyond is not just a virtuous ideal; Jewish legal doctrine demands it.[44]

This same idea was articulated in modern form by a different 20th century Jewish public figure, Supreme Court Justice Louis Brandeis. On holding stock in corporations, Brandeis wrote: "There is no such thing to my mind ... as an innocent stockholder. He may be innocent in fact, but socially he cannot be held innocent. He accepts the benefits of the system. It is his business and his obligation to see that those who represent him carry out a policy which is consistent with the public welfare."[45] Unlike Capitalism 1.0, in Jewish thought, the technical legal status of unethical behavior matters less and our values matter more.

Sustainable Global Development

We briefly encountered the United Nations' Sustainable Development Goals (SDGs) in the introduction. Launched by the UN in 2015, the 17 goals represent a powerful articulation of a collective global vision for 2030. They include such goals as an end to poverty, sustainable cities and clean water, gender equality, and more. But since long before the launch of the SDGs, Jewish tradition has concerned itself with sustainable global development. In particular, the Sages of the Talmud articulated the value of *yishuvo shel olam*, which literally means "settling of the world" but is best translated in context as "sustainable global development."[46]

The Sages frowned on those who sought to profit by extracting wealth from others without making any actual contribution to society. For example, the rabbis decried gambling, partly because they saw it as a kind of theft from the loser who wasn't psychologically prepared to lose, but more importantly because gambling fails to contribute to global development. It is an unproductive activity, pure speculation, zero-sum. Gamblers themselves were seen as so removed from productive contribution to society that the Sages considered them unreliable as witnesses in a court of law.[47]

The Jewish value on sustainable development prompts us to ask whether economic choices are beneficial not just to us but the world at large. Parts of our modern financial system do in fact contribute to sustainable development. But a significant part of financial and investment activity today does not contribute anything to sustainable development, and in fact detracts from it. (If any of the terms below are unfamiliar, feel free to explore the Glossary).

Rabbi Yitz Greenberg explains that the **stock market**, rather than gambling, is in fact providing a significant service of financing valuable economic activity.[48] The stock market enables companies to raise new capital from investors by assuring investors that if they no longer want their stock, there will be a ready market of buyers.[49]

Futures contracts also have an important role. Futures contracts involve paying a fixed price now to purchase a certain quantity of food or other items—for example, $50 per bushel of corn, to be delivered in September. Futures contracts help smooth out the market for volatile commodities, providing farmers with certainty and needed cash early in the growing season.

Day trading is more complicated. It represents a trader buying and selling stocks, profiting from daily fluctuations in price. However, Rabbi Greenberg notes that most economists agree that this trading provides important liquidity to the market. Contemporary Rabbi Eliyahu Abergel (Morocco and Israel), former head of the rabbinical court in Jerusalem, wrote a responsum in 1999 distinguishing between long-term investment and day trading. He prohibited day trading as one's sole profession, akin to gambling, but considered it permissible to dabble in such trading (though he argues the most pious approach would be not to).[50]

On the other hand, what about collateralized mortgage obligations, CMOs, essentially bundles of mortgages resold as securities, which were one of the precipitating causes of the 2008 financial crash? What about **hedge funds** that seek to short the market, in essence betting that certain companies will fail or lose value? What about high-frequency trading, which seeks to take advantage of millisecond-long gaps in information to profit from quickly buying and selling stocks?

It seems clear that *yishuvo shel olam*, sustainable development, becomes a serious concern as one examines the current state of the financial arena. This is the same financial arena whose complex products brought down the economy in 2008, and where investment bankers essentially sent the message that their products were so complicated even rocket scientists couldn't understand them. Less than one percent of the trillions of dollars flowing through financial markets every day goes to productive use, providing capital to companies to hire, expand, or develop new products.[51] The financial arena has often ignored concerns of whether its actions are productive for society's development, violating a key rule of Jewish money ethics.

Modesty

Modesty as an ethic might sound foreign to some ears, but it is a strong Jewish value. Far beyond concerns of, for example, what parts of the human body are covered by clothing, modesty is about communal norms that limit ostentatious displays of wealth.[52] In the past, when Jewish communities had enough political autonomy to legislate standards of economic behavior, communal authorities used Judaism's value of modesty to legislate a standard of how much is "too much."[53] For festivities like weddings, they limited the number of attendees and money spent, to avoid an unnecessary focus on material opulence.[54] While rabbis no longer have the authority to place limits on the extravagance of modern celebrations like bar and bat mitzvah parties, many continue to encourage modesty as a communal standard.[55] This is especially important given the already-high financial burden that Jewish life imposes on families today in everything from holiday observances to Jewish education. A modest approach to consumption has become countercultural in American consumerist society, but it is a core principle of Jewish money ethics.

Shmita—Sabbatical Year

We have already seen the *shmita* year appear earlier in this chapter as well as the introduction, and it will continue to reappear throughout this book, because of the deep connections between *shmita* and money ethics.

The Torah instructed the Children of Israel, wandering in the wilderness, that, once they entered the Promised Land, they would need to maintain a regular practice of renouncing its ownership. Once every seven years, all the land was declared ownerless for a year with the fruits available to everyone. This was an act of radical economic justice, returning the entire community for a full year to an Edenic society free of private land. It was also an act of faith, requiring landowners not to sow their fields and simply to trust in the abundance that would come that year and the following.

Additionally, the entire community experienced a collective debt cancellation. Creditors were required to forgive their debtors, and the slate was wiped clean. The Torah expressly warned against a tendency to withhold credit as the *shmita* year approaches, out of fear that one will lose the opportunity to collect the debt. The Torah motivated creditors by appealing to them to have faith in abundance: "for in return God will bless you in all your efforts and in all your undertakings."[56]

With some context, it is easy to see the divine inspiration in the *shmita* year's focus on debt cancellation. David Graeber, writing in *Debt: The First Five Thousand Years*, notes that "for the last five thousand years, with remarkable regularity, popular insurrections have begun the same way: with the ritual destruction of debt records… in the ancient world, all revolutionary movements had a single program: 'cancel the debts and redistribute the land.'" The Torah takes those same urges and builds them into the very fabric of society, offering a sustainable approach to lending and investing, and potentially preventing a tremendous amount of violence.

Some might think of the *shmita* year as an idyllic time, and the precepts of *shmita* do embody certain societal ideals, but in lived experience in ancient Israel, it was also a time of crisis. The Torah commanded Jews to let fields lie fallow, leading to a scarcity of farmed food. The Torah itself acknowledged the challenge and anxiety, reassuring the Israelites that God would divinely provide for them during the sixth year enough to sustain them during the seventh.[57] But naturally they remained anxious, leading to an ongoing struggle between the people, who sought to circumvent the technical rules of *shmita*, and the rabbis, who sought to patch the holes.[58]

Contemporary scholar Aharon Ariel Lavi argues that part of the point of the *shmita* year was providing a planned opportunity for crisis. When we intentionally force ourselves into crisis for a defined period of time, we become more resilient as individuals and as a society. Indeed, without *shmita*, our economy experiences a recurring cycle of booms and crashes, which in recent history come every 7-8 years, like the dot com bubble of 2001 and the Great Recession of 2008. The difference is that they come unexpectedly, and we are poorly prepared for the outcomes. Lavi argues that investors themselves caused these crises, and that an average of 7-8 years is no accident—this is the amount of time it takes an investor to forget the previous bubble and join the next one. *Shmita* provides a regular and forced opportunity to practice resilience.[59]

In Chapter 8, we will explore the ethical problems with our current approach to loan capital and explore an alternative, inspired by *shmita*. In Chapter 4, we will explore how ancient communities developed pooled endowment mechanisms to navigate the loan cancellation requirements of *shmita*. In Chapter 5, we will see how the *shmita* year's restrictions on selling produce informed other restrictions on doing business in other prohibited food.

The approach of the *shmita* year suggests that the right answer to the problems with our current version of capitalism is not a violent revolution to cancel the debts and redistribute the land. Instead, we need to work to build a more sustainable system, like *shmita*, that offers its own brakes on profit accumulation and concentration of economic inequality.

Limits on Profits and Monopolies

In 2015, when hedge fund manager Martin Shkreli raised prices on a drug that treats a life-threatening parasitic infection from $13.50 a tablet to $750 overnight, it was just the most blatant example of greed in the pricing of pharmaceutical drugs.[60] The action from Shkreli (now a convicted felon for securities fraud) drew condemnation from both major party presidential candidates, who decried not just Shkreli but the rising cost of prescription drugs across the board.

The pharmaceutical industry is rife with examples of extreme price gouging of necessary medicines, and the industry is severely lacking in transparency. At the same time, one in four adults in the US today will not fill a prescription, will cut pills in half, or will skip doses because of cost.[61] The logic of our current approach to capitalism has led us as a society to allow industries providing life-saving resources to charge exploitative prices.

In Judaism, on the other hand, communal leaders throughout history have intervened to prevent monopolistic price-gouging. Rabban Gamliel (1st century CE), famous head of the rabbinic academy in Jerusalem, once navigated a case where merchants inflated the price of doves purchased by new mothers as sacrificial offerings. Standing up in the public study hall, Rabban Gamliel announced that the dove sacrifices would no longer be required as frequently of mothers, and by the end of the day the price fell to approximately one percent of the high.[62] The Talmudic Sage Shmuel (165-254 CE, Nehardea/Babylon) similarly used his status as legal authority to threaten sellers not to price-gouge, whether in ritual items like willow branches for the holiday of Sukkot[63] or ceramic cookware after the holiday of Passover.[64] In 19th-century Poland, Rabbi Yisrael Meir Kagan approved a ban on eating fish for Shabbat for several weeks if the price of fish became too exorbitant, until sellers regretted their decision and returned the price to normal.[65] Even today, the rabbinical court of the *Eida HaChareidit* in Jerusalem has removed its stamp of kosher supervision from stores found to have jacked up prices during the *shmita* (Sabbatical) year, when produce is harder to obtain.[66]

Jewish tradition also sets explicit restrictions on profit for essential items. In the Talmud, the same Shmuel who intervened to stop price gouging also articulated a prohibition on earning more than an 18 percent profit on essential items like food.[67] Medicine is even more clearly off-limits as a source of windfall gains. Ramban, writing in Spain in the 13th century, outlawed exorbitant profits from the sale of pharmaceuticals, instead allowing drug producers to earn only the cost of producing the medicines plus a modest fee for time spent in their production.[68] These rules were adopted by the Jewish legal codes[69] and remain in force today.[70]

The drive to increase prices on pharmaceutical drugs is a product of our current economic mindset. For example, reports have drawn a direct correlation between executive pay incentive packages and price increases. AbbVie's CEO Richard Gonzalez's compensation exceeded $22 million in 2017 in large part due to sales performance on its blockbuster drug Humira, which has more than doubled in price since 2014 and now costs more than $60,000 per year.[71]

Price gouging is also made possible by monopoly power. In the case of pharmaceutical companies, the monopoly on production is often reinforced through devious (but legal) mechanisms to extend trademarks. Monopolies are not confined to pharmaceutical companies, of course, and are growing ever more prevalent. In the United States, there are now four major airlines and three major drug stores. Online retailer Amazon's market capitalization is bigger than all the publicly traded department stores in the United States combined.[72]

Monopolies play a key role in the mainstream investment arena. In 2018, *The Nation* magazine published a profile on Warren Buffett. Unlike most profiles of Buffett, who is usually lionized as the conscience of American capitalism as well as a successful billionaire investor in companies, *The Nation* critiqued Buffett's investment strategy. In short, a core element of Buffett's approach is to look for companies that hold monopolies or near-monopolies, buy them, and strengthen their monopolies in order to profit from them. Warren Buffett is quite open about the practice, which in his investor letters he terms a "moat" around a company. In 2010, investigators representing a federal commission visited his office in Nebraska to probe Buffett's role as a major owner of Moody's, the rating agency whose approvals of rotten investment instruments the US government identified as a key enabler of the 2008 financial crisis.[73] According to *The Nation*, Buffett explained he knew nothing about the management of Moody's. He bought the company because they're one of only three players that together control 95 percent of their market. "The single most important decision in evaluating a business is pricing power," Buffett said. "If you've got the power to raise prices without losing business to a competitor, you've got a very good business." Buffet went on to explain that "if you've got a good enough business, if you have a monopoly newspaper or if you have a network television station, your idiot nephew could run it."[74]

Buffett has indeed taken a courageous moral stand when calling for the government to close tax loopholes, like capital gains, from which he and other billionaires benefit. Yet his investment philosophy raises real questions when analyzed from the perspective of Jewish tradition. Jewish tradition has legislated against monopolies for thousands of years.[75] Theoretically, the United States' economic approach also opposes this kind of monopoly power and seeks to break up concentrated industries to encourage competition, but the government has frequently failed to act, and corporations have gotten larger and more concentrated than ever, enabling problems like price gouging of vital medicines.

In response to escalating drug prices around key medicines, some socially responsible investors have launched campaigns in recent years calling on pharmaceutical companies to limit their annual price increases. These investors have also sought to pressure corporate boards to change the way they compensate pharmaceutical executives and remove the link between executive pay and price hikes on key drugs. This advocacy even led to shareholder resolutions at five major pharmaceutical companies in 2019.[76] Jewish values can inspire us to continue this fight and others, and to ultimately seek a mindset of sustainability and societal benefit rather than short-term profit.

"Exxon Knew" and Stealing Awareness

In June 2021, staff members at Greenpeace's investigative arm caught an ExxonMobil lobbyist on video discussing efforts to undermine the presidential administration's push for action to mitigate climate change. The investigators, posing as headhunters, recorded the lobbyist revealing that the company "aggressively" fought against climate science and funded shadow groups to deny global warming, and that the company advocated for certain proposals like a carbon tax precisely because they knew such proposals would be unlikely to pass and would prevent climate action.[77]

This was not the first time journalists exposed ExxonMobil's efforts to undermine climate science. In 2015, investigative journalists discovered internal company memos indicating Exxon knew as early as the 1970s the impact of its products on climate change, including "dramatic environmental effects."[78] Exxon's predictions were shockingly skillful and accurate. Yet the company spent decades sowing doubt and spreading misinformation about climate science.[79] In 2015, the New York attorney general opened an investigation to determine whether ExxonMobil lied to the public about the risks of climate change.[80] That same year, activists launched a coalition called Exxon Knew, building off the investigative reports and seeking to hold the corporation accountable for its misinformation. Before the fossil fuel industry's misinformation campaigns, the basic insights central to understanding climate change were in place in the 1950s and could have led us on a very different trajectory. Climate science was widely accepted in 1965, even quoted in reports from the United States president's Science Advisory Committee.[81]

In 2021, New York City sued ExxonMobil for violating false advertising and deceptive trade practices.[82] Yet even today, ExxonMobil continues its narrative war, running an ad campaign on Twitter in January 2021 about how "natural gas is helping to shape a cleaner world around us," and, through its membership in the American Petroleum Institute, advocating against President Biden's executive orders restricting drilling on federal lands.[83]

Our current economic mindset justifies defrauding consumers and the public in order to profit. For millennia, Judaism has held clear ground rules against this deceptive practice, known in Hebrew as *gneivat daat* ("stealing awareness"). Unlike the principle of "let the buyer beware," the rabbis place the onus on the seller to disclose any defects in the goods.[84]

Big Oil is hardly the only sector alleged to engage in deceptive marketing to mislead the public in service of profit. According to the US Centers for Disease Control, 130 Americans die every day from opioid overdoses. In 2017, thirteen years after the opioid crisis began to build, *The New Yorker* released an in-depth article analyzing the role of the Sackler family in production and distribution of opioids, reporting that the family knew and misled distributors and the general public about their products' addictive risk.[85] Public ignorance of their dangerous and addictive properties has led to an epidemic where more than 11 million people a year misuse prescription opioids.[86] It has also led to tremendous costs for the pharmaceutical companies involved. As of the time this book's publication, the Sackler family had already committed $6 billion dollars to compensate communities and individuals ravaged by the opioid epidemic, as a part of legal proceedings,[87] alongside thousands of lawsuits and potentially billions of additional dollars at stake for the 13 pharmaceutical companies linked to the opioid crisis.[88]

The Barriers

With powerful Jewish wisdom demonstrating the problematics of business as usual, we might ask why all Jewish individuals and institutions aren't already investing their money in alternatives that are more in alignment with Jewish values. Any answer to this question must recognize the challenges and barriers facing Jews doing business with the broader societies in which they've dwelt.

Jews have been falsely accused of an unethical relationship to money for thousands of years. Our tradition holds a high ethical standard in how we earn, spend, and give money, a model for the world, yet the societies in which we live have regularly accused us of being greedy and lacking loyalty.

Those who hated early modern capitalism, like Karl Marx, usually hated the Jews for "causing" it. (Despite Marx's Jewish heritage, he absorbed the antisemitic messaging that permeated his society.) Those who hated communism blamed the Jews for that, too. These accusations sometimes led to large-scale systemic violence against entire Jewish communities. There are centuries of trauma, some of it ongoing, that Jews need space to deal with as we think about the ethics of money.

The United States has been no exception. Light-skinned Jews in the United States in the early and mid-20th century were granted an opportunity to assimilate into mainstream American society. That opportunity was always conditional—the price was to give up what makes us uniquely Jewish, including our unique money ethic. To be clear, Jews did not create the current economic system. Yet Jewish tradition has a unique treasure trove of wisdom to help fix it.

Beyond the psychological barriers, it is also difficult to find the time, energy, and knowledge to make necessary shifts to our investment behavior. Remember the retirement account I described creating when I started rabbinical school? In the end, I just slotted my savings into a Vanguard target-retirement index fund. I, of all people, ought to have known the immorality of investing in an index fund profiting from tobacco, the lack of meaningful shareholder advocacy, and the horrific record of Vanguard's proxy voting on climate change issues. But it was a convenient choice. It meant I could just save money every month and not think about the impact I was having.

I did not shift my own money until I had been working for multiple years in the socially responsible investing field. I don't recall a specific event; it was an accumulation, until one day I realized I could no longer invest in a way I knew to violate my ethical standards. I logged online, did some quick research, and spent an hour shifting my investments to socially responsible, fossil-fuel-free, values-aligned funds—not perfect, but a whole lot better than where I was.

I also sat down with my spouse and we determined an amount, an actual dollar number of net worth, beyond which we would have "more than enough" and wanted to begin transitioning some of our retirement accounts out of the stock market into local-impact investments with concessionary returns. It is a realistic number that we expect to hit within the next decade. We also set a higher number that represented "too much." We might never arrive there, but if we do, we will immediately divest ourselves of whatever wealth necessary not to go above that amount.

✻ ✻ ✻

Those of us seeking to live in protest against our current "business as usual" and its increasing destruction can begin by changing our mindset around money. Judaism offers an ancient approach to living as a sustainable society: profit is not inherently evil and can do great good. But it must be balanced with an ethical system that takes into account society's sustainable development, care for the vulnerable, access to medicine, and above all, setting a spiritual limit on accumulation and growth.

These Jewish money ethics serve as the grounding for the chapters to come, where we will talk about investment capital. Investment capital is the most powerful kind of money most of us interact with, more powerful than money we may spend as consumers or earn through our work. Investment capital has the potential to transform the world, for the worse and the better. It can be a tool of exploitation for personal gain, but it is also one of the most influential tools to finance and rapidly scale solutions to global problems. In order to use investment capital responsibly, we need to begin with the economics of enough and apply them to our investments. We need to set up appropriate expectations for ourselves around how much money we will earn—our financial return—and an ethical assessment of how much we really need.

Next Steps—Chapter 2

- **Journal about the following prompts.**
  - What does "enough" mean to me?
  - Try defining "enough" in various aspects of your life (like housing, community, vacation, and recharging time) without using a dollar amount.
  - What is *more* than "enough" and what is "too much"? For what is "too much," try to specifically include a dollar amount. (We are often tempted to shift this number over time—naming it now may help you hold to it later).
  - What other values do I hold, besides the profit motive and the self-centered impulse, that I would like to guide me in my financial decision-making?

Chapter 3

Financial Return

A few years ago, I had a call with an investment professional working with a nonprofit institution. I was about to launch into my pitch for Jewish values-based investing, full of inspiring wisdom from the ancient Sages, when he interjected: "Let me start by saying that, across our portfolio, we have a mandate to grow our investments at a rate of five percent plus inflation."

I have discussed responsible investing with individuals as well as boards and investment committees at Jewish organizations across North America. Overwhelmingly, investors considering Jewish impact investing are concerned about sacrificing financial return. Whether a person who has carefully saved for retirement and relies on a projected rate of investment growth to support themself in old age, or a Jewish institution providing thousands of free meals annually to vulnerable community members that has adopted an endowment model to partly fund its operations, pretty much everyone is worried about giving up the opportunity to make as much money as a market-rate return provides. (We will define "market-rate" shortly.)

The search for profit is legitimate, acknowledge the Talmudic Sages, who are always pragmatic in their approach to social change. We have already seen the idea that the *yetzer hara*, the self-centered inclination, plays a vital role in building human society. And we have already encountered fiduciary duty, the responsibility of nonprofit boards to manage the organization's financial resources to support the organization's mission (for example, a mandate to grow the portfolio at five percent plus inflation).

At the same time, profit cannot be our ultimate motive. To those who argue for making as much money as they can and using the proceeds to "do good" in the world,[1] Jewish wisdom teaches that how we make money is as important as how we give it away. The Sages of the Talmud offer the analogy of a man who stole a bushel of wheat to turn into bread. Even though he gave the baker a tip, he fed the bread to his children, and he made the appropriate blessing to God before bringing the food to his mouth, his act can never be considered admirable; it is really just offensive to God.[2]

The old myth that investing with values requires sacrificing returns has been disproven by impact investors in recent years (we will see statistics shortly). When aligning our investments with our values doesn't require any financial sacrifice, Jews have a religious obligation to do so. When socially responsible investments do require a financial trade-off, Judaism does not obligate us but does encourage us to consider giving up some return to achieve more impact. Above all, we need to carefully rethink the concept of a "market rate" of return when it involves investing in activities antithetical to Jewish values and human dignity. Judaism would encourage us to reflect deeply on what constitutes an ethical expectation of financial return. This chapter will provide us the guidance to do so.

Doing Good While Doing Well

Common critiques of impact investing from previous decades assumed that bringing values into investment decisions would require sacrificing financial returns. Because of this, most investors concerned with financial return would have nothing to do with impact investing.

Market rate of return, by the way, means the average amount an investor would earn investing across all the stocks in the market. This number fluctuates, and the amount looks different when investing, say, in Europe versus Japan, but as an example, an investor in a broad-based United States stock index has generally earned around seven or eight percent annually for the past 70 years.[3]

As the impact investing arena has matured over the past fifty years, research has conclusively debunked the myth that ethical investing requires sacrificing financial return.

The number of studies proving this has itself grown into the thousands. In 2020, researchers from New York University's Stern Center for Sustainable Business and from Rockefeller Asset Management performed a meta-analysis of over 1,000 studies published in the previous five years about socially responsible investing. The study concluded that investing with an eye to Environmental, Social, and Governance (ESG) factors was either neutral or boosted financial performance.[4]

Another analysis of over 2,000 academic studies on how ESG factors affect corporate financial performance found "an overwhelming share of positive results."[5] New studies are constantly emerging that reinforce the fact that it is possible to bring ethics into investment decisions and still achieve market-rate returns.

ESG is "a set of considerations that investors are using to try to understand risks and opportunities not accounted for in traditional financial models," according to one helpful definition.[6] The term developed as most responsible investment issues began coalescing into Environmental, Social, and Governance subject areas. Governance includes technical and obscure issues like how board directors are elected and how

CEOs are compensated. Governance issues are important for ethical investors. They determine how possible it is to hold companies accountable for their behavior on environmental and social issues.

Some researchers offer evidence that investments aligned with ESG principles even outperform "standard" investments, a phenomenon known as impact alpha.[7] While there is research on both sides and the debate remains inconclusive, the idea has proven inspirational enough that a major industry publication named itself after the premise.[8] Even shareholder engagement, which we will explore more in Chapter 7, can increase financial performance. In one recent study, companies that had recently been the subject of a successful shareholder campaign outperformed in the years following the campaign.[9]

There is a current pushback against ESG investing, which we'll discuss more in Chapter 7. Detractors of ESG like to claim that a company's non-financial impacts have nothing to do with financial performance. This claim is just plain wrong: it is rebutted by the extensive data we just surveyed. Further, the pushback against ESG investing runs counter to the religious framing of the Sages.

Jewish wisdom itself espouses the spiritual concept that doing good leads to doing well. The Book of Ecclesiastes says, "Cast your bread upon the water, for after many days you will find it." The Sages understood this to refer to the benefits that circle back to us from a practice of charitable giving.[10] This attitude is echoed by Jewish thinkers throughout the ages.[11] The Sages of the Talmud offered a pun on the word from the Torah for tithing (from the root *aser*), which sounds like the word for "growing wealthy" (from the root *asher*), to make the spiritual point that charitable giving can lead to an increase in wealth, not a decrease. (It's nice to know the rabbinic penchant for puns is at least two thousand years old.)[12]

Some understood doing well by doing good as a spiritual axiom; others tried to explain it as a natural consequence.[13] For example, the great, medieval Jewish scholar Rambam argued that benevolent actions benefit society at large, which has a direct causal relationship when they rebound to benefit to the original actor.[14] This kind of logic also appears in the socially responsible investing arena, which argues that ESG issues are "material," meaning financially relevant: a company's actions on environmental and social issues affect its financial performance, which justifies us acting on them.

My former organization, JLens, launched its Jewish Advocacy Strategy in 2015 as a concrete example of an investment vehicle that seeks to consider Jewish values, mitigate harm, and generate positive impact from a Jewish perspective, all while achieving market-rate returns. The strategy was designed to perform comparably with a common benchmark. According to JLens' Director of Communications Jake

Herman, investment accounts implementing the strategy have matched and even slightly outperformed the benchmark since inception.[15]

Some of the most impactful and transformative investment opportunities available do require being willing to sacrifice and achieve a lower financial return. These are known as **concessionary returns** because one is conceding the maximum possible profit in order to achieve impact. Some will argue, as we will see later, that true social change requires those with the most wealth to begin ceding financial return.

However, all investments have an impact. It is possible to avoid some of the worst harms and achieve a meaningful degree of values-alignment across an entire investment portfolio without sacrificing financial return. JLens, for example, offers investment strategies that screen out certain sectors like tobacco and fossil fuels. They achieve positive impact through shareholder advocacy, like successfully pressuring Amazon (which owns Whole Foods) to reduce its food waste, an issue that affects both climate change and hunger.

It is possible to bring values to bear on one's entire investment portfolio, without sacrificing financial return. But most investors have yet to do so. So, what does Judaism have to say? To learn more, we will need to scroll back almost two thousand years to the era of the Mishnah.

The Character of Sodom

The Sages of the Talmudic era compiled a Mishnah, a teaching, which speaks directly to our question. This remarkable text will require some unpacking.

> There are four characters of people:
> The one who says "what's mine is mine, and what's yours is yours": Some say that's an average character. But there are some who say that is the trait of Sodom.
> "What's mine is yours, and what's yours is mine": an *am ha'aretz* (uneducated person).
> "What's mine is yours, and what's yours is yours": a pious person.
> "What's yours is mine, and what's mine is mine": a wicked person.[16]

Of the four characters described in the Mishnah, it is easy to comprehend the two extremes. We all understand the nobility of offering our own resources without expecting anything in return; on the other extreme, we recognize the evil of a life lived seeking to take without giving.

The other two cases are more complex. Some of us might theoretically like to live in a world of "what's mine is yours and what's yours is mine." Many of us live this principle in relationships with loved ones. Yet on the societal level, the 15th-century commentator Ovadiah Bartenura (Italy, 1445-1515) explains that such a person "wants the well-functioning of society but doesn't have wisdom to distinguish effective methods."[17] In other words, this approach is naïve.[18] The standard of "what's mine is yours and what's yours is mine" cannot effectively ground our economy.

The late anthropologist David Graeber from the London School of Economics notes that at a certain level, the debate between capitalism and communism becomes ridiculous, as most societies around the world are a combination of the two. When someone asks me to pass the salt, it is hard to imagine saying "what will you pay me?" Instead, we practice communism on a micro scale, from each according to their abilities and to each according to their needs.[19] At the same time, an economy based more broadly on communism is destined to fail the practical tests of human nature. The rabbis are deep pragmatists who understand human psychology and seek not only to imagine an ideal world but to achieve justice within our current lived circumstances. In the words of contemporary Israeli rabbi Elisha Ancselovits, "*Halachic* [Jewish legal] sources seek to ameliorate the human condition instead of overcome it."[20]

What about the first character in the Mishnah, a person who says, "What's mine is mine and what's yours is yours"? The Mishnah calls such a person average, yet such a person is at the same time embodying the trait of Sodom, a devastating insult.

Near the beginning of the Torah, Abraham's brother Lot lived in the city of Sodom, a city so evil that God could not find even ten people of good character to redeem it from destruction.[21] Contrary to modern associations with the word "sodomy," the Torah leaves unspecified what made the people of Sodom so evil. The Sages interpret the great sin of Sodom as a particular kind of selfishness: they refused to share access to their resources *even when it cost them nothing*.[22]

The Talmud presents anecdotes of the people of Sodom disrespecting travelers; causing property owners to be crushed by precarious walls; using deceit to uncover people's buried treasure; or, to quote a particularly vivid example: "When a poor person would visit Sodom, each citizen would give him a coin with the original owner's name written on it. And they would not give or sell the person bread, so that he could not spend the money and would die of hunger. Once he died, everyone would come and take back their coin."[23]

Saying that someone is acting with the character of Sodom means that person, while perhaps following the letter of the law, is acting in a selfish way that will destroy society. If at first this seems a more practical approach than the naïve *am ha'aretz* described above, it is also more pernicious.

Most people in the United States can relate to the paradox. In some ways it exemplifies the individualist extremes of our current society, like criminalizing homelessness or placing a greater effective tax burden on the poor than on the rich. Such norms have become second nature to many of us. At the same time, they run contrary to Jewish tradition. The Talmudic Sages taught: "If a person sits in a corner of their house, saying, 'Why should public welfare matter to me, why should I listen to their protests? Let my soul sit in peace.'—such a person destroys the world."[24]

The sin of Sodom is subtle. It begins with the assumption "what's mine is mine." Then, as a moral corollary, one's possession gives one the right to deny hospitality or benefit to others. Yet, as we've seen in Chapter 2, there is no concept in Judaism of unlimited property rights. What's "mine" is never really mine; such a claim flies in the face of the Divine nature of the world.[25] In the final book of the Torah, Moses exhorts the people before they enter the promised land: "When you have eaten your fill, and have built fine houses to live in, and your herds and flocks have multiplied, and your silver and gold have increased, and everything you own has prospered, beware lest your heart grow haughty and you forget the Lord your God, who freed you from the land of Egypt...and you say to yourselves, 'My own power and the might of my own hand have won this wealth for me.'"[26]

The Talmud discusses the trait of Sodom further in a particularly interesting case, a debate about squatters. Rav Chisda and Rami bar Chami debated the following question: "If someone lives on her neighbor's property without him knowing, does she have to pay him rent?"

They established some common bounds for argument. When the property was for rent and the squatter was looking for a place, both agreed the squatter has to pay. They also clarified that if the property wasn't for rent and the squatter had her own house (maybe she just wanted a change of scenery), and assuming no harm has been caused, she does not need to pay anything. They assumed for the sake of argument that, in this case, the squatter is taking good care of the property and is not causing wear and tear, but rather, is protecting the property from deterioration.[27] So, what if the squatter needed a place to stay, and her squatting didn't cost the homeowner anything, as he wasn't planning to rent out the vacant property anyway? They summed up the question: What if one benefits when the other suffers no loss?

The Talmud recounts the progress of the debate, including how the Sages eventually build a clear consensus. Someone who lives in someone else's property without their consent does not need to pay rent. It is a case where one benefits while the other suffers no loss.[28] Expecting the squatter to pay when she has cost the owner nothing is an act worthy of Sodom.

The Law—Helping Others While Costing Nothing

The Sages of the Talmud were so concerned with the selfishness of Sodom that they built it into the legal code, allowing the courts to force an individual who is acting like Sodom to be more generous.[29] For example, to avoid "the character of Sodom," the Sages compel a person who lives in a home with two entrances to leave by the one that will least disturb the peace and quiet of her neighbor's Shabbat observance.[30] They force two inheritors to split up property in a way that allows the one who already owns a piece of adjacent land to have his portion be contiguous.[31] And so on.

While rabbinical courts do not have the actual power to compel financial matters today, the principle still guides Jewish standards of modern behavior. Rabbi Dr. Aaron Levine, late professor of economics at Yeshiva University, offered an example of someone driving home from a benefit dinner who is asked by a passenger for a ride home along the same route—Jewish ethics would compel them to offer the ride, as one benefits while the other suffers no loss.[32]

Jewish law goes further. Not just individuals but the entire community may be forced to act in a way that avoids the selfish traits of Sodom,[33] even if the benefit will not come until after time has elapsed.[34] There are even some opinions among the medievalists that if one suffers a small expense but there is enormous benefit to another person or the community, we can compel the person to act in such a case.[35]

There are also commentators who argue that extra effort is not considered a "loss." Only financial loss counts as a legitimate excuse.[36] This could include taking the time to research values-based investments even if a target retirement date index fund (with no values alignment) might be more convenient.

It appears that Jewish law would require community members to approach all investments in a way that mitigates harm in the world and helps others when it does not cost anything to do so. Jewish investors, if they can achieve market-rate returns, have an obligation to choose investments that offer the greatest positive benefit or least harm to society. They must benefit others when they suffer no loss in doing so. They must do good while they are doing well.

But what about when a person suffers a loss, or at least loses the opportunity for maximum gain?

Concessionary Returns and Fiduciary Duty

When an investor assumes that they could be achieving market-rate returns with their money, doing anything else represents a financial concession. Such concessionary investments often have an outsized positive impact on the world compared to market-rate capital.[37] Concessionary returns could indicate a range—anywhere from one percent to five percent return, depending on the investment. It could also include a zero-percent return (like free loans, which we will explore shortly), but still a full return of all the money invested. To be clear, concessionary investments are still investments, not philanthropy.

Low-cost capital is vitally important to catalyze the development of social-purpose businesses that might otherwise never get off the ground. Some investors, including the MacArthur Foundation, even prefer to call it "catalytic capital." For example, "catalytic" investment strategies (below-market rate of return) over decades helped lay the groundwork for the biological mRNA platform used to create COVID vaccines.[38]

As another example, the community development finance arena, which grew out of the Civil Rights Movement of the 1960s, has played a crucial role moving long-term, low-cost capital into the hands of entrepreneurs and business owners of color. Such **Community Development Financial Institutions (CDFIs)** are officially certified by the Department of the Treasury and now number in the hundreds.

Lisa Mensah is CEO of Opportunity Finance Network, a trade association for CDFIs that also offers bundled financial products for companies to invest. Mensah articulates the need for concessionary returns to further the network's racial justice mission: "The most impactful capital has a couple of features. First, it's really long-term. The companies that came with us are signing on for ten years. Second, it's very low interest.... Companies are taking two percent money on our five-year notes and three percent money on our ten-year notes."[39]

As soon as we consider the topic of concessionary returns, we need to revisit the topic of fiduciary duty.

Fiduciary duty requires an investment committee to prioritize what's best for the organization—which is generally understood to be maximal profit. But we ought to think of fiduciary duty more broadly, as a responsibility to steward the organization's mission, of which financial return is a part. For example, we will learn in Chapter 9 about pension funds which have come under critique recently for investing their pensioners' money in private equity funds that buy up housing stock. Pension funds exist to enable their pensioners to afford retirement. Should we really see it as a fulfillment of fiduciary obligation for a pension to make a profit by making local housing unaffordable for its pensioners?

Fiduciary duty also looks different at different types of organizations. Notwithstanding the previous example, pension funds have a primary mission to provide financial support to pensioners in retirement while minimizing the burden on them while working. So a pension's fiduciary duty will include seeking the highest financial return possible over the long-term.

Many Jewish nonprofit organizations rely on their endowments to fund operations in support of their mission. Fiduciary duty for those organizations may require them to maximize investment returns. Of course, if it is a choice between two investments with equivalent returns, one of which also furthers the organization's values, investing in the values-aligned option is a fulfillment of one's fiduciary obligation.

But for some mission-driven organizations, fiduciary duty to the organization's mission may not require (and may even incline against) seeking market-rate returns. Certainly individuals, especially those who already have built enough wealth to have a comfortable retirement, might see concessionary returns with high impact as the best fit for their investment capital.

Young investors are more open to the idea of concessionary returns, according to a Stanford University study in late 2022. The study noted that a third of investors under the age of 40 state that they are willing to give up more than 10 percent financial return in order to bring about social and environmental improvements in companies.[40]

Faith-based investors represent another group exploring concessionary returns. A 2020 survey of faith-based investors from the Global Impact Investing Network found that 82 percent of faith-based capital currently targets market-rate returns, nine percent targets returns that are "close to market rate" but concessionary, and another nine percent of capital is invested "close to capital preservation," meaning very concessionary returns, where you preserve the money you put in but gain little to no more.[41] In other words, concessionary returns do not require an all-or-nothing approach. One pension recently suggested creating a "tiered return" system to prioritize those on fixed incomes, while still reducing the overall yield so that investments can achieve their highest impact.[42]

A recent study on faith-based investors by the University of Zurich noted that in order for investment capital to achieve "more fundamental changes, investors should look towards financing companies that provide solutions to social and environmental problems and help them grow by making capital available. Such an approach is especially effective…when investments are done on concessionary terms."[43]

Faith and Concessionary Returns

Jewish and other faith-based investors play a critical role in building the market for concessionary-return investments. Unlike public pensions and similar entities, faith-based organizations generally have a clearly articulated mission and set of values that fiduciaries have a duty to uphold. This could open the door to consideration of investments that sacrifice a bit of financial return but best embody the organization's mission and values.

Faith investors also have ready access to language to help shift our mindset. Reverend Fletcher Harper, executive director of the faith-based environmental nonprofit GreenFaith and a founding member of the clean energy investment organization

Shine, talks about "the infinite return," the idea that there are kinds of returns beyond financial that matter, or ought to matter, to faith-based investors.

Judaism believes that the profit motive, while legitimate, can never be infinite. Instead, there are numerous other values that Jewish tradition considers infinite (or at least potentially infinite). The Sages of the Mishnah taught: "These are the things that have no defined limit: leaving the corners of one's field for the poor, bringing the first fruits of one's harvest to the Temple, bringing offerings on festivals, performing generous deeds, and studying Torah."[44]

There are many different kinds of return that a Jewish investor might care about other than financial. For example, one might seek a return in the form of a reduction in poverty or improvement in education. Other returns a Jewish investor might care about include a livable climate (Chapter 10) and increased racial justice (Chapter 11).

Spiritually, Judaism encourages us to strive to prioritize a lower financial return in exchange for a higher social impact. Indeed, as the medieval Rabbi Jacob ben Asher (*Tur*, Spain, 1250-1343) writes, the very thought of "I can't possibly sacrifice my money for others" obscures the truth from a spiritual perspective that my money is not "mine," but is entrusted to me by the Divine.[45]

Concessionary Returns in Jewish Law

Jewish tradition speaks in both the language of moral guidance and the language of law. Is pursuit of concessionary returns merely an ideal and pious behavior, or would Judaism consider it an obligation?

The answer: it was a debate. The conversation began in the Talmud in a discussion about where to prioritize loans. The Sages noted one ought to favor lending to a member of one's community over lending to a total stranger. In fact, if one has a choice between a free loan to a member of one's community or an interest-bearing loan to a stranger, one should ideally choose the lower financial return and prioritize strengthening one's community.[46] It is unclear, however, whether the Talmud was decreeing a law or just describing a spiritual ideal.

The Tosafot, a group of French rabbis in the 12th and 13th centuries, argued the Talmud meant a real obligation. One is obligated to sacrifice financial return if an opportunity exists to achieve positive communal impact, even in cases of great financial loss.[47] Other commentators of the period countered that the Talmud really only intended an obligation in cases of small financial loss or no loss at all.[48]

Some practitioners in the impact investing arena differentiate between "market-rate," "near market-rate," "significantly below market-rate," and mere "preservation of capital." The Tosafot would likely argue that Jewish tradition demands we move beyond "market-rate" to pursue "near market-rate" investments if they achieve positive impact. Anyone who goes further to pursue "significantly below market-rate" investments for the sake of achieving impact is going spiritually above and beyond.

Ultimately, the Tosafot lost the debate. When the question arose again in the mid-20th century, Rabbi Moshe Feinstein, one of the pre-eminent Jewish legal authorities of that era in the United States, concluded that if one stands to lose a significant amount of money, one need not sacrifice financial return for the sake of positive impact.[49]

Rabbi Feinstein's position echoes the teaching from the Mishnah that opened our chapter. If one person benefits while the other suffers no loss, a refusal to help reflects the selfishness of Sodom. Yet if one stands to lose out, the calculation changes. High-impact investments that involve a less-than-maximal financial return are a spiritual ideal in Judaism, but we cannot consider them an obligation.

* * *

Even so, the entire Jewish discussion on market rate of return is framed by a rigorous body of Jewish law and expectations around righteous monetary behavior, including charity. An individual is already expected to be giving away at least 10 percent of one's income every year to charity[50] (or, for wealthier folks, up to 20 percent. For the wealthiest folks, Jewish law might even ask 20 percent of total wealth instead of income).[51] This kind of giving in itself slows the potential growth of one's assets.

The aspirational ideals of Judaism might also become closer to obligations the wealthier one is. Our society does a poor job of giving us an objective view of what constitutes actual wealth. For example, according to a recent calculation, someone with more than roughly $1 million in assets, a common retirement savings goal in the US, is among the wealthiest one percent of humans on earth.[52]

The wealthier one is, the more one could give up market-rate returns with less of an impact on actual quality of life. In such cases, Judaism's spiritual encouragement might sharpen toward obligation to move individuals further along the spectrum prioritizing impact over maximal financial returns.[53]

The Problems with Market-Rate

Some in the impact-investing arena have begun to argue that "catalytic capital" and concessionary returns are not just nice but necessary, and that some social problems will be impossible to solve when all of our assets are seeking market-rate returns.

For example, the US-based nonprofit Transform Finance, which envisions capital as a tool for transformative social change, released a report in April 2021 focused on the question of who gets to make investment decisions that affect communities. The report notes, "Some projects, many of those prioritized by grassroots organizations and residents of communities targeted for assistance, cannot achieve market rates of financial return. Positive change may not be profitable at all—and most likely ought not to be measured against other investments that are by their nature extractive."[54] According to Ion Yadigaroglu, partner at an investment firm that oversees the assets of former eBay president Jeff Skoll and other clients, "It's next to impossible to get families out of the mindset of expecting to compound returns at 15 percent, which is just not feasible when investing in basic needs, like access to electricity and housing."[55]

"Market-rate" itself is a difficult concept. It represents an expectation for investors actively participating in the current (broken) economic system. For example, investing in the standard stock market indices considered to be "market-rate" means investing in the production and distribution of deadly cigarettes, the growth of private prisons, and the expansion of fossil fuels. That's not to mention profiting from current and ongoing exploitation of borrowers of color, extraction of wealth from Indigenous communities and land, and instances of literal modern slavery in supply chains (which we will explore more in Chapter 11). We need to question assumptions about what constitutes market-rate, which informs the ethics behind pursuing it.

This tension undergirds the problems with the current state of Environmental, Social Governance (ESG) investing. Hans Taparia, business professor at New York University, recently called for the socially responsible investment community to radically rethink what an ESG investment ought to look like. "For far too long, CEOs have followed a 'growth at all costs' mindset to maximize shareholder value. Despite ongoing catastrophes and injustices, they are being cast in a positive light.... To be true ESG leaders, they will have to pay workers more, make products that are less addictive, and increase their costs to protect the environment. In other words, they might have to sacrifice on profit."[56]

Sara Murphy, Chief Strategy Officer at The Shareholder Commons, a nonprofit focused on systemic issues within capital markets, agrees. Investors need to focus, not on the performance of individual stocks within a benchmark, but on "the health of the benchmark itself." (A **benchmark**, by the way, is a basket of stocks or bonds by which funds commonly measure their performance. The broadest benchmark is the entire stock market.)

For example, The Shareholder Commons partnered with responsible investors to introduce shareholder resolutions at McDonald's and YUM! brands calling on the companies to address their overuse of antibiotics on livestock. Overusing antibiotics on farm animals (often to make the animals grow faster) increases "anti-microbial resistance," when the microbes that cause disease learn to adapt and avoid the effects of routine antibiotics. Antimicrobial resistance could cause up to 50 million human deaths by the middle of the century, according to the World Bank. The food producers have argued that responsible antibiotic use would drive up costs and reduce profits. Sara Murphy responds: "Ok. That's a good tradeoff."[57]

There are certain social issues, like global poverty, that can never be solved with a market rate of return. Oxfam, the international nonprofit focused on poverty alleviation, published a report in 2017 that puts it starkly: "Most enterprises making meaningful contributions to poverty alleviation lack the ability to deliver commercial rates of return." Based on Oxfam's experience, profit and impact are "more often in tension than not."[58] And the CEO of Root Capital, a nonprofit lender focused on supporting agricultural businesses in Africa, Latin America, and Southeast Asia, echoes this point: "What we can categorically say, based on 15 years of experience, data from our loan portfolio and the approaches we've developed for measuring impact, is that there is a tradeoff between financial return and some types of impact in our work."[59]

True systemic change will likely require the wealthiest among us to give up some financial return. Debra Schwartz, head of impact investing at the MacArthur Foundation, writes about a willingness to forego expected "market rate" returns: ""It is not *the* essential ingredient to achieving racial equity or justice, but I'm not sure how we get there without it."[60] What will truly transform our economy for the better is hard work and a willingness to build the economy we want to see, even at some personal opportunity cost: "These kinds of compelling impact opportunities are made, not found. They are not on the streets, for people to go window-shopping. If the market were going to just create these opportunities, we could all just go home."[61]

Rodney Foxworth, impact investing practitioner and CEO of Common Future, goes even further: "If mainstream impact investing continues to operate within the culture of the 'free market' and prioritize capital returns, by definition it will promulgate economic injustice.... If the goal is to get at *root causes*, then disrupting the concentration of power, wealth, and privilege is the solution we ought to set our sights on."[62]

Tariq Fancy, former Chief Investment Officer for Sustainable Investing at BlackRock, the largest asset manager in the world, describes an image of purpose and profit as two separate circles in a Venn diagram. Where the circles overlap, it shows where the right thing to do is also profitable. Fancy argues that the two circles overlap a lot less than he would have hoped or might have expected given the popularity of ESG investing. In his words, "if fighting climate change were cheap, we'd have dealt with it already. Morgan Stanley estimated that preventing climate change will cost $50 trillion, or close to half of the world's annual economic output."[63]

At a minimum, we need to be clear with ourselves about our motivations around impact investing. While maintaining market-rate returns, we can reduce the harm our investments cause and achieve at least a measure of positive impact—and Jewish ethics expect us to do so. But investors (including Jewish organizations) hoping to make market rates of return and heal the world from poverty, climate change, and global injustice at the same time are doomed to fail.[64]

This can be a difficult topic to bring up. After all, socially responsible investors have spent the past fifty years facing skepticism and dismissal from the "mainstream" investment community, which claimed that impact investing necessarily involves sacrificing returns and so wrote it off entirely. To use Fancy's analogy, the mainstream investment community assumed that the two circles in the Venn diagram have no overlap. Investors decided that if we need to give up either financial return or values and social impact, our values and our impact should be the thing to go. Given where society is at, talking about concessionary returns can feel like a complete non-starter.

The issue is not about the Jewish community (although Judaism has unique wisdom to offer). The whole financial arena is struggling with the topic of concessionary returns. According to The New York Times in May 2021, talking about concessionary returns "has been the third rail of socially responsible investing," precisely because "investors fear that such an approach could embolden critics who have long warned that investors will get lower returns if they want to push for change."[65] By the way, those are the same critics who themselves seem happy to profit from societal destruction for the sake of investment returns.

Another significant challenge is that it feels unfair for us to make a financial sacrifice as individuals when everyone else is continuing to profit. Tariq Fancy notes a conversation he had with a portfolio manager on staff at BlackRock, who said, "I believe in climate change. If we had a price on carbon, I'd lower my carbon footprint overnight—and so would everyone else. But it makes no sense to do it alone and put myself at a disadvantage, and it's not what I'm legally supposed to do or paid to do."[66]

Judaism recognizes the tension of being asked to make a personal sacrifice when no one else seems to be doing so. It is the same tension captured in the Talmud, which articulates that a personal sacrifice to achieve positive impact is praiseworthy but not expected. We are not required to sacrifice financial return. Yet most people are also not fund managers at BlackRock, and therefore, are not beholden to a definition of fiduciary duty that involves making as much money as possible as fast as possible. Whether individuals or mission-driven organizations, those with values inspired by faith ought to use those values to inform their approach to fiduciary duty and our investment goals.

Seeing Through the Fake Diet Gurus

In recent years, some individuals with access to significant wealth have emerged within the Jewish community have shown inspiring leadership in rethinking how they invest it. This is especially true of organizations whose missions or structure provide ample space to consider concessionary returns as a part of fiduciary duty, like private foundations.

Consider the example of Diane Isenberg. Isenberg was born to two relatively poor Jewish immigrants to the United States. Her father worked his way up and eventually built a fortune in the oil business. Isenberg herself has had a diverse life and career trajectory: for example, she worked in public health with poor rural communities in Bangladesh, then married a Welsh sheep farmer and moved to Wales.[67] When Isenberg inherited her family's wealth, she sought to invest that capital in ethical and impactful ways, aiming to address poverty worldwide.[68]

Five years in, she came to the realization that seeking market-rate returns would never solve global poverty. As she wrote in 2017, "Those of us actively allocating capital to fragile enterprises in developing markets recognize that those people who promise comfortable market-rate returns while solving global poverty are the equivalent of diet gurus promising that one can lose weight while eating limitless amounts of chocolate cake."[69]

In 2018, Isenberg's family office, known as Ceniarth, made an explicit commitment to move away from "responsible investing" strategies that focus on market-rate returns and instead aligns 100 percent of the portfolio with what Ceniarth calls its "Impact-First Capital Preservation" strategy.[70] That same year, Isenberg wrote, "We have only become more convinced that trade-offs between impact and return are real and unavoidable. Those of us with the privilege and responsibility of stewarding great wealth must confront this reality. If we genuinely wish to deploy capital in ways that will support people and places that are being left behind by market forces, then we cannot delude ourselves into believing that we can have it all. The good news is that there are many of us fortunate enough to not need it all."

Ceniarth now makes around 30-50 direct impact investments a year.[71] Isenberg's team of thirteen investment professionals is led by Greg Neichin. Neichin, himself an active member of the San Francisco Bay Area Jewish community, recounts how he met Isenberg over an argument about Israeli politics at a clean-tech conference. Neichin talks about Ceniarth's "catalytic capital" strategy (referring to concessionary returns) with a tone that suggests that it's not a radical sacrifice. Instead, "'catalytic' just means reasonable."[72]

Some other private foundations have begun to shift their investment capital from market-rate to catalytic capital investments with concessionary returns. This includes the Libra Foundation, led by Nick and Susan Pritzker and their four children, heirs to the Hyatt Hotel fortune. The Pritzkers have made impact investments in the areas of racial, gender, and environmental justice causes for years through Libra, and a few years ago Regan Pritzker, daughter of Nick and Susan, created the Kataly Foundation with more than $400 million. Kataly seeks to spend down its endowment over the next ten years through both grants and low-interest loans. Kataly is focused especially on building the economic, political, and cultural power of Black and Indigenous communities. As an example, the foundation invested in the East Bay Permanent Real Estate Cooperative, a BIPOC (Black, Indigenous and People-of-Color) cooperative based in West Oakland seeking to create affordable, community-controlled land and housing.[73]

Pritzker notes her commitment to catalytic capital stems from her own wealth and how it was created: "As someone who inherited wealth, it was maybe easier for me in some ways to hear the critique from our grantees that that wealth is not mine, and that our wealth is not ours, that it was extracted from natural resources from people's labor, has been siphoned off from our public systems through tax saving strategies, and that the call to action wasn't just to invest in better companies but really to think much bigger picture" about the overall economic, political, social systems underlying the sources of her wealth.[74]

Another powerful example of limited financial return and high social impact comes from the Hebrew Free Loan Society. The Jewish practice of interest-free loans dates all the way back to the Torah, and Jewish communities throughout history have offered free loans to vulnerable or needy community members (which we discuss more in Chapter 8). A number of Hebrew Free Loan Societies were founded in the 20th century in the United States and continue their vital work today.

The Hebrew Free Loan Society in New York (HFLS), which has traditionally built its loan capital through donations, recently created an option for high-net-worth and institutional investors to invest capital at zero percent interest with HFLS, which then lends that capital out to vulnerable or needy community members at the same zero percent interest. After several years, HFLS eventually returns it to the investors. As CEO Rabbi David Rosenn points out, since HFLS has a 99.9 percent repayment rate and a pool of money to shoulder the risk of any initial losses, the organization is able to guarantee return of 100 percent of investor capital. Rosenn compares an investment in HFLS to "getting impact out of your cash"—rather than having money sitting in a money market account, it could diversify by sitting with HFLS and create significant social impact. The organization had already raised $5 million in loan capital before the coronavirus pandemic and plans to double or triple that within the next five years.[75]

Similarly, during the pandemic, the San Francisco Jewish Community Federation and Endowment Fund made an option available to its donors to redirect some of their investment capital, held in donor-advised funds, to the local Hebrew Free Loan Society for emergency loans to community members impacted by the pandemic. The Federation was able to mobilize over $5 million over a short period of several months that was then loaned out to community members in need.

The Federation's interest-free loan pool was made possible by a $500,000 anchor investment from the Laura and Gary Lauder Philanthropic Fund. Laura Lauder chaired the Federation's endowment committee and was instrumental in moving the organization to increase its impact investing options. Since that interest-free loan, the Federation has built out an impact-lending portfolio of over $20 million.[76] The Lauders maintain a donor-advised fund (DAF) at the Federation, which they have used to seed investments like the Black Vision Fund, lending to Community Development Financial Institutions (CDFIs) to close the racial wealth gap. Thanks to the Lauders' leadership, other donor-advised fund holders are now also able to access these highly impactful investments.[77]

While large, endowed foundations and wealthy individuals might be the first to consider concessionary returns, one doesn't need to be wealthy in order to do so. One just needs to be comfortable with a lower rate of return. The authors of the Oxfam paper note that most investment opportunities having a real impact on people living in poverty in the Global South can generate average net income in the low single digits, a number that resonates in the US as well.

For example, in Oregon, anyone can become a member and invest in the Oregon Clean Power Cooperative, with a mission to increase solar installations across the state. The cooperative has worked with a number of synagogues and other houses of worship to install solar panels. According to its website, its investment offerings generally return between two to four percent annually.[78]

Similarly, a growing number of Community Development Financial Institutions are providing an opportunity for everyday folks to invest capital that is loaned out to marginalized communities who have historically been excluded from access to capital. In Chapter 11, we will learn more about Catherine Berman, who founded a social purpose company called CNote that allows average investors to invest in a diversified portfolio of CDFIs across the country. As of December 2022, CNote's Flagship Fund provided two percent annual return.[79] In Chapter 9, we will explore further the Jewish perspective on local investing; opportunities abound to make significant impact in our local communities through concessionary returns.

There are many investors for whom it may not be appropriate to shift their entire portfolio into concessionary returns, but who are interested in carving out a percentage of their assets to focus on these particularly high-impact investment opportunities. Some have started at 1.8 percent of their portfolio (the number 18 and its multiples hold special significance in Jewish tradition).

Steps Along the Journey

Jewish tradition articulates a journey of expectations around financial return. If, without sacrificing financial return, a person is able to align investments with values, minimize harm, and achieve a measure of positive impact, Jewish tradition obligates them to do so. Rather than behave with the selfishness of Sodom, Judaism expects community members to do what they can to benefit the world, expecially when it costs nothing.

Judaism would also encourage people toward a spiritual practice of exploring concessionary returns—sacrificing the maximal profit we could be making in order to achieve higher impact. This is especially true the wealthier one becomes. We saw Oxfam, Shareholder Commons, Root Capital, and others argue earlier that certain kinds of societal problems will never be solved on a market rate of return. Market rate of return is itself a problematic concept as long as the market is full of violations of Jewish ethics.

Judaism requires adherents to help others when it costs nothing, including aligning investments with Jewish ethical values through market-rate strategies. But when there would be a personal sacrifice, the calculation changes. Some investors are reliant on financial return on investments to support themselves or retire without becoming a burden on family. For others, it can feel unfair to be the one sacrificing when no one else is, like Tariq Fancy's colleague at BlackRock. Regardless, beginning with a foundation of the economics of "enough," as discussed in Chapter 2, enables us to carefully consider what kind of financial return we want to expect.

Nowhere in Jewish tradition does God promise a five-percent rate of return above inflation. While we can hope and plan for financial return, an expectation of a certain rate of return and a feeling of entitlement to receive that return is a kind of hubris. In fact, valuing profit above all else could be a manifestation of idolatry (which we discuss more in Chapter 5), which, after all, is the act of mistaking that which is truly Supreme with other substitutes.

Faith groups play a vital role here, in that they almost all believe there is something more important, more valued, more supreme in life than maximal financial return. As Martin Palmer, head of the global nonprofit impact investing network FaithInvest, has noted, faith-driven investors are the ones who have the best opportunity to question "market-rate" as a gold standard and establish more ethical expectations for their money.

Diane Isenberg, the wealthy Jewish sheep farmer, and the head of her family office Greg Neichin, echo this in an article they wrote together: "We have exhausted ourselves, unsuccessfully, in search of impact-first peers. Perhaps, like many in search of existential answers and nowhere else to turn, we have found religion at Ceniarth."[80]

I know many folks of my millennial generation and younger who are willing to question the market gospel (pun intended) about "traditional" investing and financial return. But while studies discuss the vast generational wealth transfer about to take place over the next thirty years,[81] we cannot wait for people of younger generations to

Financial Return

slowly gain more power at Jewish communal institutions or over society's investment dollars. The time is ripe for a movement to rethink the way we invest our community's capital.

> ### Next Steps—Chapter 3
>
> It is possible to bring our values into 100 percent of our investment assets without sacrificing a drop of return. It is also possible to achieve even greater impact on issues like global poverty by using concessionary return investments.
> - **Step 1: Assess where you are and what you need.** Using the frame you developed in Chapter 2, consider where you fall on the spectrum of financial return. Do you (or your institution) need market-rate returns in your investment portfolio?
>   o If you need market-rate returns: It is still possible to move 100 percent of your investment dollars into alignment with values and mitigate harm. Jewish ethics would exhort us to do so—continue your journey with Chapter 4 below.
>   o If you have "more than enough": consider allocating a percentage of your investments for "concessionary returns," sacrificing some portion of financial return in order to achieve greater impact. Some people and institutions have started with 1.8 percent or 3.6 percent of their net worth, since 18 is a mystically powerful number in Judaism.
> - **Step 2: Explore opportunities.** Learn more about opportunities that offer returns in the zero-to-five percent range and achieve tremendous positive impact. Some examples mentioned throughout this book include investing in Community Development Financial Institutions (CDFIs). You can learn more through the website of the CDFI association, Opportunity Finance Network (ofn.org), which offers a database with investment opportunities in CFDIs as well as its own field-wide investment fund. Also, see Chapter 11 for more on CNote's Flagship Fund (mycnote.com) and Calvert Impact Capital's Notes (calvertimpactcapital.org).
> - **Step 3: Continue on a spiritual path.** If your wealth is growing, you can grow over time the percentage you dedicate to high-impact concessionary return investments. Use the numbers for "more than enough" and especially "too much" that you identified in Chapter 2 as a guide.

Chapter 4

Institutional Capital and Social Change

The day before Cyber Monday in 2019, Amazon's largest shopping event of the year, the Auschwitz Memorial and Museum flagged several surprising items for sale at the online retailer: Christmas ornaments with images of the concentration camp printed on them.

Amazon responded by removing the items, but the issue was not new. For years, Islamophobic, homophobic, and antisemitic items could be found for sale on Amazon's platform.[1] The problem was severe enough to catch the attention of shareholders. At the company's annual meeting, the Nathan Cummings Foundation, a social justice foundation with Jewish heritage, had presented a shareholder resolution that the company issue a report on its hate speech policies and practices. A full 27 percent of shareholders supported the proposal,[2] representing $243 billion dollars' worth of shares, a truly impressive number.[3]

Shareholder resolutions do not usually operate like a legislature, where a majority rules. Instead, they represent an indication of investor concern and a tool for pressuring corporate boards to make different decisions. Any result greater than 20 percent usually serves as a wake-up call to the corporation to change its ways. The hate speech resolution's success is all the more remarkable when we take into account that Amazon's founder Jeff Bezos himself owned more than 10 percent of Amazon's voting shares.[4] (We will learn more about shareholder resolutions in Chapter 7).

Amazon took some steps to improve its moderation of hate content but failed to address the issue systemically, so the Nathan Cummings Foundation filed again in 2020, earning 35 percent of the vote and escalating pressure on the company.

Pressuring one of the largest companies in the world is not easy. But institutional investors have special leverage to push for social change. Some of that stems from their size: institutional investors, including faith-based endowments, own approximately 80 percent of the equity in the largest 500 US companies. But they are also uniquely positioned to make change with corporations on modern social issues because of their credibility and power to threaten a company's brand image, posing a reputational risk.[5] Socially responsible investing pioneer Amy Domini calls them "sleeping giants."[6] Recall that investment capital is the most powerful form of money most of us interact with, more powerful than the money we spend as consumers or earn as workers. Institutional capital—money invested by communities or institutions, often in perpetuity, with only the profits being spent every year—is the most powerful form of investment capital.

Even if you are a member of the nearly half of the population who owns no stocks, or someone with a modest workplace retirement account with limited options, this conversation is for you. If, for instance, you are a member of a local Jewish community anywhere in the country, you are a stakeholder in your local Jewish institutions. You may be a member of a synagogue or active in Jewish organizations that have an endowment. In most major cities in the country, there are also local Jewish Federations that act on behalf of the city's entire Jewish community, making you a key stakeholder. And the changes our institutions make with their investment capital can be far more powerful than the changes we make individually.

Recently, there has been robust debate in the Jewish philanthropic community about endowments. At one extreme, some might argue that endowments should cease to exist. The money, rather than accruing forever, to be disbursed in small sums by inaccessible trustees, should be spent down to meet immediate needs, as it was in the early years of organized Jewish life in the United States. At the other pole, some believe that communal endowments ought not to only exist and grow, but that they should focus solely on financial return as the best way to support Jewish communal continuity. In the middle, a growing number of people agree with parts of the critique of endowments and seek to deploy Jewish endowment money more purposefully and in alignment with Jewish values, to shift the world off its current destructive trajectory.[7]

There are thousands of years of history of Jewish communities maintaining pooled endowment funds, and since the beginning there has been a debate about their role in social change. Money is only truly charitable, according to Jewish sources, when it comes under the control of the community. Once it does, it has a privileged place in a Jewish charitable ecosystem. And ultimately, all a community's investment decisions ought to be aligned with Jewish values. So let's explore the Jewish approach to institutional capital, from the early days of Jewish history through today and what might be next.

Early Forms of Capital

The earliest form of Jewish institutional capital might have been the treasury of the Temple in Jerusalem, starting three thousand years ago. Aside from the actual offerings sacrificed on the altar, the Temple had an extensive treasury that supplied everything from the wood for the altar to the material for repairs. The Temple also served as repository for state and royal treasuries, as well as for charitable gifts and tithes.[8] Not only was the Temple permitted to accumulate wealth, but Temple funds had a special exemption from the normal laws prohibiting interest.[9]

Judaism is not the only faith tradition to allow Temple treasury funds to be loaned out in a way that ordinary funds are not permitted. For example, Chinese Buddhist monasteries during the Middle Ages had endowment funds literally called "Inexhaustible Treasuries" which were loaned out at interest or invested with a focus on profit.[10] In India, while Brahmins were prohibited from lending at interest, Hindu temples were allowed to do so.[11] Later, in Italy in the 16th century, the Catholic Church created monti di pietà, charitable pools to lend money at modest interest.

A second early example of Jewish institutional capital derives from the *shmita* (sabbatical) year. *Shmita*, first described in the Torah, has radical environmental and economic implications. During the *shmita* year, the land of Israel lies free from human farming interventions, all crops are available for everyone to eat, and all loans are forgiven. Recognizing how capital owners feared loans being automatically forgiven before they were repaid, the Torah explicitly commands that lending continue in the lead-up to the *shmita* year:

> Beware lest you harbor the base thought, "The seventh year, the *shmita* year, is approaching," and you turn a harsh eye to your needy kinsman and give them nothing. They will cry out to God against you, and you will incur guilt. Give willingly to them and have no regrets when you do so, for in return the Lord your God will bless you in all your efforts and in all your undertakings.[12]

Despite the explicit warning, people with available capital refused to offer loans, and poor people suffered. Hillel the Elder (Jerusalem, 110 BCE-10 CE), head of the high court, instituted a rabbinic ordinance called the *prozbul* to allow lenders to collect their debts without violating the prohibitions of *shmita*. Hillel's workaround basically involved transferring an individual's debt to the court, since courts were not subject to the *shmita* rules of debt cancellation.[13]

Before the *prozbul*, the Torah had two goals: to ensure capital flowed to the poor and to institute a regular release from the burden of debt. Hillel saw the community was unable to maintain both goals, so he prioritized the goal that poor people would be able to access capital.[14]

Thanks to Hillel the Elder's workaround, loans received special treatment when they were moved into the hands of the court, representing a kind of communal holding of loan funds.

Notwithstanding these two early examples, the fundamental conversation that established the Jewish approach to communal charitable funds came later, in the time of the Talmud. Rabbinic discussions centered around a specific, paradigmatic case: trust funds of orphaned children. To learn more, we turn to the Talmud, in the Talmudic chapter, "What is Usury."

A Talmudic Approach—Orphan Trust Funds

One day in the study hall, Rav Anan made a provocative claim: "Shmuel says that it is okay to lend money belonging to orphans at interest."

Rav Nachman immediately objected: "Do you really think that just because they are minors they are exempt from every rule? It's not like we are allowed to feed minor children forbidden food."

Then, to drive his point home, Rav Nachman added, "Orphans who take money that isn't theirs will follow their parents to the grave! Anyway, what did you actually see Shmuel do that you assumed he thought this was okay?"

"Well, the orphaned children of Mar Ukba had this beautiful copper kettle. Shmuel would lend it out on their behalf and charge the renters a fee; but he would also weigh the kettle at the end and charge them for the depreciation of the copper. He shouldn't have done both—that constitutes interest."

"Even adults are allowed to do that," scoffed Rav Nachman. "When the renters rent the kettle, they accept that the more copper they burn, the more the value of the pot is actually diminished."

Rather, Rabba bar Sheila says in the name of Rav Hisda, or maybe Rabba bar Yosef bar Chama in the name of Rav Sheshet: "One may lend out the money of orphans 'near to profit and far from loss.'"[15]

The concept "near to profit and far from loss" originates here, appearing in the middle of a paragraph about investing orphans' money. We will spend more time on this important phrase in Chapter 8 when we discuss free loans and shared risk. For the sake of our understanding now, I will offer a brief example of "near to profit and far from loss."

Suppose an investor invests money in a venture run by someone else. If the investment earns a profit, they agree the investing partner will receive half the profit and the partner managing the business will receive the other half. If the investment loses some amount, similarly, each partner agrees to absorb half of that loss.[16] This is equitably shared risk. It represents the Talmudic model of a socially just business relationship. Both partners are "near to profit and near to loss."

Suppose, instead, that the investing partner demands most of the profit—which he can get away with demanding, since he has the power as the one supplying the investment capital. He also demands that, if the business venture loses money, the managing partner will absorb most of the loss and only pass on a small amount of loss to the investor. Such an arrangement would be "near to profit, far from loss."

In Jewish tradition, one who takes advantage of the power inherent in ownership of capital by forcing excessive risk onto the borrower is considered wicked. Instead, the appropriate practice is to share risk: if we profit, we both profit, and if the business venture fails, we both lose out.

Yet there is an exception for orphans. According to the last position we saw in our Talmudic passage above, they are allowed to lend money "near to profit, far from loss."

The Talmud continues with further debate about what exactly we do for orphans:

> Rabba asked Rav Yosef what we should do with the money of minor orphans. Rav Yosef suggested: "set up a court that will hold the money and give it to them dollar by dollar as needed."
>
> Rabba objected with concern: "But that will eat away the principal!"
>
> Rav Yosef replied, "So what would you do?"
>
> Rabba explained. "Well, I'd look for a wealthy man with gold scraps. The court would buy the gold scraps from him, and then give the scraps back in a joint business venture with terms that are near to profit and far from loss. Gold scraps, by the way, because if it were finished pieces of art, they might actually have an owner somewhere who would claim them and cause everyone a loss."
>
> Rav Ashi chimed in, "Fine if you find a man with gold scraps lying around. But if not, are you suggesting we deplete the principal? Here's what I propose: find a fellow whose possessions are free of controversy, and who's trustworthy, and pious regarding the law, and is not in bad graces with the Sages. Then, in court, set up a joint business venture with him that is near to profit and far from loss."[17]

To restate the text in more modern language: the Sages discuss what to do with the money of orphans who are not yet capable of managing their inheritance themselves.

They reject the possibility of investing orphans' funds at interest—after all, the Torah prohibits lending to a fellow Jew at interest, and orphans ought to be no exception. Yet the Sages do make an exception to invest orphans' funds in certain privileged ways. Investing in a business venture "near to profit and far from loss" normally violates a rabbinic ethic of equitable risk-sharing, but the funds of orphans can be invested "near to profit and far from loss" to avoid depleting the orphans' inheritance before they reach adulthood.

A few points emerge from the Talmudic discussion. First, the Sages of the Talmud are clear that their concern is depletion of the principal. The goal is not to grow a pot of wealth, but to make sure that the amount upon which the orphans are dependent does not decrease.

There are also limits to what is allowed. Rav Anan's initial claim that the funds of orphans can be lent with interest is thoroughly debunked and even derided by Rav Nachman. Instead, what is permitted for orphaned children is an imbalanced sharing of risk. The basis of the principle of sharing risk is to prevent the investor from taking advantage of their power over the person seeking investment capital (we will explore this further in Chapter 8). However, in this case, we are dealing with one of the most vulnerable populations in Talmudic society. The Sages of the Talmud allow us to override the normal moral censure on inequitable risk-sharing if the investor is vulnerable and powerless and we are seeking to support them.

The Talmud also sets a high standard for those stewarding investment capital designated for the vulnerable. They ought to be free of controversy, scrupulous, and on good terms with communal leadership. They need to be engaged in an arrangement where, on the one hand, they have a stake in the orphans' financial success (a shared business venture). On the other hand, they minimize their own profits for the benefit of the orphans, as they agree to be on the losing end of the "near to profit, far from loss" arrangement.[18]

One final point to note about orphaned children is that they remain children for a limited period of time. At some point, they grow into adulthood and have the ability to invest their own capital, and the exemption from the rule will no longer apply.

Beyond Orphans

Medieval commentators debated whether to widen this Talmudic category of orphaned children. Some argued that communal charitable funds ought to receive the same special treatment in an advantageous "near to profit, far from loss" arrangement if they were dedicated for the general poor, just like trust funds of orphans.[19] Others disagreed and thought the special treatment was limited to the case outlined in the

Talmud of orphaned children.[20] Ultimately, the former won out, and the privileged treatment was widened to a range of communal funds.

The most expansive early list of institutions deserving preferred treatment came from Rabbi Asher ben Yechiel, also known as the *Rosh* (Spain, 1250-1327). The *Rosh* allowed communal funds to be invested with special privileges, just like orphans' trust funds, if they were dedicated funds for the poor, to support Torah learning and Torah scholars, for maintenance of synagogues or for their beautification, to support the prayer service, and to purchase and maintain a Torah scroll. The *Rosh*'s list was adopted in all the later legal codes.[21] The *Rosh* added a reminder that such funds could still not be lent out at full-fledged interest. Later rabbinic authorities also granted an exception to free loan societies, when they had low demand for free loans and extra dollars that could be invested to grow the pool.[22]

Rabbi Azaria Figo (Italy, 1579-1647) in his work *Gidulei Terumah*, also understood the category of orphan expansively to include any individual unable to manage their own finances, including people with mental or physical disabilities that prevented them from doing so.[23] A widow whose husband had died was not given this exemption, on the assumption she was capable of managing her own money.[24]

At first, these pools differed from today's endowment funds—they were not designed for the principal to endure forever and the charitable giving to be accomplished with the interest but were spent down on a regular basis. The practice of building permanent endowments began more widespread adoption in the 1600s. As it grew, rabbinic authorities responded by allowing permanent endowments to fall under the same special exemption as charitable funds,[25] expressing a comfort with capital accumulation for funds designated for the poor or vulnerable.

Today, the technical details of these legal discussions may be less relevant to Jewish institutions, as our endowments are usually not invested in business ventures based on gold scraps. However, the rabbinic conversation offers an important Jewish values framework for thinking about communal endowments.

Communal Control

Jewish law and tradition endorse communal endowments. There have been communal endowments throughout Jewish history. In fact, the rabbis not only endorsed charitable funds maintaining investment portfolios; they allowed them to bend the rules to receive preferential risk-based treatment. This was justifiable because charitable endowments are funds dedicated to the most vulnerable members of society. One should not require them to shoulder a typical fair share of the risk.

However, Jewish tradition also offers important guidelines for modern philanthropic institutions. "Charitable dollars" are only truly charitable when they have left an individual's hands and come under charitable or communal control.

Since the beginning, Jewish communities have established *tzedakah* collections to support the poor. Every Jewish community had the obligation to appoint *tzedakah* collectors to collect and disperse food and funds to the needy on a weekly basis.[26] Their communal status was always apparent, and community control was paramount. For example, the Talmud describes how *tzedakah* was always collected by no fewer than two officials working side-by-side, not because they were not trusted with the money, but because the role was one of communal authority and its honor demanded at least two representatives.[27] Indeed, at the time of the Talmud, the community had the authority to force wealthy individuals who were acting stingy to give more, based on the community's assessment of how much was appropriate for each person to give, and even to seize their possessions by force if they refused.[28] (It certainly is interesting to imagine what this ancient Jewish practice would look like if it existed today.)

Endowments for the poor were understood to *already belong* to the poor; the community was merely tasked with allocating them fairly.[29] That is why *tzedakah* funds for the poor were not subject to the periodic debt cancellation of the *shmita* (sabbatical) year, because they were considered already under the auspices of the communal court and not belonging to the wealthy individual.[30]

Rabbinic authorities are clear that funds that an individual has promised to charity but that have not yet actually left his or her control are not considered charitable funds and receive no preferential treatment.[31] This is true even if the promise is irrevocable.[32] Money is only considered charity in Jewish law once it is placed under communal ownership or distributed to poor people. Actual charitable dollars get special treatment around investment risk; pledges do not.

This deserves our attention. The way philanthropy is practiced today in the secular world represents a radically different model. Wealthy individuals sometimes create foundations endowed in their names and are considered to have already donated to charity, receiving tax benefits and positive press for their generosity. Yet the wealthy individual—or their proxies, on the board of a closely-held family foundation—often remains in control of where to donate the money, and no money has yet made it to the hands of a needy person.

On the one hand, from a Jewish perspective, such private foundations do not violate any prohibitions. Judaism sees no inherent problem with accumulating wealth and designating it for various purposes, as long as wealth is acquired in ethical ways and one's focus in life remains on the things that are truly important (such as helping those in need, deeds of kindness, and studying Torah).[33] On the other hand, in Jewish tradition, private foundations do not qualify as a communal charitable endeavor worthy of being granted exemptions from the typical rules of equitable risk-sharing in investment. Foundations are really a form of private individual capital (intended for charitable use). As such, they do not yet count as communal charity and would not receive the same preferential treatment as charitable funds.

※ ※ ※

The rabbis exempted endowments for the vulnerable and poor from normal rules of equitable risk-sharing because these charitable funds are dedicated to the most powerless members of society. However, nowhere do the rabbis suggest that it is appropriate for communal endowments to be invested in ways that contradict other Jewish values. For example, Jewish law would prohibit investing in tobacco as a violation of the Torah's precept to "not stand idly by the blood of your neighbor" (see Chapter 5). So, too, should a Jewish endowment avoid investing in tobacco. Similarly, we saw in Chapter 3 how Judaism exhorts us to do whatever we can to make a positive difference in the world, especially when doing so does not cost us anything, based on the Talmudic principle of *zeh neheneh ve'zeh lo haser* ("this one benefits while that one suffers no loss"). So, too, would Jewish ethics demand that 100 percent of our endowment capital be invested in ways that achieve positive impact, when impact investing does not require a sacrifice of financial return.

Field Leaders

Some Jewish institutions have demonstrated courageous leadership in aligning their endowments with their values to achieve positive impact. The Leichtag Foundation, based outside of San Diego and in Jerusalem, was created by Lee and Toni Leichtag, who grew up in abject poverty. As a child, Lee's family literally shared bathwater between family members. Lee might have graduated high school; Toni probably didn't. As entrepreneurs, they struck it big near the end of their lives with the first generic version of the drug Ritalin.[34]

In 1991, the same year they sold their pharmaceutical company, the couple founded the Leichtag Family Foundation, and when they died they left 98 percent of their wealth to the foundation. The foundation also transitioned to an independent foundation (where no family members are on the board nor on staff). In the words of Charlene Seidle, executive vice president, this put the foundation in a rare position: "We had the ability to take a lot of risk, and to be urgent about that risk, to lead and to fail forward, using a full spectrum of tools to address challenges. Our board had a real mandate that we should be at the forefront of risk."[35]

The foundation set a goal to align 100 percent of its investment portfolio with its mission by 2025. It has already reached 60 percent. Included in the portfolio is the Leichtag Commons, a unique 67 acres of real estate that includes agricultural land rented out to farmers, growers, and research scientists; a hub of coworking and office space for nonprofits and social enterprises; and space used to host educational programs and arts and culture events.[36]

The foundation has also invested in venture capital in Israel like the Jerusalem Venture Partners,[37] emphasizing the founders' deep love for Israel and its thriving. The foundation instituted an incredibly robust do-no-harm policy for its investments, screening out investments that profit from child labor, human trafficking, entities who deny the right of the State of Israel to exist as a democratic Jewish state, discrimination, detrimental effects on human health, environmental destruction, and more. Influenced by the devastation of wildfires in California, the foundation has already begun to move part of its portfolio out of fossil fuels and is currently exploring a bigger no-fossil-fuel commitment.[38]

The foundation experienced additional challenges aligning investment capital with values because the foundation is "limited-life," meaning it has an explicit commitment to spend all the money in the endowment and cease to exist. This is unusual, as most secular foundations plan to exist in perpetuity through their investment returns. Instead, the Leichtag Foundation seeks to spend money to meet the urgency of the moment. That means the foundation needs the ability to sell its investments at a moment's notice, which is not possible for certain kinds of illiquid investments like early-stage startups.[39]

Being limited-life also affects the Leichtag Foundation's goals of financial return. The foundation has aimed for a five-to-seven percent return over time but does not rely on that financial return to sustain itself. Instead, it seeks to be opportunistic to make change "in this generation" as much as possible. The foundation also makes interest-free loans, which provide no financial return, while other investments, like Israeli venture capital, are expected to outperform in the long run.[40]

Another foundation leading the way is the Nathan Cummings Foundation mentioned earlier. It was founded on the fortune Nathan Cummings built with the Consolidated Foods empire (later Sara Lee Corporation) after growing up in Massachusetts as a poor first-generation Jewish immigrant from Lithuania.

In 2002, the foundation began an impact investing journey. The foundation had screened tobacco and weapons companies from its portfolio since the early 1990s, but beyond those sectors, the foundation found it easier to implement an active ownership and shareholder advocacy approach rather than adding negative screens. It based its approach on the writing of a Jewish business ethicist, Albert O. Hirschman. In his book *Exit, Voice, and Loyalty*, Hirschman noted that investors can choose different courses when confronted with corporate behavior they find problematic, whether the unfettered burning of carbon, complicity in human rights abuses, or even poor governance. An investor can sell her stock, but there is likely another investor willing to buy it, and the investor gives up her voice. Or an investor can exercise her voice, through voting proxies and filing shareholder resolutions (which we explore more in Chapter 7).[41] The foundation embraced this strategy of voice and active ownership—the foundation has filed at least eight or nine shareholder resolutions every year for the past 15 years, and far more some years.[42]

The foundation's shareholder resolutions played a key role moving Apple, UnitedHealth Group, and other companies to adopt "say-on-pay" provisions that allow investors to influence the company's executive compensation policies, rather than leaving the decision in the hands of the board. This practice was eventually legislated in the Dodd-Frank Act as mandatory for all US public companies after the 2008 financial crisis.[43] More recent wins include a shareholder resolution at Occidental Petroleum in 2017 calling on the company to conduct an assessment of the long-term impacts of climate change on its business. The resolution received more than 50 percent of the vote, a first for a climate-risk proposal at a major US oil and gas company.[44]

As the foundation continued its journey, trustees began considering making a commitment to align 100 percent of the foundation's assets with its mission. Members of the investment committee held a range of opinions. James Cummings, who lived on a commune in the 1960s and sports an earring in one ear, was a strong proponent, while John Levy, the investment committee chair and a New York tech venture capitalist, was more skeptical at first. But after a year of learning more about mission-aligned investing, the board voted unanimously to commit 100 percent of the endowment.[45]

Implementing the commitment has taken time. When the foundation made the commitment, nearly half of the portfolio fell in the category of investments that were unacceptable to the foundation because they failed to avoid harm to key stakeholders. Today that number has fallen to a tiny fraction of the portfolio, most of it illiquid investments that the foundation will be able to sell in the next five to ten years. The foundation has also grown its portfolio of direct investments, contributing to solutions to global problems, from nearly zero to nearly a fifth of the portfolio.

An organization doesn't need to be a private foundation in order to be a leader. The Reform Pension Board (RPB) serves the Reform Jewish movement by providing retirement and insurance programs to its congregations and, collectively, their thousands of employees across the country. The Pension, stewarding over $1.5 billion,[46] had been exploring values-based investing since the 1980s, when the fund joined the boycott on companies doing business with apartheid South Africa. In 1992, the organization joined the Interfaith Center for Corporate Responsibility and in 1997 began investing 1.8 percent of its assets into community development agency bonds. In 2014, the RPB formally adopted a Jewish-values investing policy. The RPB works with a proxy advisor to vote its proxy ballots in line with its values. Where they are able, the RPB screens out tobacco, coal, predatory lending, private prisons, and other types of companies that go against the Jewish values espoused through over 100 years of Reform movement resolutions.[47]

Institutions do not need to be enormous to make meaningful change. The synagogue Kolot Chayeinu in Brooklyn has less than $1 million in its endowment. In 2016, the synagogue joined the Standing Rock Sioux Tribe's effort to protest the Dakota Access Pipeline, which would run just upstream of the reservation. The synagogue learned that among the banks funding the pipeline they opposed was their own, JPMorgan Chase.

JPMorgan Chase has faced significant pressure from climate activists and investors over the bank's investment in fossil fuels, but the company has continued to finance over $317 billion in fossil fuel infrastructure since the Paris Climate Accords were signed, the most of any bank, earning it the unfortunate award "Still the Worst" from the nonprofit advocacy group BankTrack.[48] In 2018, the synagogue pulled its savings from JPMorgan Chase "to explicitly oppose the funding of fossil fuel and other related projects dangerous to the world in which we live," and moved them to Amalgamated Bank, a much smaller, values-oriented bank that originally served labor unions.[49]

Some institutions are embodying the communal nature of their charitable funds by opening up access to their investment committees beyond a typical cast of characters: older folks with long careers in investments. The United Jewish Israel Appeal, which makes an appearance in Chapter 12, launched its Si3 impact-investing initiative by recruiting a cohort of investment committee members from the broader community, including younger people. Wealth was not a requirement for sitting on the committee.

Temple Israel of Boston has devoted investment and resources to partner with the Boston Ujima Fund, a unique, participatory investment organization with an investment committee comprised of local community members, who may not have a business degree but bring on-the-ground intelligence.[50] (We will learn more about the Ujima Fund in Chapter 9.)

In working directly with Jewish institutions to transition their investment portfolios to Jewish values-based investing, I have witnessed first-hand how pressure is mounting on Jewish institutions to move past "traditional" investing and transform investment capital into a tool for making a positive impact on the world. Some of that pressure is external, reflecting a growing awareness of the problems with business as usual—accelerating climate devastation, growing inequality, and the compounding

Institutional Capital and Social Change

effects of systemic racism. Some of the pressure is coming from within the Jewish community and organizational stakeholders, including people of younger generations like mine (I am a millennial) who understand that change is easier than many might claim and are demanding that it happen faster. Whatever the motivation, the landscape is rapidly shifting.

Endowments and Difficult Choices

During the coronavirus pandemic, aside from the enormous death toll, human suffering in the United States and globally increased drastically through economic closures and poverty. In response, a number of leaders of color in the philanthropic sector articulated a call for foundations to pay out more than the legally required minimum distribution of five percent of their assets each year. In the words of Vu Le, former nonprofit executive and author of a popular blog critiquing the philanthropic sector, "Funders, this is the rainy day you have been saving up for."[51]

The medieval scholar Rambam noted that when encountering those in need, an individual ought to give up to 10 percent of one's assets.[52] The spiritual ideal would be to give up to 20 percent (more than that risks bankrupting the giver over time). Less than that falls under Rambam's category of "a miserly eye."[53] Does a gift to a foundation count as "charity"? Or, from a Jewish framework, since the foundation's assets have yet to fall under communal control or make it to the hands of a poor person, ought a foundation to apply the same goals of maintaining a minimum payout rate of 10-20 percent?[54]

The argument many foundations and funders make—that if I let this money sit and grow for years through investments, I will have more money to give—belies the fact that the problems facing society often also grow at a compound rate when not addressed. As Vu Le noted, there is no point saving these charitable dollars for another day if we are going to let people die in the streets in the meantime.

The problem is compounded (pun intended) when most foundation assets are invested in investments that exacerbate the very problems they may be trying to solve. I remember when news broke about the Bill & Melinda Gates Foundation, which funds public health around the world. The foundation's endowment was profiting from investments in companies that were emitting fumes and massive pollution that undermined public health, directly contravening its good works.[55] All investments have an impact, and we would be deceiving ourselves to think that money could just magically grow for twenty years without externalities worsening in the process.

Some advocate even more aggressively for spend-down of foundation capital and individual wealth. Resource Generation is a multiracial membership community of young people, ages 18-35, with wealth and/or class privilege who are committed to the equitable distribution of wealth, land, and power. Specifically, the organization advocates for young, wealthy inheritors (and their family foundations) to redistribute their inherited wealth. The organization was founded in 1998 and currently has around 1,000 dues-paying members across the US who collectively expect to control $22 billion in their lifetimes.

Many foundations are not comfortable going as far as Resource Generation and may not even be prepared yet to give out more than 5 percent of their portfolios. Regardless, we need to be thinking about what happens to the remainder of a foundation's corpus, invested for profit. As Edgar Villanueva, author of *Decolonizing Wealth*, notes, "*What about the 95 percent?* This is a question all of us need to be asking."[56]

As we have seen, Jewish tradition considers endowments acceptable and useful, and they even receive special treatment when they are communally controlled and focused on care for the vulnerable. Yet Jewish values also emphasize the dignity of every human and the importance of acting to end human suffering. In this urgent moment of increasing suffering, it is important for our institutions to engage in a deep and thoughtful conversation about how best to use the power we have, including as institutional investors, to help heal the world.

The Barriers to Change

I chose to ground this chapter in Jewish history and text and to highlight inspiring examples of leaders because I believe that will be most effective in inspiring social change within values-driven communities. But the same challenges and barriers we explored in Chapter 2 exist for Jewish institutions: a legacy of Jewish trauma informed by false historical biases of Jews as greedy, the high price of assimilation in the United States in order to avoid that discrimination, and a lack of time, energy, and knowledge to engage in values-based investing.

It took me years to align my assets with my values, despite the reality that I believe deeply in the cause and have literally written the book on Judaism and values-based investing. That gives me compassion for the broad Jewish community, and especially its institutions. Institutions move slowly, but when change comes, they can move mountains.

At the same time, the issues are urgent, and some solutions are simpler than we think. In 2019, Vu Le published an article about what he termed "solutions privilege," when people currently in power fail to recognize solutions being proposed unless those solutions are within one's comfort zone and already align with one's worldview. In his characteristic humor, he quoted Tarah Wheeler, a cybersecurity expert

Institutional Capital and Social Change

at Harvard University's Kennedy School of Government, who posted on Twitter a (probably hypothetical) conversation with a man about fixing the gender pay gap:

> Dude to me: what will fix the gender pay gap
> Me: pay women employees the same as men
> Dude: but how do we solve in the short term
> Me: pay all your women employees the same NOW
> Dude: but how
> Me: literally change their pay
> Dude: maybe we could teach women to negotiate better
> Me: (knife emoji)[57]

We could, literally, just make a commitment to align all of our community institutions' investment assets with our values. We could do it tomorrow. I know this to be true; I have spent years working with investment committees and boards across the country.

Such an abrupt change would fall outside the comfort zone of many of the people who sit on investment committees today. They would need to address concerns like financial return and how they want their institutions' values to be reflected in their investment portfolios. And they might not be able to execute the transition immediately. But investment committees and boards could make the commitment and begin the process of learning and growing together. A lot of capital could be moved quite quickly, more quickly than some might realize is possible, in alignment with communal values. The most effective way to get there will be for all of us together to lovingly pressure our communal institutions on this path.

We All Have a Role to Play

Many people in our communities, especially young people, are already recognizing both the power of investment capital and the urgency of shifting it away from the business-as-usual of our current version of capitalism.

There are people like Ophir Bruck, a Jew of mixed Sephardi-Ashkenazi heritage who grew up between Israel and Vancouver and has had a longstanding interest in environmental sustainability. Bruck graduated from the University of California, Berkeley, in 2014. As a student, he started a campaign to pressure the university to divest from fossil fuels. As he tells the story, "I was shouting at the University of California to divest from fossil fuels, and then the Chief Investment Officer did something really interesting—he hired me to work in the investment office." Bruck went on to serve as a senior manager at the UN Principles on Responsible Investment, the world's largest responsible-investment initiative.[58] In May of 2020, the story came full circle when the University of California announced it had divested completely from fossil fuels.[59]

There's the Jewish Youth Climate Movement, which was founded in 2019 to make collective climate action a defining feature of what it means to be Jewish over the coming decade.[60] JYCM is led by a board of middle school and high school students. In 2021 JYCM collaborated on a campaign to push the largest institutional investor in the world, BlackRock, to reduce its financing of fossil fuels. Among other investments, BlackRock financed the disastrous Line 3 tar sands pipeline in Minnesota, which traverses land that its opponents claim is protected by US treaties with Ojibwe nations,[61] and which would have the yearly climate change impact of 45 new coal-fired power plants.[62] In fall of 2021, the youth, along with an intergenerational cohort of rabbis, risked arrest and succeeded in the first full blockade of BlackRock's New York headquarters to make their point about the urgency of climate transition.[63]

Jewish institutions have been maintaining pooled endowment funds for thousands of years, and our community will certainly maintain endowments for the foreseeable future. They ought to seek, and increasingly are seeking, to bring Jewish values into their decisions and to invest in ways that transform the world toward a more sustainable future. Every community member has a role to play to help them get there.

Next Steps—Chapter 4

Institutional endowments and investments are one of the most powerful forms of investment capital. Even if you do not have significant investments, you may be a stakeholder in an institution that does. Jewish ethics would exhort all of our communal capital to be invested in alignment with our values, just as it would for individuals' investment dollars.

- **Step 1: Journal prompt:** where are you a stakeholder? We often have relationships with more communities and institutions than we realize. Do you have any relationship with your local synagogues? Did you have a relationship with one growing up? Do you live in a city with a Jewish Federation?
  - If you are resistant to thinking of yourself as "belonging" to any of these places, journal about that. Judaism is a communal religion. Being in community is often not easy, but the most powerful and sustainable change we can make comes from joining in community.
- **Step 2: Research each institution.** How much is your institution investing, and where? Who makes decisions about those investments—is it an investment committee, the board, or somebody else?
- **Step 3: Begin a conversation.** Talk with like-minded people at the organization. Share examples of other organizations leading the way.
- **Step 4: Be persistent.** Institutions sometimes move slowly, but when they do move, the effects can dramatically ripple outward.

Chapter 5

Negative Screens and Stumbling Blocks

By now, you may have caught on to a central theme of this book: The financial system we are in is broken, so those of us seeking to make ethical choices with our money are left with a difficult set of decisions about how to live in resistance to the brokenness.

It can feel lonely and confusing to be part of a small community of people committed to ethical and just choices, living in a broader society whose very structures obstruct ethical and just choices. How does one manage daily life? Opting out entirely is only available to the very privileged, and even then, does not change unjust systems. Further, the Jewish way is to engage in the world as it is, not to wait until it becomes as it should be. Yet pretending things are normal while ignoring that the world is burning around us (literally, as I write from the West Coast of the United States on another smoky day) is a morally devastating choice.

We are not alone, and we are not the first to ask these questions. The Jews at the time of the Talmud faced a similar challenge. They were a small group committed to a way of life that, while not without challenges, was grounded ultimately in a belief in the dignity of every human being and the importance of being in right relationship with society and with God's creation.

They were surrounded and dominated by cultures that, they perceived, maintained corrupt ethical standards and lacked a sense of respect for basic human worth. In the Torah's language, these were cultures of idolatry.

The word idolatry can sometimes feel distant to contemporary ears, but it is a useful concept. Idolatry is mistaking something that is not truly important for that which is most important. It can be seen as worshipping something that does not deserve to be worshipped, or as living a life without an ethical core while rationalizing one's unethical choices. One medieval commentator even understood "idolatry" to mean barbaric societies not bound by common decency.[1]

Throughout the Tanakh (the Jewish Bible), the Israelites understood the surrounding nations to be idolatrous, fundamentally not grounded in justice and a shared sense of human dignity and worth. The late Rabbi Sacks, Chief Rabbi of the United Hebrew Congregations of Great Britain and the Commonwealth, noted that the story of the Tanakh is a long-term battle against both the system of idolatry and the acts that sustain it. "The world against which Judaism is a protest is one in which conflict is endemic, power the ultimate victor, and society the hierarchical ordering of power."[2] The same continued to be true through the time of the Talmud. The Sages experienced many societies surrounding them that cared only about power: allowing state-sanctioned violence against individuals and property, appointing rulers who extorted the community, persecuting minorities, and holding a general lack of accountability or justice for those who took advantage of marginalized people.

Rabbi Sacks's words resonate in our current moment: "Every age has its idols. What are ours? One is politics. We fall out of love with the government of the day and into the lap of a new party that promises to solve our problems without pain.... The next comes from economics. People believe the market will solve problems. We then see banks pursuing short-term gain at the long-term cost of customers and the economy." Rabbi Sacks explains, "Idol worship and magical thinking happen when we believe some institution or person will bend the world to our desires, making problems vanish without effort on our part."[3]

A focus on profit at the expense of everything else is emblematic of idolatry. In the most infamous example of idolatry in the Torah, the Israelites created and then bowed down to a golden calf, literally worshipping a form of money as God.[4] On the very first page of the Talmudic volume aptly named Idol Worship (*Avodah Zarah* in Hebrew), the Sages imagine the Roman Empire, under whose oppressive rule many of them lived, on the Day of Judgment. Rome enters before God and brags about its actions: "We established many markets, we built many bathhouses, we accumulated much silver and gold." This, of course, is rejected by God, who is more interested in those who lived an ethical life.[5]

Medieval thinkers also identified a profit-at-all-costs mentality to be a key feature of idolatry. The *Book of Education*, a 13th-century anonymous work written as a letter from father to son, notes that money earned through theft and destruction is considered a "tool of idolatry" and is off-limits.[6] And 20th-century figures like the prolific Rabbi Yisrael Meir Kagan, known as the *Hafetz Hayim* (1838-1933, Russia and Poland), note that trusting in one's money, rather than in a Divine power, is a form of idolatry.[7] There are too many examples to list here.[8]

Idolatry is not a superficial issue; it is a fundamental flaw in society's orientation. The Sages considered idolatry as important as all the other precepts in Torah combined.[9] It doesn't matter how much one gives to charity, or how many good intentions one has, if one has built one's life on an unethical foundation.

Idolatry is not just a concern for Jews but for all humans. The Sages of the Talmud draw from the story of Noah early in the book of Genesis, when the world was still quite young and creation had gone terribly wrong—at least, the human part of it. Humanity was violating God's expectations and engaging in terrible sins, the worst that one being could do to another: destruction,[10] theft,[11] rape and forced marriage,[12] and general lack of value placed on human life. God sent a flood to destroy the world, but spared Noah and his family, the righteous of that generation. After the flood, God made a covenant with Noah never to wreak such destruction again. Noah recommitted himself and all his descendants to seven basic precepts of human behavior.

The seven Noachide Laws, as they are known, prohibit idolatry (our topic), blasphemy, murder, stealing, and sexual violations (including rape and incest), and set the requirement to establish systems of justice and courts of law. They also prohibit eating a limb from a living animal. This served as an ethical guardrail for preventing cruelty to living creatures following the permission to eat meat that was granted to humans, formerly on a Garden of Eden diet, after the flood.[13]

The Sages of the Talmud perceived members of surrounding societies regularly violating these seven core principles of human ethics. In this context, every daily decision became morally fraught. Can I buy or sell goods in the market, or might doing so abet unethical behavior? How much should I even benefit from the structures of the broader society? Should I avoid using the roads, or going to the barber for a haircut? Similar ethical questions resonate for those of us today: How, and to what extent, we should interact with a society whose norms run counter to our values.

For those of us who come from marginalized or minority identities, interacting with mainstream society can mean sacrificing our own cultural heritage. Edgar Villanueva describes his experience as a minority (Native American) in a white-dominated financial system: "For a lot of us, it is actually harder than it sounds to stay true to yourself, to maintain integrity, in a world where so many adopt the way of the colonizer in order to wield influence.... It's literally about keeping the shape of your whole self intact. In my case, in the worlds in which I travel, staying authentic is often a vulnerable thing to do."[14] Jews in the United States have faced similar pressures, including a pressure to assimilate and hide the "Jewish" parts of our identity to be accepted and avoid violence.

The challenge of navigating unethical systems manifests differently for those of us with class or economic privilege. For an exaggerated, comical version, see the opening sketch from a popular television show (based in my state) about a couple who sits down at a restaurant to order roast chicken. The bird is organic, heritage-breed, local, with acres of free range, fed a diet of sheep's milk and hazelnuts, and the restaurant offers a picture and dossier on the chicken to confirm to the couple that the chicken led a happy life, yet the couple insists on visiting the farm where the chicken was raised to confirm it avoids as many ethical pitfalls as possible. They end up settling on the fish instead.[15]

The more mundane version hits some people every time they enter a grocery store and need to decide which kind of eggs to buy (conventional, free-range, or organic), what kind of plates to eat them on (paper, compostable, reusable), even which store to shop at and what product to purchase in the first place. The "egg dilemma" would not be a dilemma at all except that most eggs in this country are produced in ways that do not align with our values, in giant factory farms that cause significant suffering to the animals themselves, pollute waterways with animal waste, build antibiotic-resistant diseases through farm overuse of routine antibiotics, and fail to honor the dignity of human laborers.

The same ethical questions arise when we struggle with how to navigate a society full of structural racism. Contemporary Rabbi Avi Killip elaborates on her own journey toward claiming the title "anti-racist" and how the Talmudic tractate *Avodah Zarah* (Idol Worship) inspired her: "The rabbis understood that living in a society permeated by a toxic ideology requires us to actively and frequently negate the culture. Living as a committed Jew is not enough. We have to be 'anti-idol.' The requirement to reject the surrounding ideology can be applied to racism too. If we swap out 'idolatry' for 'racism,' the entire tractate can be read as a guide to living an anti-racist life. How should we behave when the bathhouse has a statue of Aphrodite? The answer to that question can help us assess how to enter a building that has been named after a slave owner."[16]

* * *

The same challenge manifests in our investment portfolios. Lift the hood on most socially responsible investing or ESG funds and you will find at least one company that has engaged in behavior we would consider immoral or abhorrent. True alternatives are sometimes difficult to access or are the province of the very wealthy.

One natural response to encountering societal injustice is to throw one's hands up in despair and opt out of the entire project, seeking to destroy systems as they exist in the hopes that something better will arise. Yet however bad the system seems now, the chaos of its destruction could be even worse. Judaism believes in transformational change, not destructive change. Three pages into the Talmudic tractate *Avodah Zarah*, discussing idol worship, the Talmud quotes a teaching from the deputy high priest, Rabbi Hanina: "Pray for the welfare of the government, for if it were not for them, men would swallow each other alive."[17] This teaching was promulgated under Roman rule, during the era when troops advanced on Jerusalem, destroyed the Temple, and sent the Jews into exile. Despite the barbarism of the government at the time, the Sages were acutely aware that societal collapse could have been even worse. While standing up for our values, we also need to live within whatever framework we find ourselves.

To put it another way, we need to (re)learn the spiritual skill of living near and within societies we consider unethical without ourselves aiding and abetting immoral acts.

❊ ❊ ❊

This chapter is about **negative screens**. Negative screens are when investors exclude certain kinds of companies or certain sectors of the economy from an investment portfolio, often on ethical grounds.

Early on, the modern socially responsible investing (SRI) field focused heavily on negative screens. The field has evolved to include a focus on ways to make a positive impact with investment capital, which we will explore later in this book. But most socially responsible investment strategies still begin by asking which sectors should be off-limits as negative screens.

Since the modern SRI field was catalyzed by the efforts of American and European Protestant denominations (who deserve great credit for inspiring what is today a global movement), the early screens included what are termed "Christian sin stocks": alcohol, gambling, tobacco, and weapons. A screen on alcohol also plays a prominent role in Islamic finance, as do screens on usury and other financial practices Islam sees as unethical (see Chapter 8 for more). Even today, many Socially Responsible Investing or ESG investment approaches, including secular ones, still begin with the Christian sin stocks. They have become "part of our tradition" in the field, according to Joe Keefe, CEO of one of the largest mainstream SRI fund managers, Pax, that launched the first modern SRI fund in 1971.[18]

These screens do not always line up with a Jewish approach. For example, alcohol is a substance regularly used for ritual purposes on holidays in Jewish tradition. While Judaism advocates drinking in moderation, alcohol is certainly not a negative screen. Marijuana is slightly more controversial in the Jewish community, with some sectors of the Orthodox community considering it off-limits. Part of the reticence is also related to the substance's historic illegality, a reality that is rapidly changing as more states pass laws legalizing recreational marijuana (though marijuana remains prohibited on a federal level). Marijuana does not have the same chemical properties of addiction and can also be used in medicinal settings—in fact, the Orthodox Union certifies some medical marijuana varieties kosher for use by kashrut-observant consumers.[19] As such, many rabbis would be comfortable with an investment in a marijuana company, at least where the substance is legal.

Gambling is a concern in Jewish tradition, as we noted in Chapter 3, but Jewish tradition did not censure occasional dabbling in gambling as a game, so a negative screen on casinos would not be relevant for a Jewish-values investment strategy.

Another common investment screen for certain groups of Christians is abortifacients, chemicals that induce abortion, and companies that offer abortion services. There is a range of Jewish opinions on abortion, but they nearly all fall within certain bounds: on the one hand, abortion is a weighty act that is not to be taken lightly, and on the other hand, a fetus is not considered a human and abortion (at least up to a certain stage) is not considered murder.[20] Jewish communities are strongly pro-natal, celebrating and supporting families and education. At the same time, there are cases where Jewish law requires aborting a pregnancy. It is understandable why some other faith groups maintain a screen on abortifacients. Yet while the matter is weighty in Jewish tradition, abortifacients are not a part of a Jewish screen for investors.

Jewish values do include certain negative investment screens: for example, this chapter addresses tobacco, for-profit prisons, and certain weapons companies, and Chapter 10 explores a Jewish perspective on fossil fuel divestment. Yet overall, Judaism does not see unethical investment behavior as concentrated in a few sectors, but rather as a systemic question. A Jewish-values perspective on negative screens is nuanced, focused on behavior, causation, and implication. Jewish tradition asks questions like: When am I complicit in harm, or a violation of my ethical principles, to such an extent that I need to divest from the situation? And if I am not called upon to fully divest, what am I called upon to do to live my ethics as best as possible in our not-yet-redemptive world?

This chapter will explore five Jewish approaches leading to five key potential negative screens. Most of them are discussed in the Talmudic tractate Idol Worship (*Avodah Zarah*), which, out of all forty Talmudic volumes, is the central location where the Sages debate the question of our financial relationship with unethical systems.

First Approach: A Stumbling Block Before the Blind

To understand the first approach, we need to zoom back to the time of the Torah, in a dense section of laws that Moses delivers to the people as they journey through the desert, liberated from slavery and learning to create their own society. The Torah instructs:

> Do not insult the deaf or place a stumbling block before the blind [in Hebrew, *lifnei iver*]. Don't favor the rich in judgment. Do not stand idly by the blood of your neighbor. Do not hate your fellow in your heart; rebuke them, and do not bear sin on their account.[21]

The prohibition regarding a stumbling block is not meant to be taken literally (the immorality of tripping a blind person is obvious). The Sages instead understood *lifnei iver* to be broader and more metaphorical. The Torah is teaching us not to cause those who are spiritually blind to stumble by aiding and abetting their transgressions.[22] Paired with the commandment to offer constructive rebuke two verses later, this verse paints for us a picture of human interconnectedness. I must rebuke my neighbor when they act in an unethical way. If I fail to do so, thereby aiding in an unethical act, I bear some responsibility for the ethical stumbling.

In this broader, metaphoric understanding of *lifnei iver*, putting a stumbling block before the blind is problematic in two ways. First, I am aiding someone to commit an unethical act, which morally injures them. Moral injury is not a light thing—it creates real, palpable damage. In this framing of *lifnei iver*, the focus is on a relationship between people, and how my actions affect others.

Second, by putting a stumbling block before the blind, I am also doing spiritual harm to myself. I am violating the Torah's precept and "standing idly by the blood of my neighbor." I am responsible for a different kind of reprehensible behavior—one of those who "remain neutral in times of great moral conflict," as the popular quote goes. Contemporary Rabbi Aryeh Klapper comments on this second approach: "The law of *lifnei iver* is an environmental rather than a relational obligation—it is about one's responsibility for the context in which every other human being makes decisions."[23]

There may be moments when Judaism does not consider me culpable for the unethical acts of another person, but the role I play in those acts might still be harmful enough to my own soul that I need to avoid them. This leads to a wide range of questions. If I offer friendly words to someone who works for a cause I find unethical when we pass on the street, have I placed a metaphorical stumbling block before them? If I purchase something from any company that has a history of any kind of problematic behavior, am I enacting *lifnei iver* for the corporation and its employees?

Without constraints, the *lifnei iver* umbrella could become so large as to be unlivable. Rabbi Klapper articulates:

Almost every action we take as members of an imperfect society can be seen as violating *lifnei iver*, by supporting or participating in sinful activity. We are always entering into situations where acting for the sake of one value brings us into real conflict with other values and principles we hold dear.... Understood most broadly, the *lifnei iver* legal complex makes almost any interaction... fraught. Every sympathetic interaction encourages transgressors; every helpful interaction enables their transgressions, however indirectly. Every choice we make privileges one value and eventually contravenes another. Such a maximal understanding of *lifnei iver* would require Jews to be hermits and would preclude their participation in such an imperfect society.

However, the Talmud recognizes the value and necessity of belonging to society, even if the society you perforce belong to does not completely share your values and commitments.[24]

Instead, the legal parameters of *lifnei iver* play out like a pendulum over time. The Torah declared a prohibition on aiding and abetting sin that we might have interpreted with a maximalist approach: any helping of a transgressor is prohibited. The Sages of the Talmud came to understand the prohibition in a much narrower way. And later rabbis, as we will see, expanded its reach once again.

"Stumbling Block" in the Talmud

The Sages of the Talmud explore and limit the reach of the *lifnei iver* prohibition in the very first teaching of tractate *Avodah Zarah*. This teaching prohibits trading with idolaters (narrowly defined this time as actual worshippers of idols) in the days leading up to their major holidays. Let's walk into the study hall in the middle of the Sages' debate.

Why are we prohibited from conducting business with idolaters in the days leading up to their festivals? Is it because they might profit, believe their idol was responsible, and worship it in gratitude? Or is it a violation of "Do not place a stumbling block before the blind?"

"Why does it matter?" Some unnamed student jumped in. "Well, the difference is if the idolater had his own sacrificial animal already. If the problem is helping him profit, conducting business with him still allows him to profit. But if the problem is a 'stumbling block,' well, he already has an animal ready to sacrifice to his idol. He's already 'stumbled.'"

"Oh, really?" rejoined another student. "If he already has what he needs to sin, am I not still at fault for trading with him? What about Rabbi Natan's teaching? He taught that 'stumbling block' includes extending wine to a Nazirite [a person who took a special vow not to drink wine], and offering flesh from a living animal to anyone to eat [which is off-limits to everyone, as it violates the Noachide laws], presumably even though they can get it anyway."

"No," the answer came. "Rabbi Natan was talking about standing on two sides of a river. If there is no wine on the Nazirite's side, and I extend them a cup of wine from across the stream, I am violating 'putting a stumbling block.' Rabbi Natan even literally said that the person 'extends' the wine."[25]

To summarize: the Sages debate the origins of a prohibition to trade with idolaters in the days leading up to their festivals. Is it about not wanting to help them earn any profit, or more narrowly about aiding them in their idol worship? The Talmud tries to invoke the Torah's prohibition on "placing a stumbling block before the blind," which includes aiding anyone to commit a transgression. However, the Sages introduce a limit: if the person is able to engage in the transgression through other means and my support is not necessary, then my support is also not forbidden by the Torah.

Here we see the most important limitation placed on *lifnei iver*: that it only applies when the person seeking to transgress would be unable to do so without my help.

It is as though we are standing on two opposite sides of a river and the forbidden item is on my side. Without my tossing it across the river they could not access it. If, however, the person seeking to transgress could do so without my help, then my help is not considered a "stumbling block."

As the conversation continues, the Sages add a number of other qualifications that further limit the application of *lifnei iver*. They make clear the Torah is concerned only with direct aiding and abetting: the Torah would not prohibit a Jew from selling a product to a non-Jewish person who then resells it to a third person who uses it for nefarious purposes.[26] Also, if there is a good probability the person will not go on to commit a transgression, there is no Torah prohibition on supporting them.[27] Further, if in the process of aiding and abetting an unethical act I am actually preventing the person from committing an even worse deed, "stumbling block" doesn't apply.[28] All of these limitations narrowed the prohibition on *lifnei iver* so much that it became relatively easy to avoid in practice.

The pendulum began to swing back in the Middle Ages. Several medieval European commentators expressed astonishment that Judaism could condone helping someone commit an unethical act, just because they might have gotten help from elsewhere instead. Even though the Torah's stumbling block prohibition might not apply, they explained, surely the Sages held a communal expectation that we not actively assist a person to commit an ethical transgression.[29] This was adopted, with some debate, as the normative Jewish approach, and is known as "not aiding the hands of transgressors," or *mesayea* for short.

This rabbinic enactment is both more and less restrictive than "stumbling block." The rabbis only imposed "not aiding" on someone playing an active role. I would not bear responsibility for passively allowing someone to commit unethical acts. On the other hand, "not aiding" applies to any active support one provides, regardless of how helpful it is. Recall that one's action violates "stumbling block" only if one were providing indispensable help that couldn't have come from elsewhere, as if the person sinning and the accomplice were standing on two opposite sides of a river. "Not aiding" goes further and encompasses any action helping another person sin, regardless of where else they could have gotten help.

Let's see how this plays out with tobacco as an example.

The Torah commands us to care for our bodies, which rules out smoking cigarettes.[30] Providing others with cigarettes violates *lifnei iver* ("stumbling block") because I am supplying an object they will use to engage in harming their bodies, a prohibited act.

If they could have gotten a cigarette from someone else, then the Torah prohibition of *lifnei iver* doesn't apply. But the rabbinic rule on *mesayea* ("not aiding") still applies, since I am actively providing others with an object they will use to violate the Torah's precepts on caring for our bodies.

If a tobacco company goes public and I purchase stock in the initial public offering, I am providing capital to the company to produce more cigarettes, so I would be liable. If, on the other hand, I buy a share from another investor on the stock market a few years later, no new capital flows to the company. We could argue this is a passive act, so under the rabbinic rule of "not aiding," I am not liable for the actions of one who chooses to buy and smoke those cigarettes.

However, Judaism is also concerned with the spiritual effect playing a role in unethical systems will have on me and my moral compass. In the same Torah quote we just read introducing "stumbling block," the Torah also taught, "do not stand idly by the blood of your neighbor." Profiting from tobacco stock may not be actively helping others transgress, but profiting from the sale of a deadly substance is the epitome of standing idly by the blood of my neighbor. This causes moral injury to my own soul. The ethics of Judaism demand that I divest from tobacco stock.

The conversation regarding investments doesn't end there. What about investing in a mutual fund that holds a small amount of tobacco stock? One might try to argue that such an investment is technically permitted, as the investor in the mutual fund is not making stock decisions and instead turns that responsibility over to the mutual fund's partners. Even an investment in an index fund, which seeks explicitly to own all the companies available in the market, might be permitted, since the profit accrued comes from many companies of which only a small number are distributing prohibited products like tobacco.

This argument rings false in our hearts. Judaism makes a claim on our moral conscience even beyond the technical obligations of the law. Any ownership of tobacco stock is an ethical problem even within a mutual fund, and we ought to be advocating with our mutual fund providers to drop tobacco, or else we should drop the mutual fund and find a socially responsible fund that will screen out tobacco (such funds now number in the thousands).

What about investing in a pharmacy like Walgreens that sells thousands of products, including cigarettes? In such a case, investment in the company would be permitted, but we as shareholders would have a moral responsibility to offer feedback and advocate with management of the company until they agree to stop selling tobacco.

In fact, a group of shareholder advocates in 2015 launched an advocacy campaign targeting Walgreens Boots Alliance (the parent company of Walgreens) about the company's choice to carry tobacco. Walgreens is the only major retail pharmacy that still carries tobacco products, and to do so runs against the company's image as a champion of community health. From an investor perspective, this decision also exposes the company to significant risks. In 2016, the company promised shareholders that dropping tobacco would be on the board agenda, yet failed to act to remove tobacco products, so shareholders sent a statement to the company's board of directors and spoke up at the annual meeting. When there is a shareholder campaign like this, Jewish investors have an obligation to join and offer constructive rebuke to improve behavior (see Chapter 7).

* * *

In the past two centuries, Jews have gained unprecedented acceptance and access to wider society. Despite the amazing advances in human dignity over the past two centuries, there have also come astonishing inequality, human suffering, climate disaster, and more. As the 20th century scholar and teacher Nechama Leibowitz noted, "The Torah teaches us that even by sitting at home doing nothing, by complete passivity and divorcement from society, one cannot shake off responsibility for what is transpiring in the world at large, for the iniquity, violence and evil there. By not protesting, not marking the...danger spots, you have become responsible for any harm arising therefrom, and have violated the prohibition: 'Thou shalt not put a stumbling block before the blind.'"[31] *Lifnei iver* provides a vital frame for Jewish investors to think carefully about the ethical values they hold dear and then to refrain from aiding or abetting the transgression of them.

Second Approach: A Market for Theft

Sometimes the ethical issue arises not in a product itself, like tobacco, but in the way it is created. In that case, Judaism offers a second frame for investors and consumers, focused on their role as part of an economic context that makes ethical violations profitable.

In the words of a Mishnah that appears a little bit later in the same Talmudic tractate *Avodah Zarah*: "One may not purchase wool, milk, and kids from the shepherds who tend the flocks of others, due to the concern they may have stolen these items from the owners of the flocks. And similarly, one may not purchase wood and produce from the produce watchmen.... One may purchase eggs and chickens from everywhere, as it is unlikely that someone would steal and sell these commodities."[32] The Talmud then generalizes: "The overarching principle is that anything the owner would notice if it were stolen, one may buy it from the shepherd tending the flocks. But if the owner would not notice its absence, one may not buy it from them."[33] In other words, the Sages prohibited buying objects we suspect were likely stolen.

The principle was quoted broadly in the *Shulkhan Aruch*, the most famous Jewish legal code, written in the 16th century: "It is forbidden to purchase a stolen object from a thief. Purchasing such an object is a grave sin, as it enables thieves to steal again, for if he would not find customers he would not steal.... Likewise, it is forbidden to assist a thief with anything that enables him to steal."[34] Commentators invoke the Talmudic aphorism "It's not the mouse that steals, it's the hole."[35] When a mouse steals a piece of cheese and escapes through a hole, the hole (metaphorically) bears responsibility. In other words, those who enable unethical behavior are largely responsible for it.

As an example, consider private prisons. Today, 25 percent of people in prison across the globe are imprisoned in the United States. The United States incarcerates more people—both per capita and in total—than any other country.[36] Judaism understands the point of criminal consequences to be a tool for restitution for the victim and for a criminal's repentance, ultimately changing their ways and reintegrating into society. The modern system of mass incarceration works in exactly the opposite way. There are severe and lifetime consequences for anyone caught in the system, including the loss of the right to vote, the stigma of needing to "check the box" on a job application that often leads to reduced employment opportunities, and restricted access to public benefits like food stamps. The incarceration system discriminates against people of color (and especially Black people) at astonishing rates and at every step of the process, from arrest through conviction, imprisonment, and parole.[37] Incarcerated individuals are the only exception to the 13th amendment to the United States Constitution prohibiting slavery and are frequently expected to work for poor or nonexistent pay, playing a role in the supply chains of more than 4,000 companies (see Chapter 11 for more). The private-prison sector operates on a business model reliant on these injustices.

We could say that in a sense, private prisons in the United States today profit on stolen freedom. In such a case, investors provide the economic context that enables theft of freedom. Jewish values guide us to avoid being complicit in that theft and to screen out private prisons from an investment portfolio.

Third Approach: Weapons and Self-Defense

A third approach Judaism offers for negative screens relates specifically to weapons, which are a sector frequently considered by secular investors for divestment.

Judaism views weapons as unfavorable tools to be used only when necessary. In the ideal world, proclaimed the prophet Isaiah, "they shall beat their swords into plowshares, and their spears into pruning hooks. Nation shall not lift up sword against another nation, nor shall they learn war anymore."[38] The Sages of the Talmud prohibited wearing weapons as accessories on Shabbat, contrasting them with jewelry and proclaiming they are "nothing other than reprehensible."[39]

On the other hand, life is of highest value in Jewish tradition, and self-defense is wholly legitimate. The Sages instructed that because of this value, nearly any Torah precept can be violated for the sake of saving a life.[40] This value goes beyond self-defense to defense of others: When someone is pursuing someone else to murder them, Judaism condones defending the victim even at the cost of the life of the would-be murderer. (The details of this law are complex and I will leave them for now).[41]

Jews have been an often-persecuted minority without the right to political self-determination for most of the past 2,000 years. Defending oneself against enemies is a legitimate value. Unlike Christian sin stocks, Judaism would not call for a broad negative screen on defense companies.

Yet weapons, traded into the wrong hands, can threaten that same highest Jewish value, to save a life. What count as legitimate reasons to trade in arms, and when has a person crossed a moral and spiritual line?

Weapons in the Talmud

The discussion on selling weapons to unscrupulous people arises in the same Talmudic volume of *Avodah Zarah*. The conversation begins in the era of the Mishnah, around 200 CE: "One may not sell weapons to idolaters, nor the auxiliary equipment of weapons, and one may not sharpen weapons for them. And one may not sell them stocks used for fastening the feet of prisoners, or iron neck chains, or foot chains, or iron chains."[42] A similar text from the Mishnah, quoted shortly afterward, echoes: "One may not sell bears, or lions, or any item that can cause injury to the public, to idolaters."[43]

Recall that idolaters represent societies that the Sages of the Talmud experienced to be violent, unjust, and oppressive. Selling weapons to active participants in such a society crosses a moral line because the weapons will likely be used to murder. The prohibition is not unique to violent societies but applies to anyone who will use weapons to harm innocent people. In the next paragraph, the Sages say this explicitly when they also prohibit selling to a Jewish bandit. The debate even extends to selling shields for protection. The Talmudic text is worth exploring in some depth:

> The Sages taught that one may not sell shields to idolaters. But some say one may sell shields to them.
>
> Why? If it is because shields protect and sustain them in wartime, then even wheat and barley should be off-limits to sell for the same reason.
>
> In fact, Rav agreed: If it were possible to avoid selling produce to idolaters without inciting hatred, it would actually be prohibited to sell them. But such a position isn't feasible.
>
> There are those who say: The reason one is not allowed to sell them shields is because when they run out of weapons, they will use the shield to kill.
>
> There are those who say we do sell them shields. When they run out of weapons, they won't use the shield as a weapon—they will flee. Rav Nachman concludes in the name of Rabba bar Avuha: The law follows the opinion we can sell them shields.
>
> Rav Adda bar Ahava adds: One may not sell them blocks of iron. Why? Because they forge weapons from them.

> The Gemara asks: If so, then even hoes and axes should be a problem, as they too can be used to forge weapons. Rav Zvid explains: we are talking about Indian iron, which is high quality and only used for crafting weapons.
>
> And as for the fact that nowadays we do sell all weapons, Rav Ashi said: We sell the weapons to the Persians, who protect us.[44]

There is a lot of content packed into this excerpt. Let's review for a moment. The Sages debate selling shields to idolaters. One opinion holds that Jewish people should not sell them shields because Jews should not be selling anything to people whose societies are built on fundamentally unethical principles; every single act of doing so sustains them and makes those who sell to them morally complicit. But the Talmud acknowledges that cutting off all economic ties is an unrealistic expectation.

The other approach argues that the question of shields is the same as the question of weapons. If a shield is likely to be used, in cases of last resort, as a murder weapon, selling it should be prohibited just like a weapon. But since it is not generally used as a weapon—someone who is left with only a shield is likely to flee the scene—the Sages permit selling shields. This is the direct source for Judaism's comfort with investing in defense companies.

The Sages also add a prohibition on selling idolaters blocks of iron, but clarify it only applies to iron that is clearly used to make weapons.

Finally, the excerpt ends with a short but transformative sentence. Apparently, there was a robust arms trade between the Jews and the Persians at the time; the Sages justified it because the Persians used those arms to protect Jews, not to murder them.

Medieval rabbinic authorities debated the logic behind the Talmud's approach. One approach explained the Talmud's reason as a concern for "placing a stumbling block before the blind," supplying weapons to someone who will use them to commit violence. But recall that the Torah only prohibited aiding and abetting unethical acts when one's support uniquely enabled the ethical violation. If there is already a ready market for weapons, my participation in the market does not constitute a "stumbling block."[45]

Another medieval position held that the Talmud was concerned about self-defense, and in particular not selling weapons to those who might hurt the Jewish community. In that case, selling to groups like the Persians at the time of the Talmud is understandable. The Persians were protecting the Jews, though they might have used the weapons to hurt others. In fact, a range of medieval French Talmudic commentators all note that Jews of their own era traded in arms and justified the practice because they were selling weapons to those who would protect them in times of violence.[46]

A third position held that the prohibition on sales of weapons was about a more fundamental concern for human life, over and above any formal prohibition, and Jewish religious tradition calls on its adherents to avoid participation in destruction of life to the extent possible.[47]

Regardless of the Jewish-values approach we follow, there are certain investments that all would agree are permissible, like defense companies. There are also kinds of weapons trade that most would agree are ethically unacceptable. For example, Rabbi Yaakov Toledano, who served as rabbi in Morocco and Egypt and chief rabbi of Tel Aviv in the 1940s and 50s, prohibited an individual to trade in recreational weapons to those who had a potential to use them to harm the Jewish community.[48] And a growing number of Jewish individuals or institutions screen out companies doing business with violent and extremist regimes like Iran, even if the product being sold is not clearly a weapon, on the assumption that such business strengthens the hands of those who explicitly seek the destruction of Jews and others.

While a small number of civilian firearms are sold to Jews and Jewish institutions for self-defense in the United States, a much larger number are sold to unspecified individuals, with a background check system riddled with mistakes and gaps,[49] where it is easy for unscrupulous people to acquire them and use them for nefarious purposes—precisely the example prohibited by the Talmud. Judaism's approach to the problematics of weapons trade might lead a Jewish investor to screen out civilian firearms manufacturers. As for companies that distribute such firearms (like Dick's Sporting Goods or Walmart), a Jewish values-based investor ought to pressure the companies to impose strict standards on the sale of weapons to ensure that they do not end up in violent and unscrupulous hands.

The Modern Israeli Arms Trade

The issue of trade in weapons became significantly more pressing after the founding of the State of Israel. Jews are in a unique historical moment when we have not just the political autonomy to defend ourselves against violence, not just the ability to produce weapons to do so, but also the capacity to sell those weapons to other friendly (or not-so-friendly) actors.

The State of Israel has had a robust trade in arms almost since its inception, and especially since the 1970s. After the Six-Day War, world governments refused to sell arms to Israel, and the Jewish State was left to produce its own weapons for self-defense. Given the small size of the country, the only economically viable way to do so was to produce more than needed and sell the extra arms. Israel has also sold weapons for the purposes of strategic political alliances, similar to how the Talmudic Sages were comfortable selling arms to the Persians. Some of these sales are easy to understand from a Jewish moral perspective. But some of them pose a real problem for Jewish values-based investors.

Rabbi Avidan Freedman grew up in a strongly Zionist Orthodox home and made *aliyah* (emigrated to Israel) early in his adult life. As a schoolteacher, he never considered himself an activist, until in 2017 he heard a guest presenter at his school in Jerusalem speak about Israel's arms deals to some of the worst regimes in the world. As he put it, "I was shocked—I had never really heard about this issue before...somehow I missed the fact that, not as of last week or last year, but for a long time, since the 70s, Israel has sold weapons to many of the world's most brutal and aggressive regimes."[50]

For example, several months before the Saudi government's murder of journalist Jamal Khashoggi in 2018,[51] the iPhone of his wife was targeted by a secretive software that enables its owner to take over another's cellphone at will with no effort, including revealing all private information on the phone. Forensic analysts were unable to determine if the phone was breached and whether the spyware may have played a role in his death. But they know for certain that the iPhone of another woman close to him was hacked in the week following his death.[52]

The unique spyware was provided by NSO Group, an Israeli cybersecurity company. Following accusations that NSO Group's spyware played a role in Khashoggi's murder and other heinous crimes, NSO Group terminated its contract with the Saudi government. But several months later, the government of Israel urged the company to resume a relationship with Saudi Arabia and issued a license to do so, overriding any concerns about human rights abuses.[53]

Spyware is a fast-growing front for international warfare and a key part of the cybersecurity industry. Israel has staked a position as a global leader in cyber, with over 40 percent of investments in the sector globally in 2020 going to Israeli companies and entrepreneurs.[54] This makes up a substantial part of Israel's economy: 43 percent of Israel's exports are attributed to tech, and cybersecurity is one of the hottest sectors.[55] Many of these companies are legitimate and scrupulous. Unfortunately, some are not.

All Israeli weapons manufacturers, cyber companies included, need permission from the Israeli Ministry of Defense in order to enter into contracts with foreign governments.[56] Israel insists that if any Israeli spyware were used to violate civil rights, it would revoke the company's license.[57] Yet *The New York Times* notes that "Israel secretly authorized a group of cyber-surveillance firms to work for the government of Saudi Arabia despite international condemnation of the kingdom's abuse of surveillance software to crush dissent, even after the Saudi killing of the journalist Jamal Khashoggi."[58]

Spyware can be used for legitimate purposes—in criminal investigations, or to prevent drug trafficking and human trafficking, for example. Within Jewish tradition, some have argued that weapons trade on a national level is different from trade on an individual level.⁵⁹ Maybe we can assume that a country is generally purchasing weapons for at least somewhat legitimate purposes, to increase stability rather than destruction.⁶⁰

But spyware can also be used by oppressive regimes to violate human rights. For example, NSO Group's software was reportedly used by regimes with a known history of human rights abuses to target people in high-profile national security positions who are "allies of the US," as well as journalists and human rights defenders.⁶¹ And while the Sages justified selling weapons to the Persian Empire because they were then used to protect Jews, it seems harder to justify Saudia Arabia's use of spyware with a similar argument.

Beyond privacy violations and harassment, spyware attacks often have a direct link to physical violence against their targets, according to researchers at Goldsmiths, University of London, who specifically mapped out all known targets of NSO Group's spyware app Pegasus.⁶² This has led to calls from civil-society organizations like Amnesty International and the Electronic Frontier Foundation for a moratorium on the sale and use of surveillance technology until world governments can adopt a legal and regulatory framework that protects human rights.⁶³ Indeed, in late 2021, the Biden administration placed NSO Group and another private, Israeli cybersecurity firm on the Commerce Department's "entity list," preventing it from accessing American technologies after the administration determined the spyware companies had acted contrary to the "foreign policy and national security interests" of the US.⁶⁴

The growth of spyware as a weapon has also affected the investment arena. NSO Group is owned by a private equity firm, but other Israeli spyware companies are publicly traded. When Israeli spyware company Cellebrite debuted on the New York Stock Exchange in 2021, civil-society organizations criticized the company's business deals with repressive regimes including China, Saudi Arabia, Myanmar, and Russia, and even sought to prevent the exchange from listing the company publicly until Cellebrite addressed its human-rights concerns (which it still has not fully done).⁶⁵

Rabbi Freedman notes that NSO Group's spyware is just the latest in a long stream of weapons deals to reprehensible regimes. While much of Israel's arms trade may be justified, some weapons sales are clearly serving "to aid and abet the most oppressive regimes to do the worst things, to do the most heinous acts that undermine democracy all over the world." When he learned of it, Freedman was devastated by the idea of Israel's Start-Up Nation brilliance being used "to cause so much suffering."

Freedman began organizing protests and found that the issue resonated across the political spectrum in Israel, from the center to the far right to the far left. The barrier to passing legislation to set a higher standard, he realized, was not moral argument but political will. So in 2021, he started an organization called Yanshoof—in Hebrew, the name is an acronym that stands for oversight of weapons sales, but also the word for owl. The image of an owl peering into the darkness and discerning the reality is an apt one.

While Yanshoof is, so far, focusing on legislative change in Israel, the questions apply to every Jewish investor as well. To the best of our ability, Jewish values-based investors need to assess whether a company they own is engaged in legitimate sales to protect vulnerable individuals (including their own communities) and uphold systems of justice. If not, Jewish tradition might demand that investors screen out such companies.

Fourth Approach: Trading in Forbidden Foods

Another frame for Judaism's approach to negative screens arises in the Talmud's discussion of non-kosher meat. Jewish tradition sees nothing inherently bad or evil with non-kosher animals, and the main focus of the Torah's exhortation to eat kosher is on maintaining a spiritually disciplined food practice. The Sages of the Talmud, as an extra step in this spiritual discipline, created a prohibition on trading in non-kosher meat.

The topic appears in the Mishnah, circa 200 CE, in the section dealing with *shmita*, the Sabbatical year. (As we have seen, there are several surprising connections between the *shmita* year and Jewish ethical investing, and here is another.) The *shmita* year was a powerful social institution for keeping inequality in check. Every seven years, the entire land was declared ownerless, and anyone could eat fruit growing anywhere. The fruits that grow during *shmita* are off-limits for trade—they are designated for eating, not for profit, according to the Mishnah.

In that same section, the Sages took the opportunity to articulate a list of other foods prohibited for Jews to trade in, including non-kosher food. It was no longer enough to avoid eating *trayf* (non-kosher); the Sages insisted that Jews add an extra layer of spiritual discipline by not profiting from it. The Mishnah, however, noted an exception: while an animal trapper cannot intentionally seek to trap non-kosher animals, if they accidentally trap a non-kosher animal, they can sell it.[66]

Later commentators included running a non-kosher food business in the prohibition, by oneself or even jointly with a non-Jewish person.[67] Grocery stores received an exception; since everyone prefers the convenience of a one-stop shop and the storeowner would lose customers otherwise, a Jewish grocery store owner is allowed to stock non-kosher items alongside kosher ones (which is great news for those of us who want to invest as members in our local food co-op).⁶⁸ But until the 1960s, few rabbis addressed the question of a shareholder in a food or restaurant corporation.

Unlike banks and manufacturing corporations, food corporations of the kind and scale we recognize didn't arise until the mid-20th century. For example, Hershey Chocolate Corporation first traded publicly in 1927, and General Mills was formed as a corporation in 1928; and anyway, the Torah doesn't prohibit Jews from eating flour or chocolate. The first McDonald's restaurant opened in 1940, and Ray Kroc didn't join the company until 1955, turning it ultimately into the behemoth food corporation we know today. Jewish law's prohibition on trading in prohibited foods has only intersected with public equities very recently from a Jewish perspective.

In 1970, Rabbi George Lintz wrote an article in the *Journal of Halacha* titled, "May a Jew Invest in McDonald's?" Rabbi Lintz offered several reasons to say yes, dependent on the intent behind the Mishnah's prohibition against trading in non-kosher food. Some say the original prohibition was instituted lest one come to eat non-kosher food; but there is no risk that my owning McDonald's stock will lead me to eat a non-kosher hamburger. Some say the prohibition was intended to categorically minimize Jewish ownership of non-kosher food; but owning a share of stock isn't really actual ownership of the food (see Chapter 7 for more). And some say the prohibition was a rabbinic concern for appearances; but owning a share in McDonald's looks nothing like actively running a non-kosher restaurant.⁶⁹

Other contemporary rabbis disagree. For example, Rabbi Ethan Tucker, head of Yeshivat Hadar, an egalitarian institute for traditional Torah learning based in New York, posits that owning stock in Burger King would count as "trading in prohibited food" and be off-limits. However, Rabbi Tucker allows for investing in mutual funds that own a bundle of stocks that include Burger King. He justifies this by relying on rabbis who expand the exception for animal trappers mentioned in the Mishnah to any case of 'financial loss.' Rabbi Tucker argues that avoiding investments in Burger King and similar companies would count as a 'financial loss' in comparison to the normal way people invest, since successful investing requires diversification and buying stocks from a variety of different sectors.⁷⁰

The actual effects of this prohibition are limited today. There are occasional Jewish investors who seek to avoid investment in companies that profit from non-kosher meat. For example, at the Jewish Impact Investing Summit, speaker Nigel Savage recounted his former work with a pension fund for kosher butchers in Britain, which avoided investing in companies that profited from non-kosher food.⁷¹ The Bais HaVaad Rabbinical Court in Lakewood, NJ, decreed on behalf of their Hareidi Orthodox population that one should ideally screen out companies whose primary product is non-kosher meat. But the vast rabbinic consensus permits owning stock in companies that sell non-kosher food.[72]

However, the principle is an important one. Today, a growing number of people are re-examining our relationship with the food we eat. Knowing where our food comes from is not just a topic for a television show parody, like the couple at the restaurant at the beginning of this chapter, but a real ethical concern. Food introduces a range of questions: How is it manufactured? What is its impact on the soil, the climate, and water use? What is its impact on agricultural workers? For animal products, what is the impact on the animals themselves?

Jewish tradition offers a spiritual practice around food that extends beyond what we eat to what we invest in. Not everything that is unfit to eat is unfit to profit from—and sometimes it is only by chance or circumstance that people find themselves invested in food that does not align with their values. But profiting on a consistent basis from certain unfit foods undermines the spiritual or ethical effect Jewish tradition is guiding its adherents to by insisting they eat kosher foods only.

Fifth Approach: Items Prohibited from Benefit

The Sages offer us a final frame for approaching negative screens, known in Hebrew as *issurei hana'ah*, items prohibited from benefit. These are a select group of items that are so paradigmatic of prohibition that they are not only off-limits to eat, but off-limits to any benefit whatsoever. This means one can't profit from their sale,[73] or even give them to a non-Jewish friend (as the goodwill we earn from gifts is a kind of benefit).[74] They are either burned or buried.[75]

For example, the singular central objects that most represent idolatry are actual, literal worshipped idols, in the narrow sense of the word, as well as the wine poured on them as libation, and they are off-limits for a Jew to benefit from.[76]

Similarly, the Torah instructs not to cook a baby goat in its mother's milk, which the Sages understood to prohibit cooking any meat in any dairy. Jewish dietary laws extend the prohibition broadly to separate silverware for meat and dairy, treating fowl as meat, and imposing a waiting period between meat and milk.[77] But kosher meat[78] cooked together with dairy in a pot—not smoked[79] or steamed[80] or fried[81]—is the paradigm of the prohibition, and it is prohibited not only from eating but from any benefit. (Note that this excludes Campbell's soups which are steamed,[82] and may even exclude MacDonald's cheeseburgers which are baked and are not kosher meat to begin with[83]).

On Passover, Jews are commanded to avoid leavened products and eat matzah instead. The rabbis imposed a further restriction that any leavened products owned by a Jew during Passover become off-limits after Passover.[84] We will discuss this more in Chapter 7 when we discuss the status of corporations in Jewish law.

Other examples include sacrifices invalidated at the Temple in Jerusalem, when it still stood[85]; fruits grown in violation of some core principles of Jewish agricultural law, which apply only in the land of Israel; and a few other esoteric categories.

All these cases carry a more potent, or one could even say radioactive prohibition in Jewish law. If one sells the item for cash, the cash becomes prohibited.[86] The rabbis even prohibit any situation that involves wanting such objects, especially wine used in idol worship, to remain in existence.[87]

In practice, the list of prohibited items for benefit is so narrowly defined that the legal category itself is likely only relevant to a modern Jewish investor in rare circumstances. I cannot remember anyone who has ever sought my guidance as a rabbi regarding investing in a local retailer selling idol libation wine. It is hard to think of a single publicly traded company that focuses on such products.[88] Even an online retailer that might occasionally carry an item on this list will make most of its revenue from selling other items. In such a case, a traditional Jewish investor might have a responsibility to encourage the company to impose limits on what it will offer for sale, as a way of distancing oneself from any desire that these objects remain in existence. But the distance between the shareholder and the business activity of the company means the Jewish investor is not really "benefiting" from these prohibited items.[89]

Yet the category of *issurei hana'ah* remains a meaningful spiritual paradigm. There are certain items that so deeply violate Jewish spiritual sensibilities that Jews need to stay as far away from them as possible and avoid benefiting from their existence. On the one hand, such items are rare and narrowly defined. On the other hand, they are practically radioactive. As investors, we have the opportunity to determine if there are sectors or products that are so antithetical to our values that we need to have nothing to do with them.

Conclusion

A Jewish approach to negative screens begins with questions about complicity. When am I financially implicated in someone else's harmful deeds, and when is the connection too distant to be my responsibility?

In the paradigm of stumbling blocks, the key questions are whether my help is uniquely necessary to carry out the transgression, and whether I am actively aiding and supporting the transgression. The Torah's teaching on stumbling blocks offers us the opportunity to think carefully about what issues we care about and to avoid playing a role in exacerbating transgressions.

Another paradigm explores the ethical problems with creating a market for stolen goods. We as investors need to be thinking actively about the broader financial systems of which we are a part and do our best to avoid creating a market for unethical behavior.

A third paradigm explores Judaism's relationship to selling weapons, which might be a concern over placing a stumbling block, but may also reflect a broader concern for the value of human life. When weapons are used in service of defending human life, they are an acceptable tool, and when they are not, Judaism would be skeptical of investing in them.

A fourth paradigm focuses on the safeguards and layers of distance the rabbis instituted when trading in non-kosher meat. Jewish values-based investors can draw inspiration in thinking about ethical food and when food that is unfit for consumption is also unfit to profit from.

A fifth approach suggests that certain items that are the paragon of prohibition ought to require even greater distance from us and our economic activity. Such volatile items are rare and narrowly defined, but extremely potent, and we need to keep away from them as much as possible.

Negative screens are an important tool for Jewish values-based investors, but there are many ways to bring Jewish values into an investment portfolio and achieve a positive impact on the world. The next section of the book explores these ideas on a more practical level.

Next Steps—Chapter 5

This chapter offered five different Jewish lenses to the question of negative screens. Unlike the model of "Christian sin stocks," Judaism's approach to negative screening depends on context and questions like what harm is being caused and what complicity one has in aiding it. Specific screens the chapter mentioned include:

- Tobacco companies (because of the precept "do not stand idly by the blood of your neighbor")
- Private prisons (inspired by the prohibition on providing a market for theft, like the stolen labor of prisoners)
- Manufacturers of certain kinds of weapons (especially civilian firearms that can easily be used to harm innocent people, including members of the Jewish community)
- Companies doing business with terrorist regimes (depending on the investor, Iran is often on this list, and sometimes others)
- Companies that produce non-kosher meat (a small minority of Jewish investors use this screen)
- Fossil fuels (which we will discuss in-depth in Chapter 10)

- **Step 1: Journal.** The chapter outlined five frames for negative screens:
    1. Do not put a stumbling block before the blind
    2. Complicity in creating a market for theft
    3. The ethics of investing in weapons
    4. Trading in prohibited foods
    5. Items prohibited from any benefit
    - Which of the five frames outlined in the chapter resonates the most with you as you think about negative screens? Why?
- **Step 2: Make a list.** List the screens you find most meaningful.
    - Remember: The goal of this list is not to exclude every potentially problematic behavior. Judaism believes in the power of constructive rebuke through owning a company's stock and advocating to change its actions, as we will see in Chapter 7. There is no such thing as a perfect company from a Jewish perspective. Instead, focus on the question of when your values conflict at their core with corporate actions or core business models, and when, by remaining invested, you become complicit in unethical behavior.
- **Step 3: Analyze your current investments.** Investors will often invest through funds rather than selecting individual stocks. For tobacco, weapons, private prisons, and fossil fuels, you can research whether any mutual fund or ETF owns companies in those industries through the Invest Your Values tool created by nonprofit organization As You Sow (investyourvalues.org).

Asset Classes

Chapter 6

Getting Started: Asset Classes and Investment Advisors

The Talmudic sage Rabbi Yitzchak advised that "a person should divide their money in three parts: one third in land, one third in business investments, and one third in cash on hand."[1] Modern investors call these asset classes and Rabbi Yitzchak's recommendation an asset allocation, which represents a fundamental way to structure an investment portfolio.

Rabbi Yitzchak lived in the land of Israel two hundred years after the destruction of the Second Temple, in the era of Roman rule, amidst a significantly impoverished community and recent political upheaval, so his particular asset allocation may not be as relevant to us.[2] Yet the idea of asset classes is central. They are important not only to financially smart investing, but to thinking about the impact our investments have.

All of our assets have an impact, and that impact varies based on the asset class. If we seek to align our investments with our values, we need to look at each of the asset classes where we are invested and consider how they are impacting the world.

Cash

Consider Rabbi Yitzchak's third category, cash on hand. In popular discourse, cash refers to literal wads of dollar bills and rolls of coins. But in the investment arena as well as in Talmudic thought, cash refers to any money that is saved and stored somewhere, available for immediate use, rather than being spent or invested.

At the time of the Talmud, cash was usually deposited with trusted individuals who would watch over a pool of funds. This parallels the origins of many modern credit unions that formed when a group of people would pool money in a shoebox in someone's basement.

Today, most people and organizations deposit their cash in a bank. This might be a bank like Chase that takes those deposits and underwrites loans to fossil fuel projects like the Keystone XL pipeline or Enbridge's Line 3 pipeline in Northern Minnesota (both routed through Indigenous land and opposed by Indigenous tribes),[3] earning the company the dubious title of the leading global financer of fossil fuel companies. In fact, the "dirty dozen" of banks, including household names like Bank of America, Morgan Stanley, and Citi, collectively hold over $2 trillion in fossil fuel loans.[4] Or it may be a financial institution like Wells Fargo, which has used that cash to issue predatory subprime loans, taking advantage of low-income and minority borrowers,[5] and in the meantime generated business through fake accounts and unethical sales.[6]

Or maybe your cash is held at one of 19 international banks that are currently invested in billions of dollars of ties to the military junta and its conglomerates in Myanmar, which in February 2021 staged a coup of the country's government. "The Myanmar military's campaign of terror is enabled by the complicity of international companies that continue to do business with the illegal junta and its conglomerates," claims Yadanar Maung, spokesperson at Justice For Myanmar. "Banks have a responsibility to take action against investees that are complicit in the junta's atrocities."[7]

As Ebony Perkins, Director of Investor Relations at Self-Help Credit Union, likes to say, "Are you comfortable where your money sleeps? If you're not comfortable with your answer, then consider moving your money."[8]

Cash is not often considered when we think about impact investing, but it's often the very first asset class one should consider. That's according to Sharlene Brown, senior fellow at the justice-oriented finance-research institute Croatan Institute.[9] Cash should be first because it offers the greatest number of opportunities of any asset class to funnel money into organizations grounded in the communities they seek to serve, and without needing extensive research.[10] In other words, you and I could make this change right now.

A great place to start when considering where to park one's cash is a credit union. Credit unions are nonprofit financial cooperatives owned entirely by their members. They have a long and proud history, including in the United States, where second-generation German Jew Edward Filene (of Filene's department stores) played a pioneering role in their development. Many communities, especially communities of color shut out of traditional financial systems, have been practicing cooperative finance for centuries. As noted David Graeber, the late professor at the London School of Economics, these cooperative finance vehicles were part of the practical resistance to the problems with our current economy. "The late nineteenth century saw the first creation of modern corporate capitalism in the United States, and it was fervently resisted, with the centralization of the banking system being a major field of struggle, and mutualism—popular democratic (not profit-oriented) banking and insurance arrangements—one of the main forms of resistance."[11]

Getting Started: Asset Classes and Investment Advisors

Credit unions and financial cooperatives play a vital role in ethical banking today.[12] When you deposit funds at a credit union, they are not being used to enrich the pockets of outside investors or international companies with dubious human rights records. Instead, credit unions are committed to serving their members; your deposits will likely be loaned out to another member from your same community.[13]

Credit unions serve a combined membership of over 100 million in the United States. At most credit unions, deposits are insured by the government, just as they are at banks, making them a safe and low-risk choice.[14] Beyond the services they provide, credit unions support our broader cultural resilience. They position us not as victims of broader systems beyond our control, but as mutual and equal owners of our financial institutions. A narrative of powerlessness can often slow the adoption of ethical finance. One key problem identified by a recent report from the Nonprofit Futures Lab is that "we lack identification with our own role in relation to money and see finance as belonging to others."[15] Credit unions help overcome that apathy and helplessness.

Another vital place to look when considering where to deposit your cash is the growing national movement of Community Development Financial Institutions, known by their acronym CDFI. CDFIs have been around since the 1970s but gained increased prominence when the Treasury Department began officially certifying them in the 1990s. In short, these are organizations that provide financial services to communities that have been traditionally shut out of the financial system, considered not worth the time or investment by mainstream banks. Some CDFIs are small banks or credit unions which accept deposits and then use those deposits to make loans to marginalized communities and minority entrepreneurs who may otherwise not have access to capital. Ebony Perkins's Self-Help Credit Union, mentioned above, is a credit union that is also certified as a CDFI. CDFI credit unions and banks carry guarantees on their deposits as well, making them a safe choice.

Holding cash at a local institution like a credit union or CDFI also aligns with the Jewish value of investing locally, which we will visit more deeply in Chapter 9. There are a growing number of websites offering to search for banks or credit unions in your area, like Green America's Get A Better Bank website, Mighty Deposits, bank.green, and Bank for Good, and there will likely be more by the time this book reaches print.

Beyond where you deposit your money, you can also pay attention to which credit cards you use. Green America's website offers a resource for selecting a credit card from financial institutions that may align more closely with your values and still offer competitive deals. You can also explore options offered by your local credit union or CDFI.

This section has introduced us to cash—money deposited at a financial institution for daily use. The next several chapters are organized by the modern version of Rabbi Yitzchak's asset allocation. Rabbi Yitzchak had three categories; the modern equivalent has five, plus or minus a few. In addition to cash, they include public equity, private equity, and public and private debt.

Chapter 7 discusses **public equity**, meaning companies with shares listed on public stock exchanges and available for trade. These companies, especially the large ones, make up the bulk of most individuals' and institutions' investment portfolios. Chapter 8 discusses investing in debt (public and private), meaning making loans or purchasing bonds. Chapter 9 discusses private equity, meaning investing as an owner of a business but not doing so through the stock market. Think of investing $50,000 to become a part-owner of your local organic microbrewery. This chapter will especially focus on investments in local businesses and explore Judaism's approach to prioritizing local needs.

There are other asset classes we won't have time to cover—for example, **venture capital**, which is a risky and potentially highly profitable investment in startup or early-stage companies, seeking to benefit from their rapid growth.

Before we explore all these modern asset classes, though, it is important to note that this book is not investment advice. It really can't substitute for a relationship with a financial advisor. Unless you want to research all the proxy ballots you receive in the mail from funds you may be invested in or do a deep personal dive on your local microbrewery's financial statements—and who has time for all of that today?—you will want the help of a trusted advisor. And that choice, in and of itself, is an opportunity to bring our Jewish values into our financial decisions.

Investment Advisors

A crucial tool for those of us seeking to achieve positive impact through our investments is a financial advisor who understands impact investing, and who ideally shares a belief that it is important. Unfortunately, many investment advisors are not familiar or comfortable with values-based investing. This is especially difficult for faith-based investors, notes a recent report from the University of Zurich. "Faith-based investors face challenges from their traditional... managers who are bottlenecks for driving more capital towards impactful opportunities, since these managers lack the expertise or willingness to change their investment behaviors due to inertia, lack of incentives, and misconceptions about return."[16]

For example, a few years ago, the Leichtag Foundation, the Jewish independent foundation based outside of San Diego and in Jerusalem (profiled in Chapter 4), sought to make an initial investment in Jerusalem Venture Partners, an Israel-based venture capital firm. The foundation's investment advisor, inexperienced with impact investing, forced the foundation to sign a document that the advisor would not be responsible for the performance of the investment. That investment ended up performing best financially of all the investments in Leichtag's portfolio.[17]

As you begin to shop around for financial advisors, this is a good first topic to explore. Is your advisor someone who has expertise in or focuses on values-based investing? The University of Zurich recommends "the seeking out of specialized advisors for the implementation of impact-driven investment strategies."[18] Does the advisor have other clients (and how many) who are engaged in values-based investing? More philosophically, what do they understand to be the point of investing, and does that align with your goals and values?

Another question to ask your investment advisor is where they are directing money. Investment advisors serve as gatekeepers, meeting with you, the client, and funneling your money into various funds. To date, investment advisors have a terrible track record on selecting funds run by diverse people.

A committee of the Securities and Exchange Commission published a report in July 2021, citing credible studies that find "widespread gender and racial bias" within the investment industry.[19] To be precise, approximately one percent of all professionally managed investments are managed by women or people of color.[20]

The overwhelming bias in favor of white men is hurting our collective investment returns. To be clear, the gender and racial identity of an investment manager isn't the main qualifier—their performance is. But research by Illumen Capital demonstrates how woman- and minority-led firms perform at least as well as firms managed by white men, and in fact, tend toward outperformance. Daryn Dodson, founder of Illumen Capital, points out that the goal is not to find women and people of color, but rather to find the most skilled people in the world, which includes women and people of color, who are otherwise shut out of the investment industry. In an industry ostensibly focused on getting the highest financial return, the fact that the percentage of assets invested with woman- and minority-owned firms has hovered around 1.3 percent indicates a serious problem to address.[21]

Part of the problem is that the investment advisors themselves, and in fact most of the financial industry, is homogenous. 90 percent of the chief executives and senior leadership are white. 70 percent of venture capitalists are white, as are 87 percent of angel investors.[22] This affects who these investors are likely to fund. On the receiving side, 2.6 percent of venture capital funding went to African-American and Latinx entrepreneurs. Black entrepreneurs are three times as likely to be denied a request for funding as their white counterparts.[23] I am proud of my prior role working for JLens, a woman-led investment organization and part of the one percent of capital in this country managed by firms owned by women and people of color.

Another problem is the hurdles that advisors require fund managers to jump over. These could include a certain minimum size (known as assets under management, AUM) as well as a minimum number of years of solo track record. These litmus tests might sound reassuring. But according to research from the Securities and Exchange Commission, they do not actually predict how an investment manager will perform. At the same time, such litmus tests have the effect of screening out most firms owned by women and people of color, who are denied the opportunity to build those track records and reach those levels of assets under management in the first place.[24]

Some within the industry have begun taking proactive steps to commit to diversity and equity. In early 2021, a group of investment advisors and asset owners (with contributions from over a dozen asset managers who are Black, Indigenous, and people of color) launched the Due Diligence 2.0 Commitment. Signatories commit to finding alternative ways to assess investment potential rather than minimum years of track record, minimum assets under management, or similar requirements that might prove barriers to entry for women- or minority-led firms. Signatories also commit to having the courage to be the first investor or advisor in a new fund.[25]

For now, most of your money will likely be invested in funds that are not run by women or people of color. There just aren't that many options yet. But this is a good question to ask your advisor—are they taking steps to try to increase the diversity of the investment managers they recommend? Could they get you started with a fund run by women or people or color to add to your portfolio? You can remind them that the goal is to find the best funds, and that working against the current industry bias is likely to lead to new and under-explored opportunities.

When selecting an advisor, it is important to think about the kind of impact you would like to have. For example, we will learn more in Chapter 7 about public equities. Today, a majority of our investment dollars are invested in stocks of large public corporations, or in mutual funds or index funds holding corporate stock. An important tool for socially responsible investors is shareholder advocacy, which involves using one's position as investor and part-owner of a company to pressure it to improve corporate behavior on a range of values-aligned issues. There are many funds that focus on shareholder advocacy as a tactic. Does your investment advisor value shareholder advocacy and are they willing to recommend funds that engage in it?

Investment advisors also need to be able to see through the growing haze around socially responsible investing. A couple of terms and examples will be useful here. In the past 15 years, corporations have responded to the advocacy and pressures of socially responsible investors by building out extensive Corporate Social Responsibility (CSR) programs and departments. Judith Rodin and Saadia Madjsberg, two long-time impact investing practitioners, note that despite the recent exponential

Getting Started: Asset Classes and Investment Advisors

growth in CSR, it has been "often limited to charitable donations or company investments in communities around their offices or factories. At its worst, CSR involved little more than public relations and a new mission statement."[26] On the other hand, some companies have taken CSR quite seriously: they have set and achieved explicit goals for greenhouse gas reductions, rectified pay gaps between people of different ethnicities or genders and achieved a more diverse board and senior leadership.

Another industry term is Environmental, Social, and Governance investing (ESG). ESG investing is now often used to refer broadly to investing with an eye to risks posed by non-financial metrics. But it can also refer to the specific practice of grading companies on their E, S, and G scores and then investing in the best-performing companies. The "E" and "S" buckets may be the easiest for average folks to understand. The "G" bucket encompasses many traditional governance concerns, like the length of a board term and whose votes count for how much at the annual general meeting.

The problem is that it has become hard to distinguish between actual efforts toward environmental preservation and social change, instead of an attempt to cash in on the growth of ESG-interested investors. The growing problem has earned several catchy names. Duncan Austin, a former partner at Al Gore's investment management firm, says the problem goes beyond "greenwashing" to "greenwishing"—widespread wishful thinking that overestimates the positive impact of ESG funds.[27] Tariq Fancy, the former Chief Investment Officer for Sustainable Investing at BlackRock, the largest investment manager in the world, refers to the problem as "sustaina-babble."

The good news is that there are a growing number of investment advisors, authentically motivated by values, seeking to be held accountable and hold others accountable to making a positive difference. The landscape is rapidly changing, so this book will not recommend specific advisors, but it is becoming more and more possible to find the right investment advisor who will be a trusted partner in this work. You can begin by asking friends and family who share your values if they have any recommendations. A growing number of synagogues have committees interested in social justice and environmental sustainability, which may be a resource. There are also a growing number of resources online. *The Wall Street Journal* has a helpful guide titled, "How to Find a Socially Responsible Investment Adviser."[28] The organization Resource Generation, mentioned in Chapter 4, which is primarily focused on wealth redistribution through giving, also maintains a list of values-aligned financial advisors who have answered a rigorous set of social justice questions.[29] You can look for advisors who are members of socially responsible investing organizations, such as the Interfaith Center on Corporate Responsibility, the UN Principles on Responsible Investing, or Ceres.[30]

Perhaps the most important qualification of an investment advisor is that they be someone explicitly committed to thinking about you and your needs. The Torah itself offers clear expectations of a financial advisor. The Torah's prohibition of *lifnei iver* (placing a stumbling block before the blind, which we saw in Chapter 5), also applies to advice—someone who is blind in knowledge, as it were. One violates this precept when one gives advice that is not in the best interest of the person.[31] The Sages of the Talmud prohibit offering purely self-serving advice: "Do not advise someone to sell a donkey and buy a field when you want to buy a donkey and sell a field."[32]

A secular parallel to this ethical standard, known as the fiduciary rule, nearly took effect in the United States in 2017. Simply put, it would have required an investment advisor to put their clients' interests above their own and disclose any conflicts of interest.[33] A significant number of investment advisors came out against the rule, and it was eventually voided.[34] But the standard remains a Jewish value. It is worthwhile to ask your investment advisor whether they have a personal commitment to fiduciary responsibility to their clients. Does your advisor earn commissions off products they sell? What are the details, and are you comfortable with them?

Regardless, shop around and find the best fit and relationship for you, with someone you can trust. And then dive in to explore all of your assets, across asset classes, and see how you can bring Jewish values to bear and make a positive impact.

Next Steps—Chapter 6

This chapter offers two steps you can take right away to get started.
- **Step 1: Move your "cash."** You can transition your bank deposits (and credit cards) to an institution that aligns with your values. Examples include credit unions and Community Development Financial Institutions. Resources include:
  o Get a Better Bank (greenamerica.org/getabetterbank)
  o Mighty Deposits (mightydeposits.com)
  o bank.green
  o Bank for Good (bankforgood.org)
- **Step 2: Find a financial advisor.** Seek someone who is committed to socially responsible investing and can help you on your journey.
  o To read more on the topic, *The Wall Street Journal* has a helpful guide titled, "How to Find a Socially Responsible Investment Adviser" (wsj.com/articles/how-to-find-a-socially-responsible-financial-adviser-11633020657). Green America maintains a list of socially responsible financial planners (learn more at greenamerica.org/socially-responsible-investing). The organization Resource Generation also maintains a list of values-aligned financial advisors that have answered a rigorous set of social justice questions. (The link is currently resourcegeneration.org/financial-advisors-database/).
  o You can also look for advisors who are members of socially responsible investing organizations such as the Interfaith Center on Corporate Responsibility (iccr.org), the UN Principles on Responsible Investing (unpri.org), or Ceres (ceres.org).
- **Step 3: Go deeper with your advisor.** Ask the following questions:
  o Do you have expertise in or focus on values-based investing?
  o Where are you currently directing money? (What percent of your clients' funds are directed to socially responsible options?)
  o What commitments have you made to socially responsible investing or Diversity, Equity, and Inclusion? What coalitions have you joined?
  o Are you committed to being a fiduciary and putting my best interests first, as I understand them, in your advice?

Chapter 7

Public Equities

What is the first thing you think of when you hear the word "investing"?

If you are like many people, you think first of the stock market. The vast majority of investments held in retirement accounts in the US are comprised of **public equities**, meaning stocks of companies traded publicly on the stock market. These companies are categorized by their size, or capitalization (cap), but all of them are truly huge. The biggest large-cap companies are bigger than the economies of many countries.[1] Even the smallest "microcap" companies have **market capitalizations** (total worth) of $50 million or more.[2] These companies wield huge influence in our lives as well as our investment portfolios. Already by the 1880s, US President Rutherford B. Hayes said, "This is a government of the people, by the people, and for the people no longer. It is government by the corporations, of the corporations, and for the corporations,"[3] and that adage remains true today.[4]

Many investors do not pick individual stocks or public equities, instead preferring the convenience of **mutual funds** and **ETFs**. These are usually nothing more than bundles of stocks and public equities (or sometimes bonds). Public companies make up the majority of an investment portfolio for most Jewish investors today, but that was mostly not the case historically (and might not be the case forever). It is easy to forget that the stock market as we know it and the corporations that trade on it are a recent phenomenon, unique and exotic from a historical perspective.[5]

All of rabbinic literature prior to the mid-19th century addresses sole proprietorships or relatively small partnerships. Those were the legal forms that existed in practice in society.[6] The past 200 years have seen the rapid transformation of the investing marketplace from primarily agricultural and small-business investing, familiar in most of Jewish history, to primarily enormous corporations owned by total strangers spread out across the world. Jewish legal scholars have had to race to keep up.[7]

If you were a rabbi in the 19th century trying to navigate the growth of corporations, your first challenge was defining what a public corporation even was. Public corporations are more properly known as publicly traded joint-stock corporations, and they have a number of distinctive characteristics. They are historically unprecedented in size and scope. They have the ability to issue shares that can be traded publicly (a process we will revisit in Chapter 9, when we learn about local investing and the difficulty for small companies to issue public shares). At first, public companies were required by governments to limit their activities to one or two specific worthy aims, but now they can do business in any sector or all of them at once.[8] Aside from all these qualities, two of the innovations of public companies stand out in their implications for Jewish thought.

First, a corporation has a unique legal identity as an "artificial person." That is, a corporation can do business just like a real person. This also means a separation between ownership and control. The corporation's assets are controlled by the corporation, not by the individuals who invest in the corporation.[9] In a partnership, at least one of the partners has the right to manage the inventory of the business and enter the premises. In a publicly traded chocolate corporation, for example, no shareholder can walk unannounced into the factories to taste the chocolate. Instead, shareholders exercise power indirectly through a board of directors that hires executives.[10]

Second, corporations today have what the president of Columbia University in the early years of the 20th century called "the greatest single discovery of modern times," outshining steam and electricity: limited liability.[11] Without limited liability, whether a business partnership had two people, 200 people, or 200,000,000 people, they would all be liable to pay civil damages if the business cheated or injured its customers (known as "joint and several liability"). In contrast, in the 19th century, secular law began to recognize the idea of "limited liability," where an investor's liability in case of damages would be limited to the amount of money they invested in a company. For example, somebody who was injured by the company could claim assets of the company to pay medical bills but had no claim on the houses or bank accounts of individual shareholders.

Limited liability provided plenty of benefits in secular law, including to synagogues and other charitable entities. But it is a concept in many ways foreign to Jewish law. As Jewish authorities debated the status of a corporation over the past 150 years, limited liability became a central question.

❊ ❊ ❊

While the stock market and public corporations are new and unusual developments of the past several hundred years, it has become hard to imagine a world without them. This chapter will explore what Judaism has to say about these strange young creations and their role in our investment portfolios. We will see early Jewish approaches to corporations, including the question of whether Judaism condones investing in them at all. As corporations grew more complex, so did rabbinic approaches to them. Ultimately, Jewish wisdom encourages (and maybe demands) that we use our voice and power as investors in public companies to pressure and influence those companies to act in ethical ways. We will close the chapter with some examples of investors doing exactly that. But to begin, we need to rewind to a time before corporations and explore how they came to be.

A Brief History of Publicly Traded Corporations

John Micklethwait and Adrian Wooldridge from *The Economist,* who wrote a book on the history of companies, note that there are two things we mean when we say "company." One meaning is simply an organization engaged in business. These companies have existed for thousands of years. The other meaning is the limited-liability joint stock company, which has come to dominate our modern world.[12] These companies began rapidly spreading in the second half of the 19th century, but the groundwork for their growth was laid a bit earlier.

One Japanese construction company has been around since the late 500s CE.[13] Others identify the Finnish manufacturer Stora Enso as the oldest corporation to issue shares starting in 1288.[14] But most agree that the legal foundation of the limited-liability joint-stock corporation began to develop in Europe in the High Middle Ages, when what used to be merely groups or partnerships of people began to morph into something more.[15] Monasteries, churches, and universities became entities unto themselves, somewhat akin to actual people, able to accumulate property and enter into contracts. Religious institutions led the way, and these early models for the limited liability joint-stock corporation had a distinctly religious tone. One medieval European historian compared angelic beings, a popular topic of conversation at the time, with corporations in their ability to live forever and act like a natural person.[16] In some ways the Temple treasury in Jewish tradition serves as a parallel, an independent entity that held its own assets. Indeed, some rabbinic scholars, when faced with the task of explaining modern corporations, have sought the Temple as an analogy.[17]

The next major development came in the 16th and 17th centuries, with the growth of companies chartered by governments, especially England, France, and Denmark. Previously, investors would join together in a basic partnership to finance a single ship's voyage to a distant land for a share of the colonizing proceeds.[18] The partnership would then disband and each investor would go their own way. Now, the British, French, and Dutch governments all chartered East India trading companies intended to endure beyond a single voyage. They issued stock and paid dividends on all the voyages the company took.[19]

Government played a central role.[20] Publicly traded corporations were created through a special act of a monarch for specific public purposes.[21] They often held monopolies in their sector. For example, the British monarchy backed the East India Company's monopoly, making the shares attractive to purchase and leading to a frenzy of speculative activity.[22] This was just the first of hundreds of new start-up joint stock company offerings,[23] in almost every case built around a prospective colonial venture.[24] They targeted nearly every known place on earth, and some unknown ("The Company of Distant Parts").[25] This investment activity in chartered companies led in 1720 to one of the largest financial bubbles in history, known as the South Sea Bubble.[26] The bubble caused a series of disastrous economic collapses, and the British government concurrently banned the offering of stocks until 1825 (about 25 years before emancipating its Jewish residents).[27]

Governments held firm authority over companies, and corporate charters were as easily revoked as issued. Before Virginia was a colony, it was the Virginia Company, with 700 shareholders who paid the equivalent of an ordinary worker's six months' wages for a share. After two decades, 85 percent of the European settlers had died. King James I revoked the company's charter in 1624, forcing the company to become a colony instead.[28]

The role of corporations in the economy expanded slowly at first. In 1801, there were only 317 publicly traded joint-stock corporations in the United States, most of them accomplishing some public function. There were bridge companies, turnpike companies, and eventually banks and insurance companies (which were both seen to have public purpose).[29] As governments permitted more widespread chartering of corporations, the number and purpose of corporations expanded. By 1815, 128 new corporations had been formed in Massachusetts alone, a number that doubled again by 1830.[30]

In the US, corporations were fervently resisted on the federal level until the late 1800s.[31] During the Constitutional Convention debates in the nascent United States, James Madison proposed granting Congress the power to grant charters to new corporations. The other representatives objected that it would be divisive, obstruct public welfare, and lead to monopolies. The proposal was roundly defeated.[32]

Instead, US states maintained tight control over the corporate chartering process, imposing a whole range of conditions. Corporate charters were granted for a limited period of time and could be easily revoked. Corporations could not own stock in other corporations, and corporations could not make any political or charitable contributions.[33] Banks, in particular, faced fierce opposition from multiple US presidents. Their charters required them to honor a distinctively public mission, with heavy restrictions on things like where they could operate and for how long.[34]

Since the early 1800s, the role of corporations has changed from primarily public purpose to primarily capital accumulation.[35] Britain's Joint Stock Company Act of 1862 began the process of acceleration, making it easier to charter a corporation for any purpose.[36] Gilbert and Sullivan even wrote one of their comic operas, *Utopia Unlimited*, parodying the Act and society's growing tendency for everything to become a corporation.[37] The Companies Acts were rapidly copied in other countries.[38]

Despite the slow start, the past 75 years (and especially the past few decades) have seen drastic acceleration in publicly traded stocks. Corporations have gotten larger and more concentrated than ever. There are now four major airlines and three major drug stores. Online retailer Amazon's market capitalization is bigger than all the publicly traded department stores in the United States combined.[39]

Making everything more complicated, companies are now allowed to own shares in other companies. In 1950, individual investors owned 90 percent or more of corporate shares; today they own less than 30 percent. Part of the difference is made up by financial intermediaries, many of whom are large companies themselves.[40] In 1940, investors held a stock for an average of seven years; by 2007, that fell to seven months or shorter.[41] And while corporations in the US may face more regulation today than they did in the Gilded Age, now that they are permitted to make political contributions, they also have more direct influence than ever on the political processes that shape those regulations.[42]

Modern joint-stock corporations were controversial at first (and still are). The famous economist Adam Smith, writing in 1750, disparaged the joint-stock corporation. He critiqued both its concept of limited liability and its outsourcing of decisions to corporate management, two concepts we saw earlier in this chapter. Smith thought granting shareholders immunity from liability for the company's acts would make them more likely to take imprudent risks. Also, corporate management would be less careful with other people's money than with their own. Smith thought it far better to have a private business where each of the partners was liable for the business being run well (and morally).[43] Early corporations were also problematic for their ethics. The British East India Company exemplified this problem when it colonized and ruled India with a private army of 260,000 troops, double the size of the British army.[44]

Another early critique of corporations centered on fears of their monopoly power. This critique resonates in our experience today. The six largest private banks in the United States hold 67 percent of all the assets in the financial system,[45] corporations are significant contributors to political campaigns, and nearly every corporation owns at least some stock in other corporations somewhere on its balance sheet, leading to a powerful and interlocking system.

Public equities have come to dominate most investors' portfolios, including those of socially responsible investors. Often, depictions of impact investing focus on private deals like a loan to an agricultural cooperative in Rwanda or an investment in a local organic microbrewery. Yet public equities make up by far the largest allocation for most impact investors. The membership of the United Nations Principles for Responsible Investment, the largest socially responsible investing coalition in the world, allocates more than twice as much capital to public equities as any other asset class.[46] According to the Global Impact Investing Network, faith institutions on average hold about 40 percent of their portfolio in public equity (plus another 25 percent in public debt).[47]

And while some individuals and institutions have begun to move their investment dollars out of the stock market (see Chapter 9 on local investing for more), most people and institutions plan to keep investing in public corporations for the foreseeable future.

Business Partnerships or Something Else?

Historically, a Jewish investor knew exactly what it meant to invest Jewishly: any business one owned needed to follow every single letter of Jewish law, just like individuals. Whether a sole proprietorship or a small partnership, Jewish tradition expected business entities to observe all the laws that individuals observed.[48]

The Torah obligates Jews to promptly pay workers and to pay a fair wage; so too must Jewish businesses. The Torah forbids borrowing or lending money on interest to other Jews; similarly, a Jewish-owned financial company could not lend to or borrow from Jews. The Torah prohibits owning leavened products, known as *hametz*, during the holiday of Pesach; the same prohibition would apply to businesses.

Similarly, businesses must close on Shabbat and holidays. The Torah commands the entire community to rest once a week for the holiday of Shabbat, including businesses. The Torah explicitly includes workers and servants in Shabbat rest, a powerful societal guardrail to limit inequality. For Shabbat as a societal institution to function, businesses must close on Shabbat as well. The entire body of Jewish law, which is both an ethical system for societal relations and a spiritual system of personal and communal practice, would apply directly to one's business investments.

We saw earlier a key innovation of modern corporations that set them apart from a Jewish perspective: the corporation has a unique identity as a "legal person," with separation between ownership and control. Jewish legal scholars debated the extent to which this secular innovation could be imported into Jewish law.

Does Jewish law acknowledge a corporation as its own entity with limited liability, or does it regard a corporation as just a big partnership? This was a pivotal issue in

19th-century Jewish approaches to investing in public equities. For example, if a corporation is just a partnership, I could not invest in retail establishments that are open on Shabbat. But further, virtually every other company on the stock market would also be off-limits, as these companies are always open when a Jewish holiday like Yom Kippur falls on a weekday. I could not invest in any financial services companies that charge interest; but I also couldn't invest in any company that sells bonds,[49] as this would violate the prohibitions of usury.[50] And I would be prohibited from owning shares in General Mills on the holiday of Pesach, when a Jew is prohibited from owning *hametz* (leavened products like bread). But I would similarly be prohibited from owning shares in any company that owned even a speck of bread anywhere in a locker or a company cafeteria. In multiple ways, considering a corporation a partnership would mean that a Jewish investor could not participate in the modern stock market.

Jewish Legal Approaches to a Corporation

In fact, the first rabbi to publish an opinion on the topic took that very approach. In 1864, in what is present-day Ukraine, Rabbi Shlomo Ganzfried wrote a handbook for Jewish life designed for laypeople, the *Kitzur Shulkhan Arukh*. Rabbi Ganzfried's handbook prohibited owning shares in a bank or even depositing money. Since other Jews were borrowers, this would violate prohibitions on a Jew lending to another Jew at interest.[51]

A year later, Rabbi Joseph Saul Nathansohn published a response in his magnum opus, *Shoel U'Meishiv*. Replying to a letter from Rabbi Ganzfried, he argued that Jewish law should permit depositing money at a bank. While he offered several arguments against Rabbi Ganzfried, he seemed less concerned about justifying his point and more concerned about how Rabbi Ganzfried's opinion might disrupt Jewish life. He even called on Rabbi Ganzfried to retract his opinion in the next edition of his book (which Rabbi Ganzfried did not).[52]

A few years later, another rabbinic authority, Rabbi Moshe Shick, chimed in with a responsum. Already by his time, there was a common practice of creating pooled loan funds (similar to early credit unions). He quoted the earlier rabbinic exchange and argued a powerful new idea: that a loan fund is its own entity, not merely a partnership of its owners, and so avoids the prohibitions of usury.[53] And the floodgates of the debate were opened.

A strand of Jewish thought continued to agree with the stringent opinion of Rabbi Ganzfried into the 20th century, arguing that it ought to be off-limits for a Jew to invest in a company that does business on Shabbat or owns *hametz* during the holiday of Pesach.[54] Other authorities were lenient (see the footnotes for a list).[55]

Those who prohibited investing in public companies argued that a corporation is a straightforward business partnership, no matter how many millions of shareholders it has. And each shareholder is a part-owner, no matter how small the part. The company must obey Jewish law or be off-limits for investment.

Those who allowed investing in public companies had a range of justifications. Many saw a corporation as its own separate entity, parallel to secular law. Others crafted definitions of a corporation based on lending relationships or were vague on the exact legal definition but argued that the attenuated relationship between an individual shareholder and a public corporation couldn't possibly be considered a partnership.[56]

These positions have evolved in meaning over time. Public corporations have grown immensely more complex since the late 19th and early 20th centuries. Some of the early rabbis who advocated for the stringent opinion clearly did not intend to prohibit owning stock entirely. For example, Rabbi Menashe Klein, who argued in 1960 that one must sell shares in a company owning leavened bread during the holiday of Pesach, thought it was fine to purchase the shares back afterward.[57]

The first wave of rabbinic opinions on the status of a corporation were written at a time when corporations were not allowed to own stock in each other. Yet the growing complexity of the corporate landscape means that we can no longer disentangle specific issues or sectors and need to address the system as a whole. Corporations are now permitted to own shares in each other, and the practice has become ubiquitous, like a web of ownership where owning any single company inevitably means investing in the web itself. Practically speaking, if one follows the more stringent approach of treating a corporation as a partnership under Jewish law, it is impossible for a Jewish investor today to invest in publicly traded stocks.[58]

Jewish Approaches in Practice Today

There are rare instances today of Jews taking the approach that investing in the stock market ought to be entirely off-limits. For example, in 2008 the Badatz of Jerusalem, a *Haredi* Orthodox kosher supervision group, created an investment committee to grant kosher certificates to financial instruments. The Badatz committee found that practically every Israeli publicly-traded company ran afoul of Jewish law, and the committee could not find a way to permit investment. The Badatz published a pamphlet in 2010 explaining, "Even 'innocent' shares such as the Darban land development company owns a mall that operates on Shabbos, and Bank Leumi is a partner in the Fox fashion chain.... Strauss shares include branches of the Coffee ToGo cafe chain, which operates on Shabbos."[59]

Shortly thereafter, the Badatz created an investing group, Besadno, which they called "the first kosher alternative investment group." Investments are approved by the Badatz's own finance committee to be in conformity with Jewish law.[60] After securing nearly 2,000 investors from the Israeli market, the organization launched an equity crowdfunding investment platform called Investination open to accredited investors in the US. Investors choose from a range of Israeli start-ups and can invest a minimum of $10,000 in each.[61] Investment opportunities include Earways Medical, a medical technology company marketing an enhanced tool to remove earwax, and SolidBlock, a financial technology company whose digital products provide access to increased liquidity for real estate investors. The investing platform mostly focuses on early-stage (not yet public) innovative technology startups, and all of its investee companies observe Shabbat, keep kosher, and follow Jewish laws.[62]

Others seek to avoid investments in public equities from a more progressive perspective. One example is Diane Isenberg, whom we met in Chapter 3. Over the past several years, Isenberg has sought to move her family office, Ceniarth, into "impact-first capital preservation" investments and decrease her investments in the stock market. She has done so not out of a sense of Jewish legal obligation but out of a similar moral concern with the implications of being an owner in stock, and the sense that investing in the stock market will never solve global poverty. Other social-justice focused economic organizations have taken a similar stance. Resource Generation, mentioned in Chapter 4, is a membership organization of young people with wealth, including a number of Jewish individuals. The organization seeks not only to encourage its membership to give away or redistribute excess wealth, but also to divest from Wall Street and reinvest funds in local investments that build community wealth.[63]

Both the Badatz of Jerusalem and Ceniarth have taken a principled approach. They have assessed the fundamental structure of corporations and allowed their integrity to guide them to opt out of the entire system of public equities, in preference for more ethical alternatives. But this approach is quite difficult to put into practice. The Badatz represents an extremely committed religious constituency and is dealing with a specific circumstance of Jewish-owned companies based in Israel. Ceniarth and Resource Generation both represent constituencies with significant wealth, which makes taking a principled stance easier. Both remain outliers even among impact investors, at least for now.

In the Jewish conversation, the vast rabbinic consensus agrees that when a public corporation is under majority non-Jewish ownership, Jewish shareholders are not liable for the corporation's violations of Jewish law. They can own stock in a company that operates on Shabbat, charges interest to Jews, and owns *hametz* on Pesach.[64] According to this consensus, as a shareholder, I am not responsible for the unethical acts of the corporation—a kind of religious limited liability, as it were.[65]

Moral Challenges to Each Approach

Beyond the legal arguments, all of these approaches face moral difficulties. On the one hand, saying that a corporation is its own entity leads to the same unsavory ethical ground in Jewish law that it does in secular law. If I hold shares in a corporation that sells cigarettes, pollutes the environment, or employs forced and child labor in its supply chain, do I have no responsibility at all for the actions of the corporate entity? And even if my individual stock ownership plays a miniscule role, Judaism still holds us accountable to avoid making a mockery of a religious life through shameful acts (known in Hebrew as *hillul Hashem*). How much spiritual harm does it contribute to the world when I invest in such injustice?

Maybe the most ethical approach is to consider a corporation a partnership and consider each individual shareholder responsible for all the acts of the company. Corporations have become the dominant force in our society and across the globe. They are legally required to pursue profit at the expense of other externalities, an approach contrary to Jewish values. This, plus the size of modern public corporations, means it is difficult to find a corporation that is not complicit in some kind of human rights abuse or environmental degradation at some point in its supply chain. The power of corporate influence in the US prevented more comprehensive financial reform after the 2008 economic meltdown,[66] gun reform[67] after the 2012 school shooting in Newtown, Connecticut,[68] and attempts to curb pharmaceutical prices in recent years.[69] Perhaps Judaism's legal compass calls on us to divest from the system.

On the other hand, Judaism has never been a religion of asceticism. As we saw in Chapter 2, Judaism does not eschew wealth or participation in business. Further, the rabbis, with their keen awareness of human psychology and communal life, avoided making decrees that most of the community would fail to follow (as we will see in Chapter 10). Participating in the stock market has become a regular part of Jewish life across the world.[70] And beyond merely investing in corporations, most of us engage with some of them every day. Considering a corporation a partnership would not only prevent a Jewish investor from owning public equities but might even prevent being a consumer or interacting with the many corporations that define our modern economy, so as not to place a stumbling block before the blind (see Chapter 5). Who could truly uphold this standard?

A growing number of people are actively working to change the moral problematics of the status quo, whether through alternative structures for corporations (like the public-benefit corporation we encountered in the introduction) or through making it easier to invest in non-publicly traded entities (which we will learn more about in Chapter 9). While it may take time and energy to find and engage with these efforts,

Jewish values would certainly encourage us to, as they offer paths to participating in business according to one's values and without living an ascetic life.

In the meantime, avoiding the stock market entirely is not realistic for most Jewish investors. Neither is it appropriate for faith-based investors to abandon all moral responsibility for the actions of corporations in which we invest. We need a middle approach, ideally one that allows us to work in complement to others working to transform our economic system for the better.

The Influence of a Shareholder

We can find a middle path in one of the most interesting and evocative rabbinic approaches to public corporations, by Rabbi Moshe Feinstein, a prominent 20th-century Orthodox rabbi and legal scholar. Rabbi Feinstein was asked about corporations in 1960 and again in 1974, and he replied with two different answers.

In 1960, Rabbi Feinstein published a responsum permitting an individual to invest in public companies. He based this permission on an assumption that shareholders had no interest in influencing the company and were merely seeking to hold stock and profit from it. He argued that the founders of the corporation always reserve a majority of stock for themselves, and a minority shareholder is just along for the ride, even for decisions like election of the board chair.[71]

Rabbi Feinstein's early position reflected the reality of the time. The most common approach to corporations in the 1960s was to invest in them and leave moral qualms behind. We noted in Chapter 2 that Milton Friedman's influential essay, "The Social Responsibility of Business Is to Increase Its Profits," was published in The New York Times in 1970. It is likely that most shareholders of the time were investing simply for a share of the profits and losses, not to have moral responsibility for a business, exactly as Rabbi Feinstein noted.

However, Rabbi Feinstein published a different approach in 1974. This time around, Rabbi Feinstein introduced the idea that the role of the shareholder is not one of decision-making power but one of influence.

He grounded his assessment in a concept of "ownership of work," based on a farming arrangement described in the Talmud, which he applied to the role of a shareholder in a public corporation today. Shareholders own the corporation itself; the board and senior management own the work and can decide when and how it is done; and shareholders influence management by offering advice and input.

Rabbi Feinstein's earlier responsum had assumed that shareholders have no interest in influencing the company—unless they have actual control, in which case the full panoply of Jewish-related obligations kick in. His later framing captures a very different approach that shareholders might take. The "work" and its responsibility are owned by the corporate directors and the executives they hire. At the same time, all shareholders have the potential for influence.

Rabbi Feinstein's change in position in the intervening 14 years echoed a broader change. Society was shifting in its perception of the role of a shareholder in a corporation, thanks to the birth of one of the most important developments in socially responsible investing in the past fifty years: the modern shareholder advocacy movement.

An Introduction to Shareholder Advocacy

Shareholder advocacy involves an investor using their stock ownership as a platform to advocate with a corporation to improve its behavior. Here is shareholder advocacy's origin story, as told by the leading coalition of faith-based and values-based shareholder advocates, the Interfaith Center on Corporate Responsibility:

> During the twentieth century, the international centers of power began shifting from the capitals of national governments to the headquarters and boardrooms of the world's biggest companies. Corporations and the capital they wielded developed an extraordinary influence on global economies, government policies, and hence, people and the environment. In the early seventies, the abhorrent policy of apartheid, the legislated segregation of races in South Africa, became a clarion call to action for faith communities. In 1971, the Episcopal Church in the United States filed the first religious-sponsored shareholder resolution with General Motors requesting that the company withdraw its operations from the country until apartheid was abolished. Other faith organizations soon joined the campaign.[72]

Any investor who is concerned with a corporation's behavior can reach out to that corporation to seek change. When a corporation fails to respond to outreach or dialogue, an investor who owns even one share can escalate by attending the annual shareholder meeting and speaking directly to the CEO and board. If that fails, they can go further and file a shareholder resolution to appear on the company's annual ballot. This requires $2,000 worth of stock held for at least three years (under current rules from the Securities and Exchange Commission) and a certain amount of technical expertise to craft a shareholder resolution that will pass the SEC's review process, but it is a powerful tool to highlight an issue and increase public attention. Once a resolution makes it to a company's annual ballot, every shareholder is invited to weigh in.[73]

Since the 1970s, shareholder advocacy has grown tremendously as a tactic used by values-based investors. In one recent count, over $10 trillion of investment assets in the United States make use of this tactic, seeking change on social and environmental issues.[74]

Hundreds of shareholder resolutions are filed each year at major corporations, on a wide range of issues. Some resolutions are filed by private shareholders, like the Nathan Cummings Foundation that we met in Chapter 4. Others are filed by socially responsible asset managers and funds, which we will learn more about later in this chapter. In 2021, shareholders asked companies to conduct a racial justice audit of a company's operations (filed by Zevin Asset Management), align a company's business practices to the Paris Climate Accords (filed by Boston Trust Walden), adopt paid sick leave for a company's workers (filed by Trillium), phase out overuse of antibiotics in livestock that lead to the growth of antibiotic-resistant superbugs (filed by Green Century Funds), and more.

For a long time, many corporations sought to ignore or dismiss shareholder resolutions. But in recent years corporations have come to understand the cost and reputational risk of avoiding action on the issues being raised by shareholder advocates. In response, corporations have built out an entire field of Corporate Social Responsibility (CSR). In 2013, only 20 percent of large US corporations published a Corporate Social Responsibility report; in 2020, nearly 90 percent did.[75]

Shareholder proposals can be filed by investors of any political background, though they are more often filed in favor of progressive causes. In 2023, of the more than 500 shareholder proposals filed, the vast majority reflected ESG concerns. Over 120 addressed climate change, and over 50 focused on curbing corporate lobbying and supporting free and fair elections. But over 40 proposals were filed from a conservative, or more specifically "anti-ESG," perspective. The most popular topic was a challenge to corporate diversity, equity, and inclusion (DEI) initiatives, including board diversity efforts.[76]

The tactics of shareholder advocacy have their limits. In general, shareholder advocacy campaigns are more likely to be successful if they reflect a growing social movement or grassroots campaign. For example, thanks to the work of scientists, climate campaigners, and environmental justice activists, there is now a strong and growing grassroots movement to combat climate change, and that has often translated into higher voting percentages on climate-focused shareholder resolutions.

The anti-ESG proposals filed in 2023 averaged a measly 2.8 percent vote,[77] probably because the concerns they reflected were not grounded in the needs and goals of grassroots movements. For example, far more working Americans support diversity, equity, and inclusion (DEI) practices than don't, and even among conservatives there is significant support.[78] Most people can understand intuitively the value of diversity of thought in leadership, and research demonstrates that diverse boards perform better.

Progressive shareholder resolutions face the same pitfalls. Shareholder advocates can accelerate a company's response to growing movements for justice. But if shareholders become too ambitious in their demands without building enough public and grassroots support, shareholder resolutions will receive low votes and corporate management might feel comfortable ignoring the issue.

There are other issues with shareholder advocacy. Shareholder resolutions in the United States are generally non-binding. Shareholder resolutions are garnering majority votes with increasing frequency, but even if more than 50 percent of shareholders support a resolution, the board and management of the company are under no obligation to act. In certain other countries in Europe, shareholder resolutions are binding, but the threshold for filing them is much higher, sometimes as much as five percent of the total shares of the corporation, making the tactic inaccessible for many values-based investors.

Nevertheless, shareholder advocacy is an important tool, in conjunction with community organizing and building grassroots movements, to move the cost-benefit analysis for corporations. If a company knows that "business as usual" will attract the scrutiny of trillions of dollars of investor capital, it will be more motivated to change its behavior.

Shareholder advocacy has only accelerated in recent years. In 2021, a full 20 shareholder resolutions on Environmental, Social, and Governance issues at major companies received a majority vote, including resolutions on racial justice, political lobbying, and the climate crisis, more than double the previous year.[79]

Shareholder advocacy begins with knowing an investor's own values and ethical expectations for corporate behavior. Thankfully, Judaism has an entire ethical framework that outlines basic expectations of all people (and companies)—the Noachide Laws.

Universal Standards

The Torah focuses mostly on the spiritual practice of Jews, but it also articulates universal expectations of human behavior. These appear at the beginning of the Torah, when God renewed a covenant with Noah and his descendants after the flood. The rabbis understood this covenant to encompass seven core precepts. They are known in Hebrew as the *sheva mitzvot b'nei Noach* (the seven practices of the children of

Noah), and usually referred to in English as the Noachide laws. For example, there is no expectation in Judaism that all humans will eat kosher. But there is an expectation that all humans will avoid stealing, will not murder, and will establish a system of laws and courts to ensure justice and societal functioning. (See Chapter 5 for more).

Corporations ought to live up to these standards too, according to several modern Jewish scholars.[80] In other words, while a corporation may not be a Jew, it is a "person." It should be obliged to follow the same basic standards of behavior that Judaism expects of all people, Jewish or not. A company such as Wells Fargo, which harmed millions of people through deceptive and fraudulent practices that became public in 2016, was violating not just secular law but the Noachide laws that prohibit stealing and require upholding a system of justice.

In Chapter 5, we discussed the Torah's prohibition on placing stumbling blocks before the blind and aiding the deeds of transgressors. We learned that this prohibition applies only if I am taking active steps to support those engaged in ethical violations. Purchasing shares from another investor on the secondary market (like a stock market) is not actively assisting a company in its misdeeds, as no money flows back to the company from my purchase.

However, I do have the opportunity actively to assist management every year by voting on a company's annual proxy ballot.

If you owned shares of Exxon Mobil in 2021, you were invited to vote on several proposals. One demanded disclosure of the company's lobbying activities and political spending. Another asked the company to account for if and how its lobbying aligns with the Paris Climate Accords. Both passed with majority shareholder votes. Even more remarkably, you were invited to vote to replace four of Exxon's twelve board members with more climate-focused board members nominated by an activist hedge fund. Three of the new candidates were voted in.[81]

When one votes one's shares in line with management, one is directly assisting the company to continue in business as usual. If business as usual violates Judaism's fundamental values and principles of human behavior, Judaism would obligate me to vote my proxies according to my conscience.

Contemporary Rabbi Dr. Barry Bressler, dean of business at Touro College, puts it as follows: if there is a shareholder movement at a company aligned with Jewish values, "an investor wishing to be in accord with Jewish law is obliged to participate or divest himself of company holdings. Failure to do so is tantamount to supporting the status quo power of unethical management."[82]

Unless you are blessed with a tremendous amount of free time, you likely are not able extensively to research each of the shareholder proposals and board directors at the hundreds of companies you may own in an investment portfolio. This is similar to how much time we might (or not) spend researching candidates in the political realm.

Further, many investors do not invest directly in individual companies but instead in mutual funds and ETFs. This means that proxy ballot votes are not actually the choice of the individual investor, but of the fund manager. The fund manager is responsible for voting the annual proxy ballots for the entire fund at each company the fund is invested in. Investors rely on these asset managers to make decisions about the proxy ballots on their behalf.

Some of the largest and best-known asset management firms may not be making decisions in a way our Jewish values would support. BlackRock, the largest asset manager in the world, supported only 14 percent of the climate-related resolutions it voted on in the 2020 proxy season. The second-largest, Vanguard, was not much better.[83] The specific ESG or SRI funds at these asset managers have a better track record of votes on shareholder resolutions but still are not exemplary.

Instead, it is important to choose an asset manager who will vote in an active way and be unafraid to challenge management. You can look to invest with an asset manager with a strong voting record. We will see more resources for finding funds and asset managers in the next section.

What about ESG Funds?

Some investment funds, known as ESG funds, seek to score every company on its Environmental, Social, and Governance practices, and to invest in the best-scoring companies.

There is currently a pushback against ESG investing among both progressives and conservatives. Some conservatives, afraid of a perceived growing trend of investment capital being used to further social change on progressive causes, have sought to increasingly ban funds from using ESG metrics. This is misguided. Investors with a range of values and approaches should acknowledge the risks posed by ESG concerns, though they may take different approaches to mitigate them. Further, the claim that financial profit ought to be the only consideration in an investment decision is antithetical to a Jewish approach to money ethics.

Of note, news reports have revealed that fossil fuel companies likely originated and promoted the wave of anti-ESG sentiment as a backroom campaign beginning in state legislatures in 2021,[84] suggesting that perhaps these companies themselves prioritized spending time on their own "social" concerns rather than finding a long-term sustainable business model.

Progressives sometimes critique ESG funds as failing to achieve any actual change.

The Stanford Social Innovation Review recently ran an article with the headline, "The World May Be Better Off Without ESG Investing," noting that the current system of ESG ratings sets the bar too low and looks at the wrong criteria. For example, tobacco company Phillip Morris has made it into the Dow Jones Sustainability Index, and oil giants Exxon and BP get a relatively decent score from ratings agency MSCI.[85] The Wild West variability of ESG standards has also caught the attention of investment regulators such as the Securities and Exchange Commission, and regulators are actively working to create minimum standards for ESG.

There is no such thing as a perfect company from a Jewish perspective, and ESG funds are far from an ideal solution to the problem of ethical investing. And some funds do even less—they merely "consider" ESG in their investment decisions.

That said, ESG funds may help investors avoid being complicit in the worst violations of our values, a definite improvement over "traditional" investment vehicles. Some ESG funds, especially the more rigorous ones, will also maintain a list of negative screens—they may avoid any investment in tobacco or fossil fuels, for example—which is a meaningful commitment.

If you cannot access a fund that engages in shareholder advocacy and you only have a choice between a "traditional" fund and an ESG fund, selecting the ESG fund might mitigate some of the most negative potential social and environmental impacts. It will also mean you are joining a broader movement for social change, which is an important movement to support.

A Jewish Approach to Shareholder Advocacy

Beyond merely avoiding complicity in harmful acts, Judaism provides an affirmative frame for shareholder advocacy. Two sentences after the prohibition on placing a stumbling block before the blind, the Torah articulates: "Do not hate your fellow in your heart; rebuke them, and do not bear sin on their account."[86]

In Judaism, constructive rebuke is crucial to relationship. A 13th-century work, the *Book of the Pious*, notes that when possible, one should offer constructive rebuke to everyone, Jew or Gentile. The author brings the example of the prophet Jonah, sent by God to rebuke the city of Nineveh.[87] Expanding on Jonah as a model, presumably this advice applies not only to individuals but also to entire collectives like cities or corporations.

There is even a Jewish process for rebuke. The *Book of Education*, another 13th-century work published anonymously in Spain as a letter from father to son, elaborates on the commandment of rebuke. The author notes that one ought to begin with private conversation and calm words, to avoid embarrassment and make the feedback more effective. If the recipient does not respond, one should respectfully escalate to the point of calling out the person's misdeeds publicly and continue to offer them rebuke until they are literally ready to strike out in response. On the other hand, if it becomes clear the person will not respond—the harmful behavior is too deeply ingrained—then one is absolved of the responsibility to rebuke.[88]

Modern shareholder advocates follow almost word-for-word the *Book of Education*'s description of rebuke. Advocates begin with private conversations with a company. When a company fails to respond, or makes only token changes, shareholder advocates publicly call out the company at the annual meeting, file resolutions, and recruit other investors to campaign.

Unfortunately, sometimes businesses do make it clear they will not respond in a productive way to constructive feedback. For example, companies will sometimes respond to feedback by filing a lawsuit against those speaking out that is not intended to prevail in court but to be so costly in legal fees for the defendants as to discourage any criticism. These lawsuits have earned the moniker Strategic Lawsuits Against Public Participation, or SLAPP, and many come from polluting industries and are aimed at environmental organizations. In 2016, the environmental group Greenpeace was sued by a logging company in a suit that was later deemed by a judge to be a SLAPP lawsuit under California law. The company was required to reimburse Greenpeace for some of their legal fees, but other costs were never recovered.[89] When an investor gives feedback and a person or a corporation makes clear they will not respond productively, one should end the investment relationship.

My former organization, JLens, created the Jewish Advocacy Strategy in 2015 to represent Jewish communal capital in the investor advocacy arena. The investment vehicle has investments from dozens of Jewish institutions across the country. In my time at JLens, we filed shareholder resolutions on gender and racial pay gaps with TJ Maxx, climate change impacts with utility company AES, and the opioid epidemic at multiple pharmaceutical companies. (As of the time of publication, the JLens offering is available only with a minimum investment of $250,000).

You can find many other investment funds that engage in shareholder advocacy on a range of social and environmental issues. A number of them are mentioned in this chapter or throughout this book, though you should do your own research to see if their approach aligns with your goals. The most robust asset managers (the ones who are willing actually to file shareholder resolutions) will be members of coalitions like the Interfaith Center on Corporate Responsibility, mentioned above, or other responsible investing coalitions. One useful tool is Green America's Socially Responsible Investing Heart Rating (on the organization's website, greenamerica.org/socially-responsible-investing). These funds will also be the most likely to vote their proxies in an active and values-aligned way, even when that means disagreeing with corporate management.

Conclusion

Public equities dominate our investment choices, and corporations dominate our modern world. Both of these developments are very new from a Jewish perspective. Jewish law has evolved in step with the rapid growth in corporate power and complexity of corporate structure. Early on, public corporations in the United States were a dynamic topic, faced with a range of controversies. At first, corporations were founded by acts of the state and focused on public welfare rather than profit maximization. Early corporate charters included building roads and bridges, and bank and insurance companies which were explicitly chartered for the public welfare. Jewish scholars in the 1860s debated whether a Jew could participate in banks and loan funds without violating prohibitions of usury, doing business on Shabbat, or owning *hametz* on Pesach. As corporations grew more complex, so did rabbinic conversations about them.

The more stringent position would consider a corporation to be a straightforward partnership under Jewish law, and therefore a shareholder would be liable for all the actions of the corporation. Since most corporations are not run in accordance with Jewish precepts, a Jewish investor would basically need to divest from the stock market. A select few take this approach today. A more lenient position, held by the vast rabbinic consensus on the topic, permits owning stock in a corporation.

Neither position is fully morally satisfying. It is nearly impossible to find a corporation without some form of harmful behavior somewhere in its supply chain or global operations. The most ethical approach might be to divest from the system entirely. Yet Jewish tradition seeks to avoid untenable standards of communal behavior and to engage in the world as it is, not as we wish it would be.

Rabbi Moshe Feinstein, in his later position published in 1974, articulated an understanding of the ways that shareholders have influence, though not total control, over a corporation's behavior. Based on the principles of "not putting a stumbling block before the blind" and "constructive rebuke," Judaism would obligate an investor to join in shareholder campaigns to influence management and to vote proxies in accordance with one's conscience. If, after ongoing rebuke, it becomes clear that a corporation will not cease its harmful behavior, it might be appropriate to divest and end the relationship. According to a number of modern Jewish scholars, a corporation ought to at a minimum be held to the ethical standards of behavior Judaism expects of every person, the Noachide laws.

Judaism is a spiritual path. We are invited by the tradition to be in a continual practice of stretching ourselves to be the most ethical people we can be. In a world so dominated by public corporations, Judaism may not demand we divest from public equities. But we are meant to be concerned about complicity in corporate structures that prioritize profit at all costs. We need to move beyond having our investment portfolios dominated by stocks of public corporations whose legal imperative is profit above all else. The next several chapters will provide us a few ways to do so.

Next Steps—Chapter 7

Public equities (stocks of companies, or funds made up of stocks) represent the largest allocation for most investors. One of the most impactful and Jewish values-aligned approaches to investing in public companies is shareholder advocacy.

- **Step 1: Engage in shareholder advocacy.** Or, more realistically, move your public equity allocation to investment funds and strategies that engage in shareholder advocacy on your behalf.
  - This chapter is full of examples of investment firms engaging in shareholder advocacy to move the needle on corporate actions, including Boston Trust Walden, Green Century Funds, Trillium Asset Management, and Zevin Asset Management, as well as my former organization JLens, which engages in shareholder advocacy specifically from a Jewish perspective. Visit the websites of these investment firms to learn more about their work. Ask your investment advisor for recommendations of other funds to invest in that have a robust commitment to shareholder advocacy.
  - Remember, shareholder advocacy is only a tool, and it is often only effective when used to amplify and accelerate broader grassroots movements. Research opportunities for activism—focused on broad systemic change, not just individual action—on whatever issue most inspires you. Share what you have learned with a friend. Consider making a regular time commitment volunteering in a way that builds movements for change.
- **Step 2: Pick ESG over "traditional."** When you do not have access to funds that engage in shareholder advocacy, you can select an ESG or other socially responsible fund.
  - ESG funds may be an improvement over "traditional" funds. Some ESG funds, especially the more rigorous ones, will also maintain a list of negative screens—they may avoid any investment in tobacco or fossil fuels, for example—which is a meaningful commitment. ESG is growing in popularity and becoming more widely available.
  - If you cannot access a fund that engages in shareholder advocacy and you only have a choice between a "traditional" fund and an ESG fund (maybe you have limited choices in your company's 401(k)), the ESG fund might mitigate the most negative potential social and environmental impacts of your portfolio and build support for a broader movement for social change.
- **Step 3: Reallocate toward greatest impact and values alignment.** Consider what it would take to move a portion of your investment portfolio away from public equities and to local investing (Chapter 9) or other alternatives mentioned throughout this book.

Chapter 8

Debt:
Free Loans and Shared Risk

Jerry and Marcie Martinez had stopped playing Monopoly. The game, with its real estate theme, reminded them too much of a painful reality: that in the midst of the biggest financial crash in recent decades, their mortgage was underwater.

A mortgage falls underwater when the value of the home drops below the amount left on the mortgage, at which point a family is saddled with debt even if they were to sell the house. The Martinezes had bought their home in early 2005 for $630,000, using an interest-only mortgage, a popular loan during the economic boom. As of early November 2008, the home's value had plummeted to $420,000. Income was scarce as Jerry's contracting business suffered. The family cut back on family bowling night and movies and stuck to board games at home—but avoided Monopoly.[1]

Their story of homeownership is far from unique. According to *The New York Times*, nearly a quarter of all homes with mortgages in November 2008 were either underwater or nearly so.[2]

Families like the Martinezes were left wondering why the economy crashed so severely and how it could be prevented from doing so again. Several years after the Great Recession, Atif Mian and Amir Sufi, economists from Princeton and the University of Chicago respectively, sought to probe that very question. Part of a new generation of economists with access to modern computing power and reams of financial data to analyze, they were able to reconstruct a well-grounded story of the crash.

A part of the story was extraordinary household debt. Prior to 2000, household debt grew at a steady pace, but in the years between 2000 and 2007, the total amount of household debt doubled. This incredible increase was matched by only one period in US history, the years 1920-1929, preceding the Great Depression. The spike in household debt was accompanied by a sudden drop in household spending, also unparalleled since the Great Depression.

However, the crash was not the fault of any individual, even individuals with high debt. Mian and Sufi identified a key problem with the way many mortgages, and really most forms of debt, are structured in this country. Mian and Sufi use the term "inflexible debt contract," which is exactly what it sounds like: the lender doesn't provide any flexibility, and the borrower is expected to pay no matter what.[3]

These two economists demonstrate in their book *House of Debt* that the economic crash was a direct result of the fact that most of the debt in the economy was "inflexible." The inflexibility of the debt put the Martinezes and borrowers across the country in a weak position, many defaulted on their loans, and the entire economy suffered. Mian and Sufi argue that we can move away from painful episodes of economic bust only if the financial system moves away from inflexible debt contracts and toward an alternative—shared risk—that we will discuss more in this chapter.

In Chapter 3, we learned the Talmudic teaching that the sentiment "what's mine is mine and what's yours is yours" is an average, common sentiment, and yet at the same time represents the destructiveness of Sodom. According to Mian and Sufi, inflexible debt contracts in our society are a paradigmatic example. Mortgages, student loans, auto loans, and credit card debt are the building blocks of most people's lives in this country. Yet they are all inflexible debt, which, as the book *House of Debt* documents, plays a key role in causing economic crashes like the Great Recession of 2008.

This is worth saying again. The subject of this chapter is investing in debt. The average American today is in debt representing 130 percent of their annual income.[4] The asset class known as "fixed-income" is made up of entirely of debt, including corporate and municipal bonds, which are essentially loans from an investor to a corporation or the government. The average building blocks of our society are these inflexible debt contracts. Yet according to economists Mian and Sufi, the inflexibility of these contracts is precisely what led to the 2008 economic crash. Inflexible debt contracts represent the norm; at the same time, they are the building blocks of economic collapse.

The pervasiveness of inflexible debt contracts in our society was not inevitable. In fact, dependence on inflexible debt contracts has been frowned upon by most civilizations throughout history and even today is far from universal across the world (especially in Islamic countries). There are many alternative financial vehicles that ensure everyone who wants can access capital as a tool for building wealth and developing society, while not allowing capital accumulation to lead to economic collapse.

Faith traditions have a long history of sustainable approaches to debt. Judaism, along with Islam, Christianity, Hinduism, and other of the world's major religions, has statutes against usury (charging interest to someone in need).[5] Judaism in particular has a long and sophisticated history of navigating issues around debt and usury. The Torah prohibited lending at interest, a prohibition with a moral as well as practical valence. The rabbis of the Talmud clarified the differences between an interest-bearing loan and an investment. In short, investments were permitted when they were partnerships that shared risk equitably between the investor furnishing the capital and the partner using the capital. Later, the rabbis of the medieval era, in an increasingly sophisticated and global economy, developed new Jewish legal investment instruments, continuing to ensure capital was available to borrow for entrepreneurs who needed it while maintaining ethical limits to prevent runaway capital accumulation by the richest at the literal expense of everyone else. These practices of shared risk still exist today in Judaism and can serve as a guide for an ethical approach to investment in debt.

Interest that Bites

Shortly after emerging from slavery in Egypt, the Israelites stood together at the foot of Mount Sinai and received the Torah. The Israelites were instructed on a set of ethical precepts for society. Following an exhortation to care for needy community members, widows and orphans, the Torah records: "If you lend money to my people, to the poor among your people, do not act like a creditor toward them; do not take any interest from them."[6]

The same prohibition on charging interest to a fellow in need appears in the next book of the Torah as well. This time it comes right after the laws and precepts of the *shmita* year (we saw more about *shmita* in Chapter 2, and the connection between *shmita* and ethical investing keeps recurring throughout this book).[7] And a third time, forty years later, before the Israelites enter the land of Israel, Moses reiterates the commandment and adds details: "you shall not deduct interest from loans to your countrymen, whether in money or food or anything else that can be deducted as interest; but you may deduct interest from loans to foreigners. Do not deduct interest from loans to your countrymen."[8]

Early Jewish tradition framed the prohibition against interest in both ethical and spiritual language. For example, King David composed a psalm praising righteous behaviors and included not lending at interest.[9] The prophet Ezekiel, in a list of righteous acts, describes marital fidelity, not stealing, feeding the hungry, clothing the naked, and not charging interest.[10] The Torah itself connects the prohibition against interest to God's covenant with the Jewish people: interest is prohibited because "I am the Lord your God who brought you out of Egypt." In the final book of the Torah, Moses explicitly links the prohibition on usury to God's blessings: "so that the Lord your God may bless you in all your undertakings in the land that you are about to enter and possess."

The rabbis knew the deep temptation to loan at interest; they put the weight not just of their legal authority but also spiritual authority behind this prohibition. One who charged interest was seen as having a lust for money and was deemed unfit to serve as a witness in court.[11] The Talmudic sages, in a chapter appropriately titled, "What is Usury?", note that the Hebrew word used for usury in the Torah, *neshech*, literally means to bite—charging interest is taking a bite out of someone.

The prohibition was not absolute. Jews, who all joined the same social contract described in the Torah (and often geographically formed a unified community), were prohibited from lending at interest to each other. They were also prohibited from accepting a loan at interest from each other, as the prohibition described in the Torah falls on both parties to a loan. Non-Jews, who had not bought in to the same social contract, could both lend to and receive loans from Jews at interest.[12] In fact, non-Jewish neighbors would regularly serve as intermediaries in the lending process, and the rabbis extensively discuss the nuances of paying interest to a non-Jewish intermediary. (We will discuss this more in-depth in a few pages).

Why Not Interest?

Jewish tradition does not actually view interest as inherently immoral; it is merely inappropriate for Jews to charge it to each other.[13] There are two primary ways we can understand this prohibition: spiritual and practical.

Spiritually, charging interest to a fellow community member leads me away from the Divine. Our possessions are not truly ours; they belong to God. I am unlikely to forget the Divine source of my possessions while tending a tree dependent on rain and its own miraculous process of budding and flowering. The moment I am most likely to forget the Divine origins of my possessions is the moment when my own money seems to generate more money for me with no Divine intervention.

To put it another way, Judaism has no problem with me renting out my possessions. I can rent out my ox to a neighbor and receive a payment in exchange; I am unlikely to fool myself into thinking I can create an ox myself without Divine input. But under Jewish law, I cannot rent out my money and receive the money plus an interest payment. Doing so could lead me to an assumption that I am multiplying my money by myself without any input from God.

The 17th-century commentator Turei Zahav points out that someone who chooses to lend at interest despite the prohibition on doing so is demonstrating that they think they know better than God. The person argues, "if only God had known how much profit I could earn." They may even see themselves as righteous: "if only God had known how much an interest-bearing loan could help this poor person." These misguided justifications chip away at the foundations of faith that underpin Judaism's vision of economic justice.[14]

From this angle, the prohibition on interest is a spiritual test. Indeed, the Jewish legal codes grouped charging interest with transgressions like denying the fundamental principles of Jewish faith, denying the liberation of the children of Israel from Egypt, and even denying the divinity of God.[15] In the most popular code of Jewish law, the laws concerning usury are included not in the volume dedicated to economic issues but in the volume dedicated to spiritual issues, alongside keeping kosher and avoiding idol worship.[16] Rabbi Samson Raphael Hirsch (Germany, 1808-1888) notes the Torah's goal in banning usury is to remind us of God as the source of all our funds and to inspire us to direct excess funds to charitable use.[17] This is also why Judaism makes no distinction between interest rates—a loan at 2 percent interest is just as prohibited as a loan at 50 percent interest, since both multiply one's money by themselves and risk disconnecting one from the true Source of one's wealth.[18]

On the other hand, practically, we can understand the prohibition on interest as a communal norm, a way to sustain society. We saw above in the text of the Torah that the prohibition of avoiding interest itself stems from the obligation to offer support to community members in need. Once we are already considering a loan to help a vulnerable or needy person, we ought to avoid charging interest, because interest would undermine the purpose of such welfare. This might be a reason why the prohibition applies to community members with whom one shares a social contract, but not to strangers (non-Jews) in what are likely one-off transactions.[19]

Interest has a particular quality of compounding, of starting so small that we can barely feel it but then growing so quickly it overwhelms human relationships. The *Book of Education*, a medieval Jewish work that outlines the moral wisdom behind the Torah's commandments, comments on the prohibition on interest. The book notes that God desires a developing and functioning society and so "commanded to remove this obstacle from their path, that one should not swallow up the wealth of his friend without his [even] feeling it, until he finds his house empty of all good. As that is the way of interest, and the matter is well-known."[20] The medieval rabbi Rashi adds that interest is called *neshech* (literally, a bite) in Hebrew because, like a snake bite, it begins with only mild discomfort that then increases in severity.[21]

In other words, interest is not bad, and it is legitimate to charge interest to strangers. But a community cannot support its needy through loans, cannot ensure loving and generous human relationships, cannot be sustainable on this earth, with a norm of interest.

In-Group and Out-Group

Some have sought to cast Jewish law as backward for maintaining different sets of rules for Jews and non-Jews. The truth is that making some distinctions between my group and others is a universal human experience. Nearly every culture across the world considers it acceptable to charge high prices to tourists but cut locals a break. We all live within certain social contracts. Those who buy into a social contract and make a commitment to others receive the benefit of reciprocal treatment.

Regarding capital in particular, in-group lending is common among many minority affinity groups. In the Korean *kye* system, groups of Korean immigrants to the United States, usually women, pool capital monthly and extend rotating loans to members of the group.[22] Chinese lending circles are known as *hui*, West Indian ones as *susu*, and Ethiopian ones as *ekub*.[23] Nearly a third of the population of Mexico participates in lending pools known as *tandas*.[24] Even secular groups like mutual aid societies, designed to help members of a particular community or affinity group support each other, feature in-group and out-group rules. These mutual aid societies saw a revival during the coronavirus pandemic in 2020.

The same in-group/out-group dynamic exists in Christianity, which prohibited Christians lending at interest to each other but allowed for non-Christians to fulfill the moneylending function. Because of laws that prevented Jews from owning land or joining other professions, many of the moneylenders in medieval Christendom were Jews. These moneylenders played a crucial role in ensuring a continued flow of capital. Unfortunately, the role also furthered inaccurate stereotypes, grounded in anti-Jewish oppression, of Jews as money-hungry, which have fueled everything from discrimination to massacres and expulsions.[25]

The Torah's wording itself suggests that the laws concerning usury are really about mutual social contracts. The common word for non-Jew in the Torah is *ger*, translated as sojourner or resident alien, someone who has at least some interaction with the community. Notably, this is not the word used when permitting interest. Instead, when permitting interest, the Torah uses the word *nochri*, meaning foreigner, stranger, someone totally outside the community.[26]

Despite these clear ethical grounds for charging interest to strangers who had not bought in to the social contract, the Sages of the Talmud were concerned about the psychological and spiritual effect of relying on interest for one's income long-term. They limited such loans to occasional affairs and discouraged Jews from making a living in such activities. Some of the Sages of the Talmud went so far as to condemn any lending at interest, to Jews or Gentiles.

More importantly, Jewish thinkers sought to transform the nature of relationships around capital from "lending" to investing, through the mechanism of shared risk.

From Lending to Investing: Sharing Risk

The Jews of the Bible lived in an agrarian society, where most loans were sought for personal purposes, like a farmer whose crops failed one year who sought a loan to sustain himself until the next year.²⁷ By the time of the Talmud, some Jews had begun to engage in commercial pursuits as merchants. This shift became widespread in the Middle Ages when a significant percentage of European Jews were forbidden by local governments from owning land.²⁸

Lending can be a tool to generate tremendous productivity through credit. To do business as a merchant, one needs investment capital to acquire goods to sell.²⁹ Even in a thriving economy at the time of the Talmud, without loans there were still few options for landless people to rise above poverty or access investment capital, instead remaining stuck in poverty and dependence.³⁰

Investment capital is a vital tool for business and wealth creation. Yet the Torah recognized that among a local community, lending at interest, especially to those in need, begins a vicious cycle that can bring a community to ruin. Like the idea of living in balance that we explored in Chapter 2, Jewish tradition has for thousands of years navigated these poles of the ideal and the possible in its rules around access to loan capital.

The Sages of the Talmud saw investment focused on wealth creation as a legitimate business enterprise. Lending, on the other hand, was viewed as a charitable and society-sustaining endeavor (and is in fact considered the most noble form of charity).³¹ The Sages pinpointed a key feature that distinguishes lending from investment: the sharing of business risk.

In a loan, the risk of the business's success falls entirely on the borrower. Regardless of whether one makes a business mistake, the economy crashes, or one's house burns down, a borrower is obligated to repay a loan. The Martinezes, the family at the beginning of this chapter, were still obligated to pay the bank the full $630,000 they had borrowed even though their home mortgage went underwater.

Of course, lenders face other kinds of risk over the course of time, most notably credit risk. A borrower may go bankrupt. Even if the lender is able to take possession of collateral, like a home, the home's value could fall underwater, or the cost of repairing and selling it could outstrip the value of the loan. Some home mortgages are "non-recourse," limiting the amount a lender can seize beyond the value of the home (and maybe making those mortgages slightly less "inflexible").³² Banks today mitigate these risks, among other tools, by setting limitations on what percentage of a home's value the borrower needs to bring as a down payment. But the vast majority of loans today are repaid in full, even by borrowers whose business ventures have failed. And at least in the initial agreement, the borrower shoulders the entire risk of the business venture, agreeing to pay the lender regardless of the business's success or failure. The Sages of the Talmud instead promoted an upfront agreement to share the risk of the success or failure of the business venture itself. And, according to economists Mian and Sufi we saw at the

Put Your Money Where Your Soul Is

beginning of this chapter, such an arrangement might even reduce the number of loans that end up defaulting.

To take a more extreme example: in the 1950s and 60s, many white people offered predatory mortgages to Black families in cities like Chicago. The white homeowners structured the contracts to be able to claim for themselves all the home equity built up by the Black family if the Black family missed a single mortgage payment, leaving the Black family with nothing.[33] Over 80 percent of homes sold to Black families in Chicago were sold this way. The exploitative practice, known as "contract selling," represents the opposite of equitable sharing of risk. It also transferred between $3 and $4 billion from Black families to white families in Chicago during the course of those two decades.[34]

According to Jewish tradition, among community members, the only time it is legitimate for the lender to assume none of the upfront business risk is when the lender is also earning none of the business profit. Loans without interest are legitimate. They represent a charitable endeavor that benefits vulnerable and needy members of the community. In fact, in early Jewish history, loans were cancelled every seven years at the end of the *shmita* (Sabbatical) year, but this stopped in practice at the time of Hillel the Elder. Hillel noticed people with wealth refusing to lend to their fellows in need immediately prior to the Sabbatical year because of the fear of *shmita*-related default. He instituted a decree to avoid the debt-cancellation and incentivize lending.[35]

When an investor seeks to profit from a business investment, according to Jewish tradition, they must also share in the business risk (and not just the risks that come from borrowers who default or file bankruptcy). According to the Sages, in a legitimate ethical investment, the borrower and lender are in a business partnership and both of them share the risk. If the business venture fails, the investor must be prepared to lose their money. If the venture succeeds beyond everyone's wildest dreams, the investor and the "managing partner" (the investee) both profit accordingly.

For example, the Talmudic Sages of the commercial city of Nehardea, in ancient Babylon (present-day Iraq), crafted a model of an investor investing in a business run by a managing partner. The investor structured half of their capital as an investment and half as a loan. The half that was an investment carried risk of total loss as well as potential for profit. The half that was a loan had no upside, as the investor could not profit through interest, but also no downside, as it must be repaid completely.[36] The Sages of the Talmud adopted this half-loan, half-investment as the standard arrangement for an investment partnership, known in the Talmud as an *iska*.

Even within such an investment partnership, Jewish tradition considers it immoral for the investor to use their power to disproportionally benefit. The Sages of the Talmud prevented this possibility in two ways. First of all, the Sages required the investor to pay the managing partner a salary for their work. They reasoned that if the recipient of investment capital works for free to increase the value of the investment, their free labor constitutes a form of interest paid for use of the capital.[37] To use the modern terminology we encountered in Chapter 6, asset owners in an investment venture were required to compensate the investment manager.

The second key protection the Sages of the Talmud instituted was that the risk not only needed to be shared between an investor and the investee: it needed to be shared equitably. The Sages stated that if there is a business venture between community members, with an investor and a recipient, in which the investor is "near to profit and far from loss," then the investor is a wicked person. We first encountered this concept in Chapter 4, when discussing orphans' trust funds.

Let's see an example. Suppose an investor invests some capital in a startup and demands 70 percent of the profit should the business make money. The investor can get away with making such a demand because the business owner is beholden to them for capital. At the same time, the investor only accepts 30 percent of the loss should the business fail. That arrangement is unethical according to Jewish law. It represents abusing one's power as an investor to force excessive risk onto the "borrower."

On the other hand, if an investor accepts 50 percent of the profit and 50 percent of the loss (or even 100 percent of the profit and 100 percent of the loss), that represents a fair sharing of risk. This is what happens, for example, when one invests in stock: one becomes a part-owner of the company and shares in its gains as well as its losses.

At the extreme, if the investor demands 100 percent of the profit and accepts 0 percent of the loss, that is a straightforward interest-bearing loan. It is an inflexible debt contract, which is prohibited by the Torah.

The Talmud puts it this way: "If the investor is first to profit and second to loss, that is a wicked person. If the investor is first to loss and second to profit, then the investor is an especially pious person. If the investor and recipient share the risk and reward, this is a general business practice."[38] In other words, being willing to have one's capital be more at risk makes one especially pious. Sharing risk equally is an appropriate norm. Offloading the risk of failure onto the person operating the business who relies on one's investment capital is unjust.

Rabbi Yitz Greenberg, whom we met in Chapter 2, comments on this line in the Talmud. He notes (in a continuation of his remarks from that chapter):

> The Gemara, the tradition, the halakha, accepts the idea of "general business practice." And in fact, as we heard several different ways, profit motive is legitimate; self-interest is legitimate. One of the most powerful truths about covenantal partnership I mentioned

> before is that you have a right to start with your own family; that you have a right and in fact an obligation to start with the poor of your own city and extend outward, rather than simply say "equal at every step of the way." So it recognizes the human reality. The human reality is that people working for themselves, people investing, do better, or apparently are more productive, are more effective, than others. And this is something that has to be done—because in the long run, when you produce more, there is more for everybody if you handle it and manage it correctly. So the tradition does recognize and accept profit and self-interest as a legitimate working principle.
>
> On the other hand...[the Talmud] is saying: the profit motive should not be absolute. It is not self-validated. You know, the answer is not like Vince Lombardi, that the only thing that matters is winning. If you load it so "winning" that in fact you're being unfair and taking advantage of the other side, this is a violation.[39]

The Talmud recognizes that it is legitimate to seek profit through investment. On the other hand, it is illegitimate for a quest for profit to be so dominant that it leads an investor to take advantage of someone seeking investment capital. Jewish tradition navigates between these two poles by requiring equitable sharing of risk.

Rabbi Greenberg goes on to frame this tension more broadly. Respect the profit motive, take advantage of it, use it, strengthen society with it; but do not give it a blank check. On the contrary, it has to be controlled. If it is not controlled, it will lead to destructive behavior. And as we saw in Chapter 2, Rabbi Greenberg continues to broaden this further, noting that our current civilization has accumulated staggering power while harboring a disproportionate focus on the profit motive.[40] Instead, we as a civilization need to move toward a more equitable model of sharing risk; we need to offset the profit motive with an ethical motive as well.

Contemporary Jewish artist Alicia Jo Rabins describes this same principle in a more poetic way. Her award-winning independent musical film, *A Kaddish for Bernie Madoff*, features songs Rabins composed based on interviews she conducted. Inspired by an interview with the Zen teacher Norman Fischer (of Jewish heritage), Rabins sings:

> Something happened in the last 100 years,
> with ever more elaborate financial instruments
> allowing us to make fabulous amounts of money

from nothing.
We start to believe it's possible to escape.
It never could happen before, but now there's a way.
We start to develop this unconscious faith
that money can protect us from tragedy and old age.
And there will only be an upside.
There will only be an upside.
The only transcendence is fully embracing the ups and the downs,
and even then, we all grow old and die.[41]

Medieval and Modern Developments: The *Heter Iska*

In the Middle Ages, with the collapse of empires, regulation of local markets became increasingly the responsibility of local religious authorities.[42] These authorities continually sought to limit or prohibit lending at interest, and lay businesspeople sought to circumvent them.

For example, the Sages of the Talmud had frowned on someone making a living from interest-bearing loans to non-Jews, even if they were technically permitted. Instead, they limited profit to just what one needs to cover the cost of basic necessities of life.[43] Yet already by the time of the medieval rabbi Rabbeinu Tam (France, 1100-1171), most people were not carefully observing this prohibition. Rabbeinu Tam attempted to justify it by noting that the cost of living had risen with extensive governmental taxes. Regardless, in the end, Rabbeinu Tam concluded that a hard limit on profit from interest-bearing loans was untenable.[44] Indeed, sometimes the rates were quite high, to compensate for the high risk of such loans; on occasion, instead of merely defaulting on a loan, a ruler would exile Jews from his kingdom or incite violence against them.[45]

Related developments were happening across the Christian world. In the commercial economy of medieval Italy, Christian lenders developed a model of a "partnership" (which we will explore in detail shortly) that operated suspiciously like a fixed-interest loan. The "partnership" structure was only applied to business loans, and interest remained forbidden on consumer loans. Yet in practice, it was clearly a loan with interest, which is why Martin Luther attacked these partnerships, calling them evil and sinful. This did nothing to stem the tide of such loans, which provided vital seed money for people who wanted to improve their economic position.[46]

Following the Italians, German cities and some areas in France and Spain similarly developed loopholes to enable moneylending, against the Church's wishes. The same development happened in Islam, where oral law allowed for an escape clause to permit interest.[47]

In response to these developments, and the increasing sophistication of the world economy, Jewish authorities also developed a form of partnership contract that avoided prohibitions on interest. By the time of the Middle Ages, investors were not satisfied with the arrangement we described in the last section, equitably shared risk. It was, after all, risky. Not only could an investor fail to profit, but they could also lose a significant chunk of their investment. Many investors were reluctant to invest under these conditions, despite the need for capital.

Instead, Jewish legal authorities sought a permitted way to earn an interest-like profit on an investment, while ensuring likely repayment of at least the principal. They developed a contract known as the *heter iska*, which reframed what otherwise would have been a straightforward loan as something more flexible, closer to an investment relationship. In fact, it served in practice as a Jewish "flexible debt contract," to use the language of Mian and Sufi at the beginning of the chapter.

The first *heter iska* was published by Rabbi Israel Isserlein (Austria, 1390-1460) in the 15th century.[48] The *heter iska* had three parts. First, the *heter iska* articulated the monetary amount and time frame of the investment relationship. Second, it imposed a set of onerous requirements on the managing partner (who would otherwise have been the "borrower"). These included extensive financial reporting, a public oath of integrity, and more. Third, it offered a way out of those requirements. The managing partner could forgo the onerous requirements by just paying back the investment plus a predetermined amount. This ended up looking a lot like principal plus interest. But it differed in two key ways, one regarding the principal and one regarding the interest.

First, regarding the principal: unlike a loan, the *heter iska* did not contain an actual guarantee that the capital of the "lender" would be returned. Instead, in the event the business failed, the *heter iska* allowed the "borrower" to avoid paying back the money if they could bring witnesses to testify to the business venture's failure. The contract included tight restrictions on those witnesses, which made it unlikely except in extreme cases that the witnesses would testify. Far more likely, the "borrower" would simply repay the money. But since there was a theoretical possibility of bringing witnesses and avoiding repayment of the investment capital, the *heter iska* was not a loan. It transformed a loan from an "inflexible debt contract" into a "flexible debt contract." It may not have been all that flexible; but it wasn't an ironclad guarantee of repayment, either.

Second, regarding the profit: here, the *heter iska* went even further. There was no requirement of witnesses to avoid paying the profit. Payment of the assumed profit depended solely on the borrower choosing to pay it, in order to maintain a good credit

Debt: Free Loans and Shared Risk

rating.⁴⁹ In a worst-case scenario, the borrower could just swear they were telling the truth about not having earned any profit and then return the amount of the original investment. Their credit rating would suffer, but they would not be obligated to pay interest on a loan. This truly made the *heter iska* into a flexible debt contract (and also distinguished it from Christian models of the same time period).

Since the *heter iska* frames what might otherwise seem like a loan as an investment, it can only apply to business loans. A student loan, for example, could never be permitted with a *heter iska*, since it cannot realistically be framed as the lender and the borrower going into business together. The same is generally true with consumer loans like credit cards.

Mortgages, on the other hand, could be the subject of a *heter iska*, since a home is an investment.⁵⁰ In fact, a home is often the single most valuable asset of a family.⁵¹ Homeownership has been a crucial source for generational wealth-building, as well as a cause of growing inequality between white people and people of color in the United States, given its long history of discriminatory mortgage lending.⁵² As we saw economists Atif Mian and Amir Sufi describe in the introduction to this chapter, home ownership is a type of investment where it would be very appropriate to seek ways to more equitably share risk.

In its origins, a *heter iska* applied to individual business transactions. Each investment required a new *heter iska*. With the growth in complex business transactions, and especially the growth of public corporations over the past 200 years, a blanket version was developed that could apply to all of a corporation's lending activities.⁵³

The *heter iska* remains a live practice in occasional situations in the investment arena today. For example, Dan Gilbert, who is Jewish, founded Quicken Loans in 1985 with two collaborators. With its focus on online service, the company grew in 2014 to become the largest online mortgage lender nationwide and the second largest mortgage lender of any kind.

In April of 2018, the Agudath Israel of America, a *Hareidi* Orthodox Jewish membership organization, realized that Gilbert's ownership of the company posed a problem. They flagged the issue of usury and issued a general prohibition on taking out a mortgage with Quicken.⁵⁴ Gilbert announced that he would assemble a committee to research the subject and find a solution, which the company did by June of that same year, adopting a universal *heter iska* (known as a *heter iska klali*) that applied to all mortgages that might otherwise violate the Jewish laws of usury.⁵⁵

All the banks in Israel use a universal *heter iska*, as does the Israeli government itself (which issues Israel bonds).⁵⁶

The need for a *heter iska* arises only rarely in the impact investing arena. Recall that the Torah only prohibits usury between Jews or Jewish institutions. The laws of usury do not apply to non-Jewish entities like corporations, governments, or municipalities. For this reason, Judaism's ethical guidance on usury would see no issue with federal and municipal bonds, like Treasury bonds.

The restrictions also do not apply to an individual who invests in stocks and mutual funds. Stocks and mutual funds are already structured with equitable risk. If the stock rises, the investor gets all the profit. Yet the opposite is also true—the investor shoulders the entire risk of loss, which is why mutual funds are required to disclose that the investment is not guaranteed and may lose value. The laws of usury only apply in the somewhat rare case when a Jewish investor invests through private debt in a private company owned or managed by a Jewish person.

In Chapter 7 discussing public equities, we learned the current rabbinic consensus that the prohibitions on usury do not apply to large corporations owned and controlled mostly by non-Jews. In fact, one of the early rabbis in the 19th century to discuss modern banking, Rabbi Moshe Shick, permitted a Jew to participate in such lending societies precisely because they were not set up primarily for the benefit of the shareholders but for the benefit of people needing loan capital.[57]

Regardless, the *heter iska* is an important model to learn, and not just because of its occasional real-world use. It represents the latest development in a rabbinic tradition seeking to navigate between two opposing forces: the problematic ethics of lending at interest, and the need for investment vehicles and access to capital to develop society and build wealth. It can help us remember the ethical importance of de-centering the investor, and re-centering the relationship between investor and investee, in the modern investment arena.

Re-Centering Impact

Jewish tradition offers us a vital perspective on debt: investing ethically means thinking beyond what is best for the investor. On the one hand, it is legitimate to seek a profit from one's capital. On the other hand, the benefits and risks of the investment ought to be shared equitably. To put it another way, Judaism's ethical inspiration on investing in debt involves de-centering the investor and re-centering the impact of the loan capital on society.

Investors seeking to apply Jewish wisdom to their debt allocation can begin by assessing their current allocation. What is your loan capital going to support? Are you supporting the federal government and municipal governments to provide the cash flow to pay Social Security and Medicaid, engage in economic development, or pay the defense budget? Are you supporting companies with questionable ethical stances? Are you profiting from the exploitation of families like the Martinezes from the beginning of the chapter?

There are a growing number of socially responsible fixed-income funds that are accessible to everyday investors. These funds seek to avoid the "profit at all costs" approach that Jewish tradition rejects. For example, Community Capital Management offers an impact-bond fund that invests in fossil-fuel-free bonds with social and environmental impact. Most of the bonds in the fund qualify for the Community Reinvestment Act of 1977 that encourages financial institutions to direct capital to low- and moderate-income neighborhoods.[58]

Green-bond funds are an important and rapidly growing subset of this ecosystem. A number of investment managers, including BlackRock, Van Eck, and more, offer green-bond funds that avoid investment in the most harmful or polluting companies and focus on financing companies building an environmentally sustainable future. You can research many more opportunities online, or a trusted financial advisor with experience in values-based investing can support you.

Share the Access

Judaism's wisdom on risk-sharing can inspire a range of other important questions for our debt allocation. For example, where is money flowing in the first place? Are mainstream impact investors acting like the people of Hillel the Elder's time, who withheld loans from those in need for fear of default? Who are we willing to create investment relationships with, and have we overlooked people or institutions who need access to capital?

Currently, in the socially responsible investing arena, "the crowd is overwhelmingly white," according to Edgar Villanueva. He quotes a conversation with an African American consultant at a social finance conference. "The white folks in social finance feel more comfortable investing in some sustainable opportunity in Africa than they feel investing in African Americans," the consultant explained. "There's an overlord mentality: they don't trust Black or brown entrepreneurs to handle money."[59] Are those of us who are white willing to examine our own biases regarding whom we trust with investment capital?

Ryan Bowers, a former staffer in municipal public service, was troubled by the long history of cities' municipal budgets reinforcing racial oppression dynamics. Committed to making change, Bowers founded the organization Activest. Activest calls itself a voice for "fiscal justice," which it uses to refer to municipal practices around criminal justice, economic development, public health, and other areas of social impact that are not traditionally considered in investment decisions (but should be).

Activest operates based on a conviction that communities who treat their residents justly will have stronger fiscal outcomes, a belief aligned with the Jewish principles we saw in Chapter 3. As an example, in 2015, after the fatal shooting of Michael Brown in Ferguson, Missouri, and the ensuing protests, credit rating agencies began downgrading Ferguson's bonds (similar to how a credit score works for an individual). In other words, they assessed Ferguson as an investment risk, and investors began moving their money away. Key drivers of the credit deterioration included "unbudgeted expenditures, and escalating expenses related to ongoing litigation and the (U.S.) Department of Justice (DOJ) consent decree currently under negotiation."[60]

Activest rates cities based on the fiscal justice of their budgets. It recently partnered with investment advisor Adasina Social Capital to make it possible for individual investors to invest in fiscally just communities. The Adasina Social Capital Fiscal Justice Investment Strategy launched in 2020.[61]

Share the Risk

Actual financial vehicles that involve sharing risk remain somewhat fringe in mainstream finance, but these principles are beginning to appear more in the field of impact investing. For example, Transform Finance, a secular, nonprofit organization with a mission to mobilize the investment arena to serve as a positive contributor to a just and equitable society, published a report in April 2021 about the growing field of "Community-Engaged Investing." (We will learn more about this field shortly). The organization defined such an investment as effective and ethical when: "1) it meaningfully engages communities in the design and governance of investment processes; 2) it adds more value than it extracts; and 3) it fairly balances risk and return between investors and non-investors."[62]

One example comes from South Africa, where Black-owned businesses were historically excluded from economic opportunity. That disadvantage persists despite attempts to rectify it. A few years ago, the government, the largest purchaser in the country, set a goal to spend over 300 billion rand (around $20 billion) ordering supplies from small businesses. But many Black-owned businesses aren't able to scale quickly enough to meet the need.[63]

In 2017, South African entrepreneur Luyanda Jafta founded a startup called The People's Fund, a crowdfunding platform to help Black business owners scale their businesses.[64] Individual investors in South Africa can participate for as little as 100 rand. Rather than receive repayment like a loan, investors receive a percentage of the small business's profit. The People's Fund has already supported 2,000 businesses with capital supplied by thousands of investors since its inception several years ago.

The fund is explicitly modeled after community savings and lending circles common in Africa and elsewhere.[65]

In another example, the recently launched Elevate/Elevar Capital fund in St. Louis provides entrepreneurs an opportunity to pay based on their revenues, not based on a fixed interest rate. Business owners will pay between 2 percent and 10 percent of their revenues after a repayment holiday of three to 12 months, up to a cap of 1.5 times of the amount of the loan.[66] The fund is Black woman-led and designed to specifically target historic racial injustices. It looks for Black and Hispanic-owned companies and does not require collateral or a high credit score.[67]

We have far more work to do to bring principles of shared risk into our economic system. Atif Mian and Amir Sufi, in *House of Debt*, describe ways that contemporary inflexible debt contracts (like mortgages, credit card loans, auto loans, etc.) could be structured as investments with shared risk. If the Martinezes had a flexible debt contract (a contract based on shared risk) with the bank, the family might still have suffered during the economic downturn. But the mortgage would not have ended up underwater, because the amount to be repaid would have shrunk with the plummeting value of the house.

Societies across the world are actively pursuing shared-risk banking and investing, especially Islamic banking, a trillion-dollar industry. Islamic banking offers interesting similarities to a Jewish approach, a topic that deserves a book of its own. In the Western world of impact investing, shared-risk investing remains on the fringe. But the model provides an important correction to our societal approach to debt, urgently needed before the next crash hits.

Share the Decision

Investors inspired by Judaism's wisdom on shared risk can take these ideas even further. How about literally sharing decision-making power over where investment dollars flow?

Alyssa Ely and Denise Hearn, two leaders in the impact-investing field, published an article in the Stanford Social Innovation Review in April of 2021 arguing that, to achieve meaningful impact, impact investors need to share more with their investee partners. They need to share risk more equitably than current practice; they also need to share more decision-making power over investment choices, more control of the time frame, and more knowledge and transparency.[68] Edgar Villanueva, expert on race and philanthropy, proposes, "what if funders no longer assumed that disadvantaged communities and individuals needed to be empowered at all? What if we acknowledge how powerful they inherently are?"⁶⁹ A key step to do so is to share decision-making authority.

Transform Finance calls this "Grassroots Community Engaged Investment." Local grassroots communities have input and decision-making power over capital being invested in their communities.⁷⁰

Many other investment practitioners representing historically marginalized communities agree: the goal is to have the communities most impacted be more proximate to control of capital. Daryn Dodson, managing partner at Illumen Capital, puts it this way: "The idea that people who are investing large amounts of money to transform the world would sit down with the communities that they're trying to transform is a really important pillar of what we're trying to accomplish."⁷¹ Ebony Perkins at Self-Help Credit Union, whom we met in Chapter 6, echoes: "It's easy to throw money at a problem—I don't have to be close to it, I don't have to touch it. But Brian Stevenson notes that in order to solve a problem, you have to get proximate. Racial injustice cannot only be solved by money."⁷²

The Ujima Fund, based in Boston, describes itself as the first "democratic investment fund" in the United States. Investors cede power over their investment capital to a committee of Ujima Project members, made up of residents of Boston or those displaced from their homes by rising rents, who are either low-income or people of color. Each Ujima Project member gets a vote on where money is invested or loaned; non-resident investors do not. This model has resonated with many, including the local Jewish community; a notable group of funders and investors is the congregation of Temple Israel of Boston.⁷³

Investors and investees could also literally share ownership of new infrastructure being developed. For example, low- and moderate-income communities who do not yet have high-speed internet access are in significant ways cut off from the modern economy and modern educational systems. Internet and telecommunications companies may seek to develop new infrastructure in those communities but will expect to own it.

In 2013, entrepreneur Donnel Baird founded a social enterprise, BlocPower, seeking to develop high-speed internet in low- and moderate-income communities, with a twist: communities will own their own internet infrastructure. The project is focused on equity, as he puts it: "Not just equity in terms of social justice, but equity in terms of literal ownership of stock in a special-purpose entity that owns a set of infrastructure assets. In this case those assets are broadband connectivity assets that will close the digital divide." BlocPower's advocacy even managed to include this approach in the United States' bipartisan infrastructure bill in 2021.⁷⁴

Some of the examples above remain fringe, are difficult to invest in today, or are accessible only to wealthy investors. Activest's investment vehicle offered by Adasina

Social Capital is restricted to those with a minimum of $1 million to invest and a time horizon of five years or more. The Ujima Fund has stopped accepting investments for now as they have reached their goal of capital raised. BlocPower has raised more than a million dollars from everyday investors through the Raise Green crowd-investing platform, but the offering is currently closed at the time of this writing.[75]

But there are opportunities available for everyday investors. Calvert Impact is a global nonprofit investment organization originally founded as a branch of the well-known socially responsible investment firm Calvert, when the parent firm wanted to begin allocating a percentage of its mutual fund capital directly to impact investments in communities in need throughout the United States. The original Calvert is now owned by Morgan Stanley, but Calvert Impact remains an independent nonprofit.

In 1995, the organization launched the Calvert Impact Note, an investment vehicle with a $20 minimum. Certifying a low-minimum impact investment offering like that with the regulators was no easy task. But the organization succeeded, and the Notes are now available for investment in all 50 states.[76]

Amanda Joseph, former Director of Faith-Based Initiatives at Calvert Impact and a member of the Philadelphia Jewish community, notes that this offering aligns deeply with Jewish values.[77] Joseph has more than two decades of experience with community development finance. She even worked at an early Jewish impact-investing organization, Jewish Funds for Justice, that sought to bring more Jewish capital specifically to the field of community development finance. Jewish Funds for Justice no longer exists, but the broader field is thriving. As of the end of September 2021, Calvert Impact Capital's Impact Notes had nearly $600 million invested, with financial return between 0.40-2.5 percent at terms of one to ten years.

The Ongoing Journey

Judaism offers an ethical framework for debt: debt is an ethical investment when the risk is shared equitably.

The technical details of this law led to the development of the *heter iska*, a document that transforms a relationship that might have been a loan into an investment. It shifts the relationship away from "inflexible debt contracts" (like we saw in the introduction to this chapter) toward a more flexible alternative. *Heter iska*s are still in use today (especially in Israel, where more financial companies are owned by Jews), though they rarely apply to a modern investor's portfolio.

However, the principles of equitably shared risk can inspire us to think more broadly about the relationship between us as investors and our investee partners. Is our capital invested in ways that focus exclusively on our needs as investors: earning as much financial return as possible, as quickly as possible, with as much flexibility for us as possible? If so, Judaism's teachings can inspire us to de-center our needs and re-center the relationship between us and our investee partners. While it is legitimate to seek a profit, our debt allocations also can serve those who need capital in order to grow a business or lift themselves out of poverty. Longer-term, we as a society need to think about how we can transition our norm of inflexible debt contracts into a more flexible alternative, in line with faith-based teachings of Judaism and other religions, to put us on a more sustainable path.

> ## Next Steps—Chapter 8
>
> - **Step 1: Assess where you are right now.** Explore where your debt allocation is currently invested. Is the bulk of your loan capital primarily flowing to entities that you believe will use it to further economic development and fund the functioning of our society? Are you financing companies that are polluting the atmosphere or taking questionable ethical stances on issues you care about?
> - **Step 2: Research opportunities.** Look for opportunities to invest in socially responsible bond funds, which, by definition, seek to expand beyond what's best for the investor and to incorporate criteria of social responsibility. A growing subset of this field is green bonds, which avoid financing the biggest polluters and instead finance energy efficiency and the clean energy transition.
> - **Step 3: Reach out.** Think about what your debt allocation might be overlooking or failing to invest in. Are there communities that need your capital yet don't have access to it?
> - **Step 4: Get advice.** Opportunities mentioned in this chapter include: Raise Green's crowdfunding investment platform (and the company BlocPower), Adasina Social Capital Fiscal Justice Investment Strategy, Calvert Impact Capital's Impact Notes, Community Capital Management's impact bond fund, BlackRock's Global Green Bond ETF, VanEck Vector Green Bond ETF, and others. Ask your financial advisor for recommendations.

Chapter 9

Private Equity and Debt: Local Investing

The first time Abdulkader Hayani had to interview for a job, it was in a foreign language. Hayani, 29 years old, was a refugee from Syria. He had spent his entire working life building a small business as a tailor, until he was forced to flee the war that had devastated his country. He managed against the odds to bring his wife and their four children to safety in the United States. When he arrived, Hayani began working with Jewish Vocational Service of Greater Boston (JVS) to learn job skills and work-related English. With the help of JVS, Hayani managed to secure employment at a clothing store several months after arriving.[1]

JVS has met a similar need in the community for decades. Founded in 1938 during the Great Depression to assist Jewish immigrants struggling to enter the workforce, the nonprofit organization today serves clients of all religions from more than 60 countries facing the same struggles.[2]

Workforce preparedness and English-language education are growing concerns in Massachusetts. Today, adult English-language learners in the Boston area experience higher rates of unemployment and earn roughly $24,000 less annually than individuals with similar credentials who speak English fluently. Thirty percent of the greater Boston labor market is based on immigrants entering the workforce, yet one in ten residents, many of them refugees or immigrants, lacks the basic skills and credentials to enter college or family-sustaining employment.[3]

The Commonwealth of Massachusetts began experimenting with creative ways to address these concerns. One model that looked especially promising was a **Social Impact Bond**. In this unique investment vehicle, also known as a pay-for-success investment, private investors provide upfront capital to a high-performing nonprofit social-service agency to deliver services. The government repays those private investors with interest if the program outcomes are achieved.[4] At varying degrees of success, the investors receive varying degrees of payout, and if the project completely fails, investors stand to lose their investment entirely.

The state selected Jewish Vocational Services as its nonprofit partner for a Social Impact Bond focused on immigrant and refugee workforce development. This was a natural fit. JVS was seeking to expand to five additional communities on the outskirts of Boston. The organization had a successful track record of fundraising; it had recently completed a $6 million capital campaign to move to a new building. But JVS's leadership knew that philanthropy alone could not bring them the funding they needed to scale their important workforce development programs to new communities. So they were receptive when approached to participate in the state's Social Impact Bond.[5]

An early challenge was identifying investors for this innovative and risky model. That's where Combined Jewish Philanthropies of Greater Boston came in. CJP serves as the endowment pool for the Boston Jewish community. It invests the collective assets of a number of Boston-area institutions, including synagogues, as well as charitable funds from individuals and foundations. CJP held a hefty $1.5 billion in assets. The vast majority of that money was invested in large public companies with global footprints headquartered across the world.[6] In 2016, the organization began exploring this opportunity to invest closer to home.

Forty impact investors, including Combined Jewish Philanthropies, invested a total of $12.43 million in the Social Impact Bond. That money went to JVS, which accepted the challenge of meeting four metrics identified by the state. If JVS met all four metrics, including successful increases in earnings or transitions to higher education with 2,000 adults in Boston over three years,[7] investors would earn back a total of $15 million.[8]

From JVS's perspective, serving as an impact investment vehicle posed significant reputational risk. "There has never been more attention on anything we have ever done," said Carol Ozelius, JVS's chief operating officer. "It's like putting a national spotlight on yourself and saying, 'I can deliver.'"[9]

The Social Impact Bond also required significant monetary outlay from JVS before ever receiving a payment. "The due diligence involved was 18 times more in-depth than for a grant," said Ozelius. At the beginning, "we didn't know what we were getting into. We assumed this deal would be completed in a year." Instead, the deal took 22 months to sign and an additional six months before receiving payment. Meanwhile, JVS was contributing substantial staff time and energy to establishing the project. Senior staff recalled discussing, "how long can we hold on in order to close this deal?"

On top of everything, shortly before the deal was supposed to close in early 2017, newly inaugurated President Trump signed his first executive order, drastically limiting immigration and throwing a wrench into the plans. What would happen to the refugee community in Boston? Would this wreak havoc with the designated metrics? Ultimately, all the parties decided to proceed, and the deal was signed in March of 2017.

Combined Jewish Philanthropy's contribution was uniquely valuable to enticing the other investors to join the effort. The organization offered its investment as "first loss capital," meaning if the venture failed to earn back the anticipated profit, CJP was willing to lose its money first, adding a layer of protection for the other investors. This is a concrete example of the "far from profit, near to loss" approach mentioned in Chapter 4 that the Sages of the Talmud identified as particularly pious and generous.

Some in the community raised concerns about the "cannibalization of philanthropy." Once donors saw an opportunity to invest and earn a potential return through a Social Impact Bond, they would stop giving philanthropic dollars directly to human service agencies. Most of these agencies, including JVS, rely on direct donations to fund their operations.

But JVS staff wasn't worried. Instead, as Ozelius noted, it is "a brilliant model that people can earn money, money is invested at a level that government is not going to do, and thousands of people get served where they wouldn't have otherwise."

Shu Dar Yao, an impact investment advisor who worked on the Social Impact Bond and is a member of San Francisco-based synagogue The Kitchen, notes that this particular Social Impact Bond was carefully crafted to offer something to gain for every stakeholder.[10] As Karin Blum, chief development officer at JVS, puts it: "Capital is sitting in an investment fund somewhere, so why not bring it to a Jewish agency?"

The first Social Impact Bond was launched in 2010, and more than 100 have been launched since. They are a complicated form of investment, and not for the faint-hearted. But this particular Boston-based investment provided a unique opportunity for Jewish investors to partner with a Jewish nonprofit service provider in ways that measurably benefited the local community.[11]

This chapter is about **private equity** and **private debt**. Private means that these companies and investments are not traded on a public stock exchange (like in Chapter 7). We explored **debt** more broadly in the previous chapter. **Equity** means being a part-owner—buying part of the company, instead of lending money to the company.

It is possible to invest in private equity and debt globally (including opportunities in Israel, which will be discussed in Chapter 12). But some of the most values-aligned and impactful opportunities that private capital opens up are investing in local businesses. This chapter will explore private debt and private equity through the framework of investing locally. Securities laws differ from country to country, and this chapter will focus on the United States. As we will see, being listed on a stock exchange involves a tremendous set of legal hurdles and costs that only the largest companies can afford. For those seeking to support local business, private equity is a key asset class. And supporting local businesses and organizations with our investment capital is one of the most important steps we can take to transform our Capitalism 1.0 into something more sustainable.

The Benefits of Going Local

The past three decades have seen a surge of the "locavore" movement for eating local, growth of farmers' markets, and a parallel movement for buying local.[12] Investing local is the vital next step in building a more sustainable economy. The hard statistics bear this out. Small businesses, defined by the US's Small Business Administration as companies with fewer than 500 employees, generate half of the Gross Domestic Product of the US and create three out of every four jobs.[13] Small businesses are net job creators, while large companies are net job destroyers.[14] Yet most of our investment capital is invested in large companies, not small businesses.

A dollar spent at a locally-owned business generates three times more economic activity in your local community than a dollar spent at a corporate peer headquartered elsewhere.[15] Recall from Chapter 2 that investment capital is the most powerful form of money most of us interact with. So it stands to reason that investing locally and in small businesses can have a far greater economic impact than investing in large companies with a global footprint.

We might assume, based on the news we hear, that the thing businesses want more than anything else is tax breaks. But that is true only for major corporations in excess of $1 billion.[16] For small businesses, access to capital through loans and equity investments is far more important to spurring growth and job creation than a potential tax break.[17] Investors play a crucial role.

Just as investing locally can strengthen our economies, failing to pay attention to the needs of our local communities can undermine investment goals. A number of pension funds have come under criticism recently for investing their pensioners' money in private equity funds that buy up housing stock,[18] making local housing unaffordable for the very people invested in the pension.[19] A focus on investing locally can help us ensure our investment dollars are not undermining the very communities we seek to support.

Broadly speaking, local investing is a key tool for transforming our current version of capitalism into something more sustainable. When investors described in Chapter 7 sought to move their money out of the stock market because of its moral problematics, they turned to local investments. When investors in Chapter 8 sought to hand decision-making power over their investment capital to local communities, they similarly were embracing the power of investing local. In Chapter 10, we will discuss climate change, and local investing is a vital tool there as well. Our society needs to be promoting goods made locally and to reserve use of energy-intensive long-haul transport for cases when goods cannot be produced locally or when local production is more carbon-intensive.

Beyond external benefits, the Jewish community should care about local investing because local investing is a deep and ancient Jewish value.

The Poor of Your City

In Jewish tradition, every human life has infinite dignity and value. But caring for one's local community is of special importance. We are first responsible for ourselves and our own family, then our community, then our society, then the whole world. This is as true about loan and investment capital as it is about charity.

The Talmud teaches about loan dollars:

> Rabbi Yosef expounded on a verse from the Torah: "If you lend money to any of My people, to the poor who is with you..." (Exodus 22:25). The term "My people" teaches that if one of My people and a stranger both come to borrow money from you, My people take precedence. The term "the poor person" teaches that if a poor person and a rich person come to borrow money, the poor person takes precedence. And the term "who is with you" teaches that if your poor person [one of your relatives] and a different poor person living in your city come to borrow money, your relative takes precedence. If it is between one of the poor of your city and one of the poor of another city, the one of the poor of your city takes precedence.[20]

Elsewhere, the Sages of the Talmud extend the principle of local investing and local charity to encompass a wide variety of needs.

> Regarding a well belonging to the townspeople, when it is a question of their own lives or the lives of strangers, their own lives take precedence; their cattle or the cattle of strangers, their cattle take precedence over those of strangers; their laundering or that of strangers, their laundering takes precedence over that of strangers. But if the choice lies between the lives of strangers and their own

> laundering, the rabbis state that the lives of the strangers take precedence over their own laundering.[21]

Judaism understands an obligation to all humanity to coexist alongside a unique obligation to those to whom we are closest. We need to care about humans in great need; we also need to care about those to whom we have the greatest connection or obligation.

As humans, we naturally connect more on an emotional and psychological level with those to whom we are closest. This remains true today even with the miraculous capabilities of technology. While we have a responsibility to help end suffering for all people, to ignore the suffering of those with whom we are closest is a greater moral travesty.

Jewish tradition sees us as so bound up with our local communities that we are responsible for our community's actions and their impact:

> Whoever is able to protest against the transgressions of his own family and does not do so becomes responsible for the transgressions of his family. Whoever is able to protest against the transgressions of the people of his community and does not do so becomes responsible for the transgressions of his community. Whoever is able to protest against the transgressions of the entire world and does not do so becomes responsible for the transgressions of the entire world.[22]

Judaism's principle of investing and community-building on a local level is the subtext for an amazing Talmudic story. This story is also one of the great moments when the Talmud, written and normally dominated by men, directly compares a particular woman's deeds to those of a man's, and the woman's deeds are considered superior.

> Mar Ukba had a poor person in his neighborhood into whose door-socket he would throw four coins every day. One day, the poor person said: "I will go and see who does me this kindness." On that day, Mar Ukba happened to be late at the house of study, and his wife was coming home with him. As soon as the poor man saw them jostling the door, he went out after them. They fled from him to protect their anonymity. They ran into a furnace room from which the fire had just been swept. Mar Ukba's feet were burning from the hot floor. His wife said to him: "raise your feet and put

them on mine." Her feet, miraculously, didn't burn. Seeing that she had merited this miracle, he became resentful. She explained to him, "[I merited a miracle because] I am usually at home, so my charity is direct—I give actual prepared food, while all you give are coins.[23]

Mar Ukba thought he was engaging in meaningful charity by regularly giving money, anonymously, to a poor person in his neighborhood. Yet he also expected a reward for that charity (for God to protect his feet in the still-hot furnace) and grew resentful when he learned his wife's charity was preferred.

Mar Ukba's wife, who is not given a name in the Talmud, is the hero of the story. She not only reassures her petulant husband but also gives more effective charity. The point of the story is that her charity is better because she is not merely throwing coins, but instead entering into relationship with those in her local community in need. Normally, Judaism highly values anonymous giving. But in this case, Mar Ukba's wife is getting to know the members of her local community and their needs, and treating them with dignity, which is the higher form of charity.

Whether through charitable giving, sharing of resources like well water, or investment capital and loan dollars, Jewish tradition has a long history of prioritizing local community. Today, the growing movements for buying local, eating local, and investing local are all aligned deeply with Jewish values and tradition.

The Challenges of Local Investing

So why have we not already brought more investment capital to our local communities, to our human-service agencies, to local impact-focused businesses? Social Impact Bonds that we described in the introduction are a particularly complex example with a unique set of challenges and risks. But surely there are plenty of straightforward options?

In fact, all local investing in the United States is far more difficult than it seems at first glance. Journalist Amy Cortese, in her 2012 book *Locavesting*, offers more detail. Rewind a hundred years or so, and it was a lot easier for a United States citizen to invest in anything one might want. In fact, it was too easy. Everyday people were being fleeced on a regular basis by entrepreneurs selling distant gold mines, miraculous oil wells, and other fraudulent transactions which had no more basis than selling a patch of blue sky. State legislators in Kansas, seeking to protect the public from catastrophic losses, instituted the first "blue sky" laws in 1911. Similar laws were adopted by most states over the next two decades. After the crash of the stock market in 1929 and the start of the Great Depression, the federal government instituted its own securities laws in the 1930s and early 1940s. These laws regulated sales of securities (a **security** is any investment that can be bought and sold—a loan, a bond, a share of stock, a part-ownership in a company), and led to the creation of the **Securities and Exchange Commission** (**SEC**). The SEC provided a new era of significant protection for everyday investors. But the new laws required people wanting to offer securities for sale to register them, a complicated and costly legal process that only larger businesses could afford. The laws also built an exception for wealthy investors who were assumed to be able to fend for themselves or sustain risk of loss. Further securities laws in 1982 built on this foundation to establish the category of **accredited investors**.

In other words, large public companies can afford the legal fees to register publicly traded stock, but your local small business probably can't. And the wealthiest of investors, accredited investors, can invest in ways that avoid the most expensive filing requirements, but the majority of investors can't.

According to Cortese, "just like that, the universe of investors was cleaved in two. If you had a net worth of $1 million or more, or annual income of at least $200,000 (later amended to $300,000 for couples), you were among the top 2 percent of Americans and could invest in pretty much anything you like." More recent estimates put the number of accredited investors at 10 percent of the US population.[24] On the institutional side, nonprofits with $5 million of investments qualify as accredited investors, which includes some of our Jewish communal institutions but also leaves many out.[25]

For nonaccredited investors, most local investing opportunities became inaccessible. Michael Shuman, author of the book *Local Dollars, Local Sense* and longtime advocate for local investing, paints a stark picture of the investment arena today: Americans hold collectively tens of trillions of dollars in stocks, bonds, mutual funds, pension funds, and life insurance, and "not a penny of that goes into local business."[26]

Some reading this book will be accredited investors or represent Jewish institutions that are accredited. Others will not. Let's take a moment to look at some examples available to each.

Investing Locally as an Accredited Investor

In 2017, the Jewish Community Foundation of San Diego (JCFSD) launched its impact investing pool. The organization had historically operated donor-advised funds for Jewish donors in the San Diego area. **Donor-advised funds (DAFs)** are analogous to a convenient and pared-down private foundation. Donors contribute money to a sponsor organization (which itself must be a registered charity) and then "recommend" distributions to nonprofits. Donor-advised funds are held by individuals and

Private Equity and Debt: Local Investing

families; synagogues, local Jewish institutions, and secular nonprofits also hold assets at the San Diego foundation. Like private foundations, most donor-advised funds do not distribute all of their capital immediately but instead donate a portion and leave a portion invested for later allocation to nonprofit grantees.

Beth Sirull, president and CEO of JCFSD, understands the importance of local investing. Prior to her role at JCFSD, she served as president and CEO of Pacific Community Ventures, a community-development financial institution. Sirull identified a problem with the investments she saw being held by charitable institutions across the Jewish world: Jewish investors were not investing with Jewish values. As she articulated in an article published in the *Forward* in 2019, Jewish institutions were often checking their values at the door to investment-committee meetings. "Why does a synagogue community go to great lengths to ensure its kitchen's kashruth, but allow its endowment to prosper from companies whose environmental, labor and community practices are at odds with Jewish values?"[27] These issues felt especially pressing because the money invested by JCFSD was all designated in the long-run for values-aligned charitable causes.

In response, Sirull led her organization to create the country's first Jewish impact-investing pool available to donor-advised fund holders and organizational funds. At first, her own investment committee was nervous. The pool was designed to achieve market-rate financial return (see Chapter 4), yet the committee was worried that the pool's financials would perform poorly and investors would not be inspired to invest. The opposite ended up happening; the impact-investing pool has been the highest performing investment option of the entire suite of options offered by JCFSD over the past five years.[28]

The pool is available for fundholders at JCFSD, and only charitable dollars can be invested (as opposed to retirement savings). The pool invests in a range of asset classes including public equity. But some of the most innovative work of the pool has involved finding opportunities to invest locally in San Diego.

For example, JCFSD was the first and largest investor in the Homebuilding Investment Fund created by San Diego Habitat for Humanity. The $2 million fund acts as a line of credit to allow the nonprofit organization to build more homes faster, supporting affordable housing in San Diego.[29] This partnership with Habitat for Humanity offers a powerful example of a Jewish institution that is an accredited investor moving its capital off Wall Street and into investments that positively impact its own local community.

Other Jewish institutions have begun building out local investment options, including the Bay Area-based Jewish Community Federation and Endowment Fund. The fund has created opportunities for donor-advised fund holders to invest in loans to local businesses, local Jewish nonprofits engaged in impactful projects, and building sustainable cities in Israel. The possibilities abound.

Local Investing for Nonaccredited Investors

For the rest of us nonaccredited investors, the current possibilities are fewer. Many businesses will not bother to spend the tens of thousands of dollars necessary to file complex paperwork and be able to offer their investments to nonaccredited investors.

There have been a few examples of companies that have navigated the regulatory thicket in order to enable local investment. Ice cream maker Ben and Jerry's was a rarity when it raised early capital decades ago through an option in the securities law known as a Direct Public Offering.[30] With the growth of the internet, Direct Public Offerings have seen a small resurgence, including companies like TechSoup, a company providing technology and networking for civil, society organizations.[31] But Direct Public Offerings remain complex to navigate and are infrequently used.

Local businesses have explored a range of ways to raise capital while avoiding the most expensive and onerous filing requirements. For example, some local businesses have sought interest-free loans, which are not considered "investments" in the same way and face less regulation. Some have limited themselves to a single state's boundaries to earn an exemption from the SEC, especially in states whose regulators are willing to smooth the registration process for local businesses. Cooperatives also present another way to avoid the thicket of regulations—a communally owned co-op can raise funds from its members with fewer problems. These opportunities remain less common but are important for locally-focused investors to know about.

A major step forward for local investing was Regulation Crowdfunding, finalized under the Obama administration in 2015. The regulation allowed for companies to raise up to a million dollars and make their investment offering available to non-accredited investors, and up to $5,000,000 in some cases.[32]

A handful of platforms have already gained prominence for their ability to facilitate deals through Regulation Crowdfunding. For example, on the online portal Small Change, you can find investment opportunities like San Francisco Community Land Trust's BIPOC Homeownership project that seeks to finance the purchase of cooperative apartment buildings for Black, Indigenous, and people of color (BIPOC) in the Bay Area. The project has a $1,000 minimum and returns 2 percent over an expected term of nine years.[33]

Another growing opportunity for investing in small businesses comes through Community Development Financial Institutions (CDFIs, which we have seen recur throughout this book). Historically, CDFIs have received capital from banks and other large investors. A small but increasing number have navigated the complex regulations to enable individuals to invest.[34] A group of Christian religious congregations based in New Jersey and the tri-state area, mostly nuns, were among the first modern adopters of responsible investing. In the early 1980s, seeking a way to address poverty more directly with their investment assets, they created the Leviticus Fund, a community-development financial institution that bases its name on the verses from Leviticus that describe the *shmita* year. The fund's first two loans in 1984 were a tenant-owned cooperative in New York City and a workplace and training center for mentally challenged adults in Nyack, NY. It has grown to over $140 million in capital today.[35] Individuals can invest in the Fund for as little as $1,000 and select whether they want to receive 2 percent interest or make their capital available interest-free.[36] (For those interested in investing more in CDFIs, you can learn more about the organization CNote in Chapter 11).

These opportunities have a lower rate of return, but there are also local opportunities that offer a market rate of return. Those opportunities, including investing directly in local businesses in your neighborhood, tend to be the ones that require the most legwork and effort.

A vital step you can take if you are a "main street" nonaccredited investor is to join the growing movement of people working on the national level to make local investing accessible to all. Michael Shuman, author of the book *Local Dollars, Local Sense* quoted above, recently founded the Main Street Journal, an online newsletter dedicated to covering opportunities for local investing. Signing up for his newsletter provides a glimpse of the truly inspiring opportunities that are possible with local investing and provides an up-to-date assessment of what is available with local investing.

Shuman and Amy Cortese, author of *Locavesting*, both serve as advisors to the new organization National Coalition for Community Capital, which is similarly devoted to building the regulatory and practice framework for investing local.

Another relatively new resource is The Next Egg, a community of learning and practice made up of people seeking to learn how to move their retirement savings out of the stocks of multinational corporations and into local community-based investments. The Next Egg offers tools and resources to create something called a "self-directed 401(k)," which means that rather than hold your 401(k) retirement account at a major financial institution, it is held through an institution that specializes in facilitating investments beyond just stocks and bonds. The work still falls on you to identify the investment opportunities in your region, but The Next Egg helps provide resources to do so.

These organizations and newsletters are all great opportunities for those interested in doing a little extra work to move investment capital in truly transformative ways.

Investment Opportunities are Made, Not Found

Local investing, through private equity and private debt, has the potential to transform our economy. The locavesting movement is growing, paralleling the locavore movement of eating local and movements for buying local. It is impeded by securities laws that prevent most investors from accessing local opportunities. But the landscape is rapidly shifting, and there are many opportunities for those willing to put in a little extra work to move their capital off Wall Street and onto "main street," investing in local businesses and entrepreneurs.

These investment opportunities are not simple to find. But truthfully, the most impactful opportunities never are. As Debra Schwartz, Director of Impact Investing at the MacArthur Foundation, notes, "Creating positive opportunities that move money to places it doesn't want to go—because of prejudice, because the areas are too rural and too dispersed, because people look too risky, because the breakthrough climate technology looks too speculative—whatever has pushed people away from access to capital, it's the proactive agents of change that create the opportunities we need."[37]

Jewish wisdom acknowledges the importance of starting where we live with our investment capital. We have a universal obligation to all humans, but we have a unique obligation to our local communities. And the work ahead can be joyous and exciting.

※ ※ ※

Since the time of the Talmud, investors have diversified their investments across asset classes. The modern asset classes of cash, public equity, private equity, and debt/fixed income each present a unique opportunity to apply Jewish wisdom to our investment portfolios and make a positive impact.

The next four chapters approach our investment portfolios through a different lens, that of issue areas. Judaism has wisdom that can guide us in our approach to every contemporary issue, but four of them are especially relevant for the investing arena: climate change, racism, investing in Israel, and investing in coexistence and peace.

Next Steps—Chapter 9

Local investing requires more effort and time than investing in publicly traded stocks, but it is both Jewish values-aligned and deeply impactful. Local businesses are net job creators; large corporations are net job destroyers.

- **Step 1: Explore organizations** promoting local investing, including Main Street Journal, Next Egg, the National Coalition for Community Capital, and others. Sign up for their email lists.
- **Step 2: Assess your status.** Based on your income or net worth (or, for organizations, your total assets), determine if you are an accredited or non-accredited investor.
  - If you are a non-accredited investor: research crowdfunding investment opportunities. Create an account at Small Change (smallchange.co) or other crowdfunding platforms.
  - If you are an accredited investor: you have a world of potential open to you, including exciting investments in Israel and elsewhere mentioned throughout this book. Seek a financial advisor who can help you vet local investments (Resource Generation's list mentioned at the end of Chapter 6 might be particularly helpful).

Issue Areas

Chapter 10

Changing Climates

One of the most successful advertising campaigns in history premiered in 1971. The "Crying Indian Ad," as it was dubbed, featured a Native American man clad in buckskin with a long braid, paddling through a river full of trash, past a factory with pollution spewing from smokestacks. A blond woman throws a bag of fast-food waste that lands on his beaded moccasin. The camera pans to his face, where a single tear rolls down. The narrator announces in a somber voice, "People start pollution. People can stop it."[1]

You might naturally assume the purpose of this commercial was to encourage recycling. And it was—but for the advertiser, it had a more important, deeper objective: to change the common societal understanding in the United States around garbage to place blame on the individual, rather than the manufacturer producing it.[2]

We did not always have a manufacturing class that intentionally sought to create more waste. The real formation of the waste industry in the country came after World War II, when manufacturers' capacity grew tremendously in keeping with a burst of post-war consumption. In 1956, a presenter at a premier plastics industry conference sang the virtues of trashable products—because they led to more consumption.[3]

Similarly, consumers in the United States did not always know how to throw things away. It was a skill that literally had to be taught in the post-war years: manufacturers took out ads in magazines and radio educating people about what could be thrown away and how to do so.[4]

When the state of Vermont, recognizing the problem, passed a ban on single-use disposable containers in the 1950s, a number of corporations sought to prevent the spread of similar legislation to other states. They banded together to form the organization Keep America Beautiful. The organization ostensibly dedicated itself to anti-litter and beautification. But, more importantly for its funders, it also sought to divert responsibility for the litter problem onto individual consumers.

The Crying Indian Ad, designed by a New York advertising agency contracted by Keep America Beautiful, was deceptive on a number of levels. The man hired to play the Native American was not actually Native but of Sicilian descent. He refused

Put Your Money Where Your Soul Is

to cry for the ad, so the ad firm used glycerin to create a fake tear rolling down his cheek.[5] The ad firm did not seek permission from nor offer payment to actual Native Americans before culturally appropriating an Indigenous persona.

Nevertheless, it worked. In fact, the narrative that individual choices cause the environmental crisis remains pervasive today. I was educated from childhood to turn off lights in my house when not using them, to turn off water when I was brushing my teeth, and to recycle my packaging when possible. I was not educated to protest governmental inaction or to put pressure on companies to reduce their wasteful packaging in the first place. Only as an adult did I learn about the vital role of advocacy and activism in making change.

As our society has understood more about human-caused climate change in the past few decades, the same narrative of personal responsibility remains pervasive. Fossil fuel corporations have reinforced and harnessed this narrative. Consider the widespread fixation with calculating one's personal "carbon footprint." This term was, in fact, coined and promoted by oil company BP as part of its strategy to focus public attention on individual instead of collective action.[6]

Certainly, Judaism believes in the power of individual actions. In our framework of *mitzvot*, commandments, every single act has the power to ripple outward to the entire world. In fact, in medieval Egypt, the rabbinic scholar Rambam wrote that one should behave as if one's deeds were always equally balanced between righteous and evil, and a single good deed would tip the scale.[7]

Individual actions are also vital from an environmental perspective, especially when well-organized, collectively, toward a large-scale impact. Thanks to the individual efforts of millions of people, up to 40 percent of the United States' fresh vegetables came from local and household "victory gardens" during World War II, a practice that saw a resurgence during the 2020 coronavirus pandemic.[8]

But Judaism is also a profoundly communal religion. The Talmud teaches *kol yisrael arevin zeh bazeh*: all members of our community are bound up with one another.[9] This justifies Jews getting in each other's business and offering loving feedback. The Sages of the Talmud recount a story of a man who was dumping debris from his yard into the public thoroughfare. A wise person interrupted him: "why are you throwing debris from a place that does not belong to you into a place that does belong to you?" The man laughed off the critique. A while later, the man had to sell his field, and was walking along the public thoroughfare when he tripped on the debris he had thrown. He acknowledged ruefully, "the wise person critiqued me well."[10]

Jewish tradition requires a quorum, a *minyan*, to pray, because it teaches that certain prayers are stronger and more powerful when recited communally. In fact, some prayers for personal welfare and safety are written and recited only in the plural.[11] These are not merely spiritual ideals. In autonomous Jewish communities throughout the generations, rabbis and community leaders have held the power to enact communal legislation related to environmental issues. The Talmudic Sages limited the locations of manufacturing processes that produce foul smells, instituted a communal tax for infrastructure improvements, and more.[12]

The story behind the "Crying Indian Ad" reveals that while our society may currently focus more on individual environmental actions, corporations hold immense power to influence environmental crises. That means we can have the greatest impact when we shift how they wield that power.

One half of all human-generated fossil fuel emissions globally have been released since 1990, and a full third since 2005.[13] These emissions come primarily from large corporations. The twenty largest fossil fuel companies have contributed up to 35 percent of the world's carbon dioxide and methane emissions.[14] If left unchecked, the hundred largest oil and gas companies will use up 80 percent of the world's carbon budget: Their operations alone will prevent the world meeting the United Nations' goal of keeping global warming less than 1.5 degrees Celsius above preindustrial levels.[15]

Investors, as owners of companies, have a unique lever of power to change corporate practices. Here's an example. The Australia-based Minderoo Foundation published a report in 2021 detailing that over half of the world's single-use plastic waste comes from just 20 companies.[16] That same year, a group of investors including the shareholder advocacy nonprofit As You Sow filed shareholder resolutions at several major manufacturers to support the "right-to-repair" movement. Investors sought to pressure companies to make it easier to repair, rather than trash, broken devices. The investor advocacy has achieved some surprising early wins. Microsoft agreed to study how increasing access to the parts and information needed for repair can reduce its contributions to climate change and electronic waste and explicitly committed to act on the findings of that study by the end of 2022.[17] Other recent shareholder resolutions have been successful at pressuring some corporations to reduce single-use plastic packaging, which, while insufficient by itself to combat pollution, is nevertheless a significant victory.[18]

True, like the "Crying Indian Ad" suggested, we need to be reducing our own individual waste. We even need to be reducing our individual carbon footprints. Yet we should remain clear-eyed that doing so will not actually solve the problem of global carbon and methane emissions. In 2008, researchers at MIT calculated a minimum amount of carbon emissions that an individual living in the United States could never avoid, even a person who slept in homeless shelters and ate in soup kitchens.[19] The amount was still several times what the world could sustain if every person used that amount of carbon emissions,[20] because the infrastructure of the country still relies to a significant extent on fossil fuels. Even despite a global pandemic and stay-at-home orders in 2020, the global level of carbon dioxide emissions did not fall at anywhere near the pace needed to stem climate change.[21] Most of the greenhouse gas emissions are not tied to individual choices, but rather are embedded in our economy.

Rabbi Jennie Rosenn, founder of *Dayenu: A Jewish Call to Climate Action*, likes to paraphrase the environmental activist Bill McKibben: "The climate crisis no longer yields to individual actions. There's no way to make the math work one vegan dinner or Tesla at a time. At this point, the most important thing an individual can do is be less of an individual and join movements sharp enough to make change."[22]

Clearly, there is a vital need for our investment capital and our political will to be pressuring companies and politicians with urgency to shift business as usual.

❃ ❃ ❃

Investment capital touches on a wide range of environmental issues—plastics pollution, access to water, food waste, deforestation, and agriculture, to name a few. But perhaps the most pressing issue facing environmentally conscious investors today is the climate crisis, which requires massive collective action.

There are many reasons why Jewish investors today seek to help combat the climate crisis, and those reasons are becoming more visceral and personal every year. A growing number of Jewish communities are themselves impacted by once-rare weather events, like the Vancouver Jewish Federation, which jumpstarted its journey to climate action after heat waves, wildfires, and flooding affected the local community.[23]

Those who care deeply about Israel ought to be especially concerned about climate change. Israel is already a hot and water-scarce country. The Middle East is the most sensitive place on earth to climate change after Antarctica, according to Mariana Bergovoy, the senior audit manager of the State Comptroller of Israel. Bergovoy recently conducted an audit on the Israeli government's response to climate change. The audit noted that on the current climate trajectory, the country will see a rise in temperature of 2.6 degrees Celsius by 2050. Precipitation will reduce by 24 percent. The resource scarcity and environmental impact could spiral into deeper geopolitical issues.[24]

This chapter will explore Judaism's approach to investing and climate change. To begin, we will take an unexpected detour.

We need a model for how a community can change its relationship to fossil fuels—a change in social climate, so to speak, or in society's narrative. One surprisingly apt model is the evolving approach of traditional rabbinic legal authorities to tobacco. Rabbis' attitudes to smoking cigarettes transformed over the second half of the 20th century from widespread acceptance to widespread rejection. The Orthodox community in particular is bound by a legal approach to Jewish practice; when a rabbi declares something forbidden by Jewish law, that has real and immediate impacts on communal behavior.

The evolution of these rabbinic approaches to tobacco provides an important case study for a path the Jewish community could chart in its relationship to fossil fuels.

Cigarettes and Communal Edicts

Jewish tradition has a long relationship with smoking, extending back hundreds of years before the modern tobacco industry.[25] Setting aside the potential health effects of pre-industrial-era tobacco,[26] we now know that the modern tobacco industry's products are deadly—in fact, the leading preventable cause of death in the United States—and cause hundreds of thousands of deaths a year.[27]

In January of 1964, the United States Surgeon General released a report documenting the connections between cigarette smoking, lung cancer, and heart disease. At the time, a whopping 42 percent of the US population smoked, and the number may have been even higher in certain parts of the Jewish community.[28] It is hard for us to recall today, when smoking is so universally understood for the lethal activity it is, but a significant minority of the public expressed doubt about the dangers of smoking even until the 1990s. These doubts were amplified by the tobacco industry's concerted efforts to promote smoking and obfuscate the science. The industry hired scientists and a top public relations firm to challenge the already-existing scientific evidence that smoking could kill you. Decades later, that eventually led to the tobacco industry being found guilty of a massive and ongoing fraud, according to the Justice Department, to "deceive the American public about the health effects of smoking."[29]

In 1963, the year before the Surgeon General released his report, the prominent American Orthodox rabbi Moshe Feinstein had issued a responsum saying that although smoking might have negative health impacts, it could not be considered prohibited. Smoking was widespread among laypeople and communal leaders alike. Other rabbinic authorities of the time echoed similar perspectives, refusing to forbid smoking according to Jewish law because such a position would be untenable for the community. Rabbi Feinstein even quoted a verse from Psalms, "God watches over fools."[30]

* * *

To understand Rabbi Feinstein's motivation, we need to rewind further, to a previous societal shift, that of the destruction of the Second Temple by the Romans in 70 CE.

The destruction of the Temple was a tragic and apocalyptic event for the generation that witnessed it. Some in the Jewish community sought refuge in ascetic impulses, eschewing all worldly goods in despair over the loss of the Temple. But the Talmudic Sage Rabbi Yishmael encouraged restraint in the community's mourning. He based this on his acute sense of compassion and political awareness of what the community could handle: "From the day that the Temple was destroyed, ideally we should not eat meat or drink wine. But a court does not decree restrictions on the community which they cannot uphold."[31]

This tempered approach is significant coming from Rabbi Yishmael, who had plenty to grieve about Roman rule. He was kidnapped by the Romans as a child and was ransomed from prison by a future rabbi of his who recognized his brilliance.[32] His son and his daughter were themselves stolen into slavery.[33] He was one of ten sages targeted with gruesome assassination by the empire, according to Jewish tradition.[34] Despite his personal motivations for deep mourning, Rabbi Yishmael recognized the importance of a mild approach to setting communal norms: Do not decree restrictions on a community that a majority of the community will fail to uphold.

Rabbi Yishmael's principle was adopted into Jewish tradition, providing a general guideline for legislation in gray areas: Do not issue a decree when most people cannot uphold it.[35]

This principle of respecting the community's inability to uphold a decree directly influenced the Orthodox rabbinic approach to smoking in the 20th century. It is reported that Rabbi Feinstein and other rabbinic authorities personally held that smoking is prohibited under Jewish law. They refrained from writing those opinions publicly because they knew many people in their community would reject their opinions. Publishing such an opinion would begin to fray communal unity and their ability to maintain standards of practice in other areas.[36]

As the risks became more universally acknowledged, and as the number of smokers fell, the tone among traditional rabbinic authorities began to shift. Rabbi Eliezer Waldenburg, a renowned Orthodox authority on medicine and Jewish law, opened his 1982 responsum with a lengthy description of the scientific evidence against smoking. He noted the overwhelming scientific consensus that smoking is harmful, and he explicitly critiqued Rabbi Feinstein's lenient approach. He instead offered a carefully worded "There is ample room to prohibit smoking," and defended the right for individuals in public spaces to demand that smokers stop smoking there.[37] Near the end of his life, Rabbi Feinstein finally agreed it would be prohibited to smoke in a shared space like a study hall because of its impact on others sitting there.[38] Yet he refused to retract his position that smoking, however ill-advised, was permitted.[39]

The first Orthodox rabbinic authority to explicitly prohibit smoking was the chief Sephardic rabbi of Tel Aviv, Chaim David HaLevi, in 1976.[40] Rabbi HaLevi noted the drop in the number of smokers and the growing clarity of the science as factors in his ability to take a stand.[41] As smoking became universally recognized as lethal, a wide range of Orthodox rabbinic authorities joined the chorus calling for its prohibition, including rabbis like Rabbi Waldenburg, who had earlier ruled ambiguously but in 1985 adopted a stricter position.[42] Other denominations began taking action around this time as well. In 1987, the Reform movement passed a resolution declaring smoking a health hazard and banning it at meetings and functions.[43] Around the same time, the Conservative movement approved a responsum declaring smoking to be a violation of Jewish law and ethics.[44] Finally, the story came full circle when the largest Orthodox rabbinic association in the United States made a public proclamation in 2006 prohibiting smoking.[45]

The discussion then spiraled outward to activities ancillary to smoking. For example, a decade after Rabbi HaLevi came out as the first Orthodox rabbi against smoking, he explicitly prohibited purchasing cigarettes for someone else, even if that someone was one's own father.[46] Similarly, offering someone a light aids and abets them to harm their body and becomes a violation under the umbrella of "Do not put a stumbling block before the blind," which we discussed in Chapter 5. In 1995, Rabbi Waldenburg called for publicizing a broad prohibition against production and sale of cigarettes, barring a few individual exceptions.[47]

Rabbi Dr. Aaron Levine, the late professor of economics at Yeshiva University, noted that if one understands smoking to be prohibited, then there is a moral obligation to help other people stop smoking. He suggests admonishing those who smoke and lobbying the government to prevent the sale of cigarettes. And investing in cigarette companies? Regardless of what proactive steps one takes, investment in a tobacco company is unthinkable, a clear violation of the Biblical injunction, "Do not stand idly by the blood of your neighbor."[48]

There remain a few voices who are wary of condemning smoking or investments in tobacco companies, but they have become the far fringe. The overwhelming consensus of Orthodox rabbis today is clear: Smoking is prohibited by the Torah.[49]

Fossil Fuels: The Tobacco of Our Time

The similarities between the tobacco industry of the 1960s and the fossil fuel industry of today are striking. Both industries manufacture and distribute products that are ultimately hazardous to human health. Cigarettes do not immediately kill but rather significantly increase the likelihood of illness and death. Similarly, global use of fossil fuels over the past several hundred years, but especially over the past several decades, has led to a world that is already demonstrating extreme and unpredictable weather patterns. These are literally killing people and will only continue to accelerate.

Cigarettes are chemically addictive. And while fossil fuels are not addictive in the formal sense, they are certainly a hard habit to break, and our society has been described allegorically as "addicted to fossil fuels."[50] We have begun to seek explicitly to reduce our dependence on fossil fuels, including for electricity and travel. Yet few of us are able to entirely avoid using fossil fuels.

Fossil fuel companies have used an eerily similar playbook to the tobacco industry. Both industries knew they would no longer be profitable once consumers understood the risks.[51] Both funded scientists to spread doubt regarding the danger of their products. They even hired the same research consultants to sow misinformation.[52] After the surgeon general's warning, it took decades for Big Tobacco to be universally understood as the life-threatening danger that it is, a shift that only took place more fully in the 1990s.

Rabbi Feinstein lived at a moment of significant societal change, when smoking cigarettes, a behavior that was nearly universal, became understood as deadly and destructive. And we ourselves are at a similar moment of significant social change. Our society desperately needs to change its relationship to fossil fuels to limit global warming to the global consensus of 1.5 degrees Celsius, beyond which catastrophic impacts accelerate more rapidly. If we do not change, the world will change for us, becoming more unfriendly to human life within the next 100 years, with an increase in natural disasters expected to kill hundreds of millions of people, on top of the millions of lives it already impacts.

Every action we take—how we eat, how we work, how we visit family—impacts and often exacerbates the climate crisis. Yet wrapping our collective mind around the problem is difficult. It is disconcerting to discover that behavior we considered normal is nevertheless detrimental to society, according to Yale researcher Dan Kahan in a study on beliefs around climate change[53]—as disconcerting as it might feel to learn that a widespread several-times-a-day habit of smoking is slowly killing us.

Judaism is a communal religion that has survived drastic social transformations before. The Sages were practical in their approach to social change. They knew that whatever ideals we might hold, a standard that is set too high is ultimately useless. To take solitary action is ineffective; to not take action at all is defeatist. Instead, we need to focus on moving the entire community, and society, on a collective path.

❊ ❊ ❊

The cultural change around tobacco did not happen by itself. In the United States, tobacco became universally understood as harmful thanks to a long-term, grassroots movement. Activism managed to overcome millions of dollars spent by the tobacco industry on public relations, disinformation, and lobbying. It took decades to make the culture shift and then to embed that culture shift into law.

The concept of a window of public opinion within which a politician can operate without seeming extreme and out-of-touch is known in political theory as the Overton window.[54] Just as politicians understand how far would be too far to push the community in any given moment, so too rabbis (at least those who retain any communal credibility) understand the range of acceptable discourse at any given historical moment.

The window is shifting in our society. As I write this chapter, the news is proclaiming several hundred people dead in my region of the Pacific Northwest due to a record-setting heat wave. 2020 was one of the most extreme wildfire seasons on record, with smoke literally darkening the skies of the entire United States. Then 2023 was worse. The Intergovernmental Panel on Climate Change, the body of the world's leading climate experts, which releases a series of reports roughly once every seven years, published its latest reports beginning in summer 2022, painting a devastating picture of extreme weather taking hold in every part of the planet.[55]

As we saw, fossil fuel companies are by far the biggest contributors to the climate crisis. And despite clear science about the need to reduce carbon emissions, from 2014-2019 the major publicly traded and state-owned oil companies all increased their production. Even today, few fossil fuel companies have "climate transition" plans that extend at least 20 years into the future and of those, even fewer actually involve reducing carbon emissions.[56]

Faith communities are helping move the window of discourse. In spring of 2022, the nonprofit organization Greenfaith publicly released a platform of five standards for all banks and asset managers. Those standards, developed in conjunction with Indigenous communities, human-rights experts, and faith-based experts, feature commitments like "exclude across all investments any assets that include production of fossil fuels" and "provide all clients fossil fuel- and deforestation-free investment options as a default."[57]

The window of discourse is also shifting within Jewish communities. For example, July 2021 marked the first time an Orthodox rabbi, Rabbi Haggai Resnikoff, came out publicly with a responsum explicitly prohibiting the use of fossil fuels except in cases of need, because of the danger they pose to civilization. Significantly, Rabbi Resnikoff recognized that the Jewish obligation extends beyond merely refraining from use of fossil fuels; we also should not be invested in fossil fuel companies in our investment portfolios.

Society increasingly recognizes burning fossil fuels as a direct contributor to the climate crisis. Awareness is growing daily of the devastation human-caused climate change is already wreaking on our world and the moral call to stop profiting from that devastation. And daily more Jews are moving their assets from fossil fuel companies to more environmentally sustainable investments.

If the change feels daunting or impossible, we should remember the amazing shift that society and the Jewish community made regarding tobacco in just a few decades. As we all join the movement to reduce our dependence on fossil fuels, we can achieve a culture shift like that which happened with Big Tobacco, toward a sustainable and resilient future free of burning fossil fuels. It is no longer enough to just pray that "God watches over fools."

The End of the Fossil Fuel Era

There are several tools in a values-based investor's toolbox to confront the climate crisis. One is shareholder advocacy; another is negative screens. Often, values-based investors will begin with efforts toward shareholder advocacy. After a company demonstrates its unwillingness to respond or change its harmful business practices, investors move their money elsewhere.

We saw in Chapter 7 the Jewish value of feedback, or rebuke, as a crucial part of being in relationship. Judaism prefers engagement when possible, rather than terminating a relationship. We saw in Chapter 5 that there are also moments when screening out a stock or a sector is the appropriate Jewish decision: when the sector's core business model runs contrary to Jewish values, for example, or when companies fail to respond to repeated and escalated advocacy.

Shareholders have been pressuring oil and gas companies like Exxon for over three decades to shift their business models into renewable energy and stop contributing to climate change. When companies have made any changes, they have been minor or superficial. And despite recent major wins—like new board directors at Exxon, which we will discuss shortly—at this point, the change is too little and too late. For example, Shell in 2021 agreed to pay more than $100 million to communities in southern Nigeria impacted by a crude oil spill in 1970. In other words, justice took more than 50 years—the children affected by the oil spill might now be grandparents.[58] Given the urgency of the climate catastrophe brought about by years of business as usual and Big Oil's failure to take action when it could have been easier and more effective, it might be time to concede that advocacy has failed.

In the early 2010s, a movement launched to encourage institutional endowments (including colleges and universities) to divest their holdings in fossil fuels and reinvest that money in renewable energy and environmental sustainability.[59] The campaign grew out of 350.org, the climate nonprofit founded by environmentalist Bill

McKibben, along with other grassroots organizations. A growing number of institutions, including Harvard and Brandeis University, have joined the campaign for fossil fuel divestment, along with some of the largest names in philanthropy: the Rockefeller, Ford, and MacArthur foundations.[60] As of the end of 2022, more than 1500 institutions, representing more than $40 trillion dollars, have pledged to move their money out of dirty energy. That is an amount larger than the total of the two largest global economies, the United States and China, combined.

Joining this broader movement also happens to offer a reduction in our personal carbon footprints. One of the biggest contributors to our individual and organizational carbon footprints is our banking and investment relationships. The four largest US banks—Chase, Citi, Wells Fargo, and Bank of America—are also four of the world's largest financiers of fossil fuels. A bank account with $5,000 held at one of these banks creates more emissions than a cross-country flight. An account with $125,000 creates more emissions than the entire annual carbon footprint of an average American.[61]

The social climate is changing along with the physical climate. Investors are increasingly recognizing fossil fuels as a volatile, risky investment. For example, the fossil fuel sector, which used to top the lists of ten largest companies in the country, has underperformed the broader market over the past ten years.[62] Increasingly, investors are screening out fossil fuels not out of any moral or ethical conviction, but because fossil fuels are volatile and have demonstrated poor performance over the long term.

In 2019, Rabbi Jennie Rosenn founded the organization Dayenu. Dayenu seeks to meet the climate crisis with "spiritual audacity and bold political action," and has achieved significant legislative wins, including playing a key role in the Inflation Reduction Act of 2022 that saw hundreds of billions of dollars of increased funding for climate solutions for United States institutions.[63]

In 2022, Dayenu launched a report, *All Our Might*, providing a baseline of Jewish communal investment dollars invested in fossil fuels. The report offers both Jewish and financial arguments for why now is the right moment for Jewish institutions to join the movement screening out fossil fuels.

Dayenu offers a six-step process for organizations ready to meet the challenge. First, begin by understanding the issue from a Jewish perspective. Then, research your current investment portfolio. Educate yourself and your institution. Engage with your asset managers to signal your intentions. Make a plan; and finally, move your money. Dayenu's approach is to invite organizations into the process, rather than to call out or shame anyone. It provides extensive resources to Jewish organizations along the journey.

Addressing the Arguments Against Divestment

Some still argue for retaining stock in fossil fuel companies in order to advocate with them to transition their businesses away from fossil fuels. Of course, investors would then be responsible to regularly engage in this advocacy. No one in the socially responsible investing community claims that it is acceptable to own fossil fuel companies—the largest contributors to the climate crisis—without advocating with them to transition their business to cleaner energy. Judaism echoes this moral position. We saw in Chapter 7 that if there is a shareholder campaign targeting a corporation to improve its behavior, and I fail to support the campaign and instead default to management's perspective, Jewish law implicates me in the outcome.

Investors on the side of own-and-advocate have argued that divestment is ineffective. They claim the point of divestment is to make it more expensive for a company to do business and raise capital, but divestment will never be successful in doing so. According to one estimate from Stanford Business professor Jonathan Berk, to actually raise the cost of capital for companies, even by a minimal 1 percent, requires an astronomical 86 percent of the investment market to be committed to divestment.[64]

However, recent research demonstrates otherwise. Academics from Harvard University and universities in Stockholm and Brussels have released a paper featured in 2023 in the *Financial Times* that made this point. Fossil fuel divestment pledges over the past few years that gained traction on social media have actually had an outsized impact on fossil fuel companies' share prices, mainly by "changing the economic narrative." The researchers noted that divestment builds on itself, highlighting the risk of continuing to hold fossil fuel companies and inspiring other investors to avoid that risk.[65]

This is an important point: The goal is not only to raise the cost of new capital, but to challenge a company's social license for doing business. Berk's calculations fail to account for that cost. Bill McKibben of 350.org made a similar point in an op-ed in *The New York Times* in October 2021 titled, "This Movement Is Taking Money Away From Fossil Fuels, and It's Working." McKibben celebrated that the movement had reached over $40 trillion dollars: "If money talks, $40 trillion makes a lot of noise."

Those arguing for own-and-advocate might point out that for the moment, our society still needs fossil fuels to power our homes, synagogues, and hospitals. But investors screening out fossil fuels are not seeking to immediately destroy fossil fuel infrastructure. Rather, they are aligning their investments with their values and stemming the tide of ongoing expansion of fossil fuels that leads us in the opposite direction we need to go.

Proponents of owning and engaging companies argue along the lines of Alfred O. Hirschman, the Jewish economist we encountered in Chapter 4 who wrote *Exit, Voice, and Loyalty*. Hirschman argues that divesting from a company means giving up one's voice, which ultimately means one is less effective in pressuring the company to move.[66] More recent research argues against this claim, offering evidence that faith-based investors retain significant voice even after they exit.[67] But some investors are not yet convinced and believe they will be more effective at influencing oil and gas companies to change their business models through owning stock.

Proponents of the own-and-advocate approach might even point to wins like a recent shareholder campaign targeting ExxonMobil, the largest oil company in the US, in 2021. At Exxon's annual meeting, the company experienced what some called a shareholder revolt. A group of organizations led by an activist hedge fund, Engine No. 1, proposed a slate of four new board members for Exxon's twelve-member board. Incredibly, thanks to the support of values-based investors working alongside mainstream investors, three of the four were elected. News outlets called this unprecedented churn-up of an oil company's board by an investor concerned about climate a "milestone in climate-driven activism" and a "stunning victory."[68]

A few weeks after the momentous win at Exxon, Anne Simpson, Managing Investment Director at California's giant public pension fund CalPERS, noted with chagrin that if fewer major institutions concerned with climate change had divested from oil and gas, the activist hedge fund's fourth director would probably have been voted on as well.[69]

However, when I spoke to Engine No. 1's managing director and leader of its impact strategy, he disagreed with Simpson. To him, it was crucial to have a robust global divestment campaign from fossil fuels. The campaign forced all investors to reckon with their oil and gas holdings even if they did not choose to divest. From Engine No. 1's perspective, without the global fossil-fuel-free movement, zero of the four new directors would have been elected.[70] Surprisingly strong words, from one of the leaders of the own-and-advocate approach, for the value of fossil fuel divestment.

In the time since those board members have been elected, there has been little meaningful change.[71] Because of this, in 2023 faith-based investors began voting against reelection for the entire board at Exxon (including the three new "climate competent" directors) for failure to take meaningful action on climate.[72] The success of appointing three new board directors at Exxon was itself a symptom of the shift in public opinion that the fossil-fuel-free movement is creating. And whatever the new board members do accomplish will be thanks to the social climate shift that created the conditions for them to succeed. The time is increasingly ripe for investors to move their investments out of fossil fuels and invest in a clean energy future.

Investor Advocacy on Climate

Advocacy and divestment are complementary because even for those who have taken the courageous step to divest from fossil fuel companies, it is nearly impossible to avoid other investments that in some way impact the climate. There are banks that finance fossil fuel projects, insurance companies that insure them, food and agriculture companies whose supply chains impact the soil and deforestation of agricultural land, and more. Our world still runs on fossil fuels for now, and so do our investment portfolios.

The good news is that advocacy with these sectors can make a meaningful difference. Consider the financial sector. Banks and investment companies play a crucial role financing new fossil fuel infrastructure. The finance industry as a whole has a failing track record of taking action on climate change.[73]

At the same time, banks and investment companies across the world are facing increasing pressure for their financing of fossil fuel expansion. When Bloomberg broke the news that Russia's largest coal producer and coal plant operator was issuing bonds with the support of Bank of America and Citi as well as a number of European and other banks, investors immediately began calling on the banks to terminate their role in the bond offering and end financing of new coal projects.[74]

In 2017, shareholder advocates filed a resolution with BlackRock, the largest asset manager in the world. BlackRock owns trillions of dollars of shares of major companies. The company has the right, and the responsibility, to vote the proxy ballots of each of those shares for each company's annual general meeting (we saw more about proxy voting in Chapters 6 and 7). Yet BlackRock has a historically atrocious track record on the environment (and on other issues, like racial justice, which we will explore more in Chapter 11). Investors filed a resolution demanding the company change its voting record on climate issues. In this case, the act of filing itself was enough to motivate the company to agree, so investors withdrew their resolution prior to the annual meeting.[75] The following year, BlackRock indicated its willingness to vote in favor of more shareholder resolutions and supported a climate-related resolution at oil giant BP.[76]

The company still has plenty of work to do. We saw in Chapter 4 how the Jewish Youth Climate Movement in 2021 blockaded BlackRock's headquarters to protest the investment company's continued investment in fossil fuel infrastructure despite its stated commitment to combat climate change. And the wave of anti-ESG efforts in 2023 caused many banks and asset managers to pull back on even the meager climate commitments they had made a few years prior. However, most investors believe that climate change is real and poses a material threat to our investment portfolios. Moving these institutions will be slow going, but we need to advocate and ensure our majority voice is heard by banks and asset managers.

Changing Climates

Or consider climate lobbying. As we saw in Chapter 7, public companies used to be prohibited from lobbying the government. Today, they regularly spend millions to lobby national, state, and local politicians. Many companies use their lobbying power to advocate for gutting restrictions on the production and burning of fossil fuels. The environment-focused investor organization Ceres noted in 2021 that while a significant majority of companies acknowledge climate change as a risk to their operations, fewer than half align their government lobbying to support climate change policy.[77]

When the government will not hold companies to account, investors have a crucial role to play. While values-based investors have been pressuring corporations for decades to be more transparent and accountable in their lobbying,[78] investors have escalated pressure in recent years. In August 2021, Fiona Reynolds, CEO of the largest responsible-investing organization in the world, called on investors to advocate with regulators and policymakers around the world to end anti-climate corporate lobbying.[79]

Investor pressure has played an important role over the past decade, especially in conjunction with broader movements for social change. Several companies, including AIG, Entergy, and FirstEnergy, committed to change their direct and indirect lobbying (for example, which trade associations they join) to more closely align themselves with the goals of the Paris Climate Accords to limit global warming to 1.5 degrees Celsius. Companies including CSX and Duke Energy agreed in 2021 to issue a report examining their lobbying in light of the climate crisis.[80] Thanks to a combination of investor and grassroots pressure, more than 100 companies have renounced membership in the trade association that most undermines climate change regulations.[81]

Climate change is a systemic issue in our economy, which means that opportunities abound for us to address them. For example, food waste is a major issue in the United States that affects both climate change and hunger. Estimates suggest one third of all available food in the United States goes uneaten through loss or waste,[82] while over 50 million people in the US face questions about where their next meal will come from.[83] Food waste that is thrown away instead of being eaten or composted also contributes to climate emissions.

In my previous work with the impact investing organization JLens, we filed a shareholder resolution with Amazon, which owns Whole Foods as well as brands like Amazon Fresh and Amazon Go, calling on the company to take more action to reduce its food waste. The resolution garnered over 30 percent of shareholder votes, and the company ultimately conceded to the investor pressure to implement steps to reduce its food waste.[84]

Deforestation is another issue directly related to climate: trees are nature's best "carbon sink," meaning they capture and sequester carbon currently in the atmosphere. Fewer trees means less carbon sequestered and more of it in the atmosphere.

185

The World Resources Institute notes that deforestation globally increased 12 percent between 2019 and 2020, representing an area the size of the Netherlands.[85] A significant percentage of this deforestation is caused by companies that produce agricultural commodities. Investors have scored recent wins on deforestation, including a shareholder resolution by Green Century Funds in 2021 targeting one of the "Big 4" global agricultural commodity traders that earned an unprecedented 98 percent of the shareholder vote. Investors also filed a successful shareholder resolution on deforestation at consumer-goods company Procter and Gamble.[86]

If you are looking for a place to get started, there are a number of socially responsible mutual funds that screen out coal, oil, and gas companies. A great place to start is to rate your own investments and their exposure to fossil fuels. As You Sow, a nonprofit shareholder advocacy organization, offers an easy online tool that calculates your investment portfolio's exposure to fossil fuels at fossilfreefunds.org.[87]

There are also a growing number of mutual funds, available to even a modest investor, that engage in advocacy with a range of companies across sectors on climate change. Some funds like Green Century aim to do both, divesting from fossil fuels while advocating with companies to reduce their environmental pollution, like encouraging Coca-Cola to reduce its reliance on virgin plastic.[88]

Investing in Climate Solutions

In the introductory chapter, we explored how saying "no!" to current unsustainable systems is not enough. Divesting from fossil fuels is a crucial form of "no." Yet when we divest, we are inherently putting our money elsewhere—that's a "yes," which is why some call the global fossil-fuel-free campaign DivestInvest.[89] We need both.

To stem the tide of the climate crisis, we need to stop funding the expansion of new fossil-fuel infrastructure. Dayenu, the Jewish climate change nonprofit we encountered earlier, quotes that for every dollar we keep investing in fossil fuels, we would need an astronomical four dollars in clean energy investments. Dayenu notes: "Impact investing in climate without also screening out fossil fuel companies is like undergoing lung treatment while continuing to smoke."[90] But, once we have ensured our investments are not funding and profiting from the expansion of fossil fuel infrastructure, we also need to think about how they can fund the clean-energy transition.

When we engage in shareholder advocacy with public companies to reduce their reliance on climate-destructive technology, that is a "no." But, ideally, we are articulating a vision for what business operations should look like, in line with justice and science, which is a "yes."

The same balance is true on the personal level. On the one hand, it is important for those who use more than our fair share of the world's energy to scale back.[91] This includes climate-efficient ways of living our daily lives as well as simply using less—not in ways that cause deprivation, but, rather, in ways that actually increase happiness. In Chapter 2, we spoke about "right-sizing" our lives, Judaism's value of living with gratitude, and how the moment does not call for deprivation for those with the privilege to have more than enough but rather to "give up poison." Following Rabbi Rosenn and Bill McKibben's earlier advice, getting involved in movements sharp enough to make change also provides us a sense of nourishment and purpose in the face of what can feel like an overwhelming crisis.

We also need to be seeking out the "yes" of a more sustainable way of life. That will need to include widespread sources of renewable energy. 750 million people still lack access to modern energy sources, most of them in sub-Saharan Africa.[92] Access to modern energy is a key pillar of environmental justice. Today, lack of energy access primarily affects the global poor, preventing storage of lifesaving vaccines, forcing people (especially women and girls) to spend hours fetching water, and making it harder for business owners to compete in the global marketplace.[93]

We need widescale ways of generating renewable energy, and investment capital is an essential tool. Investors contribute the money needed to rapidly grow sustainable energy solutions. The United Nations recommends tripling clean-energy investment by 2030. The UN even adopted access to clean, affordable energy as one of its 17 Sustainable Development Goals. And a growing number of investment funds (too many to explore in this book) offer a range of approaches to fund renewable energy and other climate solutions.

Jewish ethics exhort us to use our resources to solve problems affecting the public. In fact, when a hazard has arisen in the public domain that poses a danger to life, Jewish law places an obligation upon each of us to take action to clean it up. This law originates in the Torah, which commands, "beware for yourself, and guard your life."[94] The Torah also warns against failing to act, and one who could have dealt with a hazard and failed to do so is included in responsibility for whatever happens.[95] These laws were incorporated into the Jewish legal codes, including the comprehensive works of the Rambam in 12th-century Egypt.[96]

Rabbi Yerucham Fishel Perlow (1846-1934, Poland) builds on this point. If a public thoroughfare is high enough to pose a threat to those who fall from it, the responsibility falls on the communal authorities to build a fence to protect the public. If they fail to do so, the obligation devolves onto each and every one of us.[97] So too, the public hazard that is the climate crisis requires each of us to step up to take action.

Some of the most innovative and promising climate investment opportunities will be available only to accredited investors, the wealthy class of investor described in Chapter 9 with more than a million dollars in net worth. But one category of climate solution investments is accessible to every individual or organization that owns its own building—investing in greening your real estate assets.

For example, the Jewish Alliance of Greater Rhode Island has been on an environmental journey for a number of years. The organization underwent a strategic planning process, and, due to the encouragement of community members and stakeholders, social responsibility in general and climate specifically became key themes of the strategic plan.

The Alliance has a large facility. It serves as the community's Federation, Jewish Community Center, Jewish Community Relations Council, and more, all literally under the same roof. That roof was not large enough to hold solar panels to power the facility. So the Alliance worked with a private developer to develop a solar panel array off-site (they carefully chose a site that was unavailable for other forms of development). The array went live in January 2022 and powers 100 percent of the operations of the building with renewable energy. It also saves the organization $45,000 per year. Further, the Alliance negotiated with the developer to offer a similarly beneficial rate to any synagogue or Jewish building throughout the state seeking to green its real estate assets. The Alliance also included climate change in its political advocacy through its Jewish Community Relations Council arm and is in the process of building relationships with local environmental organizations through volunteer service.[98]

An increasing number of Jewish organizations have begun moving their assets to align with the urgency of the climate crisis. This includes several foundations who have committed to screening out fossil fuels, including the Nathan Cummings Foundation we encountered in Chapter 4; Jewish organizations like the American Jewish World Service; and a number of synagogues. The list is growing on a regular basis.[99]

In 2022, Adamah, a flagship Jewish environmental organization, launched the Jewish Climate Leadership Coalition. The Coalition represents an explicit commitment by mainstream Jewish institutions to do more to address the climate crisis, with partners including all of the major Jewish denominations and other umbrella bodies of Jewish life.[100]

Member organizations commit to creating a climate action plan that aims to reduce and eventually eliminate greenhouse gas emissions from an organization's building—its carbon footprint—while also expanding an organization's impact beyond its own walls. This is an example of combining both the individual and collective orientations we talked about at the beginning of this chapter to achieve the greatest reach possible. And one of the key solution areas for expanding impact? An organization's investment portfolio.

The Jewish Climate Leadership Coalition provides interest-free green loans and matching grants, inspired by The Associated: Jewish Federation of Baltimore. Over the past number of years, The Associated has leveraged its assets to offer nearly $1 million in interest-free loans to local Jewish institutions for energy efficient installations, solar roof projects, and more. The organization reports zero defaults.

The Associated has also invested in greening its own real estate assets, installing a four-megawatt rooftop solar farm that powers the equivalent of 50 percent of the electricity consumed in The Associated's buildings and 100 percent of Adamah's electricity for its Pearlstone campus in Maryland. The solar panels save the Federation $100,000 per year. Climate change has become a regular part of the Baltimore Federation's advocacy agenda with local and state politicians every year.[101]

Definitions of Fossil-Fuel-Free

Fossil-fuel-free investing can mean different things to different people (in good Jewish fashion, there is a debate). The simplest definition is owning no stake in companies whose business is to produce oil, gas, or coal. All three of these fossil fuels contribute substantially to the climate crisis, including natural gas, which, when burned, emits the extremely potent greenhouse gas methane.

You might not own many stocks directly, instead investing in funds. As an investor in a fund, you are a part-owner of each of the investments in the fund. So if the fund owns stock in BP or Exxon, so do you. If you want to know your fund's exposure to fossil fuel producers, you can use the handy calculator at Fossil Free Funds (fossilfreefunds.org, published by the nonprofit As You Sow).

An alternative definition focuses only on the companies who own the largest 100 coal and largest 100 oil and gas reserves. This list is known as the Carbon Underground 200™ and is maintained by FFI Solutions. The Carbon Underground 200 companies collectively own more than 97 percent of those reserves, so this definition offers a more manageable list of companies that still goes a long way toward to eliminating fossil fuels from an investment portfolio.

A stronger definition of fossil-fuel-free includes utility companies that provide electricity from fossil-fuel sources. As You Sow's tool will indicate if you are invested in any of the most fossil-fuel-intensive utilities, including Duke Energy, American Electric Power, and more. A reasonable place to start, grounded in Jewish values, would be to screen out energy producers but own utility companies and advocate with them to shift their energy supply to renewables.

Judaism's Spiritual Guidance for Climate Change

Sometimes the issue of climate change can take on an apocalyptic tone. Every milestone passed feels more dire. The organization 350.org was founded in 2007 with a goal of keeping our atmospheric pollution below 350 parts per million, a goal that may now feel outlandish, as the atmosphere has surpassed 420.[102] The 2015 Paris Climate Accords' goal of keeping global warming below 1.5 degrees Celsius already feels nearly impossible. 2030 is approaching, the next major milestone, we are told, of irrevocable devastation.

Judaism can help us navigate this overwhelm. It can be easy for those living in Christian-dominated societies to forget that our frequent frame of an inclement apocalypse is a cultural choice, not a scientific fact. History as a battle between good and evil, with the world about to be destroyed and hanging in the balance—these are tropes so common in Western society that we often fail to realize they are cultural choices.

Judaism offers us a different path, a path that is not so starkly, depressingly binary. The Sages taught that a return to right relationship motivated by love is greater than a return to right relationship motivated by fear.[103] Our faith insists that actions always make a difference. On the one hand, it has always been too late to act to prevent people from dying from societal injustice. On the other hand, it is never too late to change or mitigate the conditions that might perpetuate human suffering in the future. We need to take that action together, and our investment portfolios are a particularly powerful and vital tool to join the fray.

The first modern shareholder resolution on climate change was filed in 1989, pressuring General Electric to reduce its impact on the environment.[104] In the Torah, it took 400 years and ten plagues before the Israelites went free from Egypt. As Jews, we know that change happens slowly—until it doesn't.

Next Steps—Chapter 10

Investors have been "owning and advocating" with fossil fuel companies for decades, yet progress has been superficial or nonexistent. There is a growing global movement to move investment capital away from fossil fuel producers and invest, instead, in scaling up renewable energy technology. Momentum is also building within the Jewish community. Some rabbinic authorities are even arguing that fossil fuels should be considered forbidden by Jewish law except in cases of need, so Jewish law would compel Jewish investors to screen out fossil fuels.

- **Step 1: Journal on the following prompts:**
  - Begin from a spiritual place. How do I feel about the climate crisis?
  - How do I feel about other apocalyptic fears I notice in our society, on any other issues?
  - Read the following prompt, and journal about your reactions: "Apocalyptic framings are a choice. Judaism offers an alternative. It has always been too late—and it is never too late. Change happens slowly—until it doesn't. And the best antidote to despair is action—especially action taken together."
- **Step 2: Map your current investment portfolio.** Use the Fossil Free Funds tool (fossilfreefunds.org) from the organization As You Sow.
- **Step 3: Screen out fossil fuels.** Take the leap to screen out fossil fuel companies from your portfolio.
  - Ask your financial advisor for help. If they are unable to help, find a financial advisor who has more expertise and willingness to meet you in your values.
- **Step 4: Engage in shareholder advocacy (see Chapter 7).**
  - Even once you screen out fossil fuel companies from your investment portfolio, there is more to do. Fossil fuels play a systemic role in our economy, so every company relies on them to some extent. Advocacy with other companies (like banks who are financing fossil fuel projects) will help reduce their role in supporting fossil-fuel infrastructure.
  - Organizations like Carbon Collective or Green Century Funds seek to combine these strategies: divest from fossil fuel producers, and advocate with fossil fuel financiers and other companies to reduce their climate impact.

- **Step 5: Invest in clean energy and greening solutions.**
  - Given the climate crisis we face, Jewish tradition compels adherents to seek opportunities to invest in renewable energy and other climate solutions. Can you use any of your investment dollars to invest in greening your own home or your organization's building and property?
  - Ask a financial advisor for other opportunities to invest in climate solutions.

Chapter 11

Centering Racial Justice

Cat Berman looked at her finances online one day and saw several thousand dollars in her bank account. Rather than feeling pleased, she felt perturbed. "I thought to myself, *What am I doing? Why do I have all this money just sitting in my savings account, and not doing good for anybody?*"

Berman was a particularly apt person to ask that question. On the one hand, analyzing financial statements is an area of expertise for her. She holds an MBA from Oxford and launched two successful social enterprise startups. At the moment this story took place, Berman was working as a Managing Director at Charles Schwab.[1]

On the other hand, Berman has always had a passion for social justice, inspired by her own identity.[2] Her mother, a Sephardic Jew, fled Argentina for the United States, where she met Berman's father. Once here, Berman's mother faced social barriers and lack of equal access to opportunities, an experience that strongly influenced Berman's own values. Jewish community and its focus on justice was an ongoing thread for Berman, who as a child attended Jewish camp, had a bat mitzvah, and belonged to her local Jewish Community Center. She lived in Israel twice as a young adult.[3]

Seeking to deposit her cash in an institution that could use it to benefit others, Berman attempted to invest her bank account funds in a Community Development Financial Institution (CDFI). We have seen CDFIs recur throughout this book. CDFIs can be banks, credit unions, or loan funds. They are certified by the Treasury Department. CDFIs meet stringent standards for how their capital is directed—through loans, technical assistance, and other investments—to support communities and entrepreneurs that have historically been denied access to capital, especially communities of color.

Berman found it difficult as an individual to invest in a CDFI. "It's not that CDFIs don't need the cash," she explains: "There's a huge unmet need. CDFIs have a deficit of over $600 million in loans they want to be doing but lack the capital to make happen." Yet at the same time, "they're just not equipped to handle and vet small individual [investments]."

Berman decided to launch CNote, an online impact investing platform that would enable individuals to pool their investment dollars and invest in CDFIs across the country. CNote broke new ground when it was qualified by the Security and Exchange Commission for the mass market.[4] This means that everyday individual investors, not just wealthy investors, can invest in CNote. We have encountered other investment products, like Calvert Impact's Community Impact Notes, that invest capital in community-focused institutions like CDFIs and offer low minimums appropriate for everyday investors. But those opportunities require longer-term commitments, where money is invested for years at a time. CNote is unique in that it offers higher liquidity, appropriate for investors with extra cash in their bank accounts, like Berman's experience. CNote's Flagship Fund returned 2 percent as of the end of 2022 (and has increased during this era of higher inflation) and has no minimum investment requirement.[5]

Berman and her co-founder Yuliya Tarasava, despite bringing decades of investment experience, were aware that "we don't look like today's finance executives," both because of their gender and because of their approach to using capital for social good.[6] Their product is meant to compete in the financial marketplace, and they have had to work harder than men to build credibility for it. The CNote Flagship Fund has suffered no losses since its inception.[7]

As the child of a Jewish and South American immigrant to the United States, Berman feels a special connection to people facing barriers and individuals in need. In running CNote, her goal is to "go where the need is."

The wealth gap between white and Black households is larger than between any other racial or ethnic groups, according to the Federal Reserve, with the average white family holding nearly 10 times as much wealth as the average Black family.[8] But owning a business can be transformative as a tool for building wealth. CNote's website notes that "the median net worth for Black business owners is 12 times higher than Black nonbusiness owners." The biggest problem for many entrepreneurs of color is a lack of access to startup capital. CNote, through its CDFI investments, bridges that gap. Over 50 percent of CNote's capital is invested in small businesses led by Black or Indigenous people of color, and over 40 percent is invested in women-led small businesses (eight times the national average).[9]

Racial justice is the center of CNote's work. As Berman told me, "The whole point is closing the racial wealth gap. If we aren't doing that, we might as well not be here."

This is a chapter about centering racial justice in our investment portfolios. Concretely, that means seeking to advance racial justice through our investments and assessing the overall impact of our investments by how they affect racial justice. For example, if an investment harms people of color, that overshadows other positive impacts it may seek to achieve.

Now, some might see centering racial justice and investment as mutually exclusive.

The investment arena itself has played a significant role in exacerbating racial injustice for centuries (as we saw in Chapter 1). Any effort to invest in support of racial justice requires acknowledging the full scale of that harm, ceasing to cause further harm, and making amends for the harm already caused. We also need to be advocating for national and political reckoning with our country's history of racism. We will learn more about these crucial steps later in the chapter.

At the same time, investment capital plays a unique role in building a more just society. It is possible and important for investors to bring racial justice into every asset class. In November 2021, a group of four organizations in the social impact sphere released a "Starting List to Invest for Racial Equity" with over 100 funds on it.[10]

There is an especially important role for capital invested for long periods of time at a reasonably low and not excessive rate of return. In fact, access to capital is so important that an entire movement of community-development finance arose to address it. The movement began growing in the 1970s as a response to communities and entrepreneurs of color who sought investment capital and were shut out of traditional banking channels. CNote is a direct outgrowth of that movement. Faith-based investors historically played a leadership role, and we can lead the way again today.

We will begin this chapter by understanding the Jewish imperative to center racial justice in our investing decisions. We will then explore concrete ways investors can re-align their capital to be furthering rather than hindering racial justice, inspired by Jewish values. This chapter will be heavily focused on the United States but hopefully can serve as an inspiration to people living in other geographies as well. It will mostly focus on anti-Black and anti-Indigenous racism, as those two forms of racism have played an especially significant role in the history of the investment arena. But the same principles apply broadly to racism of any form. The good news is that centering racial justice in our investment portfolios can help us tackle a wide range of problems at the same time.

Judaism's Response to Racial Injustice

This chapter uses a definition of racism as discrimination by members of a society's dominant ethnicity perpetrated against people of other ethnicities. Racism is bias and dehumanization directed against individuals because of their race, coupled with the institutional and societal power to create systems that discriminate against them.

Judaism's response to contemporary racism begins with the foundational Jewish belief that every human being is created in the Divine image (in Hebrew, *tzelem elohim*), a belief grounded all the way back in the creation narrative at the beginning of the Torah.

This powerful religious principle affirms the inherent dignity of every single person, even across differences. The Sages of the Talmud offer a metaphor: when a human stamps coins from a mold, the coins can only turn out similar to each other. Yet God has been able to "stamp" billions of humans in the Divine image, and each comes out as a different, unique person. The precept that all humans are made in the Divine image means that each human has Divine worth. As Rabbi Lord Sacks wrote in his book *The Dignity of Difference*, "We encounter God in the face of a stranger. That, I believe, is the Hebrew Bible's single greatest and most counterintuitive contribution to ethics. God creates difference; therefore it is in one-who-is-different that we meet God."[11]

The rabbis note that the principle of *tzelem elohim* also prevents one person from claiming superiority, saying to another, "my father is greater than your father."[12] It is the direct source for the Jewish belief quoted in the Mishnah that "one who saves a single life is as if they had saved an entire world."[13]

Tzelem elohim is a foundational principle for approaching racial justice. As Isabel Wilkerson describes in her book *Caste*, the systems of racism in the United States required dehumanization to make them psychologically viable, which became possible only when white people developed cultures and structures to distance themselves from people of color, and Black people in particular.[14] Contemporary racism in the United States is the result of deliberate policies instituted by our society over the course of centuries to dehumanize people of color, to deny their *tzelem elohim* and human dignity, which justified taking their wealth. This racism, especially through slavery of Black people and attempted genocide of Indigenous people, became fundamental to the investment arena.[15]

As we saw investment practitioner Ed Whitfield note in Chapter 1, the contemporary investment arena is like a poker table loaded with stolen goods. We saw in that chapter some ways that the United States loaded the table with stolen labor from Black people of African ancestry working on land taken from Indigenous people. But the theft did not stop in the 1800s.

The Center for American Progress, a research and advocacy think tank, explains: "white households first benefited from the dehumanizing system of slavery—directly, in this case, as a white slaveholding plantation class—but also from the discriminatory institutions that emerged and persisted after the Civil War."

Just one poignant example of this theft and its impact on the investment arena is the destruction of what was known as "Black Wall Street," a thriving center of successful Black businesses in Tulsa, Oklahoma, in 1921. The Center for American Progress notes this was just one of many horrid and systematic examples where "private businesses and governments institutionalized racism and discrimination. They also encouraged and sanctioned violence targeting Black lives and property."[16] Ku Klux Klan leaders, working alongside the Tulsa Police Department and the Oklahoma

National Guard, killed 300 people and destroyed millions of dollars' worth of property in the nation's deadliest massacre. In the aftermath, insurance claims were denied, and thousands of individuals were rounded up and taken to internment camps. African Americans refused to be defeated and quickly rebuilt, but their resilience does not erase the injustice of racism.[17]

Another hurdle the US government created for African Americans to build wealth and invest in themselves was redlining. Redlining refers to the practice of denying mortgages to people living in predominantly minority neighborhoods. The name came from the maps drawn by the federal agency Home Owners' Loan Corporation (HOLC) in the 1930s that marked those neighborhoods in red. The HOLC considered those neighborhoods riskier investments and allowed banks to deny loans to those communities because of the risk. The Federal Housing Authority and the Veterans Administration adopted the same lines.

Richard Rothstein, author of *The Color of Law*, notes that at the same time as the federal government was redlining districts with large populations of Black people, it was subsidizing entire subdivisions of homes for white people—with the requirement that none of the homes be sold to African Americans. These and other United States regulations, explicitly designed to segregate, ended up trapping Black people in a cycle that made it nearly impossible for them to access capital to purchase their own homes.[18] And the few African American families who did manage to purchase homes in more affluent, white neighborhoods were often targeted by their neighbors with property damage, violence, and ongoing intimidation.[19]

The Fair Housing Act that prohibited practices like redlining wasn't passed until 1968, and the impacts of redlining persist in many cities across the country.[20] This has a direct connection to the massive Black-white wealth disparity that has existed for decades. According to the Mapping Inequality Project at the University of Richmond, "As homeownership was arguably the most significant means of intergenerational wealth building in the United States in the twentieth century, these redlining practices from eight decades ago had long-term effects in creating wealth inequalities that we still see today."[21] Rothstein argues that beyond any income disparities, almost the entire gain in wealth that white families have achieved over Black families over the course of the 20th century is due to federal housing policy and its implementation.[22] Discrimination continues in various forms today, including through racial bias in home appraisals and mortgage rates, which according to the Brookings Institution have lost Black homeowners $156 billion.[23]

Those wealth inequalities were maintained through the active participation of government policy, especially the tax code. Dorothy Brown is a tax lawyer and Black woman who grew up in the South Bronx. She recently published the book *The Whiteness of Wealth: How the Tax System Impoverishes Black Americans–and How We Can*

Fix It. Brown notes numerous ways in which the tax system, designed by an all-white Congress and a president who supported segregation in the federal civil service in the early 1910s, continues to discriminate against Black Americans.[24]

The Patriotic Millionaires, a group of several hundred wealthy citizens advocating for a more just tax code that would "tax the rich," lay out detailed examples. They cite government tax policies from which the (mostly white) group has benefited that have created or maintained hurdles for most Black people who attempt to build, maintain, and pass on wealth. "Massive disparities are allowed to continue through tax preferences like a substantially lower tax rate on capital gains, and loopholes like the stepped-up basis. The stepped-up basis allows inheritors of large fortunes or assets to avoid paying taxes on their assets or inheritance while folks who earn their living through a paycheck (as a majority of Black families do in the US) end up paying a higher tax rate than the wealthy heirs."[25]

The systems of exploitation of Black labor continue into the 21st century. When the 13th Amendment prohibited slavery, it allowed an exception for involuntary servitude for people convicted of a crime. At the same time, a number of states passed vagrancy laws which made it a criminal offense not to work (or even to walk around outside without a job) and were selectively applied to Blacks, funneling them into the convict leasing system.[26] Today, United States policies of mass incarceration and the effects of discrimination still disproportionately affect Black people at every step of the criminal justice process.[27] Over two million individuals are incarcerated in prisons in the United States, and nearly all who are able-bodied work in some way, leading to a billion-dollar industry.[28] A recent report identified over 4,000 corporations benefiting from prison labor in the US, meaning many modern investment portfolios are literally profiting from this horrible offense against human dignity.[29]

We can feel the lasting impacts of racism against people of color in the investment arena today. Even today, communities of color are sometimes seen as "too risky for investment." This is simply inaccurate. Consider the experience of community development financial institutions, like Pacific Community Ventures, a CDFI that makes millions of dollars of loans to communities of color. Pacific Community Ventures' CEO notes that the organization's own lending portfolio "shows this assumption is false. Even through COVID, as we doubled the size of our small business lending portfolio—and deployed over 76 percent of our capital to entrepreneurs of color and women across the State of California, with 85 percent invested in economically distressed communities—we managed to maintain a lower than 1 percent write-off rate. This is less than the 1.3 percent average loan loss rate of US banks in 2020."[30]

The wealth that Black and Indigenous people of color were deprived of flowed instead to those higher up on what Isabel Wilkerson refers to as the caste ladder. And while not every white family grew rich thanks to racism, racism loaded the poker table with stolen goods, enabling those who won to win bigger, to use Ed Whitfield's metaphor.

It is not easy to talk about the history of racism and its effects on white families' abilities to accumulate wealth and investment capital. Yet doing so is crucial for impact investors to actually make a positive impact. Edgar Villanueva, expert on racism and philanthropy, notes that many conversations happening in the social-impact fields about wealth and grant dollars are like "rearranging the deck chairs on the *Titanic*" instead of having "frank conversations about where that wealth came from, why it's held back from public coffers," and more.[31] Anne Price, president of the Insight Center for Community Economic Development, asks: "How do we move forward with systems change work when we haven't even counted up the cost?"[32]

Once we see that racism functions as a system of dehumanization that also enables some to steal from others—theft of land, theft of labor, theft of opportunity—we can understand that rehumanizing the relationship requires addressing past and current wrongs. This frame can also be helpful in clarifying that racial justice is not about intent, but about impact. Those of us who have benefited from the thefts listed above may see ourselves as innocent of any harmful intent; those who caused the greatest harms are mostly in the past. But Ed Whitfield's metaphor of playing poker at a table loaded with stolen goods makes clear that any of us who seek to "deal into the game," so to speak, join in responsibility for those stolen goods.

Judaism calls this process of addressing past wrongs *teshuvah*. The word *teshuvah* is often translated as repentance but goes much deeper. It literally means "return"—a return to right relationship.

Shahanna McKinney-Baldon, founder and director of *Edot: The Midwest Regional Jewish Diversity Collaborative* and a Jew of color, brings a teaching from the Mishnah. The Mishnah makes a distinction between two kinds of transgressions: those between an individual and God, and those between fellow humans. For transgressions between an individual and God, the holiday of Yom Kippur serves as atonement every year. But transgressions between two fellow humans are not resolved until the one who caused the offense makes things whole with the one who was harmed, through a process of *teshuvah*. McKinney-Baldon relates this Mishnah directly to how we reckon with past and current racism. Internal remorse and spiritual growth alone are sufficient for spiritual mistakes, but harm caused to other human beings requires a more substantive response.[33]

Our country's collective process of *teshuvah* must include a reckoning with the staggering scale of theft from Black and Indigenous people. Once we do, the Torah has a clear moral response to theft: things that are stolen must be returned.[34]

Reparations

The concept of reparations for race-based slavery and genocide has existed for decades but has gained popularity in mainstream media in recent years, including through Ta-Nehisi Coates' landmark article in *The Atlantic* in 2014, "The Case for Reparations."[35] Reparations are based on the idea that stolen goods must be returned. Despite any political controversy, reparations are a fairly straightforward concept from a Jewish perspective. In fact, contemporary activist Rabbi Aryeh Bernstein grounds the Jewish approach to reparations in the Exodus narrative in the Torah: "Jews must support reparations in principle, because we took reparations for our slave labor, we were commanded by God to do so, and we were promised these reparations in the earliest Divine plan for our liberation."[36]

Let's turn to the book of Exodus to witness the scene. After the 10th and final plague, the Israelites finally left their 400-year enslavement in Egypt:

> The Israelites had done according to the word of Moses; they asked of the Egyptians silver items and gold items and clothing. God granted the people favor in the eyes of the Egyptians, so that they gave them what they asked. That is how they emptied out the Egyptians.[37]

In more modern times, Jews and the Jewish State have received reparations from the German government.[38] These reparations can never compensate for the atrocities of the Holocaust, but they have been an important part of an ongoing repentance and healing process for modern Germany. And they were quite controversial in Israel, but also crucial to the stabilization of the country's economy in the mid-20th century. Ta-Nehisi Coates himself cites this example when building a case for reparations for Black Americans.[39]

A vital place to start when we think about centering racial justice is the return of stolen capital and recompense for stolen labor. Until the theft is acknowledged and made whole, all other interventions will be temporary fixes.

This can feel overwhelming. How can our society ever pay back the millions of hours of labor and lives stolen from Black people? How can we pay back the land and the cultures and the lives stolen from Indigenous Americans?

Jewish sources themselves acknowledge the difficulty that people will have in returning stolen goods once they have been woven into the fabric of our lives. Contemporary rabbi Sharon Brous highlights this by quoting a Talmudic teaching:

> There is 2,000-year-old rabbinic dispute over what ought to be done if a palace is built on the foundation of a stolen beam.
>
> One rabbi, Shammai, argues that the whole structure must be torn down, the beam retrieved and returned to its rightful owner. No home can flourish on a foundation built illegally and immorally. Another rabbi, Hillel, offers a different take: What sense does it make to demolish it? Let the thief pay for the beam, considering its full value as the foundation of what is now a beautiful home. Neither argues that you can pretend, year after year, generation after generation, that the beam wasn't stolen.
>
> Our country was built on a stolen beam. More accurately, several million stolen beams. Only they weren't beams. They were human beings. The palace they built was magnificent, but they have never been compensated for their labor.[40]

In other words, Jewish tradition respects the psychological challenges that thieves face in returning their stolen objects. From a Jewish perspective, reparations need not look like a literal return of all stolen goods in exactly the condition they were stolen. Demanding this standard, according to Jewish tradition, would make it difficult for most thieves to pay back their victims, leaving the victims without any restitution. There is flexibility in what repayment looks like. Yet one way or another, reparations must be made.

One of the first things we as investors can do to support racial justice is to use our power to advocate for our society to pay reparations. This extends far beyond choices of how we allocate our investment dollars. The recompense for centuries of slavery and discrimination needs to be much broader than individual behavior within the investment arena. As the Center for American Progress notes, we will need the government fully on board. "The unjust obstacles to building wealth for Black households have existed for centuries, and the iterative nature of wealth begetting more wealth means that without public interventions, it will be virtually impossible for Black Americans to catch up to their white counterparts."[41] A vital step toward addressing those past and current wrongs is investor support for national movements for racial justice, whether through our choices at the ballot box, exerting influence among our often powerful peer networks, or embracing more fully potential public platforms to raise our voices in favor of national movements for racial justice.

Investors committed to advocating for racial justice have achieved concrete wins at the federal level in the past. Debra Schwartz, Director of Impact Investing at the

MacArthur Foundation and member of Chicago's Reform Jewish community, has had a bird's-eye view on this movement for decades—the foundation has been funding key impact-investing projects since as early as the 1980s. Schwartz notes that at the same time as the US government was finally beginning to undo its policies of redlining and segregation, activists and investors managed to build an entire infrastructure of federal policy to support historically under-invested communities. The movement secured wins like the Community Reinvestment Act, which forced banks to allocate a portion of their dollars to communities in need, and the creation of the official Community Development Financial Institution designation by the US Treasury, along with millions of dollars in government funding for loans to marginalized communities.

Many of the same tools of Jewish money ethics we discussed earlier can inform our racial justice process. When we begin with gratitude, and identify "what is enough," we can begin to redistribute excess wealth that came from the table loaded with stolen goods that Ed Whitfield described.

But even once those with access to wealth have given away excess money won at a table loaded with stolen goods, and even as we all advocate for governmental policies to address racism and support reparations, there is still a role for investment capital.

We Still Need Investment Capital

Investment capital plays an *"important and different* role in transforming our economic system" from charitable giving, according to the progressive nonprofit Resource Generation. Resource Generation focuses primarily on supporting young people with wealth to redistribute their excess wealth for social justice causes, but notes that investments in local communities play an important role as well.[42]

For example, recall that one of the forms racial discrimination took throughout much of the 20th century in the United States was denying families of color mortgages and business loans through redlining. Investment capital in the form of (non-exploitative) loan dollars could have made a positive difference. In the words of Andre Perry, a fellow at the Brookings Institution who studies the racial gap in wealth creation: "When you don't invest, you get social problems, you get crime, less education, all of which reduces the chances of people climbing the social and economic ladder."[43]

Finance can be a crucial tool for solving societal problems, and lack of credit can exacerbate them. The nonprofit Transform Finance notes that "entrepreneurs of color have a harder time finding capital and receive generally more costly terms than wealthier, white businesses. In the housing market, homeowners of color are discriminated against for mortgages, tend to pay more for them, and have their properties appraised at a lower value."[44] The report points out that moving investment capital to small businesses, particularly those owned by Black, Indigenous, and people of color (BIPOC) entrepreneurs, "is a critically important facet of overall wealth redistribution and helps build a class of BIPOC business owners."

Jewish tradition reinforces the idea that capital plays a crucial role in lifting people out of poverty and achieving an equitable society. In Chapter 4, we encountered the *prozbul*. Let's remember the context. The Torah commanded that all outstanding debt be forgiven every seven years during the *shmita* year. The Torah cautioned lenders against withholding loans out of fear of the loan being forgiven before it was repaid. Despite the explicit warning, people with available capital refused to offer loans, and poor people suffered. Hillel the Elder saw that the community was unable to maintain both a flow of capital to the poor and a regular release from the burden of debt. The flow of capital was so important that it took precedence. Hillel created a legal mechanism, the *prozbul*, to allow lenders to collect their debts without violating the prohibitions of *shmita*.[45]

Many leaders of color within the financial arena see a vital role for investment capital. As Monique Aiken, managing director at The Investment Integration Project, likes to say, "Justice cannot finance itself."[46] According to Mehrsa Baradaran, professor at the University of Georgia School of Law and author of *How the Other Half Banks*, "Reasonable credit not only serves as a bridge over financial trouble, but for millions of Americans, credit provides the only means to build assets, start a business, or get an education....Without this access to credit, most of us cannot take advantage of the American dream made possible by our robust market-based economy."[47]

Lisa Mensah, who leads Opportunity Finance Network, the national association of Community Development Financial Institutions, has noted, "Real liberation takes money—it takes fairly priced capital. Real liberation means you actually start to get to fight for your own life, and to me, that's so much accelerated when you actually have a shot at capital."[48]

In 2021, Mensah stood alongside vice president Kamala Harris as the federal government announced a significant increase in support for community development finance. Mensah saw it as a sign that lending to marginalized communities is no longer a sideshow, an "isn't it cool, we figured out how to lend to low-income women." Instead, "we've acknowledged that if we don't lend to the low-income women, we won't have the economy we want."[49]

Centering Racial Justice

An advantage of centering racial justice in our investment portfolios is that doing so can cause positive impact to ripple outward to a whole range of issues, an example of what economists call positive externalities.[50] Anne Price, from the Insight Center for Community Economic Development, calls this "centering Blackness," and she notes that doing so is, in fact, beneficial for everyone.[51] Every part of our economy has been touched by racial injustice, so centering racial justice positively impacts every part of our economy.

A modern example of positive externalities that provides a useful analogy is the "curb-cut effect." The term originated from ramps that provided wheelchair access for people with disabilities, but also ended up benefiting parents with strollers, skateboarders and bicyclists, and more—and centering Blackness can similarly have a wide range of positive externalities.[52] As Oakland-based think tank PolicyLink puts it, "Intentional investments in Black Americans have benefits that cascade out.... Ensuring all people live in a society where they can participate, prosper, and reach their full potential requires recognizing that the path to getting there is different for different groups."[53]

As Lisa Mensah from Opportunity Finance Network pointed out, investing in women of color can improve our entire economy. Catherine Berman of CNote puts it this way: "Women of color are the fastest growing segment of entrepreneurs in the country. They create, they deliver, they inspire, and they are the heartbeat and cultural pulse of towns and communities around the nation. Women of color, and Black women in particular, are at the core of our economy with a high rate of labor market participation throughout their lives, as small business owners, and frequently as the breadwinner in their homes."[54]

At the same time, Black-owned firms are three times more likely than white-owned firms to be denied loans. The average Black-owned firm obtains $35,205 in total start-up capital during its first year, compared with $106,720 for the average white-owned firm.[55] Centering racial justice and actively lending to communities and entrepreneurs of color would not only right a wrong but improve society as a whole.

Within the investment arena, centering racial justice can help us with a wide variety of values-aligned issues. Let's look at what centering racial justice in an investment portfolio could look like, starting with public equities.

Racial Equity Audits

In the aftermath of the murder of George Floyd in 2020, a number of companies made statements supporting Black lives and announced various initiatives to address social justice within their operations. However, these statements were mostly issued without structures of accountability. Amazon, for example, announced on Twitter its solidarity with the fight against racism.[56] Yet dozens of the company's Black employees continued to detail allegations of racial bias and discrimination on the job, and many of them said the company's human resources department is part of the problem.[57]

In response, New York State Comptroller Thomas DiNapoli filed a shareholder proposal requesting that Amazon conduct a racial equity audit. Racial equity audits are third-party, independent reviews that examine whether a company's policies and practices exacerbate racial inequalities and whether there are mechanisms to monitor whether the company is effective in its stated goals on racial justice. Racial equity audits have grown in popularity in the past few years. Starbucks, Airbnb, and other companies have conducted them. They represent a powerful tool to create structures of accountability for companies' racial justice commitments.[58]

DiNapoli sees this advocacy as rippling outward to benefit issues beyond racial justice. He notes that racial inequities have lost the United States economy over $16 trillion dollars over the past 20 years.[59] DiNapoli sees racial justice as an issue of risk: Companies that widen racial inequity through their products and services face increased risk to their business model.[60]

Johnson & Johnson's CEO issued a statement in June 2020 that racism is unacceptable and Black lives matter.[61] Yet clinical trials have failed in the past to ensure diversity, worsening racial disparities in areas like heart issues, in which J&J specializes.[62] The company's talcum-based baby powders, which have been pulled from US and Canadian shelves, allegedly led to increased cancer risk[63] that disproportionately affected women of color in Africa, Brazil, and elsewhere.[64] In response to these and other issues, Trillium Asset Management filed a shareholder proposal calling on the company to conduct a racial equity audit. Racial equity audits have also been proposed at major financial institutions,[65] including Bank of America, Wells Fargo, Goldman Sachs, and Citigroup (where the resolution received a meaningful 37 percent of the vote in 2021).[66]

Judaism strongly encourages continual accountability to acting with integrity in the world. The phrase in Hebrew for taking stock of one's behavior and whether it aligns with one's values, *heshbon hanefesh*, literally translates as "soul accounting." *Heshbon hanefesh* is a necessary component of *teshuvah* (repentance and return ro right relationship) that we explored earlier this chapter.

The Jewish calendar directs us to spend extra attention on *heshbon hanefesh* and on *teshuvah* in preparation for Yom Kippur, the holiest day of the Jewish calendar. But the tradition is explicit that soul accounting is meant to be a constant, year-round process. We need soul accounting in our country's ongoing journey to right the past and current wrongs of racism. Racial equity audits can be a vital tool.

As an investor seeking to support racial justice, you can vote in favor of these proposals or ensure you are investing in funds that vote in favor on your behalf. You can even encourage your asset manager to be the next to file a similar proposal calling for a racial equity audit at a major company.

Voting Rights and Political Donations

On January 6, 2021, a violent mob of insurrectionists stormed the United States Capitol. The insurrection threatened democracy, but it was also deeply linked to racial injustice. The insurrectionists came overwhelmingly from counties and locales dominated by fears of the "great replacement" conspiracy theory that immigrants and minorities are seeking to take over the country.[67] One prominent researcher of the Capitol insurrection drew clear ties to the far-right rally in Charlottesville, Virginia, in 2017, where crowds of white men marched with torches and shouted, "Jews will not replace us!"[68]

A number of members of Congress refused to certify the results of the election, in the wake of the insurrection that left five dead at the US Capitol building, claiming a concern with voter fraud. Since then, a wave of laws has been proposed and enacted in state legislatures limiting accessibility to voting, many including measures that disproportionately exclude Black voters and other voters from communities of color.[69] In case the link wasn't clear between repression of voting rights and racial injustice, 72 Black executives wrote an open letter in March of 2021 calling on corporate America to fight voting restrictions.[70] The list included CEOs and former executives of American Express, Merck, TIAA, and Citigroup.

Yet corporate America in general has not only failed to respond; it has continued to exacerbate the problem. A number of companies, including those who put out public statements in the summer of 2020 affirming that Black lives matter, also donated to politicians who supported the January 6 insurrection. Many of the same politicians also subsequently supported factually inaccurate conspiracies about voter fraud and sought instead to make it harder for people to cast their ballots in national elections.[71] According to the nonprofit watchdog group Citizens for Responsibility and Ethics in Washington, "Corporate contributions are now increasingly an obstacle to holding elected officials accountable—not only for pushing the baseless conspiracy theories that caused the attack [on the Capitol], but also for continuing to make excuses for it."[72]

While Jews have lived under many forms of government throughout history, Judaism places a value on integrity in governmental decision-making. For example, the Children of Israel sought someone to construct the Tabernacle as they wandered through the desert. According to the Talmud's rendition, God chose the craftsman Bezalel but did not move forward until the community itself approved of the choice.[73]

In the wake of the Capitol insurrection and voter suppression laws, many companies failed to change their policies around political donations. Socially responsible investors filed shareholder resolutions calling on companies to either cease political donations or increase transparency in their political involvement.[74] These shareholder campaigns are a powerful example of how centering racial justice in our investments can help us address a range of issues, including those core to our democracy.

Asset Managers

Recall from Chapter 6 that asset managers hold enormous power. Investors in mutual funds or ETFs do not have the power to vote their own proxy ballots. The asset manager running the fund has the privilege (and the responsibility) of voting those proxy ballots on all the issues we just described and more, which number in the thousands annually.

Yet mainstream asset managers have resisted supporting shareholder campaigns for racial justice. The four largest asset managers—BlackRock, Vanguard, Fidelity, and State Street—overwhelmingly voted against such proposals in 2021, according to a report released that same year by the nonprofit organization Majority Action partnering with the Service Employees International Union. Vanguard and Fidelity voted against every shareholder proposal calling for a corporate racial equity audit.[75]

According to the report, companies like AT&T, Home Depot, and Delta had been challenged by activists and shareholders to reform their political spending policies after their support for state-level officials alleged to be driving voter suppression was exposed. Yet the four largest asset managers failed to join the campaign and instead rubber-stamped the key directors in charge of political spending oversight at those companies.[76]

Facebook's failure to deal with rampant hate and harassment has earned strong condemnation from the Jewish community in recent years.[77] Yet BlackRock voted against a proposal calling on Facebook (now Meta) to report on the misuse of its platform to promote hate speech, disinformation, and violence.[78] Fidelity even served as sponsor of an organization that has supported the pushback against ESG, despite claiming on its website that robust sustainability practices are important to an investor's success.[79]

Asset managers have a powerful role in influencing, or failing to influence, corporations. We noted in Chapter 6 that it behooves Jewish values-based investors to pay attention to the behavior of our asset managers. In this case, centering racial justice allows us to address the larger issues of accountability and good stewardship that asset managers ought to be engaging in.

We as investors can take several concrete actions. If you are like many investors who invest through funds, you can carefully choose funds that have an active record of proxy voting. If you are investing through one of the major four asset managers listed above—Vanguard, BlackRock, State Street, and Fidelity—you can call on them to do a better job voting proxies in alignment with your values. If they fail to respond, there are plenty of other funds and asset managers who are willing to vote your proxies in favor of racial justice.

Indigenous Rights

Pope Francis, in his address to the Vatican multifaith conference we visited in Chapter 1, drew attention to "a special group of religious persons, Indigenous peoples. Although they represent only five per cent of the world's population, they look after about twenty-two per cent of the earth's landmass.... In a strongly secularized world, such peoples remind us all of the sacredness of our earth."

From an investor perspective, caring about Indigenous rights, beyond just being the right thing to do, can help investors mitigate risk. As extractive industries like the fossil fuel industry continue to expand, they encroach on Indigenous land and communities. The responsible investing field has adopted a standard for how companies ought to seek permission from Indigenous people for use of their territory. The standard, referenced in the United Nations Declaration on the Rights of Indigenous Peoples, is known as Free, Prior, and Informed Consent (FPIC). Companies who fail to seek consent at all, or do so only after the project has begun, or through coercion, are placing at risk not only Indigenous people's rights but also the company's financial future.

For example, several recent or proposed pipelines in the United States have faced opposition from environmental groups as well as leaders of Native American tribes. The Keystone XL pipeline, an $8 billion project spanning from Canada to the midwestern US, was eventually cancelled after years of active opposition from Indigenous communities and environmental activists.[80] The Dakota Access pipeline was opposed by the Standing Rock Sioux tribe, whose representatives spoke to the United Nations about their objections to the pipeline. A United Nations expert on the rights of Indigenous peoples admonished the US, saying, "the tribe was denied access to information and excluded from consultations at the planning stage of the project, and environmental assessments failed to disclose the presence and proximity of the Standing Rock Sioux Reservation."[81]

The Enbridge Line 3 pipeline, routed through the state of Minnesota, has faced significant legal challenges, raising the cost of the project. The State of Minnesota is even being sued—in tribal court, a unique development—for allowing diversion of 5 billion gallons of water for the pipeline's construction and operation. The White Earth Band of the Ojibwe assert the act is a violation of treaty rights beginning in the 1800s.[82]

The Canadian government established a Truth and Reconciliation Commission in 2008 to address the government's historic impact on Indigenous peoples and families. The Commission released a Call to Action in 2015,[83] which inspired the formation of a Reconciliation and Responsible Investment Initiative. In 2021, the Initiative released a report noting the costs of investors failing to honor Free, Prior, and Informed Consent (FPIC) in concrete financial terms: "the risks to companies that fail to develop positive relationships with Indigenous peoples are well-documented, including reputational damage, regulatory intervention, litigation, project delays and disruptions, shut downs and financial loss. For example, a world-class mining operation with $3 to 5 billion in capital expenditures could suffer a cost of roughly $20 million per week from delayed production due to company-community conflict."[84] Another recent study found that mining operations that failed to respect Indigenous rights underperformed other projects.[85]

Beyond financial risk, failing to respect Indigenous rights can also lead to a failure on other social issues. Research has linked resource extraction projects to increased crime, including sex trafficking and the crisis of missing and murdered Indigenous women. For example, in multiple sex trafficking sting operations in Minnesota in 2021, men working on the Enbridge Line 3 Pipeline were among those arrested. Victims of such sex trafficking are disproportionately women of color and Indigenous women.[86]

Indigenous communities are often the first (and sometimes the only) to defend the environment from damaging extractive industries across the world, and that role comes with significant danger. The Indigenous Peoples Rights International publishes an annual report that records hundreds of incidents of violence and attacks, including killings and criminalization in dozens of countries, against Indigenous people and human rights defenders seeking to protect Indigenous and environmental rights.[87]

Some investors are leading the way in commitment to Indigenous rights through the Investors and Indigenous People's Working Group. Founded in 2006, the group focuses on a range of issues, including Free, Prior, and Informed Consent; addressing the impact of extractive industries on the environment and Indigenous communities; and building support for Indian Country.[88] In 2017 the group engaged with investors and banks, encouraging them to adopt the standard of FPIC or else divest from the Dakota Access Pipeline. When the Dakota Access Pipeline refused to conform to this minimum standard, the efforts of activists ended up tripling the cost of the pipeline.[89] Investors can now also benefit from the wisdom of an investor toolkit on Indigenous rights published in 2023 by the organization Amazon Watch, written by Emil Sirén Gualinga, a member of the Kichwa people of Sarayaku (Ecuador) and a sustainable finance specialist.[90]

Instead of remaining complicit in violations of Free, Prior, and Informed Consent for Indigenous people, investors can take an active approach to supporting Indigenous rights. You can advocate for your investment advisor and asset managers to join the Investors and Indigenous People's Working Group, and to commit to Free, Prior, and Informed Consent in all extractive projects.

Workers' Rights

They call themselves the tomato rabbis.[91] Since 2011, more than 80 rabbis have visited Florida to learn about the flagship model of worker-driven social responsibility and an organization the Washington Post has called "one of the great human rights success stories of our day," the Coalition for Immalokee Workers.[92]

Despite the 13th Amendment to the Constitution, there are thousands of examples of modern slavery in the United States, and Florida tomato fields have been ground zero. More than 1,200 people were freed from agricultural slavery rings in Florida in the early 2000s,[93] and thousands more have faced conditions of forced or coerced labor that go unaddressed because of the difficulty of enforcement and prosecution. This is no small concern—Florida supplies approximately one third of the fresh tomatoes eaten in the United States.[94] Contemporary forced labor in the United States disproportionately affects Hispanic immigrants,[95] but the issue of forced labor and human slavery ought to be of universal concern.

In response to these abuses, a group of tomato pickers from the Immokalee region of Florida, the capital of tomato production, formed the Coalition of Immokalee Workers. The group sought to ensure more justice for farmworkers and has gained national prominence through its highly effective worker-driven model. Many national brands have signed on to the Coalition of Immokalee Workers' Fair Food Program, including McDonald's and Walmart.[96] Along with pressure from activists and faith leaders like the tomato rabbis, investor pressure has been an important tool in the fight to bring corporations on board. For example, socially responsible investors filed a shareholder resolution on Wendy's inadequate protections for farmworkers, which resulted in a strong vote among investors.[97]

We can expand beyond actual cases of modern slavery. Judaism places unique emphasis on dignified treatment of workers. Indeed, the Torah directly links its exhortations to care for workers to the historical experience of the Jewish people as slaves in the land of Egypt. Every year at the holiday of Pesach, the Jewish people recount the story of the Exodus from Egypt, with a dual emphasis on the triumph of freedom over slavery and the triumph of dignity over shame and dehumanization.[98]

The rabbis understood workers to hold an extensive array of rights, including the right to freely select when to work and when to quit. The point of going free from Egypt, argue the rabbis, was to achieve human dignity. The ultimate boss we are meant to serve is God, rather than being slaves to other humans.[99]

Judaism also addresses issues like timely pay of workers. The Torah explicitly commands us to pay workers on time, as they depend on that pay for their livelihood (and sometimes their lives).[100] This includes severance pay, which the medieval commentary *Book of Education* describes as so common-sense as to need no explanation.[101]

Yet today, wage theft is a significant issue, especially in the garment industry. For example, even before the COVID pandemic, garment workers as a global industry were paid sub-poverty wages and most were living hand-to-mouth. The Business and Human Rights Resource Centre notes that in an analysis of global apparel and footwear companies, "Forced labor allegations were identified in supply chains of 54 percent of benchmarked companies."[102]

During the pandemic, millions of workers, most of them women of color, lost their jobs, and those who didn't saw their wages dramatically reduced. On top of this, garment factories have been notorious for failing to pay their workers the money they are owed as severance (a phenomenon known as severance theft). One recent report from the Worker Rights Consortium documented more than 37,000 cases of severance theft from garment workers.[103]

A group of shareholders filed a resolution with clothing company H&M in 2021, noting the company is a buyer at multiple factories that have robbed workers of the severance they legally earned. The resolution requested the company sign on to the Severance Guarantee Fund, an international effort to ensure workers can secure their owed pay. The Persson family, which founded H&M, still owns 78 percent of H&M's voting shares, so independent shareholders are limited in how many votes they can raise. But the campaign is a vital tool to raise awareness of wage theft and pressure companies on the terrible employment situation garment workers routinely find themselves in.[104]

The garment sector is not the only place where workers, especially people of color, are suffering. Zeynep Ton, professor at MIT Sloan School of Management, offers an analogy of the US economy as a sinking ship. "Those in the lower decks are at risk of drowning. Upskilling may move some of them to a dry deck, but there isn't room there for all, and, anyway, the ship is still sinking. We need to fix the hole right now so no one drowns. ...In those lower decks, the people most at risk of drowning are Black and Hispanic Americans, who are disproportionally represented in low-wage jobs. Black workers make up 25 percent and 37 percent of two of the fastest growing (but low-wage) occupations: personal care aides and home health aides."[105]

Wages are deeply linked with racial justice. Take it from Leo Strine, the former chief justice on the Delaware supreme court. Because Delaware's state laws have been so friendly to the creation of corporations, an overwhelming number of companies officially incorporate in Delaware, so much so that Strine has been called "effectively the chief justice of US corporations." According to Strine, "The best thing that corporate America and corporations can do for Black people in the United States is to pay all people a better wage."[106]

There is a noble Jewish history of commitment to fair wages. A textbook example (literally) is Aaron Feuerstein, who in 1995 kept paying the salaries of his 3,000 workers for three months while rebuilding after a massive fire at his Malden Mills textile factory.[107] Business school students study Feurstein's case, and many business scholars have critiqued his executive approach from a financial perspective. The company went into bankruptcy six years later, following the path of most textile manufacturers in the region, and when Feuerstein tried to rescue it, he was forced out of his management role. But Feuerstein, educated in a traditional yeshiva, grounded his reasoning in the Talmud and explained that morally he could have done nothing different.[108]

❖ ❖ ❖

When it comes to centering racial justice, Jewish wisdom can help guide our choices and give us a similarly powerful moral clarity. All humans have dignity. We inherited a history and a present full of the indignity of racial injustice. This especially includes theft of resources and human bodies that built the wealth of the investment arena. Stolen goods must be returned, through reparations. Centering racial justice in our investment portfolios is one vital way to do so, and the benefits will ripple outward.

Next Steps—Chapter 11

- **Step 1: Journal prompt:** Journal first about the Jewish idea that every human being has dignity and was made in the Divine image. Then journal about your reactions to reading about how the financial arena has been built on a history (and present) of dehumanizing people of color and stealing their resources or labor.
- **Step 2: Assess where you are.** If you didn't already, do the personal work in Chapter 2 to identify what is "enough" and what is "more than enough." If you find you have "too much," begin redistributing your excess wealth.
- **Step 3: Find a trusted advisor.** Bring your concerns about racial justice to your investment advisor. If they are unable to support you in this journey, select a different investment advisor who can understand and relate to your concerns about racial justice. (See Chapter 6 for more about the process of choosing an investment advisor.)
- **Step 4: Research funds.** In fall 2021, the Bridgespan Group and three other social impact organizations released a report in 2021 entitled "A Starting List to Invest for Racial Equity." Explore the list and consider investment opportunities that might be a fit for you. Some of these products might involve concessionary returns (see Chapter 3).
- **Step 5: Advocate as a shareholder.** The campaigns described in the chapter are too much for a single investor to undertake alone. Instead, you can carefully choose funds that have a demonstrated commitment to advocacy on racial justice issues. Or you can advocate with your current fund managers to take greater action by joining the campaigns listed in the chapter (racial equity audits; political spending; committing to Free, Prior, and Informed Consent; fair treatment of workers; and more).
- **Step 6: Use your voice as an investor to call for systemic change.** Impact investing is not a panacea. At the same time, investors have a powerful voice. We can use that voice to call for racial justice at the political and societal level. As investors, we can support a fair tax code that closes loopholes for the wealthiest 0.1 percent. As investors in the United States, we can support calls for reparations, like writing to our representatives in Congress to pass the bill on studying the question of reparations that has been introduced every year for more than three decades. As investors, we can add power to broader movements for racial justice.

Chapter 12

Investing in Israel

The neighborhood of Hadar, in the northern Israeli city of Haifa, had fallen into decline. Founded in 1909, the area served for decades as a flourishing city center, housing the Technion, city hall, a public library, and a municipal theater. But beginning in the 1970s, with changing patterns of internal migration, the neighborhood faced years of disinvestment and neglect.

In the 2010s, a unique collaboration formed to reinvigorate the neighborhood. Participants included the neighborhood association, city manager, and a diversity of local organizations. To achieve the scale of transformation they sought, they needed an infusion of private capital. So in 2019, private investors created the Hadarim Fund, a long-term investment fund focused on revitalization efforts in the neighborhood. The fund holds as its guiding value United Nations Sustainable Development Goal 11: "Make cities inclusive, safe, resilient, and sustainable."[1]

The Hadarim project features a community garden (the first public green space in the area), street-side eating, long-term affordable housing, and more. In one of the buildings purchased by the fund, a group of artists renovated the common areas themselves in exchange for the opportunity to use them as workshop space. In the evenings, the artists run regular events for residents.[2]

Included among the investors in Hadarim is the London-based United Jewish Israel Appeal (UJIA). To those who knew UJIA five years prior, it would have been a surprising twist for the organization to invest in such a project. Impact investing can often be a difficult sell for institutions with a long legacy, where investments (such as an endowment) are typically divorced from the impact side (grantmaking). UJIA is a hundred-year-old philanthropic institution. It is the largest Israel-focused Jewish nonprofit in England, with an often-traditional approach. Further, UJIA does not even maintain an endowment. Instead, the organization raises funds every year from UK Jewry to support its operations and grant to Israel to reduce social inequality and disadvantage.[3]

Despite this history, in 2016, UJIA began to consider creating an impact investing arm. Board chair Louise Jacobs describes two motivations. One was to seek more financially sustainable solutions than an annual appeal for the pressing social issues that UJIA addresses. The other was the need to engage younger generations of UK Jewry in Israel, after years of declining interest and affinity. Impact investing in Israel met both needs. In 2017, UJIA launched its program for investing in Israel, known as Si3.[4]

Dalia Black, an English-Israeli impact investing consultant, served as the program's champion and built it from the ground up. Black recruited the members of the initial investment committee, encouraged the board to seed the program with an initial investment of several hundred thousand pounds, and crafted an Investment Policy Statement. The statement was important, as it specified that UJIA was not looking to achieve a market rate of return (see Chapter 3), but instead to maximize impact within Israel addressing Israeli social issues.[5]

The Si3 committee went through an extensive due diligence process on the Hadarim Urban Renewal Impact Fund before investing. On the financial side, Hadarim is structured as an equity investment, meaning Si3 invested as a part-owner. Equity investments have no end date, unlike most loans, and Si3 wanted to be sure it would eventually be able to recoup its investment capital for use in other projects. On the impact side, Si3 had a high standard for positive impact to directly improve the lives of Israelis, which the Hadarim Fund proved able to meet. The committee approved a 500,000 shekel investment (roughly 100,000 British pounds).[6]

Israel's Sustainable Development

The sustainable development of the holy land of Israel has been a Jewish value for thousands of years. Already by the time of the Talmud, the Sages codified the precept of *yishuv Eretz Yisrael*. Literally translated as "settling the land of Israel," the phrase in our context is better interpreted as the sustainable development of Israel.[7]

According to the Torah, the first Jews, Abraham and Sarah, journeyed to the land, and the first permanent Jewish landholding of any kind was the cave in Israel that Abraham purchased to bury Sarah after she died. From the book of Exodus to the early books of Prophets, the Israelites escaped from slavery and oppression in Egypt and traveled to Israel to build a free and just society.

According to Jewish mystical tradition, Israel is literally the center of the world. The center of the Holy Temple in Jerusalem built by King David and King Solomon was the place from which the world was formed, the place where Cain and Abel offered sacrifices, where Noah built an altar when he left the ark, and where Abraham bound his son Isaac.[8] Later, the prophets regularly emphasized the centrality of Jerusalem and Israel. Torah itself, according to the Sages, lives nine times as strongly in Israel as in the rest of the world.[9]

Despite two forced exiles and thousands of years, Israel has remained a focus of Jewish prayer, influencing everything from the content of the liturgy to the physical direction Jews face to pray.

Throughout most of Jewish history, the primary way to support Israel's sustainable development was to move there. Rabbi Yochanan in the Talmud found it so spiritually powerful simply to be present in the land of Israel that he taught, "Anyone who walks four paces in the land of Israel is guaranteed a place in the World to Come."[10] The Sages of the Mishnah enabled one to waive certain prohibitions in order to buy a house in Israel, even on Shabbat, because of the principle of *yishuv Eretz Yisrael*.[11] The Sages even intervened in marital disputes by ruling that either spouse who felt inspired to move to Israel could force the whole family to move there; but no one could force a spouse who didn't want to leave Israel to do so.[12]

In fact, leaving Israel once one had arrived was so frowned upon that the only truly legitimate reason for doing so was if it became too expensive to live there (at which point one could no longer call a life there "sustainable"). Even then, the Talmud recounts several stories of people who left Israel in times of exorbitant food prices, only to suffer spiritually.[13]

Donating to Israel has been another key expression of the value of support for Israel since the times of the Temple, though the practice has gained new prominence in the past few centuries. When the Temple stood, thriving Diaspora Jewish communities would regularly remit tithes to the Temple. In the centuries after the Temple's destruction and the exile of the Jews, there remained a small Jewish presence in the land that was the recipient of funds of various kinds from Diaspora communities. In the 15th century, Ottoman rule fostered the revival of Jewish centers in Israel, and emissaries from these communities began traveling to Europe to raise funds. This reflected a growing European interest in the Ottoman lands in general.[14] There was also a charitable framework among Ottoman Jewry to support Jewish communities in the Holy Land. These ongoing charitable efforts for Israel expanded significantly in the 19th century with a growing internationalism made possible by technologies like the steamship and the telegraph.[15] Charitable contributions were not just about supporting Jewish communities, but about supporting those communities' flourishing in Israel.

Beginning in the 20th century, with Israel's new statehood and the growing sophistication of the investment arena, investment capital has become an additional tool to support the flourishing of the country. The country's first prime minister, David Ben-Gurion, initiated a program of selling Israel bonds to American Jews and others. Ben-Gurion explicitly sought a way for those who were not able to move to the new country to support it through their investment capital, essentially lending money long-term to the Israeli government and financing necessary development in the country. In the 1950s, Americans purchased between $40-$60 million in Israel bonds every year,[16] a number that has grown to over $1 billion annually.[17]

Throughout the latter half of the 20th century, Israel bonds were the only way for most people to invest in Israel, and the Jewish community found them appealing. Many Jewish institutions and individuals, including those who expressed skepticism about values-based investing in general, felt compelled to add Israel bonds to their investment portfolios. Indeed, as early as the 1950s, Jewish institutions such as the United Jewish Appeal in New York and Crown Family Foundation in Chicago were willing to invest.[18] Today, many people continue to purchase Israel bonds, sometimes for a special occasion, like a baby naming or b'nei mitzvah. Some institutions dedicate 3-5 percent (UJA in New York maintains its allocation at 3 percent) of their investment portfolio for Israel bonds.[19] (This type of investment allocation is known as a "**carve-out**.")

A growing number of investors today also seek to invest in Israel through public equity, including new funds comprised of companies based in Israel or with significant ties there. Some argue that increasing one's equity allocation to Israel is simply good financial practice. Israel, having been reclassified in 2010 as a "developed" country instead of "developing,"[20] is no longer included in certain "developing market" funds, so investors need to go to additional effort to ensure the country is not underweighted in their portfolios.

Beyond just investing "in Israel," the Hebrew phrase *yishuv Eretz Yisrael* means investing in the sustainable development of Israel. It is related to the phrase *yishuv ha'olam*, global sustainable development, which we encountered in Chapter 2. Jewish tradition uses that same lens, and same language, to speak about Israel.

For example, the Torah outlines a whole set of obligations to care for the needy in society. Society at the time was mostly agrarian, so these obligations took the form of agricultural practices—and they applied only to the land of Israel. Practices included leaving the corner of one's field for the poor to reap, leaving behind bundles of food, and the *shmita*/Sabbatical year we explored in Chapter 2. The medieval scholar Rambam articulated that living in the land of Israel is important because it enables one to fulfill these unique forms of charity. Rambam saw *yishuv Eretz Yisrael* explicitly as an opportunity to increase charitable giving and build a more caring society.[21] Viewed in this light, Jewish tradition does not just value "supporting Israel;" it values contributions to Israel's sustainable development.

Even investments focused on the non-Jewish Arab population of the country can be seen as improving the country as a whole and therefore embodying sustainable development in Israel, according to Michael Lustig. Lustig is a Jewish impact investment practitioner who spent 25 years on Wall Street, many of them working for the investment giant BlackRock. In 2021, Lustig penned a guide for Jewish impact investing, where he noted that beyond Israel's special place in the Jewish values paradigm, the country is majority-Jewish. Any impactful business based in Israel is likely doing more than its share to specifically support the Jewish community. On the other hand, for a company to be truly considered an impact investment, it needs to have a (somewhat intentional) positive impact. Lustig points to Israeli pharmaceutical company Teva as an example of supporting the United Nations Sustainable Development Goal 3 of promoting healthy lives.[22]

Only in the past decade has the field of impact investing in Israel grown into an investable universe. Some Jewish philanthropists, like the Edmond de Rothschild Foundation, have spent millions of dollars in recent years helping grow the nascent field.[23] Now there are dozens of opportunities to invest in ways that directly seek to benefit Israeli society, embodying the value of Israel's sustainable development.

The organization Ogen was founded 30 years ago and originally known as the Israel Free Loan Association. In its history, Ogen has lent over $350 million, with an impressively small 0.7 percent default rate.[24] Ogen continues to offer free loans to individuals in need, but the organization recently recognized an enormous gap for small businesses in Israel seeking access to investment and loan capital. Ogen took its expertise and expanded its vision, seeking to become Israel's first social bank. Its loans to businesses include interest (within the restrictions we explored in Chapter 8, including a *heter iska*),[25] but rates are kept low, as the organization is committed to putting customers before profits and achieving positive impact in the small business marketplace in Israel.[26]

During the coronavirus pandemic, Ogen's work grew significantly, with millions of dollars of increased need that the organization raced to keep up with. For example, an events hall owner in Beer Sheva had to cease operations when the pandemic hit, but still needed to pay suppliers, which he was able to do with the help of a loan from Ogen. As weddings and other celebrations resumed, the owner was able to reinvigorate his business.

As Ogen has sought to grow its portfolio of impactful loans, it has recently begun to seek additional capital by soliciting investments. In 2021, Ogen offered investments with a five-year term and 1 percent interest. Several Jewish community foundations invested.[27] In 2022, the organization launched a bond offering, with rates ranging from 1.15 percent to 2.8 percent depending on length of time and risk involved. Ogen's vice-president of partnerships notes that while making an impact investment can be time-consuming and complex, Ogen seeks to make the process easier, using its expertise to vet borrowers and administer loans.[28]

Opportunities to invest in Israel's sustainable development are available across the spectrum of asset classes. In venture capital, ZORA Ventures offers an Israel Impact Fund that invests in early-stage tech companies focused on positive societal impact and with significant growth potential. ZORA invests in companies like CodeMonkey, which teaches middle-school students how to code and was acquired from ZORA in 2018 by a Chinese company for more than $15 million.[29] We also heard about the Leichtag Foundation in Chapter 4, who invested in the fund Jerusalem Venture Partners.

One can also follow in UJIA's footsteps, seeking out direct opportunities to invest in companies in Israel. One company I previously featured in my work with JLens is Energiya Global, run by Yosi Abramowitz, who as a new immigrant to Israel founded a solar company to leverage the readily available sunlight in the south of Israel.[30] Energiya Global takes the model of Abramowitz's earlier entrepreneurship and exports it globally, seeking to develop affordable solar projects worldwide and ensure that solar is available to all, not only the wealthiest nations.[31] These deals are growing easier to find. For example, in Chapter 7, we learned about Investination, a platform of strictly halakhically compliant investment opportunities in companies based in Israel. Other opportunities include Social Impact Bonds (recall the case study that opened Chapter 9) based in Israel, coordinated by the organization Social Finance Israel.

It is possible to make progress in Israel's sustainable development across all asset classes, including large public companies. The same tools of shareholder advocacy that help move the needle on corporate behavior across the globe can also help Israeli companies become stronger and more environmentally and socially conscious.

Along with my colleagues at JLens, I helped pioneer the field of shareholder advocacy in Israel through our engagement with Israeli pharmaceutical company Teva in 2019. Despite the company's potentially positive role in supporting healthy lives, Teva was one of a handful of major opioid pill producers sued for its role in the devastating opioid epidemic, eventually settling with all 50 US states at a cost of more than $4 billion.[32] JLens and other faith investors engaged Teva leadership, including the chairman of the board, in a dialogue seeking accountability from the company on the opioid crisis. The company agreed among other things to produce an independent report about its activity as it relates to opioids. We specifically requested that the report include details on its lobbying activities and executive compensation incentives related to opioid sales. Investors saw the engagement as a win.[33]

* * *

The additional opportunities in the impact investing ecosystem in Israel are too numerous to list and the list is growing constantly. Social Finance Israel co-authored a report in 2019 on the state of the impact-investing field in Israel, noting that it had more than doubled in size the previous two years.[34] Michael Lustig's *Greenbook: A Guide to Jewish Impact Investing* lists over a dozen opportunities specifically focused on Israel.[35]

Many of these opportunities are only available to wealthy individuals or Jewish institutions. Israeli venture-crowdfunding platform OurCrowd, for example, is limited to accredited investors (see Chapter 9), and ZORA is as well. Ogen currently requires a minimum investment of $1 million. This is understandable, as the field is new and businesses are not yet fully equipped to accept small investments of capital from abroad. Hopefully, as the impact investing scene in Israel continues to expand, a growing number of opportunities will reduce their minimums and they will become accessible to average investors.

Israel holds a unique place in the heart of Jewish tradition. Jewish tradition values supporting Israel, and especially, pursuing sustainable development in Israel (akin to the United Nations' Sustainable Development Goals). The growing impact-investment arena in Israel presents an exciting opportunity for our community's investment portfolios.

An even loftier goal—and one of the hardest kinds of investment to make—is to use our investment capital to further peace and coexistence in Israel and around the world.

Next Steps—Chapter 12

Because of its central value in Jewish tradition, Jews have been devoting resources to supporting Israel for millennia. At first, this happened mostly through donations. With the growing sophistication and global reach of the investment arena in the past 100 years, there are an exciting number of opportunities to invest in Israel through many different asset classes.

Consider the following opportunities:

- **Israel bonds.** Israel bonds were one of the first impact investments many Jewish organizations have made, and they continue to play an important role in many investment portfolios.
- **Public equity funds.** There are also a growing number of funds investing in public equities in Israel. Beyond their alignment with Jewish values, some argue these funds are simply good financial choices, since Israel might be underweighted in certain stock portfolios. Read Michael Lustig and the Jewish Funders Network's recent *Greenbook: Guide to Jewish Impact Investing* (https://www.jfunders.org/greenbook_a_guide_to_jewish_impact_investing) and explore the examples, including the Van Eck Vectors Israel ETF, Bluestar Israel Technology ETF, Ark Israel Innovative Technology ETF, and more.
- **Impact funds.** Jewish tradition goes beyond merely "supporting Israel" to facilitating Israel's sustainable development. There is a growing arena of impact investing in Israel: investments that increase access to affordable housing, ensure job opportunities for marginalized communities, support environmental sustainability in Israel, and more.
  - Research Weave Impact (weaveimpact.com), ZORA Ventures (zora.vc), Social Finance Israel (social-finance.org.il), Investination (investination.com), Bridges Israel (bridgesisrael.com), Elah Fund (elahfund.com), Takwin (www.takwinlabs.com), and Ogen (ogen.org).

Chapter 13

Investing in Peacebuilding

Gidon Bromberg is executive director of a nonprofit—one of three, in fact, since his organization, EcoPeace Middle East, insists on having equal representation from Israeli, Palestinian, and Jordanian counterparts.[1] The organization brings together people from all three societies to protect local water sources. It embeds principles of cooperation in every part of its operations, based on its belief that such cooperation is necessary to manage the growing crisis of water access in the most water-scarce region on the planet.

Bromberg frequently finds his optimistic approach more successful than the political process that has failed so far to produce peace between Israelis, Palestinians, and other Arab neighbors. Israeli-Palestinian negotiations are often all-or-nothing. The process falls apart over the final status of Jerusalem, when instead, both sides could agree on a beneficial arrangement for managing water and electricity that would improve the quality of life as well as the security of everyone in the region.[2]

I do not use the term win-win lightly, but the work of Bromberg and his colleagues at EcoPeace Middle East shows that it is possible to make an immediate difference in the lives of Israelis, Palestinians, and Jordanians. In fact, when the sewage in the Jordan River is not addressed, it hurts everyone in the region. The monumental challenge is to get political leaders on each side to agree to set aside ideological conflicts to make incremental steps toward peace and sustainability.

Investors, especially investors willing to take on risk, play a crucial role in laying the groundwork. For example, EcoPeace Middle East recently began brokering an arrangement where investors build solar fields in Jordan and Jordan sells the energy to Israel. Israel uses some of that energy to power its energy-intensive desalination plants and then sells the water back to Jordan.[3] Bromberg quickly lined up a set of interested investors based in Abu Dhabi. The organization has also worked with investors on a grasshopper farm producing inexpensive protein that seeks to move its factory to Jordan but keep its breeding area in Israel. (Certain species of grasshopper are the only kosher insects).[4]

These projects are certainly challenging to pull off. But they are not a mere daydream for idealists. Business and investment are already serving as a force for coexistence. We just don't hear about them. Projects often face such extreme pushback (from all sides of a conflict) that they rarely make the papers. One Jewish communal leader described a visit he paid several years ago to an Israeli-Jordanian agricultural venture growing a variety of produce, including *etrogs*, the fruits ritually used during the holiday of Sukkot. During the *shmita* year, Jewish religious law prohibits sale of fruit, including *etrogs*, grown within the land of Israel. The fruit grown in Jordan filled a vital market need. The farm provided employment and fair wages, education to Bedouins, and a home for Syrian refugees. The farm kept its profile low and avoided media coverage.[5]

The Jewish community has high stakes in coexistence, and not just because the survival of Israel and the existence of an autonomous Jewish community in the Middle East depend, to some degree, on sustaining peace with hostile rivals who explicitly seek its destruction. Peacebuilding and coexistence are an old and treasured Jewish value, both in Israel and across the world.

The prophets are full of exhortations toward peace, like the famous quote from Micah: "They will beat their swords into plowshares and their spears into pruning hooks. No nation will take up a sword against another nation, and they will no longer know war. Every person will sit under their own vine and fig tree, with nothing to make them afraid."[6] The Book of Psalms teaches, "Depart from evil and do good. Seek peace and pursue it."[7]

In rabbinic thought, the commandment to pursue peace took on unique importance. Peace is so treasured, and so difficult to attain, that the rabbis taught, "Great is peace, for it contains all of the blessings ... great is peace, for God's name is peace."[8] The Sages of the Talmud understood Aaron, Moses's brother, to be the ultimate exemplar: while Moses waited for cases to come before him and then judged them, Aaron proactively went out and sought to resolve disputes before they reached the courts.[9] In the Talmud, this became the model and indeed expectation for everyone: "The Law does not order you to run after or pursue the other commandments, but only to fulfill them on the appropriate occasion. But peace you must seek in your place and pursue it even to other places as well."[10]

On a more direct level, peacebuilding reflects the primacy of the value of human life. Each human life has infinite value, made directly in the image of the Divine. The Sages taught, "anyone who destroys a life is considered by Scripture to have destroyed an entire world, and anyone who saves a life is considered to have saved an entire world."[11]

The United Nations Sustainable Development Goals (SDGs) highlight the importance of peacebuilding. The 17 goals published in 2015 set an ambitious agenda to see a world in 2030 free of poverty and discrimination, with abundant resources stewarded sustainably. SDG 16, the second-to-last goal, has the heading "Peace, Justice, and Strong Institutions," and aims to "promote peaceful and inclusive societies for sustainable development, provide access to justice for all and build effective, accountable and inclusive institutions at all levels." The 17th goal is to build a global partnership to achieve the other 16 goals. Ancient Jewish wisdom aligns deeply with these goals.

SDG 16 is often seen as the hardest to invest in, or at least to invest in well, with robust accountability and transparency.[12] And it is true that peacemaking is hard work. My grandfather liked to tell a story about a time he was traveling by bus in Israel, in the early 1970s. He witnessed two Israelis fighting over who would board the bus first. A third man stepped out of line (literally) to attempt to mediate between the two. He was immediately successful: they stopped yelling at each other and started yelling at him to mind his own business.

Despite the challenges, business and investment have a crucial role in supporting peacebuilding and coexistence, both in Israel and around the world.

Investing in the Palestinian Economy

Peacebuilding requires those of us entrenched in our narratives to reach out and humanize the "other side" and explicitly work for their well-being. In the Israeli-Palestinian conflict, for example, that means recognizing that there will be no long-term security for Israelis without security for Palestinians, and vice-versa. Because I am a Jew who cares about Israel, it behooves me to pursue a robust economy for Palestinians and be literally invested in their success.

Consider the Palestinian Economic Bulletin, published monthly in English and Arabic by the organization Portland Trust. Portland Trust is a UK-based "action tank" that seeks to promote peace and stability between Israelis and Palestinians through economic development. Perhaps surprisingly, the organization was founded by Jewish venture capitalist Sir Ronald Cohen.

Cohen was born in Egypt in 1945 to a Sephardic Jewish family. When he was 12, the Suez Crisis and Egypt's persecution of Jews forced him and his family to flee to England, where he eventually won a scholarship to Oxford. He later founded what would become Britain's largest venture capital firm. Cohen is often recognized as the "father of modern impact investing."[13] Starting in the year 2000, he chaired the UK's Social Investment Task Force, well before the topic had gained its current level of popularity.[14]

In 2003, convinced of the necessity for economic opportunities for both Israelis and Palestinians as a groundwork for peace, Cohen founded the Portland Trust. The organization has offices in London, Tel Aviv, and Ramallah.[15]

When I first met the organization's executive director (now emeritus), Doug Krikler, I was struck by how much he had committed personally and professionally to understanding diverse narratives. A former CEO of United Jewish Israel Appeal, the preeminent London organization focused on relationships with the Jewish community and Israel (which we encountered in the previous chapter), he has an advanced degree in Modern Arabic Studies and spent a year living in Cairo. While in his role as CEO of UJIA, he co-founded the UK Task Force on Arab Citizens of Israel.[16]

The Portland Trust is under no illusion that business will serve as a magic solution. The organization articulates that "a lasting and sustainable peace will only be achieved through a negotiated political settlement." Instead, the organization sees business and investment as one strand of a triple helix: politics, economics, and security.

That said, economics can often make progress and lay the groundwork for peace, especially when the other two strands of the helix are deadlocked. The organization calls itself an "action tank" instead of a think tank for a reason. It helped design and initiate a loan guarantee program for small and medium-scale Palestinian enterprises. It worked with entrepreneurs to facilitate and promote affordable housing developments, like the new city of Rawabi outside of Ramallah. It launched impact-investing tools, including the first Palestinian Social Impact Bond. It offered training and expertise for Palestinian business executives.[17]

Nongovernmental organizations like the Portland Trust are an important part of the ecosystem. But for investors seeking to mobilize assets toward peacebuilding, a key area of focus is the role played by business itself.

Cisco, the information technology giant, spent years leading what the company called a "market development approach in Palestine," and ultimately published a paper sharing the lessons learned from its efforts.[18] Cisco recognized the tremendous potential for growth in the Palestinian information and communications technology (ICT) sector, which jumped from 0.8 percent of Gross Domestic Product in 2008 to over 5 percent in 2010. Despite this potential, there was significant international stigma. According to Zika Abzuk, who led the company's efforts in the Palestinian Territories, Palestinian entrepreneurs were noting that "we come and offer our services, and many companies say, 'well, you know, Palestine is a conflict area, this is an area that is colored red on our map, so we are sorry but it's too much of a risk.'"[19]

Cisco took the lead and invested $15 million of its own cash in the Palestinian technology sector. The company also used its corporate connections to bring other high-tech firms into the region to invest in Palestinian firms and newly generated funds.[20]

An early challenge was the lack of vehicles to invest in. There was no venture capital fund, no basics of an ecosystem. Instead, Cisco's Corporate Affairs team played a role in building that ecosystem. In April of 2011 Cisco invested $5 million in Sadara, the first venture capital firm targeting the Palestinian tech sector, which seeks to "build the first wave of world-class, high-growth, tech companies in Palestine."[21] Then, in March of 2012, Cisco announced a $6 million commitment to the Palestine Growth Capital Fund to provide private equity growth capital investments and management support to small and medium enterprises.[22]

The company relied on and worked closely with Palestinian ICT leaders to understand the sector ecosystem and develop a roadmap for building it. This is significant, as international development work is often done "for" the society being developed, with minimal consultation with the people whose lives are impacted. Cisco specifically sought the input of Palestinian enterprises in crafting a vision of the sector's growth.

Abzuk, leader of the initiative, recalls: "The Palestinian stakeholders said two things: we don't want you to give us charity. Our dream is for you to make a business investment here, and we want you to help us develop a high-tech industry." In fact, as Cisco's report describes, "In 2008, most of the world was unaware that Palestine had ICT service firms. Changing this mindset was and is a top priority for the Palestinian IT Association (PITA) and the leaders of the Palestinian ICT sector." As Murad Tahboub, Managing Director of ASAL Technologies, a firm based in Rawabi, put it, "We wanted to convert Palestine's image into that of an economic hub, not a political zone."[23]

There were intense challenges to Cisco's work. The company hired Palestinians alongside Israelis, and employees from both sides had to work together on projects in the midst of the previous Gaza War. Abzuk notes that having a common project and deadline made connecting with others easier during this difficult time and created space for employees to widen the conversation after the war. Abzuk also described that the company refused to engage in "the political game that is being played that is a zero-sum game that whatever my side wins means that your side loses."[24]

In Cisco's case, as in all the cases in this chapter, the political realities unavoidably affect the development of economic enterprises. The Portland Trust notes that, "According to the World Bank, Israeli constraints on the development of digital infrastructure are a key challenge to a vibrant and dynamic digital economy in Palestine."[25] On the labor front, the Portland Trust adds that "Palestinian workers' rights in Israel's labour market are often threatened by movement restrictions, a lack of formal employment contracts, and low general awareness of labour laws."[26]

None of these people making courageous attempts to leverage business as a force for good on the ground is naïve. They are aware of the deep political challenges, the power imbalances, and the need for a political resolution to the conflict that respects the dignity of all parties.

At the same time, none of these entrepreneurs and activists is seeking to frame the region as too controversial or calling for companies and individuals to divest their capital. The reason is simple: investment capital, thoughtfully deployed, is essential to making lives better on the ground and laying the groundwork for peace.

Doug Krikler from the Portland Trust argues that divestment of capital strengthens extremists on both sides of the conflict and makes a political resolution more difficult. "Economic development provides an alternative to some of the perhaps more radical or extreme solutions that others are offering. It gives people a sense of tangible hope and opportunity. In the context of the Israeli-Palestinian conflict, perhaps the development of a thriving Palestinian private sector ... creates a community with a shared language, a shared understanding, and a shared vision of what a sustainable solution can look like."[27]

Despite the political challenges, Cisco's work managed to exemplify the Portland Trust's goal of building an economic foundation for coexistence between two peoples in a complicated and protracted conflict.

Peacebuilding Around the World

While the Israeli-Palestinian conflict holds special relevance for Jews, the value of peacebuilding extends to all conflicts across the world. Business and investment capital have an important role to play.

In 2016, a group of US veterans who had served in Afghanistan realized that the country is covered with purple flowers that make world-quality saffron, one of the most expensive spices; and that the farmers in the region faced significant challenges breaking into international markets. They founded a company, Rumi Spice, which is incorporated as a public benefit corporation. We encountered public benefit corporations in the introduction (Danone Corporation is one). Unlike a normal corporation, whose executives are legally required to place profit as the highest goal, in a public benefit corporation, executives focus both on profits and on positive social benefits for all stakeholders. Rumi Spice is also certified as a B Corporation. "B Corporation" is an independent certification (and different from a public benefit corporation, though they sound similar and have overlapping areas). B Corporations are certified by the nonprofit B Lab in a process that ensures the company meets certain ethical and impactful benchmarks.[28]

The founders built the company around a mission to cultivate peace in Afghanistan through economic security.[29] The organization's model of direct sourcing provides more secure jobs to Afghan farmers, particularly women who are the backbone of the saffron industry near Herat, Afghanistan.[30] Rumi Spice also demonstrates that it is possible for a business to be financially viable while addressing peacebuilding. The woman-led company appeared on the television show "Shark Tank" in 2017, where it successfully raised start-up capital.[31] In spite of drought, the coronavirus pandemic, and other challenges, the company has since grown to employ more than 4,000 women who harvest the saffron each year.[32]

In another, more recent example, as Russia invaded Ukraine in March of 2022, Western countries imposed significant sanctions on the country. At the same time, Ukraine was in desperate need of international support, including in the form of investments. The Media Development Investment Fund (MDIF), a nonprofit investment organization founded by a *Washington Post* reporter and initially funded by George Soros,[33] exemplifies this approach. The organization has been investing in independent media outlets for decades, especially those under threat from non-democratic regimes. MDIF has had investments in media organizations in Ukraine since 1998.[34] Those organizations became essential sources of information as the war continued. As advertising dried up, the fund provided additional cash to its Ukrainian newspapers and even helped find replacement sources for newsprint paper that, prior to the war, had come almost entirely from Russia.

MDIF specifically looks for countries with some amount of political risk. In investment terms, the CEO describes, "We're betting that our investments are going to contribute to moving these countries into more accountable environments, governments, societies." The fund requires that a country have at least some level of an independent, free press (which rules out countries like China), and they must follow enough of a rule of law to make an equity investment. But beyond those criteria, the organization spreads its net wide across countries facing threats to democracy. MDIF even used to hold investments in independent media in Russia, until the fund was declared "undesirable" by Russia's prosecutor-general and banned from the country in 2016.[35]

As another example, Starbucks has sought for more than a decade to use its economic power to lay the groundwork for peace in post-conflict regions around the globe. The company was one of the first buyers to come into the Democratic Republic of Congo after the country's conflict, making a commitment to buy before even seeing the product and working with other organizations to rebuild the country's coffee industry. Similarly, in Colombia, after 50 years of civil war that devastated farmers and the market for coffee, Starbucks worked with farmers to transition from illicit crops to coffee, including providing support to make the transition. The company put its own money on the table, investing $50 million in low-interest loans to communities in need, including those impacted by climate change.

Kelly Goodejohn, Vice President of Global Coffee Sustainability at the company, notes that this was a deliberate choice. The company, which purchases 4 percent of the world's coffee, could fill its entire supply chain with coffee from three or four countries. But the company can have a much bigger impact by sourcing from 30 countries, supporting more of the 25 million farmers globally, many of them small family farms, who rely on coffee crop for income. It is hard work with financial risk, but it is also why consumers turn to the company—the company has built a brand around coffee making a positive change in the world.[36] (This is an appropriate moment to recall that there are no easy binaries, and no such thing as a perfect company from a Jewish-values perspective. Starbucks has been under fire lately for labor issues and anti-union practices. This is yet another reason why the shareholder advocacy we discussed in Chapter 7 is meaningful).

To make its work possible, Starbucks partnered with the US Agency for International Development (USAID), a key actor funding some of the riskiest post-conflict, economic-development efforts across the world.[37] Governments fund perhaps 98 percent of the peacebuilding work across the world, and everyone else makes up a measly 2 percent, quips Sheldon Himelfarb, formerly the director of a conflict and peacebuilding program at the United States Institute of Peace, an office of the United States government. In 2015, Himelfarb became the CEO of PeaceTech Accelerator, which spun out of the US Institute for Peace as an independent nonprofit. He has managed peacebuilding operations across the world, including in Bosnia, Iraq, Angola, Liberia, Macedonia, Afghanistan, Pakistan, and Burundi.[38]

Himelfarb, of Eastern European Jewish heritage, speaks with decades of experience when he notes that leaving peacebuilding to governments will never solve the world's problems, because governments have proven able to respond only to the challenges directly ahead of them.[39] The PeaceTech Accelerator itself has featured a number of successful companies. For example, Hala Systems, a graduate of the Accelerator, produces an app that uses sensing technology to track missiles when they are fired and provides civilians a vital seven to ten minutes to take cover. The app was used to successfully reduce civilian casualties in Syria by up to 25 percent and to document war crimes.

In spring 2022, Hala Systems was able to expand to Ukraine, thanks to a bridge loan from the Open Road Alliance, an impact-investing organization focused on moments of conflict and upheaval. Open Road is an "impact-first" investment, meaning that the fund prioritizes achieving positive impact over earning high financial returns (Open Road anticipates returns of 2-4 percent for investors over time).[40] The fund offered a bridge loan to Hala Systems to help the company stay afloat while awaiting a government grant.[41]

The good news is that the landscape has changed significantly. When Himelfarb used to go to a company and ask them to partner with the government on work in Liberia or Burundi, the company would dismiss the conversation. Today, more companies are likely to express interest, whether out of a desire to build a brand on peacebuilding (like Starbucks) or to seek new talent in previously untapped locations (like Cisco). The world has gotten smaller, and investing in peacebuilding, while still complex, has become a more realistic possibility.

The Challenges of Business and Peacebuilding

It is important not to sugarcoat business and investment capital. Business can be on the wrong side of conflicts, profiting from violence and destabilization. Indeed, actions of the private sector and multinational corporations have been accused of exacerbating or even creating conflicts. *The Guardian* reported that according to an investigation by the oil industry watchdog Platform, Shell "fueled armed conflict in oil-rich Nigeria by paying hundreds of thousands of dollars to feuding militant groups." Shell disputed the report and questioned the accuracy of the evidence, but pledged to study the recommendations, according to *The Guardian*.[42] We as a society need to hold corporations accountable and legislate real consequences for behavior that exacerbates conflict.

Yet it is important to realize three things. First of all, business and investment are not going away anytime soon. As we saw in Chapter 2, while Judaism offers a vision of a redeemed world without private property or borders, embodied by the *shmita* year, we cannot always, or even often, live in the *shmita* year. Jewish tradition is exquisitely concerned with living in balance, with the here and now, with how to build a better world starting with this one. Jewish tradition does not see business as inherently bad or evil.

Second, business and investment represent tremendous power. When activists think about levers of power to shape the resolution of a conflict, they often think of governments or non-governmental organizations (NGOs), but businesses are a crucial tool in the toolbox for change.

Finally, business has a unique role to play and unique strengths to bring to conflict resolution. In 2013, the Portland Trust published a report examining the role of business in peacemaking in four prominent conflict areas, including Northern Ireland and South Africa. While the business community acted differently in each conflict, it often served as a catalyst for change and "getting things done."

In Northern Ireland, business played an important role, convincing politicians of the value of seeking peace through quantifying the costs of the conflict and how much could be gained with a peace agreement.[43] In South Africa, apartheid was initially profitable to businesses, and the business community as a whole sought to "leave politics to the politicians," serving as a barrier to peace and reinforcing an unjust system. Once widespread opposition to apartheid arose on the international scene, some businesses shifted their position. Many began donating to anti-apartheid efforts including rent boycotts, school protests, and worker stay-aways. Even more radically, a group of top business leaders and journalists flew to Zambia to initiate contact with a delegation of the banned African National Congress, the first of many such visits that became known as the "Trek to Lusaka." This led Nelson Mandela himself to name the peacebuilding work of the business sector as a significant force.[44]

Peacebuilding and coexistence remain difficult and risky investments. But Judaism's value of peace and peacebuilding can inspire all of us to think about the ways we can leverage investment capital and business to strengthen coexistence, create economic stability and an economic future for people in conflict, and "get things done" when politicians and ideaologues remained deadlocked. Then we will be embodying the passage in Proverbs that describes Torah as a tree of life, whose paths are all paths of peace.[45]

Next Steps—Chapter 13

Investors play a crucial role bridging conflicts around the world and laying the economic groundwork for peace. Peacebuilding has long been considered the most difficult of the United Nations' Sustainable Development Goals to invest in, so this summary has no easy recommendations. If this is an area that inspires you, consider taking a more active leadership role to build the communal interest and logistical frameworks we will need to make investing in peacebuilding widely accessible and as impactful as possible around the world.

- **Next Step:** Reach out to the organizations mentioned in the chapter and learn more about their powerful work: EcoPeace Middle East, The Portland Trust, PeaceTech Accelerator, Open Road Alliance, the US Institute of Peace, and Media Development Investment Fund. By the way, many of those organizations accept donations to further their work building an ecosystem for investing in peace.

Epilogue

A short walk from Vatican City, you may come upon a number of restaurants that serve the Roman *carciofi alla giudìa*—literally, Jewish artichoke, a deep-fried delicacy. Continue farther and you will see the cream walls and aluminum dome of the Great Synagogue of Rome, where I prayed when I visited the Vatican. The Jewish community in Rome is over two thousand years old, older than that in any other European city, older than the Colosseum whose ruins stand a few streets farther down. After all this time, the Jewish community knows a thing or two about sustainability and resilience.

The world is at a turning point. We are rocked by the accelerating climate crisis, the compounding effects of racial inequality, and attacks on the United States' democratic institutions. At the same time, millions of people are busy building a vision of the world as it could be, transformed out of the devastation of our current iteration of Capitalism 1.0 into a more inclusive and sustainable approach.

It is a daunting time, but it is also a moment of potential. Michael McAfee, from PolicyLink, whom we met in the opening chapter, puts it this way:

> It's just messy. You think about it—we have made change in this country. But that arc of the moral universe doesn't bend unless we're deliberate about it...we've also never had such a beautiful multiracial coalition of folks fighting for a just and fair society for everyone. That is our superpower.[1]

Jewish wisdom can play a vital role supporting this movement for change. Judaism is a religion of balance, of living in tensions, as we saw in Chapter 2. Money in the form of capital, when ethically deployed, can be a vital tool with noble and ancient roots to building a sustainable society. At the same time, the profit motive alone will destroy us. Judaism offers us the language and practices of gratitude and knowing what is enough.

My hope for this book is that it supports the "no!" energy confronting business as usual with a dose of "yes!" energy, grounded in the wisdom of this brilliant tradition's ancient Sages and texts, to guide us forward. Chapter 1 quoted Rabbi Lord Sacks stating that Judaism is a religion of protest. It is also a religion of transformation, and above all, of resilience.

Acknowledgements

I am grateful to all the individuals and organizations, featured in this book and not, who are working to transform investment capital into a tool for a redeemed world. Thank you to those who read parts of the book or discussed its ideas with me, including Ari Rubenstein, Catherine Berman, Dalia Black, Laura Campos, Rabbi Haggai Resnikoff, Rabbi Jonathan Rubenstein, Jordan Brown, Julie Hammerman, Julie Weise, Rabbi Linda Motzkin (who provided the amazing cover art), Nana Francois, Ophir Bruck, Shira Rubenstein (who came up with the book's title), Greg Neichin, Elana Siegel, Shu Dar Yao, and Rabbi Ysoscher Katz. Marissa Yi served as a valuable cultural consultant on the project. Thank you to Alicia Jo Rabins for your words of support and your song lyrics in Chapter 8. Thank you to my parents, Michelle and David, for steadfast support (and for bequeathing me my sense of humor). Thank you to Larry Yudelson and the team at Ben Yehuda Press for seeing the value in this book and being such partners in bringing it to life. Thanks to Laura Logan, Markham Shaw Pyle, and Rhonda Rosenheck for your insightful and incisive edits, which made the book much stronger than it would have been otherwise.

Gratitude to the love of my life, Ruhi Sophia, who encouraged me to share this work with the world, and to my children, who inspire me daily with their resilience. And finally, to the Holy One, Blessed Be He, who has blessed me with more than enough.

Glossary of Jewish Terms

Acharonim: see *Commentaries.*

Ashkenazi: a descendant of Jewish communities originating in Western or Eastern Europe — think bagels and lox and Yiddish.

Avodah Zarah: idol worship. Also the name of a Talmudic tractate which discusses the topic of idol worship and how to distance oneself from it.

Codes: authoritative books of Jewish law (*halakha*) compiled by rabbinic scholars over the ages. Think of Jewish law like an accordion. After each code is compiled in simple and straightforward language, dozens of commentaries emerge adding nuance or debating points in the code, until, decades or centuries later, another legal authority pens a new code attempting to synthesize all of the new discussion. Then new commentaries are written on that code, and the process repeats.

Commentaries: works written by rabbis and other Jewish scholars on the core texts of the Jewish canon. There are commentaries on the Torah, on the Mishnah, on the Talmud, on other commentaries, and more. These commentaries are often divided into time periods: those of the immediate post-Temple period through 600 CE; the medieval period (known as the First Commentaries, *Rishonim*) through about 1500, and the modern period (known as the Later Commentaries, *Acharonim*).

Denominations: modern Jewish communities, especially in North America, are categorized not only by geography but also by denomination. They offer diverse approaches to interpreting accumulated Jewish tradition. These range from a continuation of the law handed down to Moses at Sinai (the Orthodox movement), to a variably binding, culturally meaningful body of text and narrative that inspire Jews to spiritual engagement and ethical action in the world (the Reform, Conservative, and Reconstructionist movements). Modern denominations began forming in the early 1800s, spurred by a number of developments including increased emancipation in Europe and the Industrial Revolution.

First Temple: see *Temple.*

Gemara: the rabbinic discussions based on the Mishnah that occurred between roughly 200-500 CE. The Gemara and Mishnah were compiled together to become the Talmud.

Gneivat Daat: lit. theft of mind. Refers to inappropriate lying or dissimulation, especially by a seller seeking to market a product.

Halakha, halakhic: *halakha* refers to the Jewish system of law. It roughly translates as "the path." Judaism is a law-based religion, like Islam, but unlike Christianity or the Dharmic religions (Hinduism and Buddhism). In Judaism, law is a rich and spiritually meaningful tool for organizing ethical behavior in the world. *Halakha* originated in the Torah and has continued to develop through the debates and proclamations of the rabbis over thousands of years.

Hametz: leavened products like bread. The Torah prohibits Jews from eating, owning, or doing business with *hametz* during the holiday of Passover, and any *hametz* that was owned by a Jewish person during the holiday of Passover becomes off-limits for consumption even after Passover.

Heter Iska: a form of contract developed in the medieval period that restructures a loan as an investment, to avoid the Torah's prohibitions on charging interest while still offering the investor strong likelihood of repayment of principal plus profit.

High Priest: the head of the priests working in the Temple when the Temple stood. Today there is no High Priest.

Hillul Hashem: desecration of God's name, usually through an act that appears morally shameful.

Israelite: the technically correct term for Jews from the time of Moses through the kingdoms of Israel and Judah.

Jerusalem: a city with ancient Jewish roots (rabbinic tradition even suggests the world was created from Jerusalem) that became the capital of ancient Israel and the site of the Temple. Remains sacred and significant to Jewish tradition today.

Lifnei Iver: (lit. "before the blind") quoting the Torah's verse, "Do not place a stumbling block before the blind." The Sages understood this commandment metaphorically to mean that one may not aid someone else to commit a transgression. The Sages also understood this commandment to prohibit giving advice that is not in the best interests of the person receiving it.

Lifnim Mishurat Hadin: the Jewish principle that one is required to go beyond the letter of the law in one's ethical behavior.

Midrash: a collection of rabbinic stories and interpretations, inspired by the words of the Torah.

Mishnah: the authoritative collection of rabbinic teachings compiled in the 2nd century CE by Rabbi Yehuda HaNasi. The Mishnah served as the foundation for the Talmud three centuries later. Note: the word Mishnah can refer both to the collected work and to an individual paragraph of that work.

Mishneh Torah: penned by the famous Jewish scholar Rambam (Maimonides, 1135-1204) in the 1100s in Egypt. The Mishneh Torah is one of the most authoritative collections of Jewish law and practice. Rambam also wrote a number of other works, including *Guide to the Perplexed*.

Mitzvah: lit. "commandment." Plural *mitzvot*. Refers narrowly to religious and ethical commandments written in the Torah or instituted by the Sages. More colloquially, the term is used to refer to any Jewish-related ethical or moral deed.

Glossary of Jewish Terms

Moses: the leader of the Israelite people in the Torah. Despite his humility, Jewish tradition views him as the greatest prophet who ever lived.

Pesach: also known as Passover, this holiday in the spring commemorates the Israelites' Exodus from Egypt. In commemoration of the Exodus, the Torah prohibits eating (or owning) *hametz* during Pesach.

Prophets: messengers who bring the word of God, but not directly (except for Moses). The writings of the prophets comprise a third of the Jewish canon (Tanakh), along with the Torah and additional later Writings.

Responsa: singular, responsum. Published rabbinic decisions, issued in places across the Jewish world, starting in the 6th century and until the present day, in response to questions submitted by laypeople (or sometimes by other rabbis).

Rishonim: see *Commentaries*.

Sages: in this book, used to refer to the rabbis of the time of the Talmud, whose opinions deeply shaped Jewish thought and practice as we know it today.

Second Temple: see *Temple*.

Sephardi/Sephardic: a descendant of Jewish communities from the Iberian Peninsula (many of whom settled in North Africa after expulsion from Spain in 1492).

Shabbes/Shabbat/Shabbos (plural Shabbatot or Shabbasim): the Jewish Sabbath, celebrated from Friday evening through Saturday night. During this period of time, all manner of work is prohibited, including commerce. Shabbat is also an echo of the seven days of creation, when God rested on the seventh day.

Shmita: the Sabbatical year, described in the Torah. Once every seven years, the land was declared ownerless and anyone could eat from all the produce. At the end of the year, all debts were annulled. The land-based practice only applies within the land of Israel and continues in Jewish practice today. The debt annulment applies everywhere. Beginning 2,000 years ago, the Sages instituted a legal mechanism to circumvent most debt cancellation.

Shulkhan Arukh: the most famous code of Jewish law, compiled in the 1500s by Rabbi Yosef Karo in Spain.

Talmud: one of the most foundational books for Jewish life today. Over 2,700 pages, and 40 volumes, the Talmud compiles commentary (Gemara) on the text of the Mishnah, plus rabbinic discussions about all aspects of how to live a righteous life.

Tanakh: the Jewish canon. The word Tanakh is an acronym: ***T*** stands for *Torah*, ***n*** stands for prophets (*Nevi'im*), and ***kh*** stands for additional writings (*Ketuvim*).

Temple: the First Temple, built by King David and King Solomon, was the center of Jewish life for 500 years in Jerusalem, from 957-587 BCE. After an 80-year exile and hiatus, the Second Temple was the center of Jewish life for another 500 years in Jerusalem, until 70 CE and its tragic destruction at the hands of the Romans.

Torah: also known as the Five Books of Moses, the Torah is the oldest and foundational text of the Jewish religion. It narrates the events of history from the creation of the world, through the enslavement of the Israelites in Egypt, their freedom and wandering through the desert to the land of Israel, and ends with the death of Moses, the leader of the Israelite people.

Trayf: colloquial term for any non-kosher food. The Torah prohibited eating it, and the Sages added an extra precaution not to trade in it (see Chapter 5).

Yetzer Hara: the self-centered (literally, the "evil") inclination. Seen by the rabbis as a necessary part of human functioning along with the *yetzer tov*.

Yetzer Tov: the selfless (literally, "the good") inclination.

Yishuvo Shel Olam: Translated in this book as global sustainable development. A longstanding Jewish value.

Yom Kippur: the holiest day of the Jewish calendar, described in the Torah. The entire community fasts and prays for forgiveness from transgressions. In ancient times, the High Priest would perform the most elaborate rituals of the year in the Temple. The day has a solemn tone but not a sad one.

Glossary of Investing Terms

1.5 degrees: signifies the goal agreed on by nations at the UN Paris Climate Accords in 2015 of limiting global warming to 1.5 degrees Celsius above pre-industrial levels. This goal represents a first limit beyond which climate-related weather disasters occur with increasing frequency and devastation.

Accredited investor: a person wealthy enough that the law presumes them to be able to sustain a high risk of loss. As a rough parameter, individuals who have over $1 million in net worth outside their primary residence, or who are earning more than $200,000 per year (or couples who earn more than $300,000 per year), qualify. So do institutions with $5 million or more of capital. Visit the IRS's website to make sure you know the detailed parameters.

Annual General Meeting: a legally required annual meeting for company shareholders. During the meeting, shareholders vote on resolutions and have an opportunity to speak directly with corporate CEOs and management. The annual general meeting can be the biggest media moment of the year for some companies.

Asset manager: a company that invests your assets in specific ways. For example, asset managers create mutual funds that people can invest in.

Benchmark: a standard against which investment funds measure their financial performance over time. A benchmark is often a popular index or a collection of stocks, usually published with a chart showing how they have performed financially over time.

Capital: see *Investment capital*.

Capitalism 1.0: one of a number of phrases representing the excesses of our current system ("business as usual"), highlighting the ways the financial arena currently operates to generally increase inequality, accelerate environmental degradation, and exacerbate a range of social ills.

Capitalism 2.0: one of a number of phrases designed to capture how our current economic system could be changed to better serve society and avoid vast inequality, combat climate change, and avoid exacerbating social ills. Contrast with *Capitalism 1.0*.

Carve-out: a percentage, or slice, of an investment portfolio dedicated to a specific use. For example, it is somewhat common for Jewish institutions to have a carve-out for Israel bonds. Some institutions wanting to begin exploring **concessionary returns** have created a small carve-out, often 1-5 percent of their portfolio, to do so.

Catalytic capital: see *Concessionary returns*.

CDFI: see *Community Development Financial Institution*.
Community Development Finance: A field that grew in prominence in the 1970s, focused on direct investments through loans or equity in businesses and communities that lacked access to loans through traditional banks. The field focused on communities of color and low-income communities. The field also engaged in government advocacy to strengthen community-based finance. This was a key early modern form of impact investing.
Community Development Financial Institution: an organization that makes loans or investments in local communities, in line with the mission of community development finance. The United States Department of Treasury began certifying CDFIs in 1994.
Concessionary returns: an investment that offers a financial return below *market rate* in exchange for greater positive social impact.
Disaster Capitalism: one of a number of phrases representing the excesses of our current system ("business as usual"), highlighting the ways the financial arena currently operates to generally increase inequality, accelerate environmental degradation, and exacerbate a range of social ills. The phrase was especially popularized by author Naomi Klein. See also *Capitalism 1.0*.
Donor-Advised Fund: like a convenient and pared-down private foundation. Donors contribute money to a sponsor organization (which itself must be a registered charity) and then "recommend" distributions to nonprofits. In the meantime, the capital is invested for growth, though it never returns to the original donor.
Environmental, Social, and Governance: See *ESG*.
ESG: ESG is "a set of considerations that investors are using to try to understand risks and opportunities not accounted for in traditional financial models," according to one helpful definition from NPR. It is a newer term for socially responsible investing that groups investors' priorities into three categories. Environmental and social are more easily understood concerns. Governance sometimes refers to more traditional investor concerns of how a company is structured and run, but it also has important implications for how and whether the company is held accountable to the "E" and the "S" of ESG. Sometimes ESG is used to refer specifically to funds that score companies on each of the three categories and select the best companies to invest in based on their score. See *Socially Responsible Investing*.
ETF: short for Exchange-Traded Fund (ETF), a relatively recent variant on mutual funds that pools money from investors and invests in a diverse basket of companies. Many individual investors will invest in ETFs or mutual funds instead of investing directly in stocks.
Ethical Investing: the practice of looking for investments based on ethical or moral principles. See *Socially Responsible Investing*.

Glossary of Investing Terms

Extractive Capitalism: another term describing the issues with our current "business as usual" economic approach. This term especially highlights environmental concerns, like the ongoing extraction of fossil fuels, which often require extracting natural resources from the lands and communities of Indigenous or historically marginalized peoples.

Faith-Based Investing: investing in a way that aligns one's financial and investment assets with one's religious practice and community.

Fiduciary obligation: Fiduciary obligation refers to a person or group's responsibility to act in their members' best interest when making investment or other financial decisions. Investment managers have a legal duty to their clients, pension fund directors have a responsibility to their pension's participants, and board members have a responsibility to their non-profit organizations. The Department of Labor has made clear that *ESG* factors are legitimate to consider when thinking about one's fiduciary obligation. It is increasingly clear that fiduciary duty ought to welcome socially responsible considerations, especially when socially responsible investments offer a market rate of return.

Free, Prior, and Informed Consent (FPIC): the process referenced by the UN Declaration on the Rights of Indigenous Peoples and adopted by the responsible investing field as a standard for how companies ought to seek permission from Indigenous people for use of their territory.

Fund: a specific kind of investment vehicle. This term is regulated by the Securities and Exchange Commission, so only certain investment vehicles may be called funds.

ICT: See *Information and Communications Technology*.

Impact Investing: a practice of investing with the intention to generate measurable environmental and social impact alongside a financial return. It sometimes refers narrowly to direct investments (private debt and private equity) in businesses. This book uses the term more broadly as a synonym for socially responsible investing.

Information and Communications Technology: a business sector focused on computing and telecommunication technologies, systems, and tools. It includes computing technologies like servers, laptops, software apps, and the internet.

Initial Public Offering: when a company, formerly owned by private investors, first sells shares of stock to the public. All money paid by investors for shares goes directly to the company to fund its operations.

Investment Capital: money that is invested or intended for investing.

IPO: see *Initial Public Offering*.

Liquidity: how easy it is to quickly withdraw one's investment. For example, if an unexpected medical bill arose tomorrow, would I be able to pull this money out quickly to pay? Most investors have a need for some of their investment capital to be fully liquid. They may also be comfortable with a portion of their money being invested in illiquid investments that may take months or years to access. To compensate investors for the inconvenience, illiquid investments may offer a higher rate of return.

Market capitalization/market cap: the total value of a company, if one were to add up the value of all of the shares or stocks. Offers a quick way to sort companies by size: the largest companies are large-cap, medium-size companies are mid-cap, etc. See Chapter 7 for more.

Market rate: the average amount an investor would earn investing across all the stocks in the market. This number fluctuates, and the amount looks different depending on geography (East Asia versus Europe, for example). A broad United States stock index would have generally grown an average of 7-9 percent annually over the past 100 years.

Mission-Related Investing: The practice of seeking investments based on their potential to deliver financial returns as well as aligning with a specific mission of an organization. See *Socially Responsible Investing*.

Mutual fund: a kind of fund that pools money from investors and usually invests in a diverse basket of stocks of corporations, based on decisions of the fund manager. Many individual investors will invest in mutual funds instead of picking stocks themselves.

Negative Screening: avoiding investment in, or divesting from, a particular company or sector.

Paris Agreement: in 2015, at the United Nations climate conference COP21 in Paris, nearly every nation on earth participated in crafting a goal to limit global warming to 1.5 degrees Celsius below preindustrial levels. This target is often referred to as the Paris Agreement or Paris Accord.

Positive Screening: selecting certain companies or sectors to invest in (or to invest in more heavily) based on their positive characteristics.

Private capital: A class of investments not publicly available on stock markets. Often, private capital investments will only be available to certain kinds of investors, like *accredited investors*. See also *private equity* and *private debt*.

Private debt: debt investments (including loans and bonds) in a business or company that is not publicly traded or available on the stock market.

Private equity: investments that involve owning part of a business or company that is not traded publicly on the stock exchange. Most private equity investments are less *liquid* than public equity investments.

Public equity: stock of a company traded publicly on a stock exchange. Contrast with *private equity*.

Public debt: a bond of a company or government body offered to the general investing public. Contrast with *private debt*.

Responsible Investing: see *Socially Responsible Investing*.

SDGs: See *Sustainable Development Goals*.

Secondary market: another phrase for the stock market. Investors purchase shares of a company from other investors, and no new money flows to the company. Contrast with *Initial Public Offering*.

Security: any financial asset, designed to make you money, that can be bought and sold. This includes stocks and bonds, private loans to a fair-trade coffee cooperative, and ownership stakes in an organic microbrewery. We could also call them investment vehicles.

Shareholder proposal: a proposal submitted for all shareholders to vote on at a company's annual general meeting. Shareholder proposals are a tactic to draw significant attention to an issue and pressure a company to respond.

Shareholder resolution: see *Shareholder proposal*. Technically, a shareholder resolution is a shareholder proposal that has successfully made it on to the company's ballot without being rejected by the Securities and Exchange Commission, which reviews shareholder proposals.

Socially Responsible Investing (SRI): investing with consideration of both the investor's financial needs and an investment's impact on society. Typically, SRI uses the tactics of screening (negative and positive), shareholder advocacy, and community investing.

SRI: See *Socially Responsible Investing*.

Sustainable Development Goals: developed by the United Nations in 2015, these 17 goals are the successors to the Millennium Development Goals launched in 2000. They represent a global consensus on a vision for the world economy by 2030, including goals like an end to poverty, achieving gender equality, building sustainable food and water systems, and ensuring quality education for all.

United Nations Sustainable Development Goals: see *Sustainable Development Goals*.

Values-Based Investing: see *Socially Responsible Investing*.

Venture capital: investments made in startup or early-stage companies. Venture capital firms seek to own part of the startup company, help the company scale quickly, and sell their portion for a considerable profit. Venture capital investment is a riskier kind of investment, as many companies fail. It is also often only accessible to wealthy investors, especially *accredited investors*.

References

These references include books and academic articles referenced in the main text of the book and endnotes. Citations for newspaper articles, reports, websites, and online videos are included in the endnotes.

Alexander, Michelle. *The New Jim Crow: Mass Incarceration in the Age of Colorblindness.* New York: The New Press, 2012.

Baradaran, Mehrsa. *How the Other Half Banks: Exclusion, Exploitation, and the Threat to Democracy.* Cambridge: Harvard University Press, 2015.

Bais HaVaad Rabbinical Court of Lakewood. "Halakhic Investing." June 2020. https://baishavaad.org/wp-content/uploads/2020/06/BHRC-letterhead-halachic-investing.pdf

Behar, Andy. *The Shareholder Action Guide.* Oakland: Berrett-Koehler Publishers, 2016.

Bleich, Rabbi J. David. *Contemporary Halakhic Problems.* New Jersey: Ktav Publishing House, 2012.

Bleich, Rabbi J. David. "Survey of Recent Halakhic Periodical Literature: The Hetter Iska and American Courts." *Tradition: A Journal of Orthodox Jewish Thought* 42, no. 3 (Fall 2009).

Blumberg, Phillip. *The Multinational Challenge to Corporation Law.* New York: Oxford University Press, 1993.

Brandow, Jonathan. *The Just Market: Torah's Response to the Crisis of the Modern Economy.* Minneapolis: Langdon Street Press, 2014.

Brill, Hal, Michael Kramer, and Christopher Peck. *The Resilient Investor.* Oakland: Berrett-Koehler, 2015.

Brown, Dorothy. *The Whiteness of Wealth: How the Tax System Impoverishes Black Americans –and How We Can Fix It.* New York: Crown, 2022.

Broyde, Rabbi Michael, and Steven Resnicoff. "The Corporate Veil: A Still Shrouded Concept." In Levine, Aaron, and Moses Pava, eds. *Jewish Business Ethics: The Firm and its Stakeholders.* Northvale: Jason Aronson, Inc., 1999.

Bush, Lawrence, and Jeffrey Dekro. *Jews, Money, and Social Responsibility.* Philadelphia: The Shefa Fund, 1993.

Coates, Ta-Nehisi. *We Were Eight Years in Power: An American Tragedy.* New York: One World, 2017.

Cortese, Amy. *Locavesting: The Revolution in Local Investing and How to Profit From It.* Hoboken: John Wiley & Sons, 2011.

Eisenstein, Charles. *Sacred Economics: Money, Gift & Society in an Age of Transition.* Berkeley: Evolver Editions, 2011.

Fraenkel, Osmond K., ed. *The Curse of Bigness: Miscellaneous Papers of Louis D. Brandeis* [1934]. Port Washington: Kennikat Press, 1965.

Friedman, Milton, and Rose D. Friedman. *Two Lucky People: Memoirs.* Chicago: University of Chicago Press, 1998.

Foer, Jonathan Safran. *We Are the Weather: Saving the Planet Begins at Breakfast.* New York: Farrar, Straus and Giroux, 2019.

Ghiridaradas, Anand. *Winners Take All: The Elite Charade of Changing the World.* New York: Knopf, 2018.

Graeber, David. *Debt: The First 5000 Years.* New York: Melville House, 2014.

Graeber, David, and David Wengrow. *The Dawn of Everything: A New History of Humanity.* New York: Farrar, Straus and Giroux, 2021.

Hawthorne, Fran. *The Overloaded Liberal.* Boston: Beacon Press, 2010.

Hersheler, Moshe, and Eliyahu Rafael Heirshik. *Sefer Torat Ribit.* Jerusalem, 2014. [Hebrew]

Hirschman, Albert O. *Exit, Voice, and Loyalty: Responses to Decline in Firms, Organizations, and States*. Cambridge: Harvard University Press, 1972.
Jacobs, Rabbi Jill. *There Shall Be No Needy*. Woodstock, Vermont: Jewish Lights Publishing, 2009.
Kimmel, Michael, and Rabbi Howard Shapiro. "Socially Responsible Investing." In Zamore, Mary. *The Sacred Exchange: Creating a Jewish Money Ethic*. New York: CCAR Press, 2019.
Kinder, P. D. and A. L. Domini. "Social screening: Paradigms old and new." *The Journal of Investing* 6(4). 1997.
Klein, Naomi. *This Changes Everything: Capitalism Versus the Climate*. New York: Simon and Schuster, 2014.
Kriwaczek, Paul. *Yiddish Civilisation: The Rise and Fall of a Forgotten Nation*. New York: Vintage Books, 2005.
Kushner, Rabbi Yosef Y. *Commerce and Issurei Hana'ah*. Jerusalem: Feldheim Publishers, 2018.
Lavi, Aharon Ariel. *Seven: Shmita-Inspired Social and Economic Ideas*. Jerusalem: Keter, 2022.
Leibowitz, Nehama. *Studies in Vayikra (Leviticus)*. Jerusalem: World Zionist Organization, 1983.
Levine, Aaron, and Moses Pava, eds. *Jewish Business Ethics: The Firm and its Stakeholders*. Northvale: Jason Aronson, Inc , 1999.
Levine, Aaron. *Case Studies in Jewish Business Ethics*. New York: Ktav Publishing House, 2000.
Levine, Aaron. *Economic Morality and Jewish Law*. New York: Oxford University Press, 2012.
Levine, Aaron. *Economics and Jewish Law: Halakhic Perspectives*. Hoboken: Ktav, 1987.
Levine, Aaron. *Free Enterprise and Jewish Law*. New York: Ktav, 1980.
Lintz, Rabbi George. "May a Jew Purchase Stock in McDonalds? (And Related Questions)." *Journal of Halacha & Contemporary Society*. 1992.
Lustig, Michael. "Greenbook: A Guide to Jewish Impact Investing." *Jewish Funders Network*. June 16, 2021. https://www.jfunders.org/greenbook_a_guide_to_jewish_impact_investing
Malkiel, Burton G. *A Random Walk Down Wall Street—Completely Revised and Updated*. New York: W.W. Norton and Company, 2015.
Marcus, Jacob. *The Jew in the Medieval World*. Cincinnati: Union of American Hebrew Congregations, 1938.
Margaliot, Rabbi Mordechai. *Encyclopedia Lechachmei Hatalmud Vehageonim*. Tel Aviv: Yavneh Publishing House, 2006. [Hebrew]
Mestrich, Keith, and Mark Pinsky. *Organized Money*. New York: The New Press, 2019.
Mian, Atif and Amir Sufi. *House of Debt: How They (and You) Caused the Great Recession, and How We Can Prevent It from Happening Again*. Chicago: University of Chicago Press, 2014.
Micklethwait, John, and Adrian Wooldridge. *The Company*. New York: Modern Library, 2003.
Monks, Robert, and Nell Minow. *Power and Accountability*. New York: HarperCollins, 1991.
O'Leary, Michael, and Warren Valdmanis. *Accountable: The Rise of Citizen Capitalism*. New York: Harper Business, 2020.
Oreskes, Naomi, and Erik Conway. *Merchants of Doubt: How a Handful of Scientists Obscured the Truth on Issues from Tobacco Smoke to Climate Change*. London: Bloomsbury, 2011.
Pittelman, Karen, and Resource Generation. *Classified: How to Stop Hiding Your Privilege and Use It For Social Change*. Brooklyn: Soft Skull Press, 2005.
Reisman, Rabbi Yisroel. *The Laws of Ribbis*. Brooklyn: Mesorah Publications, 2000.
Resnicoff, Steven. "Jewish Law and Socially Responsible Corporate Conduct." *Fordham Journal of Corporate and Financial Law*: Volume 11, Number 3, 2008.
Rodin, Judith, and Saadia Madsbjerg. *Making Money Moral: How a New Wave of Visionaries is Linking Purpose and Profit*. Philadelphia: Wharton School Press, 2021.
Rogers, Heather. *Gone Tomorrow: The Hidden Life of Garbage*. New York: The New Press, 2005.
Rothstein, Richard. *The Color of Law: A Forgotten History of How Our Government Segregated America*. New York: Liveright, 2017.

References

Sacks, Rabbi Lord Jonathan. *The Dignity of Difference, How to Avoid the Clash of Civilizations*. New York: Bloomsbury, 2003.

Sandler-Phillips, Rabbi Regina, ed. *Generous Justice: Jewish Wisdom for Just-Giving*. New York: Ways of Peace, 2016.

Satter, Beryl. *Family Properties: How the Struggle Over Race and Real Estate Transformed Chicago and Urban America*. New York: Picador, 2010.

Schwartz, Joshua, ed. *Just Balances, Just Weights: Essays on Jewish Business Ethics in a Modern World*. Uri L'Tzedek Publications. https://utzedek.org/social-justice-torah/uri-ltzedek-publications/business-ethics/

Schwartz, Mark, Meir Tamari, and Daniel Schwab. "Ethical Investing from a Jewish Perspective." in *Business and Society Review* 112:1.

Shuman, Michael. *Local Dollars, Local Sense*. White River Junction, Vermont: Chelsea Green Publishing, 2012.

Solomon, Joel. *The Clean Money Revolution*. British Columbia: New Society Publishers, 2017.

Tamari, Meir. *In the Marketplace: Jewish Business Ethics*. Southfield, MI: Targum, 1991.

Tamari, Meir. *Sins in the Marketplace*. Northvale, NJ: Jason Aronson Inc., 1996.

Tamari, Meir. *The Challenge of Wealth*. Northvale, NJ: Jason Aronson Inc., 1995.

Tamari, Meir. *With All Your Possessions*. Jerusalem: Maggid, 2014.

Tan, Kim and Brian Griffiths. *Social Impact Investing*. London: Transformational Business Network, 2016.

Teutsch, Rabbi David. *A Guide to Jewish Practice, Volume 1—Everyday Living*. Wyncote, PA: Reconstructionist Rabbinical College Press, 2011.

Teutsch, Rabbi David. *Organizational Ethics and Economic Justice*. Wyncote, PA: Reconstructionist Rabbinical College Press, 2007.

U.S. National Climate Assessment, U.S. Global Change Research Program. *Climate Change Impacts in the United States*. May 2014. https://nca2014.globalchange.gov

Villanueva, Edgar. *Decolonizing Wealth: Indigenous Wisdom to Heal Divides and Restore Balance*. Oakland: Berrett Koehler,, 2021.

Warhaftig, Itamar. "Consumer Protection: Price and Wage Levels." *Jewish Law*. In Rosenfeld, Ezra, ed. *Crossroads: Halacha and the Modern World, Vol. I*. Israel: Zomet Institute, 1987. http://www.jlaw.com/Articles/price_wage_levels.html.

Wilkerson, Isabel. *Caste: The Origins of Our Discontents*. New York: Random House, 2020.

Wrobel, Ben, and Meg Massey. *Letting Go: How Philanthropists and Impact Investors Can Do the Most Good by Giving Up Control*. 2021. https://lettinggobook.org/.

Zamore, Rabbi Mary. *The Sacred Exchange: Creating a Jewish Money Ethic*. New York: CCAR Press, 2019.

Zion, Noam Sachs. *To Each According to One's Social Needs: The Dignity of the Needy From Talmudic Tzedakah to Human Rights*. Cleveland: Zion Holiday Publications, 2013.

Notes

For full citations for books and academic articles, see the References section.

A number of sources cited are primary sources in the Jewish canon. Some are available only in Hebrew; a growing number are available in English translation online, including through Sefaria (www.sefaria.org), or through scanned copy at HebrewBooks.org.

Introduction

[1] Faith institutions own 7% of the world's landmass. Faith institutions also represent roughly one-tenth of global investable assets. Taeun Kwon and Viktoria Samberger. "Unleashing the Potential of Faith-Based Investors for Positive Impact and Sustainable Development." Center for Sustainable Finance and Private Wealth, University of Zurich. April 2021. https://ibf-uzh.ch/wp-content/uploads/2021/05/CSP_Unleashing_the_Potential_of_Faith-based_Investors_29-4-2021-pages.pdf. Page 4. Amanda Joseph. "Heeding the Call: Investing in Justice and a Livable Future." *Green Money Journal*. November 2022. https://greenmoney.com/heeding-the-call-investing-in-justice-and-a-livable-future/.

[2] Michael McAfee and Monique Aiken. "Impact Briefing: Week of July 2." ImpactAlpha. July 2, 2021. https://impactalpha.com/impact-briefing-week-of-july-2/.

[3] "Report on the Economic Well-Being of U.S. Households in 2019 — May 2020." *Federal Reserve*. 2020. https://www.federalreserve.gov/publications/2020-economic-well-being-of-us-households-in-2019-dealing-with-unexpected-expenses.htm.

[4] Nabil Ahmed, et al. "Inequality Kills: The unparalleled action needed to combat unprecedented inequality in the wake of COVID-19." *Oxfam*. January 2022. https://policy-practice.oxfam.org/resources/inequality-kills-the-unparalleled-action-needed-to-combat-unprecedented-inequal-621341/.

[5] McAfee and Aiken. "Impact Briefing: Week of July 2."

[6] Lydia Saad and Jeffrey M. Jones. "What Percentage of Americans Owns Stock?" Gallup. Aug 23, 2021. https://news.gallup.com/poll/266807/percentage-americans-owns-stock.aspx.

[7] Robert Gebeloff. "Who Owns Stocks? Explaining the Rise in Inequality During the Pandemic." *New York Times*. January 26, 2021. https://www.nytimes.com/2021/01/26/upshot/stocks-pandemic-inequality.html.

[8] Number of global millionaires: "Very High Net Worth Handbook 2021." *Wealth-X*. 2021. https://www.wealthx.com/report/very-high-net-worth-handbook-2021/. World population: Joseph Chamie. "World Population: 2020 Overview." *YaleGlobal Online*. February 11, 2020. https://archive-yaleglobal.yale.edu/content/world-population-2020-overview.

[9] Chuck Collins, Omar Ocampo, and Sophia Paslaski. "Billionaire Bonanza 2020: Wealth Windfalls, Tumbling Taxes, and Pandemic Profiteers." *Institute for Policy Studies*. April 23, 2020. https://ips-dc.org/wp-content/uploads/2020/04/Billionaire-Bonanza-2020.pdf.

[10] Michael Etzel, et al. "Back to the Frontier: Investing that Puts Impact First." The Bridgespan Group. April 2021. https://www.bridgespan.org/bridgespan/Images/articles/investing-that-puts-impact-first/back-to-the-frontier-investing-that-puts-impact-first.pdf.

[11] "New York City has the worst air quality in the world as smoke from Canadian wildfires rolls in." *NBC News*. June 7, 2023. https://www.nbcnews.com/news/us-news/live-blog/unhealthy-air-quality-canada-wildfires-live-updates-rcna88092.

[12] "Climate Change 2022: Impacts, Adaptation and Vulnerability—Summary for Policymakers." Intergovernmental Panel on Climate Change. https://www.ipcc.ch/report/ar6/wg2/downloads/report/IPCC_AR6_WGII_SummaryForPolicymakers.pdf. Page 9.

[13] Tima Bansal. "Do Hedge Funds Create Value? 3 Lessons From Danone and Unilever." *Forbes*. April 15, 2021. https://www.forbes.com/sites/timabansal/2021/04/15/how-hedge-funds-are-destroying-corporations-and-society/.

[14] Frank Van Gansbeke. "Sustainability and the Downfall of Danone CEO Faber (1/2)." *Forbes*. March 20, 2021. https://www.forbes.com/sites/frankvangansbeke/2021/03/20/sustainability-and-the-downfall-of-danone-ceo-faber-12.

[15] David Gelles. "How Republicans Are 'Weaponizing' Public Office Against Climate Action." *New York Times*. August 5, 2022. https://www.nytimes.com/2022/08/05/climate/republican-treasurers-climate-change.html

[16] Leah Malone, et al. "Biden's First Veto: Understanding the Implications of the DOL's ESG Rule." Harvard Law School Forum on Corporate Governance. April 6, 2023. https://corpgov.law.harvard.edu/2023/04/06/bidens-first-veto-understanding-the-implications-of-the-dols-esg-rule/.

[17] "US Department of Labor announces final rule to remove barriers to considering environmental, social, governance factors in plan investments." Department of Labor. November 22, 2022. https://www.dol.gov/newsroom/releases/ebsa/ebsa20221122.

[18] Andrew Ross Sorkin, et al. "DeSantis Claims Win in Campaign Against E.S.G." *New York Times*. August 24, 2022. https://www.nytimes.com/2022/08/24/business/dealbook/desantis-florida-esg-investing.html.

[19] Anne Price and Monique Aiken. "Anne Price on centering Blackness in the economic liberation of all Americans." *The Reconstruction* podcast. May 31, 2021. https://open.spotify.com/episode/404PnFR5IPDBoCZFwr1rWb.

[20] John Vidal. "Inaction on climate change will increase civil unrest, warn leading groups." *The Guardian*. November 21, 2013. https://www.theguardian.com/global-development/2013/nov/21/climate-change-increase-civil-unrest-warning.

[21] Ibid.

[22] Klein, 9.

Chapter 1

[1] The Global Sustainable Investment Alliance (2020 report) quotes sustainable assets under management as 35.9% of total assets under management. Bloomberg, on the other hand, predicts the 1/3rd mark will be hit by 2025. There are various critiques of the GSIA definitions; the important point is that this field is hot and getting hotter. "Global Sustainable Investment Review 2020." Global Sustainable Investment Alliance. 2021. http://www.gsi-alliance.org/wp-content/uploads/2021/08/GSIR-20201.pdf. Page 5. Adeline Diab and Gina Martin Adams. "ESG assets may hit $53 trillion by 2025, a third of global AUM." *Bloomberg*. February 23, 2021. https://www.bloomberg.com/professional/blog/esg-assets-may-hit-53-trillion-by-2025-a-third-of-global-aum/.

[2] "Report on US Sustainable and Impact Investing Trends, 2020." US SIF Foundation. 2021. https://www.ussif.org/files/US%20SIF%20Trends%20Report%202020%20Executive%20Summary.pdf. Page 1.

[3] See, for example, the UN Principles for Responsible Investment, an investor collaboration representing over $100 trillion in assets under management. https://www.unpri.org/an-introduction-to-responsible-investment/what-is-responsible-investment/4780.article.

[4] Schwartz, Tamari, and Schwab, 140.

[5] Milton Friedman. "A Friedman Doctrine: The Social Responsibility of Business Is to Increase Its Profits." *New York Times*. September 13, 1970. http://www.nytimes.com/1970/09/13/archives/a-friedman-doctrine-the-social-responsibility-of-business-is-to.html.

[6] Kinder and Domini, 13.

[7] The first Community Development Financial Institution, funded by religious groups and individuals, began lending to communities with limited incomes in 1973. We will learn more about CDFIs later in this book. For more information on their origins, a good resource is Opportunity Finance Network (https://ofn.org/CDFIs).

[8] "Study: 77% of Millennials have made an impact investment, but only 53% of advisors

understand the concept well." Fidelity Charitable. September 18, 2019. https://www.fidelitycharitable.org/about-us/news/77-percent-millennials-made-impact-investment-only-53-percent-advisors-say-they-understand-concept-well.html.
[9] Tamari, *With All Your Possessions*, x.
[10] Micklethwait and Wooldridge, xvi and 14.
[11] Ibid., 25.
[12] Ibid., xvi.
[13] Ibid., 25.
[14] Ibid., 17.
[15] Villanueva 6, 27. See also Micklethwait and Wooldridge, 19.
[16] Micklethwait and Wooldridge, xx.
[17] Jodi Kantor et al. "Inside Amazon's Worst Human Resources Problem." *The New York Times*. October 24, 2021. https://www.nytimes.com/2021/10/24/technology/amazon-employee-leave-errors.html.
[18] Dan Milmo and David Pegg. "Facebook admits site appears hardwired for misinformation, memo reveals." *The Guardian*. October 25, 2021. https://www.theguardian.com/technology/2021/oct/25/facebook-admits-site-appears-hardwired-misinformation-memo-reveals
[19] Micklethwait and Wooldridge, 27.
[20] Graeber, 320.
[21] Baptist, 129.
[22] Ibid.,127.
[23] Ibid., 113.
[24] Ibid., 114.
[25] Ibid. See also Brown, 17.
[26] Christian E. Weller and Lily Roberts. "Eliminating the Black-White Wealth Gap Is a Generational Challenge." *Center for American Progress*. March 19, 2021. https://www.americanprogress.org/article/eliminating-black-white-wealth-gap-generational-challenge/.
[27] Ta-Nehisi Coates. "The Case for Reparations." *The Atlantic*. June 2014.
[28] Wilkerson, 43.
[29] Ed Whitfield. "Black Economic Self-Determination: To Move Forward We Must Understand The Past." *Natural Investments* webinar. https://www.youtube.com/watch?v=1N2T_rOy5oE&feature=youtu.be (minute 63:30).
[30] Klein, 60.
[31] Graeber, *The Dawn of Everything*.
[32] O'Leary, 10.
[33] "The Reconstruction: Anne Price on centering Blackness in the economic liberation of all Americans." ImpactAlpha. June 1, 2021. https://impactalpha.com/the-reconstruction-anne-price-on-centering-blackness-in-the-economic-liberation-of-all-americans/.

Chapter 2

[1] *Talmud Yerushalmi Bava Metzia* 2:5.
[2] Talmud *Shabbat* 31a.
[3] For a more thorough summary of Jewish sources, see Tamari, *With All Your Possessions*, 6-9 and 11-24. Tamari also notes, "There is not a single major rabbinic figure who did not include in his responsa matters dealing with economic issues."
[4] Ibid., 8.
[5] Villanueva, 45. Emphasis in original.
[6] Tamari, 18.
[7] Ibid., 30.
[8] *Kuzari* 2:50.
[9] Ecclesiastes 5:9-10.
[10] Mishneh Torah, *Hilchot Talmud Torah* 3:7-10.
[11] Mishneh Torah, *Hilchot Talmud Torah* 3:12.
[12] Tamari, 29.
[13] Genesis 33:11. See Tamari, *With All Your Possessions*, xiv.
[14] Tamari, x.
[15] Ibid., xi.
[16] Lorenz T. Keyßer & Manfred Lenzen. "1.5° C degrowth scenarios suggest the need for new mitigation pathways." *Nature Communications* 12 (article 2676). May 11, 2021. https://www.nature.com/articles/s41467-021-22884-9. Also quoted in Stan Cox, "Enough For Everyone." *Yes! Magazine*. Fall 2021 (page 26).
[17] Rabbi Jeremy Benstein, "Stop the Machine!—The Sabbatical Year Principle." *MyJewishLearning.com*. Originally published May 21, 2001. https://www.myjewishlearning.com/article/stop-the-machine-the-sabbatical-year-principle/.
[18] Solnit, Rebecca, in Maor Greene, et al. "Lighting the Way: Art and Activism in the Climate Movement." Panel. Dayenu. December

2, 2021. https://www.facebook.com/DayenuAction/videos/288343133218391/.
[19] Laura E. Weber. "'Gentiles Preferred': Minneapolis Jews and Employment, 1920-1950." *Minnesota History*. Spring 1991.
[20] Riv-Ellen Prell, et al. "Antisemitism at the University of Minnesota: Minnesota Jews and Antisemitism from 1920–1948." A Campus Divided. *Anderson Library, University of Minnesota*. December 2017. http://acampusdivided.umn.edu/index.php/essay/antisemitism-at-university-of-minnesota/.
[21] Ami Eden. "(Orthodo)X-Men." *Forward*. May 23, 2003. https://forward.com/culture/film-tv/8878/orthodo-x-men-1/.
[22] Talmud *Nedarim* 38a. Moses, for example, built his wealth from the leftover shavings carved from the 10 Commandments, which were explicitly gifted to him by God. (See also *Sifrei Bamidbar* 101, *Talmud Yerushalmi Shekalim* 5:2 (49a), and *Vayikra Rabbah* 32:2.)
[23] Psalms 115:16.
[24] Talmud *Yoma* 53b; see also Tamari, 30.
[25] *Bereishit Rabba* 9:7.
[26] Talmud *Yoma* 69b.
[27] Tamari, *Al Chet*, xvi.
[28] Erica Brown. "Money, Money, Money." In Schwartz, *Just Balances, Just Weights*, Page 13.
[29] Tamari of the Jerusalem Center for Business Ethics likes to argue that Judaism does not support any particular economic system. That is not entirely true. The rabbis support a robustly regulated free market system with strong social safety nets, where the highest goal is not growth of capital but spiritual actualization—which, as this chapter and the next argue, is incompatible with what our current version of capitalism has become. Tamari's larger point may be that Judaism has been used as a cudgel synonymous with communism, or socialism, or capitalism, to prove that whatever modern movement comes next is actually what Torah meant; I agree with him that this does disservice to our tradition.
[30] Rabbis Jacob Siegel, Yitz Greenberg, Julie Schonfeld, and Aaron Panken. "Rabbinic Insights on Investment as a Force for Good." Panel: Jewish Impact Investing Summit. JLens. Dec 5, 2017. https://youtu.be/hLxZGwfI9Js.
[31] Ibid.
[32] Ibid.
[33] Sydney P. Freedberg, Agustin Armendariz and Jesús Escudero. "How America's biggest law firm drives global wealth into tax havens." *International Consortium of Investigative Journalists: The Pandora Papers*. October 4, 2021. https://www.icij.org/investigations/pandora-papers/baker-mckenzie-global-law-firm-offshore-tax-dodging/.
[34] Milton Friedman. "A Friedman Doctrine: The Social Responsibility of Business Is to Increase Its Profits." *New York Times*. Sept 13, 1970. http://www.nytimes.com/1970/09/13/archives/a-friedman-doctrine-the-social-responsibility-of-business-is-to.html.
[35] Ibid.
[36] Sarah Johnson. "'Wage theft' in Primark, Nike and H&M supply chain—report." *The Guardian*. July 2, 2021. https://www.theguardian.com/global-development/2021/jul/02/wage-theft-in-primark-nike-and-hm-supply-chain-report.
[37] Mestrich and Pinsky, 86.
[38] Friedman, 594.
[39] Walter Wurzburger, "Covenantal Morality in Business," in Levine, *Jewish Business Ethics*, 33, quoting Levine, *Free Enterprise and Jewish Law* and Meir Tamari, *With All Your Possessions*.
[40] Levine, *Free Enterprise and Jewish Law*, 20.
[41] Moses Pava. "Developing a Religiously Grounded Business Ethics: A Jewish Perspective." *Business Ethics Quarterly*. Vol. 8, No. 1 (Jan. 1998). https://www.jstor.org/stable/3857522. Page xiii.
[42] Milton Friedman. "A Friedman Doctrine: The Social Responsibility of Business Is to Increase Its Profits." *New York Times*. September 13, 1970. http://www.nytimes.com/1970/09/13/archives/a-friedman-doctrine-the-social-responsibility-of-business-is-to.html.
[43] Tariq Fancy. "The Secret Diary of a 'Sustainable Investor'—Part 3." *Medium*. August 20, 2021. https://medium.com/@sosofancy/the-secret-diary-of-a-sustainable-investor-part-3-3c238cb0dcbf.
[44] Schwartz, *Just Balances, Just Weights*, 5.
[45] As quoted in Monks and Minow, page 4. For a different version of the quote, see: Louis D. Brandeis, *Testimony Before the United States Commission on Industrial Relations*, January 23,

1915, quoted in *Fraenkel*, 75.

[46] See Talmud *Sanhedrin* 24b. For a broader approach to *yishuvo shel olam*, see Rambam, *Mishneh Torah, Hilchot Rotzeach UShmirat HaNefesh* 4:9, and Radak on *Breishit* 18:20.

[47] Talmud *Sanhedrin* 24b. See also Tamari, *Al Chet*, 7; *Mishneh Torah, Hilchot Eidut* 10. Interestingly, the Mishnah's list of disqualified witnesses also includes one who lends at interest—see Chapter 8.

[48] For a longer discussion, see Levine, *Economics and Jewish Law*, Chapter 7.

[49] Rabbi Moshe Feinstein agreed, according to author's communication with Rabbi Ysoscher Katz. See also Teutsch, 363-374, for a non-Orthodox rabbinic approach which draws similar lines.

[50] *Dibrot Eliyahu* 82.

[51] Cortese, ix.

[52] Talmud *Moed Katan* 27a-b.

[53] These were known as sumptuary laws and had secular/Christian parallels.

[54] Tamari, *With All Your Possessions*, xiv.

[55] See Rabbi Neal Gold in Zamore, 42-44.

[56] Deuteronomy 15:9-10.

[57] Leviticus 25:20-21.

[58] This occurs throughout the Mishnah and the *Talmud Yerushalmi*, Tractate *Shevi'it*. See also Lavi, *Seven*.

[59] Lavi, *Seven*.

[60] Andrew Pollack. "Drug Goes From $13.50 a Tablet to $750, Overnight." *New York Times*. September 20, 2015. https://www.nytimes.com/2015/09/21/business/a-huge-overnight-increase-in-a-drugs-price-raises-protests.html.

[61] "Access & Affordability of Medicines." Interfaith Center on Corporate Responsibility. 2021. https://www.iccr.org/program-areas/health/access-affordability-medicines.

[62] Mishnah *Keritot* 1:7. Depending on how radically one wants to read the case, Rabban Gamliel either temporarily changed the law (Rashi ad. loc. s.v. *nichnas*), allowed a delay in the sacrifices (Tosafot on *Bava Batra* 166a, s.v. *nichnas*), or didn't change anything but merely corrected a common misconception (see *Harchev Davar* Vayikra 12:1). Analyzed in Levine, "Aspects of the Firm's Responsibility," in Levine, *Jewish Business Ethics*, 80-81.

[63] Talmud *Sukkah* 34b.

[64] Talmud *Pesachim* 30a.

[65] *Mishnah Berurah* 242:2.

[66] Tamari, *In the Marketplace*, 71.

[67] Talmud *Bava Batra* 90a. There is a dispute how broadly to read Shmuel's statement. Some say only essential foods; others include all food, which is the position accepted by the *Shulkhan Arukh*. Over the centuries, various commentators added restrictions on this obligation, including that the obligation only applies when everyone is actually following it. If everyone is pricing their food merchandise to maximize their own profit, an individual is not expected to face the financial loss involved with being the only one to price food merchandise fairly. Today, this once-obligation serves instead as a values compass to guide us toward ethical behavior in pricing. See Warhaftig, *Consumer Protection*, for a summary.

[68] Ramban, *Torat HaAdam, Inyan HaSakanah*. See also Levine, "Aspects of the Firm's Responsibility," in Levine, *Jewish Business Ethics*, 77. Levine compares this to cost-plus pricing, as opposed to pharmaceutical companies' frequent attempts to justify high profits as the cost of potential future research.

[69] *Tur Yoreh De'ah* 336; *Shulkhan Arukh Yoreh De'ah* 336:3.

[70] Levine, "Aspects of the Firm's Responsibility", in Levine, *Jewish Business Ethics*, 88-90. As of 2013, the US government no longer conducts a majority of basic research, but its share is still enormous, and pharmaceutical companies do still spend a majority of their research budget on development as opposed to basic research or applied research. Jeffrey Mervis. "Data check: U.S. government share of basic research funding falls below 50%." *Science*. March 9, 2017. https://www.sciencemag.org/news/2017/03/data-check-us-government-share-basic-research-funding-falls-below-50.

[71] Berkeley Lovelace Jr. "Senate panel grills pharma CEO over executive bonuses and sales of AbbVie blockbuster drug Humira." *CNBC*. February 27, 2019. https://www.cnbc.com/2019/02/26/senate-panel-grills-abbvie-ceo-over-bonuses-tied-to-sales-of-humira.html.

[72] Wrobel and Massey, 161.

73 "The Financial Crisis Inquiry Report." *Financial Crisis Inquiry Commission.* https://www.govinfo.gov/content/pkg/GPO-FCIC/pdf/GPO-FCIC.pdf. Page 26.

74 David Dayen. "Special Investigation: The Dirty Secret Behind Warren Buffett's Billions." *The Nation.* February 15, 2018. https://www.thenation.com/article/archive/special-investigation-the-dirty-secret-behind-warren-buffetts-billions/.

75 Tamari. *In the Marketplace,* 54-55. See also Talmud *Bava Batra* 8b, *Shulkhan Arukh Choshen Mishpat* 156:5.

76 "Shareholders renew their campaign to curb escalating drug prices at U.S. drug makers." Interfaith Center on Corporate Responsibility. November 14, 2019. https://www.iccr.org/shareholders-renew-their-campaign-curb-escalating-drug-prices-us-drug-makers.

77 Alex Thomson. "Revealed: ExxonMobil's lobbying war on climate change legislation." *Channel 4 News.* June 30, 2021. https://www.channel4.com/news/revealed-exxonmobils-lobbying-war-on-climate-change-legislation.

78 G. Supran, S. Rahmstorf, and N. Oreskes. "Assessing ExxonMobil's global warming projections." *Science.* Vol. 379, Issue 6628 (January 2023). https://www.science.org/doi/10.1126/science.abk0063.

79 Shannon Hall. "Exxon Knew about Climate Change almost 40 years ago." *Scientific American.* October 26, 2015. https://www.scientificamerican.com/article/exxon-knew-about-climate-change-almost-40-years-ago/.

80 Justin Gillis and Clifford Krauss. "Exxon Mobil Investigated for Possible Climate Change Lies by New York Attorney General." *New York Times.* November 5, 2015. https://www.nytimes.com/2015/11/06/science/exxon-mobil-under-investigation-in-new-york-over-climate-statements.html.

81 Klein, 73.

82 "New York City Sues ExxonMobil, Shell, BP, and The American Petroleum Institute for Systematically and Intentionally Deceiving New Yorkers." *Official Website of the City of New York.* April 11, 2021. https://www1.nyc.gov/office-of-the-mayor/news/293-21/new-york-city-sues-exxonmobil-shell-bp-the-american-petroleum-institute-systematically.

83 Emily Atkin. "Twitter's Big Oil ad loophole." *HEATED.* February 2, 2021. https://heated.world/p/twitters-big-oil-ad-loophole.

84 *Shulkhan Arukh Hoshen Mishpat* 228. See Tamari, *With All Your Possessions,* xv.

85 Patrick Radden Keefe. "The Family That Built an Empire of Pain." *New Yorker.* October 30, 2017. https://www.newyorker.com/magazine/2017/10/30/the-family-that-built-an-empire-of-pain.

86 Figure from the 2017 National Survey on Drug Use and Health, Mortality in the United States, 2016. See "Investors for Opioid and Pharmaceutical Accountability." Interfaith Center on Corporate Responsibility. https://www.iccr.org/program-areas/health/investors-opioid-and-pharmaceutical-accountability.

87 Jan Hoffman. "An Appeals Court Gave the Sacklers Legal Immunity. Here's What the Ruling Means." *New York Times.* May 31, 2023. https://www.nytimes.com/2023/05/31/health/sackler-family-immunity-opioids.html.

88 Laura Santhanam. "What Purdue Pharma's settlement with Oklahoma means for the opioid crisis." *PBS News.* March 26, 2019. https://www.pbs.org/newshour/health/what-purdue-pharmas-settlement-with-oklahoma-means-for-the-opioid-crisis.

Chapter 3

1 For a robust secular critique of this attitude, see Anand Ghiridaradas, *Winners Take All.*

2 *Talmud Yerushalmi Sanhedrin* 2b. See another story with a similar moral in *Pesikta d'Rav Kahanna* 10:1.

3 Shuman, 2-7.

4 Tensie Whelan et al. "ESG and Financial Performance: Uncovering the Relationship by Aggregating Evidence from 1,000 Plus Studies Published between 2015-2020." 2021. Rockefeller Asset Management and NYU Stern. https://www.stern.nyu.edu/sites/default/files/assets/documents/NYU-RAM_ESG-Paper_2021%20Rev_0.pdf.

5 "Digging Deeper into the ESG-Corporate Financial Performance Relationship." *UN*

Notes

Principles on Responsible Investment. September 2018. https://www.unpri.org/an-introduction-to-responsible-investment/what-is-responsible-investment/4780.article.

[6] Michael Copley. "How ESG investing got tangled up in America's culture wars." *National Public Radio.* September 12, 2022. https://www.npr.org/2022/09/12/1121976216/esg-explained.

[7] For example: Gordon Clark, et al. "From the Stockholder to the Stakeholder: How Sustainability Can Drive Financial Outperformance." *SSRN.* March 5, 2015. https://papers.ssrn.com/sol3/papers.cfm?abstract_id=2508281.

[8] ImpactAlpha, accessible at impactalpha.com.

[9] "Summary Edition Credit Suisse Global Investment Returns Yearbook 2020." *Credit Suisse Research Institute.* February 2020. https://www.credit-suisse.com/media/assets/corporate/docs/about-us/research/publications/credit-suisse-global-investment-returns-yearbook-2020-summary-edition.pdf. Page 16.

[10] See, for example, *Kohelet Rabbah* 11:1.

[11] *Sefer HaChinukh* 480:2.

[12] Talmud *Shabbat* 119a, *Ta'anit* 9a.

[13] *Midrash Tanchuma Re'eh* 18; also Proverbs 11:4 and Rashi and Ibn Ezra ad. loc.

[14] Rambam, *Perush HaMishnayot* on Peah 1:1.

[15] Personal communication with author, June 14, 2023.

[16] *Pirkei Avot* 5:10.

[17] Bartenura ad. loc.

[18] See also Tamari, *With All Your Possessions,* xii.

[19] Graeber, 98.

[20] In Schwartz, *Just Balances, Just Weights,* 23.

[21] Genesis 18:20.

[22] Rashi on *Bava Batra* 12b s.v. *Al Midat Sdom.* See also Rabbeinu Bachya to *Avot* (Jerusalem, n.d.), 5:10.

[23] Talmud *Sanhedrin* 109b.

[24] *Midrash Tanhuma Mishpatim* 2:1.

[25] Rabbi Aharon Lichtenstein. "Alei Etzion 16: Kofin Al Middat Sedom: Compulsory Altruism?" Yeshivat Har Etzion. May 17, 2016. https://www.etzion.org.il/en/philosophy/great-thinkers/harav-aharon-lichtenstein/alei-etzion-16-kofin-al-middat-sedom-compulsory.

[26] Deuteronomy 8:17.

[27] I once taught this Talmudic passage in a class, and a participant said, "I have had squatters on my land before, and they are a pain to deal with. This is definitely 'suffering a loss.'" The Talmudic sages anticipated that question. They clarified we are talking about an abandoned house that benefits from someone living in it, whether supernaturally because of dangerous demons or more practically because we are dealing with a situation where the person living in the house also tends to it. See *Rashi ad. loc.*

[28] Talmud *Bava Kamma* 20b.

[29] Talmud *Ketubot* 103a.

[30] Talmud *Eruvin* 49a.

[31] Talmud *Bava Batra* 12b.

[32] Levine, *Case Studies,* 339.

[33] The paradigmatic example is of a public thoroughfare running through an individual's property. Under certain circumstances, that individual can exchange the path for another one that is more convenient for the configuration of the property, as long as the public doesn't sacrifice any convenience. See Encyclopedia Talmudit, *Kofin Al Midat Sedom* 533 note 55.

[34] Ibid. The example given here is of a person with a full cistern of water. The Talmud in *Yevamot* notes that such a person is prohibited to empty the cistern if they have no need for the water, when they know others need water, even if those other people are not present right now. Encyclopedia Talmudit, *Kofin Al Midat Sedom* 535 note 72-74; *Meiri Yevamot* 44a.

[35] Encyclopedia Talmudit, *Kofin Al Midat Sedom* 575.

[36] The Encyclopedia Talmudit references both sides of the debate whether "effort" is considered a loss. The language of the Rambam suggests it would be, and we wouldn't force someone to do something that cost them nothing but required extra effort. Others including the Maharik suggest that the crucial issue is money, and if it doesn't cost one any money, one is obligated to avoid *midat sedom.* Encyclopedia Talmudit, *Kofin Al Midat Sedom,* notes 335 and 337.

[37] See Michael Etzel, et al. "Back to the Frontier: Investing that Puts Impact First." The BridgeSpan Group. April 2, 2021. https://www.bridgespan.org/insights/library/impact-investing/

[38] "How these wealthy families are driving outperformance on impact." ImpactAlpha. April 6, 2021. https://impactalpha.com/how-these-wealthy-families-are-driving-outperformance-on-impact/.

[39] Monique Aiken and Lisa Mensah. "Impact Briefing June 18: CDFI's and Juneteenth hit the big time." ImpactAlpha. June 18, 2021. https://impactalpha.com/impact-briefing-week-of-june-18/.

[40] Stephen Haber, et al. "2022 Survey of Investors, Retirement Savings, and ESG." Stanford Graduate School of Business. https://www.gsb.stanford.edu/sites/default/files/publication/pdfs/survey-investors-retirement-savings-esg.pdf.

[41] "Engaging Faith-Based Investors in Impact Investing." Global Impact Investing Network. January 2020. https://thegiin.org/assets/Engaging%20Faith-Based%20Investors%20in%20Impact%20Investing_FINAL.pdf.

[42] Millard Owens. "Building the Social Justice Architecture for Impact Investing." *Nonprofit Quarterly*. April 21, 2021. https://nonprofitquarterly.org/building-the-social-justice-architecture-for-impact-investing/.

[43] Taeun Kwon and Viktoria Samberger. "Unleashing the Potential of Faith-Based Investors for Positive Impact and Sustainable Development." Center for Sustainable Finance and Private Wealth, University of Zurich. April 2021. https://ibf-uzh.ch/wp-content/uploads/2021/05/CSP_Unleashing_the_Potential_of_Faith-based_Investors_29-4-2021-pages.pdf. Page 10.

[44] *Mishnah Pe'ah* 1:1.

[45] *Tur Hilchot Tzedakah Yoreh De'ah* 247 "Ve'al yaaleh belibo."

[46] *Bava Metzia* 71a.

[47] *Tosafot Avodah Zarah* 20a s.v. "*Verebbi meir hahu.*"

[48] *Megillat Esther al Sefer Mitzvot HaRambam, Shoresh 6 Siman 1; Ahavat Chesed* I 5:5.

[49] *Igrot Moshe Yoreh De'ah* 3:93.

[50] *Shulkhan Arukh Yoreh De'ah* 247:1.

[51] If you are thinking, "Wouldn't that deplete all one's wealth in five years?," you are not the first to make that mathematical mistake. Look at it this way—the amount of money in one's account decreases every year, but so does the amount one is asked to give. Say one began with $10 million. 1/5 of that amount is $2 million, so one is left with $8 million. The next year, one gives away 1/5 of $8 million (which is only $1.6 million, so one is giving away less than the previous year). By the fifth year one would have $3.28 million. True, at some point, it might be appropriate to stop giving 1/5 of one's assets every year. But it is incorrect to suggest that one's assets would fall to $0 after five years. It might seem the Jerusalem Talmud was the first to make this mathematical slip. The apparent mistake even influenced the Jerusalem Talmud's ruling: It ruled one should give "the first year" from one's assets, and the second year onward from one's "profits" or one's annual income. The *Perisha* (Poland, 1555-1614) notes the mathematical gaffe and instead suggests a reinterpretation of the Jerusalem Talmud. Regardless, the law codes adopted a preference for giving 1/5 of one's assets once, and from then on focusing on income. Tur Yoreh Deah 247 and *Perisha* 247:3.

[52] As of 2020. "Global wealth report 2021." Credit Suisse Research Institute. June 2021. Accessed 8/11/2021 https://www.credit-suisse.com/media/assets/corporate/docs/about-us/research/publications/global-wealth-report-2021-en.pdf.

[53] See *Teshuvot HaRashba* 3:380.

[54] Andrea Armeni and Curt Lyon. "Grassroots Community-Engaged Investment: Redistributing power over investment processes as the key to fostering equitable outcomes." Transform Finance. April 2021. https://www.transformfinance.org/blog/participatory-investment-report.

[55] Michael Etzel, et al. "Back to the Frontier: Investing that Puts Impact First."

[56] Hans Taparia. "The World May Be Better Off Without ESG Investing." *Stanford Social Innovation Review*. July 14, 2021. https://ssir.org/articles/entry/the_world_may_be_better_off_without_esg_investing.

[57] "Chasing alpha is fine, but long-term returns for universal owners require beta stewardship." ImpactAlpha. September 2, 2021. https://

impactalpha.com/chasing-alpha-is-fine-but-long-term-returns-for-universal-owners-require-beta-stewardship/.

[58] "Impact investing: who are we serving?" Oxfam. April 2017. https://s3.amazonaws.com/oxfam-us/www/static/media/files/dp-impact-investing-030417-en.pdf.

[59] Ibid.

[60] Etzel, et al. "Back to the Frontier: Investing that Puts Impact First."

[61] Personal conversation with the author, March 28, 2022.

[62] Rodney Foxworth. "Wealth Inequality and the Fallacies of Impact Investing." Medium. February 18, 2018. https://medium.com/commonfuture/wealth-inequality-and-the-fallacies-of-impact-investing-eea902924309.

[63] Tariq Fancy. "The Secret Diary of a 'Sustainable Investor'—Part 3." *Medium*. August 20, 2021. https://medium.com/@sosofancy/the-secret-diary-of-a-sustainable-investor-part-3-3c238cb0dcbf.

[64] "Impact investing: who are we serving?" Oxfam.

[65] Paul Sullivan. "An Argument for Investing Where the Return Is Social Change." *New York Times*. April 2, 2021. https://www.nytimes.com/2021/04/02/your-money/impact-investing-social-change.html.

[66] Fancy. "The Secret Diary of a 'Sustainable Investor'—Part 3."

[67] "Diane Isenberg Is Married To David Freeman in Wales." *New York Times*. June 7, 1987. https://www.nytimes.com/1987/06/07/style/diane-isenberg-is-married-to-david-freeman-in-wales.html. See also Diane Isenberg. "2019 Women of Isenberg: Keynote, Diane Isenberg." https://www.youtube.com/watch?v=QHOVtVklVjM.

[68] "Ceniarth: About Us." *Ceniarth*. https://ceniarthllc.com/about-us/.

[69] Diane Isenberg and Greg Neichin. "Fighting poverty and remaining rich: Ceniarth shifts portfolio to impact-first capital preservation." ImpactAlpha. August 20, 2018. https://impactalpha.com/fighting-poverty-and-remaining-rich-ceniarth-shifts-portfolio-to-impact-first-capital-preservation/. See also Etzel, et al. "Back to the Frontier: Investing that Puts Impact First."

[70] Ibid.

[71] "How these wealthy families are driving outperformance on impact." ImpactAlpha. April 6, 2021. https://impactalpha.com/how-these-wealthy-families-are-driving-outperformance-on-impact/.

[72] Diane Isenberg and Greg Neichin. "For Ceniarth's impact-first portfolio, 'catalytic' just means reasonable." ImpactAlpha. December 19, 2019. https://impactalpha.com/for-ceniarths-impact-first-portfolio-catalytic-just-means-reasonable/.

[73] "Call No. 28: For these wealthy families, deploying catalytic capital for impact is a privilege and responsibility." ImpactAlpha. June 2, 2021. https://impactalpha.com/for-these-wealthy-families-deploying-catalytic-capital-for-impact-is-a-privilege-and-responsibility/.

[74] Ibid.

[75] Personal conversation with the author, January 20, 2020.

[76] Lillian Isley-Greene. "How Federation's impact lending program helps this Oakland business thrive." *J. The Jewish News of Northern California*. January 11, 2023. https://jweekly.com/2023/01/11/how-federations-impact-lending-program-helps-this-oakland-business-thrive/.

[77] "Impact Investing: Putting Philanthropic Capital to Work in New Ways." Jewish Community Federation and Endowment Fund. August 2022. https://reports.jewishfed.org/2022-impact-report. See also "Over $35 million loaned." Jewish Community Federation and Endowment Fund. https://impactlending.jewishfed.org/our-portfolio.

[78] "FAQ: Investing." *Oregon Clean Power Cooperative*. Accessed 12/2/2021. https://oregoncleanpower.coop/faq-2/.

[79] "CNote: Individual Investors." CNote. https://www.mycnote.com/individuals/.

[80] Diane Isenberg and Greg Neichin. "In search of existential answers and impact-first investors, Ceniarth finds religion." ImpactAlpha. August 11, 2021. https://impactalpha.com/in-search-of-existential-answers-and-impact-first-investors-ceniarth-finds-religion.

[81] See Wrobel and Massey, 166.

Chapter 4

1. "Delivering Hate: How Amazon's Platforms Are Used to Spread White Supremacy, Anti-Semitism, and Islamophobia." Partnership on Working Families and Action Center on Race and the Economy. July 2018. https://acrecampaigns.org/wp-content/uploads/2020/04/DeliveringHate-Jul2018.pdf.
2. "The Nathan Cummings Foundation: Shareholder Resolutions." Nathan Cummings Foundation. https://nathancummings.org/wp-content/uploads/Resolution-Outcomes-thru-2020.pdf.
3. "Amazon Market Cap 2006-2021." *Macrotrends*. 2021. https://www.macrotrends.net/stocks/charts/AMZN/amazon/market-cap.
4. Kerry A. Dolan. "Jeff Bezos Just Sold $2 Billion Worth Of Amazon Stock." *Forbes*. November 4, 2021. https://www.forbes.com/sites/kerryadolan/2021/11/04/jeff-bezos-just-sold-2-billion-worth-of-amazon-stock/?sh=1498f34773e1.
5. Gina-Gail Fletcher and Veronica Root Martinez. "Equality Metrics." Harvard Law School Forum on Corporate Governance. March 19, 2021. https://corpgov.law.harvard.edu/2021/03/19/equality-metrics/.
6. Domini, 19.
7. For more on this debate: Rabbi Jacob Siegel. "The Talmud and the Billionaire's Money." *Tablet Magazine*. February 3, 2022. https://www.tabletmag.com/sections/community/articles/talmud-billionaires-money-charitable-endowments. Berman, *The Jewish Philanthropic Complex*. Felicia Herman. "Jews With Money." *Tablet Magazine*. July 26, 2021. https://www.tabletmag.com/sections/community/articles/jews-with-money-lila-corwin-berman-jewish-philanthropy. Andrés Spokoiny and Lila Corwin Berman. "Lila Corwin Berman: How Political Is American Jewish Philanthropy?" On *What Gives? The Jewish Philanthropy Podcast*. Jewish Funders Network. October 13, 2020. https://www.jfunders.org/lila_corwin_berman_how_political_is_american_jewish_philanthropy. Note that all of these authors have more nuanced opinions than the extreme examples I offer in the text.
8. Tamari, *With All Your Possessions*, 175.
9. Talmud *Bava Metzia* 57b. It is unclear from the Talmud whether this was ever practiced or whether the permission to charge interest was only theoretical. (The Temple had been destroyed by the time of the discussion).
10. Graeber, 253.
11. Graeber, 256.
12. Deuteronomy 15:9-10.
13. Mishnah *Shevi'it* 10:3.
14. Rabbi Dov Linzer. "Moving From the Real to the Ideal Copy." Yeshivat Chovevei Torah Library. 8/6/2021. https://library.yctorah.org/2021/08/moving-from-the-real-to-the-ideal-copy/.
15. Talmud *Bava Metzia* 70a.
16. Rabbi Elisha Ancselovits, in Schwartz, *Just Weights, Just Balances*, 26.
17. Talmud *Bava Metzia* 70a.
18. See also *Brachot* 18b.
19. See *Teshuvot HaRosh* 13:1:10 and 13:1:17. See *Beit Yosef Yoreh De'ah* 160 s.v. vechein hadin bema'ot shel hekdesh, who cites Rabbeinu Yerucham, the Rambam, the Ri, and the *Ba'al HaTerumah*.
20. Beit Yosef ad. loc. citing the Ra'aviyah.
21. Tur *Yoreh De'ah* 160.
22. This is discussed more in-depth in *Doveiv Meisharim* 1:10.
23. *Gidulei Trumah Shaar* 46 Chapter 4 Number 5 s.v. ica.
24. *Beit Yosef Yoreh De'ah* 160.
25. The rabbis were responding to wider developments, not leading them. The first major commentator to discuss a permanent endowment fund (*keren kayemet*) and its charitable status was the *Maharit II Yoreh De'ah* 45 (1568-1639, Safed), who noted that the practice already existed in Israel. The *Machaneh Ephraim Hilchot Malveh Loveh VeRibit* 7 (1677-1735, Constantinople) responded to the Maharit. The rabbinic discussion continued with the *Mishneh LeMelech Malveh VeLoveh* 4:14 s.v. *nichsei yetomim* (1675-1715, Constantinople) and the *Havot Da'at* 160 note 10 (1770-1832, Poland). While the rabbis expressed no discomfort with permanent endowments in general, there was a debate about whether these permanent endowment funds were so far

removed from human ownership that they could even be lent out with full-fledged interest, or whether they could merely use "near to profit and far from loss." See also Hersheler, chapter 20, note 58 and 59.

[26] *Mishneh Torah Matanot Le'Aniyim* 9:1.

[27] Mishnah *Pe'ah* 8:7; see also *Mishneh Torah Matanot Le'Aniyim* 9:5.

[28] Talmud *Bava Batra* 8b. There are stories of zealous individuals fundraising for the nascent State of Israel in the 1950s in Rabbi Daniel Allen's piece in Zamore.

[29] See also Talmud *Bava Kamma* 36b.

[30] Talmud *Bava Kamma* 37a.

[31] *Mishnah LeMelech Malveh VeLoveh* 4:14 s.v. *Nichsei yetomim*, starting with *ulfi zeh hayah nireh de'afilu*.

[32] The *Erech Shai* makes a distinction between money promised as a future gift ("I will give this to charity") and money dedicated now ("this is charity"). Even so, if the money is actually belonging to charity now, the communal charitable entities ought to be able to manage it how they see fit, leading to the same conclusion. See Hersheler, chapter 20, note 55.

[33] Mishnah *Pe'ah* 1:1.

[34] "Leichtag Legacy." *Leichtag Foundation*. February 1, 2012. https://www.youtube.com/watch?v=_EJqwJKp79Q.

[35] Rabbi Jacob Siegel and Charlene Seidle. "Leichtag Foundation Goes All-In 100% on Impact Investing." JLens. August 16, 2021. https://www.jlensnetwork.org/post/leichtag-foundation-goes-all-in-100-on-impact-investing.

[36] "About Leichtag Commons." *Leichtag Foundation*. https://leichtag.org/leichtag-commons/about/.

[37] Julie Hammerman et al. "From Why to How: Jewish Institutions Discuss Impact Investing." Panel: Jewish Impact Investing Summit. JLens. May 18, 2020. https://www.youtube.com/watch?v=1ZdvduKwjI4.

[38] Ibid.

[39] Ibid.

[40] Ibid.

[41] Lance Lindblom and Laura Campos. "Changing Corporate Behavior through Shareholder Activism: The Nathan Cummings Foundation's Experience." Nathan Cummings Foundation. September 2010. https://nathancummings.org/wp-content/uploads/2018/10/Changning-Corporate-Behavior-thru-Shareholder-Activism.pdf.

[42] "The Nathan Cummings Foundation: Shareholder Resolutions." Nathan Cummings Foundation. 2020. https://nathancummings.org/wp-content/uploads/Resolution-Outcomes-thru-2020.pdf.

[43] Lowell Weiss. "18 Years in the Making: The Nation Cummings Foundation's Journey to 100% Mission-Aligned Investing." Nathan Cummings Foundation. 2021. https://impact.nathancummings.org/journey/.

[44] Rob Kozlowski. "Occidental Petroleum shareholders pass climate change disclosure proposal." *Pensions & Investments*. May 12, 2017. https://www.pionline.com/article/20170512/ONLINE/170519941/occidental-petroleum-shareholders-pass-climate-change-disclosure-proposal.

[45] Weiss. "18 Years in the Making."

[46] G. Leonard Teitelbaum. "2019 Annual Message from our Chair." Reform Pension Board. https://www.rpb.org/knowledge-center/2019-annual-message-from-our-chair.

[47] Kimmel and Shapiro, in Zamore, 101-110.

[48] "Banking on Climate Chaos: Fossil Fuel Finance Report 2021." BankTrack. 2021. https://www.ran.org/bankingonclimatechaos2021/#score-card-panel.

[49] Debra Nussbaum Cohen. "Brooklyn synagogue pulls its money out of Chase bank to promote climate change." *Times of Israel*. April 22, 2018. https://www.timesofisrael.com/brooklyn-synagogue-pulls-its-money-out-of-chase-bank-to-promote-climate-change/.

[50] Wrobel and Massey, direct communication with the author, 10/13/2021. See also "Racial Justice Initiative 2020-21 Draft Vision, Mission & Guiding Principles." Temple Israel of Boston. https://www.tisrael.org/adult-engagement/justice-compassion/justice-related-resources/racial-justice-initiative-2020-21-draft-vision-mission-guiding-principles/.

[51] Vu Le. "Funders, this is the rainy day you have been saving up for." Nonprofit AF. March 16, 2020. https://nonprofitaf.com/2020/03/funders-this-is-the-rainy-day-you-have-been-

saving-up-for/.

⁵² One could object, noting that some rabbinic opinions hold one would only be expected to give up to 20 percent of one's assets the first year, and in subsequent years could merely give from the earnings. Of course, one could object even more strongly, noting that Jewish law doesn't actually require an individual to give those percentages at all; they are just custom, albeit a strong one. I would respond quoting my rabbi and mentor, Rabbi Dov Linzer, who argues that the spiritual point of this specific giving practice, known as *ma'aser kesafim*, is to challenge us. It is part of the spiritual framework of Judaism to challenge oneself to give more. For those who are wealthy enough to have private foundations (often around the top one percent of wealth), it makes sense to follow more stringent opinions and gift by assets instead of income. See more in Chapter 3 on financial return. See also Dov Linzer. "Where Does Ma'aser Kesafim Come From, and What Can It Be Used For?"

⁵³ *Mishneh Torah Matanot LeAniyim* 7:5.

⁵⁴ Dov Linzer. "Where Does Ma'aser Kesafim Come From, and What Can It Be Used For?" Yeshivat Chovevei Torah Library. November 26, 2019. https://library.yctorah.org/2019/11/where-does-maaser-kesafim-come-from-and-what-can-it-be-used-for/.

⁵⁵ Charles Piller et al. "Dark cloud over good works of Gates Foundation." *Los Angeles Times*. January 7, 2007. https://www.latimes.com/news/la-na-gatesx07jan07-story.html.

⁵⁶ Villaneuva 182, emphasis in original.

⁵⁷ Vu Le. "Solutions Privilege: How privilege shapes the expectations of solutions, and why it's bad for our work addressing systemic injustice." *Nonprofit AF*. April 15, 2019. https://nonprofitaf.com/2019/04/solutions-privilege-how-privilege-shapes-the-expectations-of-solutions-and-why-its-bad-for-our-work-addressing-systemic-injustice/.

⁵⁸ Ophir Bruck in Rachel Cohen, et al. "Shareholder Advocacy on Social and Environmental Issues." Panel: Jewish Impact Investing Summit. JLens. December 5, 2017. https://www.youtube.com/watch?v=reqcw0VxVow.

⁵⁹ Teresa Watanabe. "UC becomes nation's largest university to divest fully from fossil fuels." *Los Angeles Times*. May 19, 2020. https://www.latimes.com/california/story/2020-05-19/uc-fossil-fuel-divest-climate-change.

⁶⁰ *Jewish Youth Climate Movement*. https://www.jewishyouthclimatemovement.org/.

⁶¹ Sheila Regan. "'It's cultural genocide': inside the fight to stop a pipeline on tribal lands." *The Guardian*. February 19, 2021. https://www.theguardian.com/us-news/2021/feb/19/line-3-pipeline-ojibwe-tribal-lands.

⁶² Hiroko Tabuchi. "Biden Administration Backs Oil Sands Pipeline Project." *New York Times*. June 24, 2021. https://www.nytimes.com/2021/06/24/climate/line-3-pipeline-biden.html.

⁶³ Rabbi Rachel Kahn-Troster [@RkahnTroster]. "Yesterday I was arrested with 8 other activists for blockading the entrance to @blackrock in support of…" Twitter. October 18, 2021. Twitter. https://twitter.com/RKahnTroster/status/1450611585140002818.

Chapter 5

¹ Meiri *Beit HaBechira Avodah Zarah* 26a.

² Rabbi Jonathan Sacks. "On Sacrifice." The Rabbi Sacks Legacy Trust. Tzav 5768/March 2008. https://www.rabbisacks.org/covenant-conversation/tzav/on-sacrifice/.

³ Rabbi Jonathan Sacks. "Challenging the idols of the secular age." The Rabbi Sacks Legacy Trust. June 15, 2013. https://www.rabbisacks.org/archive/challenging-the-idols-of-the-secular-age/.

⁴ Exodus 32. Thank you to Rabbi Max Chaikin for this framing: page 56 in Zamore, *The Sacred Exchange*.

⁵ Talmud *Avodah Zarah* 2b.

⁶ *Sefer HaChinukh* 429.

⁷ Ahavat Chesed Part II 10:3. I first learned this passage as quoted in Rabbi Joseph Telushkin's *Jewish Wisdom* (page 16).

⁸ Here's one. The rabbinic authority Rambam, in *Guide to the Perplexed*, explains that idolatrous societies rushed to benefit from the fruit of newly planted trees as soon as possible, without

Notes

regard for the tree's health. The Torah offers a direct contrast, instructing Jews to let fruit trees grow for three years before partaking of the fruit, a precept known in Hebrew as the *mitzvah of orlah*. Rambam, *Guide to the Perplexed* Part 3 36:8.

[9] Rashi on Exodus 23:13.
[10] *Hashchata* in Hebrew. Genesis 6:11.
[11] Rashi ad. loc.
[12] Various commentators discuss *gilui arayot* and these would be included. See for example *Ha'amek Davar* ad. loc.
[13] Talmud *Sanhedrin* 56a.
[14] Villanueva, 108.
[15] *Portlandia: Farm*. Aired January 11, 2011. https://www.imdb.com/title/tt1785082/.
[16] Rabbi Avi Killip. "Turn to the Talmud for instructions on anti-racism." *Forward*. June 4, 2020. https://forward.com/scribe/448059/turn-to-the-talmud-for-instructions-on-anti-racism/.
[17] *Avodah Zarah* 4a.
[18] Hawthorne, 124.
[19] "OU Medical Marijuana Statement." Orthodox Union. January 7, 2016. https://oukosher.org/blog/consumer-news/ou-medical-marijuana-statement/.
[20] The Talmud states this explicitly for Jews, and according to the consensus of the *acharonim* it applies to non-Jews as well because of the legal principle *mi ika midi*. See also a recent discussion by Rabbi Michael Broyde on the topic: https://thelehrhaus.com/timely-thoughts/what-does-jewish-law-think-american-abortion-law-ought-to-be.
[21] Leviticus 19:14–17.
[22] *Encyclopedia Talmudit Lifnei Iver*.
[23] Klapper. "'Lighting Torches for the Blind': Illuminating a Central Aspect of Halachic Business Ethics." In Schwartz, *Just Balances*, 9.
[24] Ibid., 8.
[25] Talmud *Avodah Zarah* 6a-b.
[26] Talmud *Avodah Zarah* 21a. Note that if the intermediary were a Jewish person, the Torah would prohibit; at least, that is the opinion of the Rosh (*Avodah Zarah* 1:14). See also *Tosafot Avodah Zarah* 16.
[27] *Tosafot Shabbat* 3a; Rosh; Ran.
[28] Dressler 189, quoting *Minchat Shlomo* 35.
[29] *Tosafot Shabbat* 3a, *Ran* on the beginning of *Avodah Zarah*, *Rosh* on *Avodah Zarah* 1; see *Shach* on *Yoreh De'ah* 151 note 6.
[30] This is true for Jews and non-Jews because of the principle *hovel be'atzmo assur li'vnei noach*, so selling cigarettes to both Jews and non-Jews would be problematic.
[31] Leibowitz, 178.
[32] *Mishnah Bava Kamma* 10:9.
[33] Talmud *Bava Kamma* 118b.
[34] *Shulkhan Arukh Choshen Mishpat* 356:1. See also *Pitchei Teshuva Choshen Mishpat* 356 s.v. *Liknot mehaganav*; he also quotes the Beer Hagolah, which has a slight variation in the text.
[35] Talmud *Gittin* 45a.
[36] Rabbi Lev Meirowitz Nelson, ed. "A Handbook for Jewish Communities Fighting Mass Incarceration." T'ruah. October 2016. https://truah.org/resources/handbook-for-jewish-communities-fighting-mass-incarceration/.
[37] Alexander, *The New Jim Crow*.
[38] Isaiah 2:4.
[39] Talmud *Shabbat* 63a.
[40] Talmud *Sanhedrin* 74a.
[41] *Mishneh Torah, Rotzeach UShmirat Haguf* 1:6.
[42] Talmud *Avodah Zarah* 15b.
[43] Talmud *Avodah Zarah* 16a.
[44] Talmud *Avodah Zarah* 15b-16a.
[45] *Ritva Avodah Zarah* 16a.
[46] *Nimukei Yosef* 16a.
[47] Rambam *Perush HaMishnayot Avodah Zarah* 1:7.
[48] *Yam Hagadol* 57. More recently, Rabbi Eliyahu Abergel permitted such a sale, on the assumption that most people use weapons for self-defense. *Dibrot Eliyahu* 3:13.
[49] Glenn Thrush and Serge Kovaleski. "Loopholes and Missing Data: The Gaps in the Gun Background Check System." *New York Times*. June 19, 2022. https://www.nytimes.com/2022/06/19/us/gun-background-checks.html.
[50] Daniel Gordis and Avidan Freedman. "Israel's 'Gravest Moral Stain'?" *Israel From the Inside With Daniel Gordis*. Podcast. October 17, 2021. https://danielgordis.substack.com/p/israels-gravest-moral-stain-rabbi-ad1.
[51] Conor Finnegan and Lucien Bruggeman. "Saudi crown prince 'approved' Khashoggi

⁵¹ murder operation: US intel report." *ABC News*. February 26, 2021. https://abcnews.go.com/Politics/saudi-crown-prince-approved-khashoggi-murder-operation-us/story?id=76137794.
⁵² Dana Priest, Souad Mekhennet, and Arthur Bouvart. "Jamal Khashoggi's wife targeted with spyware before his death." *Washington Post*. July 18, 2021. https://www.washingtonpost.com/investigations/interactive/2021/jamal-khashoggi-wife-fiancee-cellphone-hack/.
⁵³ Ronen Bergman and Mark Mazzetti. "Israeli Companies Aided Saudi Spying Despite Khashoggi Killing." *New York Times*. July 17, 2021. https://www.nytimes.com/2021/07/17/world/middleeast/israel-saudi-khashoggi-hacking-nso.html.
⁵⁴ Hagar Ravet. "The rotten oranges of Israeli cybersecurity." *CTech by Calcalist*. July 19, 2021. https://www.calcalistech.com/ctech/articles/0,7340,L-3912818,00.html.
⁵⁵ Ibid.
⁵⁶ Mark Mazzetti, et al. "A New Age of Warfare: How Internet Mercenaries Do Battle for Authoritarian Governments." *New York Times*. March 21, 2019. https://www.nytimes.com/2019/03/21/us/politics/government-hackers-nso-darkmatter.html.
⁵⁷ Bergman and Mazzetti. "Israeli Companies Aided Saudi Spying Despite Khashoggi Killing."
⁵⁸ Ibid.
⁵⁹ Rabbi Yaakov Epstein, *Chevel Nachalto* 1:12.
⁶⁰ *Seder Yaakov*, cited in Rabbi Yaakov Warhaftig. "Mechirat Neshek LeGoyim." *Techumin* 12. 240-244. [Hebrew]
⁶¹ Stephanie Kirchgaessner. "Officials who are US allies among targets of NSO malware, says WhatsApp chief." *The Guardian*. July 24, 2021. https://www.theguardian.com/technology/2021/jul/24/officials-who-are-us-allies-among-targets-of-nso-malware-says-whatsapp-chief.
⁶² Zack Whittaker. "A new 'digital violence' platform maps dozens of victims of NSO Group's spyware." *TechCrunch*. July 3, 2021. https://techcrunch.com/2021/07/03/digital-violence-nso-group-spyware/.
⁶³ "Joint open letter by civil society organizations and independent experts calling on states to implement an immediate moratorium on the sale, transfer and use of surveillance technology." Amnesty International. July 27, 2021. https://www.amnesty.org/download/Documents/DOC1045162021ENGLISH.pdf.
⁶⁴ Drew Harwell, Ellen Nakashima, and Craig Timberg. "Biden administration blacklists NSO Group over Pegasus software." *Washington Post*. Nov 03, 2021. https://www.washingtonpost.com/technology/2021/11/03/pegasus-nso-entity-list-spyware/.
⁶⁵ "What spy firm Cellebrite can't hide from investors." *Access Now*. May 26, 2021. https://www.accessnow.org/what-spy-firm-cellebrite-cant-hide-from-investors/. See also "Israel: Lawyer Eitay Mack's efforts bring transparency to surveillance exports that threaten rights; incl. co. comments." Business and Human Rights Resource Centre. June 17, 2021. https://www.business-humanrights.org/en/latest-news/israel-lawyer-eitay-macks-efforts-bring-transparency-to-surveillance-exports-that-threaten-rights-incl-co-comments/.
⁶⁶ See also Talmud *Pesachim* 33a and *Shulkhan Arukh Yoreh De'ah* 117.
⁶⁷ *Gilyon Maharsha* 117 note 1. *Maharam Shick* 136 permits engaging in such a partnership in a case of need. See Kushner, 86 for more.
⁶⁸ This is the opinion of the *Arukh HaShulkhan Yoreh De'ah* 117:27. But see *Igrot Moshe Yoreh De'ah* II 38, who permits this only for existing customers who have requested items, in order not to lose their business.
⁶⁹ Lintz, 69-96.
⁷⁰ Rabbi Tucker bases his position on the Mishnah on contemporary rabbi Aharon Walken. Rabbi Tucker's nuance of mutual funds is difficult to sustain. The goal of investing in a mutual fund is certainly to make money, not to protect oneself against a financial loss. Can "not making as much money as I could" really be thought of as facing a financial loss, from a Jewish perspective? See Rabbi Ethan Tucker and Rabbi Avi Killip. "Can Jews Invest in Burger King?" *Responsa Radio Episode 5*. Podcast. https://www.hadar.org/torah-resource/responsa-radio-episode-5-0.
⁷¹ Nigel Savage. "Jewish Impact Investing Summit—Nigel Savage, Hazon." Presentation:

Jewish Impact Investing Summit. Jlens. December 5, 2017. https://www.youtube.com/watch?v=S9cAfRxQbac.

[72] The *teshuvah* (responsa) literature is actually sparse on this question, except for Lintz's article, so I am referring here to my own observations of current practice in Orthodox communities. Even Kushner's book, which is focused on a Hareidi audience and inclines toward stringency, leaves the question as an open debate among rabbinic authorities.

[73] *Tosafot on Nedarim* 47a s.v. *Konam*; *Shulkhan Arukh Yoreh De'ah* 144:1.

[74] *Mishneh Torah Ma'achalot Asurot* 8:16; Rema *Orakh Hayyim* 450:6; *Tosafot on Pesachim* 22b s.v. *Ever min hechai*.

[75] Talmud *Temurah* 33b.

[76] See *Shulkhan Arukh Yoreh De'ah* 144:1 about profiting from idolatry and Talmud *Avodah Zarah* 29b and *Mishneh Torah Ma'akhalot Asurot* 11:1 about libation wine.

[77] Talmud *Hullin* 115; *Mishneh Torah Ma'akhalot Asurot* 9:1.

[78] Talmud *Hulin* 113a—this only applies to a kosher animal.

[79] *Mishneh Torah Ma'akhalot Asurot* 9:6 and *Magid Mishnah* ad. loc.

[80] *Pri Toar* chapter 7 note 3; *Chavot Da'at* 87 note 1; as opposed to *Pri Hadash* note 1.

[81] See Kushner, 43, note 6, for an overview of the sources and debates about each of these methods of cooking.

[82] Bais HaVaad.

[83] See previous notes that the prohibition applies only to kosher types of animals and possibly only kosher animals themselves.

[84] Talmud *Pesachim* 28-29.

[85] *Yibaneh bimheirah biyameinu*.

[86] *Shulkhan Arukh Orakh Hayyim* 443:3; see also *Mishnah Berurah* ad. loc. Note 17.

[87] This is known as *rotzeh bekiyumo*. See Talmud *Avodah Zarah* 64a, Rashi on *Avodah Zarah* 63b for examples regarding libation wine, and Tosafot on *Avodah Zarah* 32a s.v. *Veha* regarding *hametz* on Pesach. Whether this prohibition extends beyond libation wine is the subject of a debate between the *Tur* and *Shulkhan Arukh* (*Orakh Hayyim* 450:7) versus the *Parei Hananel* (ad. loc.) and the *Radbaz* (1:240).

[88] Another recently written responsum argues that *issurei hana'ah* are permitted because the CEO and corporate managers act as intermediaries (*arisut* in Hebrew). See Bais HaVaad.

[89] There has been little discussion of this in the halakhic literature because of how rare it is. The conversation has focused on *hametz* on Pesach, which has its own unique prohibitions. This is assuming there is no issue of *rotzeh bekiyumo* (based on the scenario in the main text). See, for example, Kushner 237, notes 5 and 6. Kushner argues the central question is whether an investor of a corporation is an "owner" (see Chapter 7) and implies the sale of some items that are *issurei hana'ah* but not part of a core business model are not a direct impact on the Jewish investor and not a concern.

Chapter 6

[1] Talmud *Bava Metzia* 42a.

[2] For biographical details: Margaliot, *Encyclopedia LeChachmei HaTalmud Ve-haGeonim*. s.v. *R' Yitzchak*. The Talmud has a variety of time- and context-specific investment advice. For example, *Ketubot* 79a (to resolve a dispute between spouses) offers recommendations of what kind of real estate to invest in.

[3] "Line 3 Pipeline Replacement Project (L3RP)." BankTrack. June 16, 2021. https://www.banktrack.org/project/line_3_pipeline_replacement_project.

[4] Billy Nauman and Stephen Morris. "Global banks' $750bn in fossil fuels finance conflicts with green pledges." *Financial Times*. March 23, 2021. https://www.ft.com/content/c1e31c6f-6319-4bfc-bde3-3ace80b46a2b.

[5] "Justice Department Reaches Settlement with Wells Fargo Resulting in More Than $175 Million in Relief for Homeowners to Resolve Fair Lending Claims." U.S. Department of Justice. July 12, 2012. https://www.justice.gov/opa/pr/justice-department-reaches-settlement-wells-fargo-resulting-more-175-million-relief.

[6] "Wells Fargo pays $2.1 billion fine over subprime mortgages." *CBS News*. August 1, 2018.

https://www.cbsnews.com/news/wells-fargo-pays-2-1-billion-fine-over-subprime-mortgages/.

[7] "New bank links to Myanmar junta and atrocities found." BankTrack. July 28, 2021. https://mailchi.mp/banktrack/new-bank-links-to-myanmar-junta-and-atrocities-found.

[8] Sharlene Brown, et al. "Leveraging Cash Allocations." Panel: Redirecting Capital to Accelerate Racial Equity Series. Croatan Institute. July 20, 2021. https://croataninstitute.org/2021/08/17/redirecting-capital-to-accelerate-racial-equity-series-leveraging-cash-allocations/.

[9] Ibid.

[10] Ibid.

[11] Graeber, 410.

[12] I sit on the board of my local credit union.

[13] Credit unions bring up a similar issue to that we encounter in Chapter 7, about the status of a corporation: is a credit union subject to questions of usury and should one use a *heter iska*? Some traditional rabbis, , such as Rabbi Moshe Heinemann and Rabbi Moshe Feinstein, held that one should ideally use a *heter iska* (see Chapter 8). But the broad consensus of Jewish legal authorities considers a credit union comprised of majority non-Jewish members (which is practically universal in the United States) to avoid any concern for the laws of usury, including Rabbi Dov Linzer, Rabbi Michael Broyde, and Rabbi Yaakov Love (personal communications with author).

[14] Up to a certain limit, bank deposits are insured by the FDIC, and credit union deposits are insured by the NCUA, both government agencies.

[15] Anna Fielding. "Private shame, public suspicion: the narrative rift that holds back ethical finance." Cohere Partners. June 6, 2021. https://coherepartners.com/private-shame-public-suspicion-the-narrative-rift-that-holds-back-ethical-finance/.

[16] Taeun Kwon and Viktoria Samberger. "Unleashing the Potential of Faith-Based Investors for Positive Impact and Sustainable Development." Center for Sustainable Finance and Private Wealth, University of Zurich. April 2021. https://ibf-uzh.ch/wp-content/uploads/2021/05/CSP_Unleashing_the_Potential_of_Faith-based_Investors_29-4-2021-pages.pdf.

[17] Julie Hammerman et al. "From Why to How: Jewish Institutions Discuss Impact Investing." Panel: Jewish Impact Investing Summit. JLens. May 18, 2020. https://www.youtube.com/watch?v=1ZdvduKwjI4.

[18] Taeun Kwon and Viktoria Samberger. "Unleashing the Potential of Faith-Based Investors for Positive Impact and Sustainable Development." Center for Sustainable Finance and Private Wealth, University of Zurich. April 2021. https://ibf-uzh.ch/wp-content/uploads/2021/05/CSP_Unleashing_the_Potential_of_Faith-based_Investors_29-4-2021-pages.pdf. Page 4.

[19] "Report and Recommendations on Diversity and Inclusion in the Asset Management Industry." U.S. Securities and Exchange Commission Asset Management Advisory Committee. July 7, 2021. https://www.sec.gov/files/spotlight/amac/amac-report-recommendations-diversity-inclusion-asset-management-industry.pdf.

[20] "Overcoming racial bias to optimize asset management for returns—and impact." Email. ImpactAlpha. March 2021. https://mailchi.mp/impactalpha.com/the-reconstruction-overcoming-racial-bias-to-optimize-asset-management-for-returns-and-impact.

[21] Interview with Daryn Dodson. Monique Aiken and Dennis Price, "Impact Briefing: Week of July 16." 2021. ImpactAlpha. https://impactalpha.com/impact-briefing-week-of-july-16.

[22] Villanueva, 5.

[23] Villanueva, 5.

[24] Gilbert A. Garcia, Scot E. Draeger, and Paul Greff. "SEC Asset Management Advisory Committee - Subcommittee on Diversity and Inclusion." Securities and Exchange Commission. https://www.sec.gov/files/amac-recommendations-di-subcommittee-070721.pdf.

[25] Rachel Robescotti. "Installment 6: Dismantling Systemic Barriers for Black Asset Managers." Adasina Social Capital. January 12, 2021. https://adasina.com/dismantling-systemic-barriers-for-black-asset-managers/.

[26] Rodin and Madsbjerg, 4.

[27] Saijel Kishan. "Corporate Climate Efforts Lack

Impact, Say Former Sustainability Executives." *Bloomberg*. July 13, 2021. https://www.bloomberg.com/news/features/2021-07-13/why-former-executives-warn-of-false-gains-in-esg-frenzy.

[28] Cheryl Winokur Munk. "How to Find a Socially Responsible Financial Adviser." *Wall Street Journal*. September 30, 2021. https://www.wsj.com/articles/how-to-find-a-socially-responsible-financial-adviser-11633020657.

[29] The latest version is available here (as of 2022): https://docs.google.com/spreadsheets/d/1WVJMFA5a4aOigkILYF__UpSTm8yckE-2-ZEQXBHDwSc/edit#gid=1224288045.

[30] Munk. "How to Find a Socially Responsible Financial Adviser." The suggestions are also available from Green America at https://greenamerica.org/media-mention/how-find-socially-responsible-financial-adviser.

[31] *Sifra Parsha* 2 *Number* 14 on Leviticus 19:14.

[32] See also Tamari, xv.

[33] "Definition of the Term 'Fiduciary'; Conflict of Interest Rule—Retirement Investment Advice." Federal Register Vol. 81, No. 68. April 8, 2016. https://www.govinfo.gov/content/pkg/FR-2016-04-08/pdf/2016-07924.pdf.

[34] Tara Siegel Bernard. "Obama-Era Investor Protection Rule Is Dead." *New York Times*. June 22, 2018. https://www.nytimes.com/2018/06/22/your-money/fiduciary-rule-dies.html.

Chapter 7

[1] See Micklethwait and Wooldridge, 176. Even by their conservative estimate, companies accounted for 37 of the 100 largest economies in the world; Walmart and Exxon both ranked in the top 50, larger than many countries.

[2] Shuman, 3.

[3] Quoted from O'Leary, page 3.

[4] See, for example, Lee Drutman. "How Corporate Lobbyists Conquered American Democracy." *The Atlantic*. April 20, 2015. https://www.theatlantic.com/business/archive/2015/04/how-corporate-lobbyists-conquered-american-democracy/390822/. In Drutman's words, "one has to go back to the Gilded Age to find business in such a dominant political position in American politics.."

[5] Graeber, 304.

[6] Technically, "corporation" is a broad category that includes many different kinds of corporations. There are close corporations, single-member limited liability corporations, corporations that are professional associations, and others. While some of these corporate forms (like the close corporation) seem very similar to historical business partnerships, the vast majority of Jewish investors' current assets are in publicly traded joint-stock corporations, which are the newest and most unusual form of corporation. That is where the bulk of the rabbinic discourse has focused and where I focus as well. See Broyde for an introductory discussion to the other forms of corporation.

[7] To be fair, even in secular law the status of a corporation remains a topic for evolving confusion. It was only in 2014 that the Supreme Court ruled, by the narrowest of margins, that corporations count as people for the purpose of political donations.

[8] Micklethwait and Wooldridge, xvii.

[9] The Jewish legal literature historically made a distinction between "large companies" and "incorporated entities." For example, Rabbi Moshe Feinstein permitted an incorporated entity to borrow money at interest even if all its shareholders were Jews (and therefore its control was clearly Jewish) since the limited liability provisions of incorporation exempted such borrowing from the category of usury. This distinction also has some grounding in secular literature that distinguishes between company law versus corporate law. However, since all public companies on the market today are incorporated, and all are also large entities with boards and management that mediate between the shareholders and the business, today the two categories overlap.

[10] Broyde, 269. Broyde notes this was stated earlier by Rabbi David Tzvi Hoffman, *Melamed Leho'il* 1:91.

[11] Micklethwait and Wooldridge, xxi.

[12] Micklethwait and Wooldridge, xvi.

[13] Joe Pinsker. "Japan's Oldest Businesses Have

Survived for More Than 1,000 Years." *The Atlantic*. February 12, 2015. https://www.theatlantic.com/business/archive/2015/02/japans-oldest-businesses-have-lasted-more-than-a-thousand-years/385396/.

[14] Albrecht Enders and Lars Haggstrom. "How the World's Oldest Company Reinvented Itself." Harvard Business Review. January 30, 2018. https://hbr.org/2018/01/how-the-worlds-oldest-company-reinvented-itself.

[15] Graeber, 304; Micklethwait and Wooldridge, 12; Blumberg, vii.

[16] Graeber, 304, quoting Ernst Kanorowicz.

[17] Broyde, 227.

[18] A practice that began in Italian towns from the ninth century onward. See Micklethwait and Wooldridge, 7. Shares being sold on the open market dates back to at least 13th-century Europe, but dramatically expanded with the "naval capitalism of the sixteenth and seventeenth centuries." Micklethwait and Wooldridge, 18-20. See also Blumberg, 4. Interestingly, 14th century Jewish authorities already addressed issues of usury when financing a shipping voyage, though certainly not for a colonizing mission (Rivash quoted in the *Minchat Yitzchak* 3:1).

[19] The first joint-stock corporations were the English and Dutch East India Companies, founded on colonization. Graeber, 320.

[20] Broyde, 207. Micklethwait and Wooldridge call the early corporations "state-sponsored charity." xv.

[21] Blumberg, 5.
[22] Blumberg, 5.
[23] Graeber, 347.
[24] Graeber 342.
[25] Micklethwait and Wooldridge, 17.
[26] Micklethwait and Wooldridge, 25; Blumberg, 14.
[27] Graeber, 341.
[28] O'Leary and Valdmanis, 2.
[29] Blumberg, 5.
[30] Blumberg, 6.
[31] Graeber, 410.
[32] Max Farrand, *The Records of the Federal Convention of 1787*. 2:615-616. https://www.loc.gov/item/11005506/.
[33] Blumberg, vii. See also "Our Hidden History of Corporations in the U.S." *Reclaim Democracy!* https://reclaimdemocracy.org/corporate-accountability-history-corporations-us/.
[34] Baradaran, 30.
[35] Blumberg, 5.
[36] Micklethwait and Wooldridge, xiv.
[37] Micklethwait and Wooldridge, xiv.
[38] Micklethwait and Wooldridge, xvii.
[39] Wrobel and Massey, 161.
[40] Cortese, 205. See also Brian G. Cartwright. "The Future of Securities Regulation." Securities and Exchange Commission. Oct 24, 2007. https://www.sec.gov/news/speech/2007/spch102407bgc.htm.
[41] Cortese, 206.
[42] For example, see Drutman, "How Corporate Lobbyists Conquered American Democracy," who noted that corporate reported spending on lobbying has surpassed the government's budget for the House and the Senate combined, and is 34 times what labor unions and public-interest groups spend combined.
[43] Blumberg, 5. For an analysis of Smith's approach to modern corporations, see also Larry Elliott. "Plc: prerogative of the unaccountable few." *The Guardian*. July 9, 2007. https://www.theguardian.com/business/2007/jul/09/politics.economicpolicy.
[44] Micklethwait and Wooldridge, xvii.
[45] Baradaran 58.
[46] "UNPRI Annual Report." United Nations *Principles on Responsible Investment*. Accessed July 26, 2021. https://www.unpri.org/annual-report-2018/how-we-work/the-pri-in-numbers.
[47] "Engaging Faith-Based Investors in Impact Investing." Global Impact Investing Network. January 2020. https://thegiin.org/assets/Engaging%20Faith-Based%20Investors%20in%20Impact%20Investing_FINAL.pdf.
[48] See also D. B. Bressler, "Ethical Investment: The Responsibility of Ownership in Jewish Law," in Levine, *Jewish Business Ethics*.
[49] Assuming even a single Jewish purchaser. See the next note.
[50] The actual *halakha* is somewhat more complicated, but the point is that considering a corporation to be a partnership means all public companies are off-limits for investment. Bear with me for a longer-than-usual endnote.

Some try to argue that Jewish law could consider a corporation to be a partnership (the stringent approach), and still allow investment in certain companies. Within the position that a corporation is a partnership, Rabbi Moshe Feinstein and others permit a corporation to pay interest, but not to receive interest. This means a company could issue bonds that a Jew could buy, if the company followed all other aspects of Jewish law. (*Iggerot Moshe Yoreh De'ah* 2:63, *Maharshag* 4:39, and *Kovetz Teshuvot* 3:124; see Reisman, *The Laws of Ribbis*, 105). Others disagree and would rule out any company that issues bonds, which is nearly all of them (*Minchat Yitzchak* 1:3, *Minchat Shlomo* 1:28, *Or Le'tziyon Yoreh De'ah* 1:5, and *Har Tzvi Yoreh De'ah* 126). Rabbi Feinstein's position would seem to lead to a negative screen on financial stocks but nothing else.

As for Shabbat, even within the stringent opinion, the *Minchat Yitzchak* permits one to own stock in a business that operates on Shabbat (see 1:72), as does the *Mishneh Halakhot* and Rabbi Moshe Feinstein in *Iggerot Moshe*. The *Mishneh Halakhot* claimed that the founders of a corporation inevitably reserve 51% of the stock for themselves in order to make decisions, which is not true of most companies on the market today; yet his halakhic reasoning may still apply.

But those who argue that one could consider a corporation to be a partnership and still invest in any company are wrong on multiple accounts. Regarding a corporation that operates on Shabbat or Jewish holidays (which includes every corporation when Yom Kippur falls on a weekday), the leniency of the authorities above only applies to non-Jewish employees. If any given corporation in a portfolio employs a Jewish person who is working on a Jewish holiday, investing in the corporation would be a violation of Jewish law (see Schwartz, Tamari, and Schwab 149; Rabbi Moshe Feinstein permits this in a case of great need, but when doing so he seems to be implicitly considering a corporation not to be a partnership).

While the rabbinic authorities have focused mostly on the three areas of *ribit* (usury), work on Shabbat, and *hametz* on Pesach, the entire body of Jewish law would also apply to a partnership. As just one example, if we consider a company a business partnership, companies that produce dough the rest of the year (not on Pesach) would need to separate a piece known as the *challah* portion. None of the strict opinions discuss similar affirmative commandments. This could be because, as noted in Chapter 7, companies like General Mills didn't become widespread investment options until the 1930s or later. But surely the stringent authorities would hold today that it is prohibited to own a business that does not fulfill affirmative commandments like separating the *challah* portion of the dough. (For more on this practice specifically and its relation to businesses, see Rabbi Yosef Dovid Chanowitz. "Challah: A guide for the Home and Bakery Industry." OK Kosher Certification. https://www.ok.org/article/challah/.

On top of everything, the practice of corporations owning stock in other corporations has become ubiquitous in the past 75 years, as I mention in the main text. And if I own stock in company A, and that company owns stock in company B, then I am also a (miniscule) part-owner of company B. If a single sector is screened out (like financials), it will render the whole market off-limits.

[51] *Kitzur Shulkhan Arukh* 65:28.
[52] *Shoel U'Meishiv* 1:3:31.
[53] *Maharam Shick* Y.D. 158 (see also 136).
[54] This includes: two of Maharam Shick's students, Rabbi Sholom Mordechai Schwadron in *Maharsham* 1:20 (1835-1911, Ukraine) and Rabbi Shimon Greenfield in *Maharshag Yoreh De'ah* 3 (1860-1930, Ukraine); one of the commentators on the *Kitzur Shulkhan Arukh*, Rabbi Hayim Yeshayah Cohen, in *Lechem Hapanim* on 65:28; Rabbi Yitzchak Weisz writing in the 1960s in *Minchat Yitzchak* (3:1, 4:16, 5:18, and 7:26); *Shevet HaLevi* 5:172; R. Menashe Klein, writing in the 1960s in *Mishneh Halakhot* 6:277; Rabbi Yisrael Rosenberg, contemporary, Bnei Brak, in *Sefer Yeshurun* 20 page 578; and *Minchat Shlomo* 1:28 (though the Bais HaVaad cited in the Bibliography notes it is unclear whether this only applies to majority-Jewish-owned corporations). See *Kovetz Teshuvot* 3:124, where *Netivot Sholom* reports

that R' Elyashiv states that this applies only to non-voting shares. *HaElef Lecha Shlomo Orakh Hayim* 238 argues that because a shareholder has no influence, one may own shares of a company that owns *hametz* during Pesach. See also Bris Yehudah, and R. Yosef Eliyahu Henkin in *Eidus LeYisrael*.

[55] R. Isaac Aaron Ettinger, writing in 1890, argued there is no problem with being a shareholder of a bank that lends on interest (*Maharia Halevi* 2:54), and also argued (*Maharia Halevi* 2:124) that owning shares in a corporation does not violate the transgression of owning *hametz* on Pesach. Rabbi Yisrael Salanter was quoted in the *Teshuvos V'Hanagos* 4:194 which states, "It is common practice for Jews to borrow and lend from banks, even though other Jews freely buy shares in those banks. They rely on the ruling of Rabbi Yisroel Salanter that the share of the Jews is *batel b'rov*." Other authorities who rule leniently include *Yad Shaul*, pp. 35-49, dealing with *hametz* on Pesach; *Gevuros Eliyahu Yoreh De'ah* 44; *Melamed Leho'il* 1:91 in his own name and in the name of Rabbi Azriel Hildesheimer; *Minchat Elazar* 2:22; and R. Chayyim David Regensberg, writing in 1966 in *Sefer Mishmeret Chayim*, Chapter 36 (134-137). The Chief Rabbinate of Israel follows this opinion and has argued that the idea of a non-human entity as collective owner of goods has precedent in Jewish tradition. They cite as examples community funds for charity as well as ownership by the ancient Temple in Jerusalem (Broyde, p. 221). Rabbi Moshe Sterbuch in *Moadim Uzmanim* 3:269n1 argues that a shareholder is really a lender, not an owner (see Broyde, in Levine, *Jewish Business Ethics*, p. 215 for an extensive critique of this argument).

[56] See Michael Broyde's long essay in Levine, *Jewish Business Ethics* for an excellent summary of opinions. See also R. Yisroel Reisman, in *The Laws of Ribbis*, 104-105.

[57] Rabbi Menashe Klein, *Mishneh Halakhot*.

[58] The Bais HaVaad articulates this as well but attempts to argue against it. Their responsum claims that an investor's responsibility doesn't extend to a company owned by another company because the original investor can't vote the shares of the second company. This is wrong on several accounts. First of all, we can take the Bais HaVaad's argument ad absurdum. According to their reasoning, if not being able to vote shares directly means I am not an owner of the business, then any Jewish business owner could create a holding company that they own in its entirety, which itself then owns a business that operates in violation of Jewish law. None of the rabbis listed above who hold stringently limited their opinions this way or suggested a holding company would make everything okay.

Second of all, The Bais HaVaad's approach violates common sense. There is a clear chain of ownership when an investor owns stock in Company A, which owns stock in Company B. Since Company A can vote the shares it owns in Company B, Company A is an owner of Company B. Investors in company A ultimately hold part-ownership Company B as well. There is no way with integrity to disentangle the web.

ואוסיף כאן שהיה נראה לי לא כדאי בכלל להביא את התשובה של בית הוועד מפני שכולל בתוכו טעויות גמורות לא רק טעויות בדבר משנה אלא בעיקרי הדת ומפרסם לשון הרע ושנאת חנם על אחינו כל בית ישראל ר״ל ולבסוף החלטתי להביא את התשובה כדי לשאת ולתת אתו אבל חייב אני להוכיח לכותביו וכן עשיתי ופה אני מפרסם שיוצא מגדר מחלוקת לשם שמים ומדבר שקר ולשון הרע והם חייבם בתשובה ולחזור למוטב ושארית ישראל לא יעשה עולה

[59] Nati Tucker. "Rabbinical Court Forbids Haredim From Investing in Israeli Companies." *Haaretz*. May 7, 2010. https://www.haaretz.com/1.5117234. See also "Badatz: Assur to Invest in Israeli Companies." *Matzav.com*. May 7, 2010. https://matzav.com/badatz-assur-to-invest-in-israeli-companies/.

[60] Timeline sourced from the Founder and Chairman's LinkedIn profile for the timeline: *Eli Gross* [LinkedIn page]. LinkedIn. Accessed 5/21/2021. https://www.linkedin.com/in/gbmcloseouts/.

[61] "Investination: Investments in Israeli Startups: About Us." Investination. Accessed 5/21/2021. https://wp.investination.com/about.

[62] "Besadno: Our Ethical Code." Besadno. Accessed March 1, 2022. https://besadno.com/our-ethical-code-of-standards/.

[63] "Transformative Investment Principles." Resource Generation. 2021. https://

resourcegeneration.org/transformative-investment-principles/.

[64] *Bris Yehudah*, Chapter 20, note 27; Reisman, *The Laws of Ribbis*, 104-105; Levine in *Case Studies in Jewish Business Ethics*, 368; Bais HaVaad Rabbinical Court of Lakewood. Contemporary poskim Rabbi Mordechai Willig, Rabbi Dov Linzer, and Rabbi Simcha Krauss (zt"l) align with this position as well.

[65] In this discussion, I have focused on the investment activity most of us engage in, which is purchasing shares of publicly traded companies on the secondary market (like stock exchanges). Rabbinic consensus is that such purchases are permitted. But other investment activities could be more problematic, like purchasing new shares of an initial public offering (IPO), investing in a close corporation (one not traded publicly), owning a majority of stock in a public company, or serving on a company's board of directors. If you engage in any of these activities, ask your local rabbi for more guidance.

[66] Matt Taibbi. "How Wall Street Killed Financial Reform." *Rolling Stone*. May 10, 2012. https://www.rollingstone.com/politics/politics-news/how-wall-street-killed-financial-reform-190802/.

[67] "How America's Gun Industry Is Tied To The NRA." *National Public Radio*. March 13, 2018. https://www.npr.org/2018/03/13/593255356/how-americas-gun-industry-is-tied-to-the-nra. In particular, "Today's National Rifle Association is essentially a de facto trade association masquerading as a shooting sports foundation. So the NRA does the bulk of lobbying for the industry."

[68] Jennifer Steinhauer. "For Gun Bill Born in Tragedy, a Tangled Path to Defeat." *New York Times*. April 18, 2013. https://www.nytimes.com/2013/04/19/us/tangled-birth-and-death-of-a-gun-control-bill.html. In particular, "Their efforts were largely trounced by the intense lobbying of gun rights groups."

[69] Ahmed Aboulenein and Carl O'Donnell. "Analysis: Drug pricing reform opponents win most pharma lobbying money." *Reuters*. October 27, 2021. https://www.reuters.com/business/healthcare-pharmaceuticals/capitol-hill-drug-pricing-reform-opponents-among-biggest-beneficiaries-pharma-2021-10-25/.

[70] This concern is echoed in many of the responsa. The *Minchat Yitzchak* describes a problematic way to sell shares of a company before Pesach, and then writes, "However, in our case, where no other way is possible, one can rely on this." Yet another way is indeed possible—not owning any stocks in the first place. Similarly, the *Maharshag*, writing in 1900, notes that his rabbi, the *Maharam Shick*, sought a permissible perspective in order to justify "the custom that has arisen in these times in our country and maybe in the entire world" of joint-stock companies with Jews and non-Jews. The *Moadim Uzmanim* writes that if the stringent position were correct, "a large percentage of Jews today who buy stocks on the market are liable for transgressing the prohibition of *hametz*, God help us...it would be fitting for us to set our souls to the *mitzvah* of finding a reason to be lenient in all of this."

[71] *Igrot Moshe Even Ha'ezer* 1:7. Rabbi Moshe Feinstein's two sons, each prominent rabbis in their own right, elaborated on this early opinion. One son, Rabbi Dovid Feinstein, framed the issue around whether or not an investor sought to engage in running the business. Anyone who actively voted proxies at annual meetings, even a minority shareholder, would be considered an "owner" by this logic (and would need to divest from all companies that are not run according to Jewish law). His other son, Rabbi Reuven Feinstein, posited that intention was crucial. If someone owned a large block of shares merely to profit from short-term market moves, that would not be considered "ownership." On the other hand, someone who owned a single share but intended to try to influence company policy would be an "owner." These positions suggest that the Jewishly permissible way to invest in a company would be to invest merely for profit and take no moral responsibility for the actions of the corporation, a position that today seems incompatible with a Jewish religious ethos but reflected the dominant approach to investing in public equities at the time.

[72] "A Faithful Voice for Justice: ICCR and 40 Years of Shareholder Advocacy." Interfaith Center on Corporate Responsibility. 2012. https://www.iccr.org/sites/default/files/

resources_attachments/_faithfulvoiceforjustic_brochure.pdf.

[73] See for reference Behar, *The Shareholder Action Guide*, page 2. Note that the dollar amounts have changed since Behar's book was published—the numbers in this text are current as of January 2022.

[74] "Global Sustainable Investment Review 2020." Global Sustainable Investment Alliance. 2021. http://www.gsi-alliance.org/wp-content/uploads/2021/08/GSIR-20201.pdf. Page 11.

[75] "92% of the S&P 500 and 70% of the Russell 1000 Published Sustainability Reports in 2020, G&A Research Shows." Governance & Accountability Institute. 2021. https://www.ga-institute.com/research/ga-research-directory/sustainability-reporting-trends/2021-sustainability-reporting-in-focus.html.

[76] "2023 Proxy Preview Report." As You Sow. https://www.proxypreview.org/2023/report.

[77] Heidi Welsh. "Anti-ESG Shareholder Proposals in 2023." Harvard Law School Forum on Corporate Governance. June 1, 2023. https://corpgov.law.harvard.edu/2023/06/01/anti-esg-shareholder-proposals-in-2023/.

[78] Rachel Minkin. "Diversity, Equity and Inclusion in the Workplace." Pew Research Center. May 17, 2023. https://www.pewresearch.org/social-trends/2023/05/17/diversity-equity-and-inclusion-in-the-workplace/.

[79] ICCR report, "Catalyzing Corporate Change." https://www.iccr.org/sites/default/files/iccrs_catalyzingcorporatechange2021_09.09.21.pdf.

[80] Schwartz, Tamari, and Schwab, 149-150.

[81] Jennifer Hiller and Svea Herbst-Bayliss. "Engine No. 1 extends gains with a third seat on Exxon board." *Reuters*. June 2, 2021. https://www.reuters.com/business/energy/engine-no-1-win-third-seat-exxon-board-based-preliminary-results-2021-06-02/.

[82] Bressler, 190.

[83] Morningstar, "How Big Fund Families Voted on Climate Change: 2020 Edition". https://www.morningstar.com/articles/1002749/how-big-fund-families-voted-on-climate-change-2020-edition.

[84] Saul Eblein. "Documents reveal how fossil fuel industry created, pushed anti-ESG campaign." *The Hill*. May 18, 2023. https://thehill.com/policy/equilibrium-sustainability/4010800-documents-fossil-fuel-anti-esg-campaign/.

[85] Hans Taparia. "The World May Be Better Off Without ESG Investing." *Stanford Social Innovation Review*. July 14, 2021. https://ssir.org/articles/entry/the_world_may_be_better_off_without_esg_investing.

[86] Leviticus 19:18.

[87] *Sefer Hasidim* 1124. While the *Biur Halachah* 708 quotes the *Tana D'Bei Eliyahu* 18 that one is only obligated to rebuke one who is "your fellow," that is in the context of Jews who deliberately and perpetually transgress, and does not address the question of non-Jews.

[88] *Sefer HaChinukh* 239.

[89] Alleen Brown. "New Federal Anti-SLAPP Legislation Would Protect Activists and Whistleblowers From Abusive Lawsuits." *Inside Climate News*. September 23, 2022. https://insideclimatenews.org/news/23092022/new-federal-anti-slapp-legislation-would-protect-activists-and-whistleblowers-from-abusive-lawsuits/.

Chapter 8

[1] David Streitfeld. "A California town drowns as home values sink." *New York Times*. November 11, 2008. https://www.nytimes.com/2008/11/11/business/worldbusiness/11iht-11home.17707597.html.

[2] Ibid.

[3] Mian and Sufi, *House of Debt*.

[4] Baradaran, 110.

[5] With the possible exception of Buddhism, which arose in a market economy—see Graeber, 235.

[6] Exodus 22:24.

[7] Leviticus 25:36-37.

[8] Deuteronomy 23:21-22.

[9] Psalms 15:5.

[10] Ezekiel 18:8.

[11] Rashi on Sanhedrin 27a; Tamari, *Al Chet*, 7.

[12] *Shulkhan Arukh Yoreh De'ah* 159:3.

[13] Tamari, *With All Your Possessions*, 181.

[14] *Taz Yoreh De'ah* 160:1.

Notes

[15] *Shulkhan Arukh Yoreh De'ah* 160:2.
[16] *Shulkhan Arukh Yoreh De'ah*; see also Tamari, 22.
[17] As quoted in Rabbi Yirmiyohu Kaganoff. "How Does a Heter Iska Work?" RabbiKaganoff.com. May 3, 2010. http://rabbikaganoff.com/how-does-a-heter-iska-work/.
[18] See also Tamari, 192.
[19] *Avnei Nezer* 157. It is interesting to note there was a suggestion among certain medieval commentators that the Torah might have expected even non-Jews to refrain from usury. See *Tosafot Bava Metzia* 70b s.v. *tashich*.
[20] *Sefer HaChinukh* 68:2.
[21] *Rashi on Exodus* 22:24.
[22] Cortese, 33.
[23] Mestrich and Pinsky, 164.
[24] Fundary. "Tandas And The Informal Economy of Mexico." *Medium*. January 3, 2018. https://medium.com/@fundary/tandas-and-the-informal-economy-of-mexico-4f3c80c1c7ce.
[25] See Graeber, 11 for one discussion.
[26] Indeed, a (very minority and rejected) opinion from Leon of Modena (1571–1648, Venice) suggests that Jews may only charge interest to the seven nations of the time of the Torah, and not to the Gentiles among whom they lived. See Marcus, 437.
[27] Tamari, 185. Tamari adds that despite their agricultural origins, interest-free loans have been a core element of Jewish society no matter where Jews lived or the sophistication of the economy.
[28] Bleich, "Survey," 54.
[29] A merchant is a middleman who purchases commodities from the producer and then sells them to consumer. The amount of capital one needs in advance to buy goods used to be modest, according to Bleich, until the Industrial Revolution, when commercial enterprises began needing "vast amounts" of capital. Bleich, "Survey," 54.
[30] See Ancselovits in Schwartz, *Just Weights, Just Measures* for a well-written review of this history.
[31] *Mishneh Torah Matanot Le'Aniyim* 10:7.
[32] Thank you to Michael Lustig for alerting me to this exception. Twelve states, including California, provide for non-recourse mortgages, which do not fit the strictest patterns of "inflexible" debt, and this may also be the case in other states for many mortgages intended for resale to US government entities.
[33] Satter, 5. The author also tells the complicated story of the Jewish community's—and her father's—relationship to the practice.
[34] Natalie Moore. "Contract Buying Robbed Black Families In Chicago Of Billions." *National Public Radio*. May 30, 2019. https://www.npr.org/local/309/2019/05/30/728122642/contract-buying-robbed-black-families-in-chicago-of-billions.
[35] Mishnah *Shevi'it* 10:3. See also Zion, 362.
[36] Rabbi Elisha Ancselovits, in Schwartz, *Just Weights, Just Balances*, 26.
[37] Talmud *Bava Metzia* 68b.
[38] Talmud *Bava Metzia* 70a.
[39] Rabbis Jacob Siegel, Yitz Greenberg, Julie Schonfeld, and Aaron Panken. "Rabbinic Insights on Investment as a Force for Good." Panel: Jewish Impact Investing Summit. JLens. Dec 5, 2017. https://youtu.be/hLxZGwfI9Js.
[40] Ibid.
[41] Alicia Jo Rabins, director and editor. *A Kaddish for Bernie Madoff*. 2021. https://www.akaddishforberniemadoff.com/.
[42] Graeber, 251.
[43] Talmud *Bava Metzia* 70b-71a; *Mishneh Torah Malveh VeLoveh* 5:2.
[44] *Tosafot* ad. loc.
[45] For a well-written and sympathetic picture in the European context, see Kriwaczek, *Yiddish Civilisation*. See also Baradaran, 104.
[46] Rabbi Elisha Ancselovits, in Schwartz, *Just Weights, Just Balances*, 26.
[47] Tamari, 180.
[48] *Terumat HaDeshen* 302 was the first to describe what a *heter iska* would look like; the first to publish an actual template was R. Mendel Avigdors of Cracow in the 16th century. Bleich, "Survey," 50. See also Bleich, *Contemporary*, 85.
[49] "Leo Strine on worker power and 'fair and sustainable capitalism.'" ImpactAlpha. July 2, 2021. https://impactalpha.com/leo-strine-on-worker-power-and-fair-and-sustainable-capitalism/.
[50] Rabbi Dani Rapp. "*Hilchos Ribbis* in Contemporary Business Settings." YUTorah.org. March 12, 2015. https://www.yutorah.org/lectures/lecture.cfm/832195/rabbi-dani-rapp/

51. hilchos-ribbis-in-contemporary-business-settings/.
51. "Chapter 5: Which Assets are Most Important?" Pew Research Center. July 26, 2011. https://www.pewresearch.org/social-trends/2011/07/26/chapter-5-which-assets-are-most-important/.
52. Rothstein, *The Color of Law*.
53. Reisman, 415.
54. Ben Sales. "Orthodox Rabbis Ban Borrowing From Quicken Loans—Because It's Run By Jews." *Forward*. May 2, 2018. https://forward.com/news/breaking-news/400133/orthodox-rabbis-ban-borrowing-from-quicken-loans-because-its-run-by-jews/.
55. "Legal Info: Disclosures and Licenses." *Rocket Mortgage*. https://www.rocketmortgage.com/legal/disclosures-licenses.
56. Tamari, 203.
57. *Maharam Shick Yoreh De'ah* 158.
58. "CCM Community Impact Bond Fund." Community Capital Management. https://www.ccminvests.com/strategies/ccm-community-impact-bond-fund/retail-shares-cratx/.
59. Villanueva, 81.
60. "Moody's cuts rating of Ferguson, Missouri, to 'junk' status." *Reuters*. September 15, 2015. https://www.reuters.com/article/ferguson-ratings-idUSL1N11N38Q20150917.
61. "Fiscal Justice Municipal Strategy: Investment Case." Adasina Social Capital. March 2021. https://adasina.com/wp-content/uploads/2021/03/Adasina-Fiscal-Justice-Municipal-Strategy-Investment-Case.pdf.
62. Andrea Armeni and Curt Lyon. "Grassroots Community-Engaged Investment: Redistributing power over investment processes as the key to fostering equitable outcomes." Transform Finance. April 2021. https://www.transformfinance.org/blog/participatory-investment-report.
63. *The People's Fund*. Accessed 11/17/2021. https://thepeople.co.za/.
64. Luyanda Jafta. "Luyanda Jafta." LinkedIn. 2022. https://www.linkedin.com/in/luyanda-jafta/.
65. Jessica Pothering. "How The People's Fund is unlocking capital for small businesses from the crowd up." ImpactAlpha. November 16, 2021. https://impactalpha.com/the-peoples-fund-is-unlocking-capital-for-small-businesses-from-the-crowd-up/.
66. "Charli Cooksey, WEPOWER." ImpactAlpha. August 13, 2021. https://impactalpha.com/charli-cooksey-wepower/.
67. "WEPOWER fund will back diverse founders to build community wealth in St. Louis." ImpactAlpha. Aug 10, 2021. https://impactalpha.com/wepower-fund-will-back-diverse-founders-to-build-community-wealth-in-st-louis/.
68. Alyssa Ely and Denise Hearn. "Impact Investors Need to Share Power, Not Just Capital." *Stanford Social Innovation Review*. April 14, 2021. https://ssir.org/articles/entry/impact_investors_need_to_share_power_not_just_capital.
69. Villanueva, 172.
70. Andrea Armeni and Curt Lyon. "Grassroots Community-Engaged Investment: Redistributing power over investment processes as the key to fostering equitable outcomes." Transform Finance. April 2021. https://www.transformfinance.org/blog/participatory-investment-report.
71. As quoted in Villanueva, 174.
72. Sharlene Brown, et al. "Leveraging Cash Allocations." Panel: Redirecting Capital to Accelerate Racial Equity Series. Croatan Institute. July 20, 2021. https://croataninstitute.org/2021/08/17/redirecting-capital-to-accelerate-racial-equity-series-leveraging-cash-allocations/.
73. Author's personal conversation with Ben Wrobel and Meg Massey.
74. Monique Aiken and Donnel Baird. "Impact Briefing: August 13." ImpactAlpha. August 13, 2021. https://impactalpha.com/impact-briefing-august-13/.
75. "BlocPower Energy Services 3 Climate Impact Note." Raise Green. Accessed June 21, 2022. https://invest.raisegreen.com/offering/bpes3cin3/details.
76. "Community Investment Note." Calvert Impact Capital. https://calvertimpactcapital.org/investing/community-investment-note.
77. Personal interview with the author, April 2021. See also Amanda Joseph. "Advancing Faith Values Through Impact Investing." Calvert

Notes

Impact Capital. March 30, 2021. https://calvertimpactcapital.org/resources/advancing-faith-values-through-impact-investing.

Chapter 9

[1] Jenna Russell. "Threads of a New Life." *Boston Globe.* May 19, 2017. https://www.bostonglobe.com/metro/2017/05/19/threads-new-life/HuhjKSPPOGdWGTahanpKjI/story.html.
[2] "JVS: Our History." Jewish Vocational Services of Greater Boston. https://www.jvs-boston.org/who-we-are/our-history/.
[3] "Massachusetts social-impact bond to fund immigrant, refugee workforce development." ImpactAlpha. June 21, 2017. https://impactalpha.com/massachusetts-social-impact-bond-to-fund-immigrant-refugee-workforce-development-23d156c1d5fb/.
[4] "Innovation at JVS: Pay for Success." Jewish Vocational Services. https://www.jvs-boston.org/portfolio/pay-for-success/.
[5] Michael Lustig, et al. "Jewish Institutions Leading the Way." Panel: Jewish Impact Investing Summit. JLens. December 5, 2017. https://www.youtube.com/watch?v=gQCDff-hGLw.
[6] The organization's recent 990 from 2019 notes $217 million in international equity, $800 million in publicly traded securities, along with significant investments in derivatives. https://cdn.fedweb.org/fed-34/2/FY2020%2520-%2520CJP%2520-%2520FED%2520Form%2520990%2520-%2520PDC.pdf.
[7] "Massachusetts Pathways to Economic Advancement Pay for Success Project." Massachusetts Executive Office for Administration and Finance. https://www.mass.gov/doc/massachusetts-pathways-to-economic-advancement-fact-sheet/download.
[8] "Massachusetts social-impact bond to fund immigrant, refugee workforce development." ImpactAlpha. June 21, 2017. https://impactalpha.com/massachusetts-social-impact-bond-to-fund-immigrant-refugee-workforce-development-23d156c1d5fb/.
[9] Rabbi Jacob Siegel. "Boston's Judaism-infused Investment Experiment." *eJewish Philanthropy.* August 10, 2017. https://ejewishphilanthropy.com/bostons-judaism-infused-investment-experiment/.
[10] Personal communication with the author, 3/30/2022.
[11] Anne Roder and Mark Elliott. "Stepping Up: Interim Findings on JVS Boston's English for Advancement Show Large Earnings Gains." Economic Mobility Corporation. November 2020. https://economicmobilitycorp.org/wp-content/uploads/2020/10/SteppingUp.pdf.
[12] Cortese, viii.
[13] Cortese, ix.
[14] Cortese, 6.
[15] Cortese, 6.
[16] Cortese, 12.
[17] Ibid.
[18] Georgia Kromrei. "Pension fund money is getting tangled in some controversial housing deals." *The Real Deal—New York State Real Estate News.* March 2020. https://therealdeal.com/issues_articles/a-pension-for-property-investment/.
[19] Ryan Dezember. "If You Sell a House These Days, the Buyer Might Be a Pension Fund." *Wall Street Journal.* April 4, 2021. https://www.wsj.com/articles/if-you-sell-a-house-these-days-the-buyer-might-be-a-pension-fund-11617544801.
[20] Talmud *Bava Metzia* 71a.
[21] Talmud *Nedarim* 80b-81a.
[22] Talmud *Shabbat* 54b.
[23] Talmud *Ketubot* 67.
[24] "How Many Accredited Investors Are There In America?" DQYDJ. June 8, 2021. https://dqydj.com/accredited-investors-in-america/.
[25] "Institutional Accredited Investors (IAIs)." Thomson Reuters Practical Law. https://content.next.westlaw.com/Document/I03f4da36eee311e28578f7ccc38dcbee/View/FullText.html.
[26] Schuman, 16.
[27] Beth Sirull. "I Should Not Have To Check My Jewish Values At The Synagogue Door." *Forward.* July 24, 2019. https://forward.com/life/428133/i-should-not-have-to-check-my-

[28] Julie Hammerman et al. "From Why to How: Jewish Institutions Discuss Impact Investing." Panel: Jewish Impact Investing Summit. JLens. May 18, 2020. https://www.youtube.com/watch?v=1ZdvduKwjI4.
[29] "Partner Spotlight: Jewish Community Foundation." San Diego Habitat for Humanity. September 27, 2021. https://www.sandiegohabitat.org/partner-spotlight-jewish-community-foundation/.
[30] Cortese, x.
[31] "The TechSoup Direct Public Offering." TechSoup. Accessed 2/2/2022. https://www.techsoup.org/direct-public-offering.
[32] "SEC Adopts Rules to Permit Crowdfunding." Securities and Exchange Commission. October 30, 2015. https://www.sec.gov/news/pressrelease/2015-249.html.
[33] "BIPOC Homeownership Project." Small Change. Accessed 2/2/2022. https://www.smallchange.co/projects/BIPOC-Homeownership.
[34] Michael Etzel, et al. "Back to the Frontier: Investing that Puts Impact First." The Bridgespan Group. April 2021. https://www.bridgespan.org/bridgespan/Images/articles/investing-that-puts-impact-first/back-to-the-frontier-investing-that-puts-impact-first.pdf.
[35] "Leviticus Fund: About." Leviticus Fund. https://leviticusfund.org/about/.
[36] "Leviticus Fund: Faith Capital for Building Communities." Leviticus Fund. March 2021. https://www.leviticusfund.org/wp-content/uploads/2021/03/Associate-Investor-Form_individual-2021.pdf.
[37] Personal conversation with the author, March 28, 2022.

Chapter 10

[1] The ad is currently available to watch on YouTube at https://www.youtube.com/watch?v=j7OHG7tHrNM.
[2] Finis Dunaway. "The 'Crying Indian' ad that fooled the environmental movement." *Chicago Tribune*. Nov 21, 2017. https://www.chicagotribune.com/opinion/commentary/ct-perspec-indian-crying-environment-ads-pollution-1123-20171113-story.html.
[3] "The Litter Myth." *Throughline (NPR)*. September 2019. https://www.npr.org/2019/09/04/757539617/the-litter-myth.
[4] Ibid. See also Rogers, 109.
[5] Auden Schendler. "The Complicity of Corporate Sustainability." *Stanford Social Innovation Review*. April 7, 2021. https://ssir.org/articles/entry/the_complicity_of_corporate_sustainability.
[6] Rebecca Solnit. "Big oil coined 'carbon footprints' to blame us for their greed. Keep them on the hook." *The Guardian*. August 23, 2021. https://www.theguardian.com/commentisfree/2021/aug/23/big-oil-coined-carbon-footprints-to-blame-us-for-their-greed-keep-them-on-the-hook.
[7] *Mishneh Torah Hilchot Teshuvah* 3:4.
[8] Tejal Rao. "Food Supply Anxiety Brings Back Victory Gardens." *New York Times*. March 25, 2020. https://www.nytimes.com/2020/03/25/dining/victory-gardens-coronavirus.html.
[9] Talmud *Sanhedrin* 27b.
[10] Talmud *Bava Kamma* 50b.
[11] Talmud *Berakhot* 29b-30a.
[12] See the Talmud, in chapter 2 of tractate Bava Batra; see also *Mishneh Torah Hilchot Shecheinim*. Examples include a sesame oil press that weakens the foundations of a nearby dwelling (*Bava Batra* 25b); an oven or furnace emitting thick smoke (*Bava Batra* 23a), where there is the possibility of endangering a neighbor's health; and those who dispose of waste in the public domain, which really belongs to everyone (*Bava Kamma* 50b).
[13] Thorfinn Stainforth and Bartosz Brzezinski. "More than half of all CO2 emissions since 1751 emitted in the last 30 years." Institute for European Environmental Policy. April 29, 2020. https://ieep.eu/news/more-than-half-of-all-co2-emissions-since-1751-emitted-in-the-last-30-years.
[14] Matthew Taylor and Jonathan Watts. "Revealed: the 20 firms behind a third of all carbon emissions." *The Guardian*. October 9, 2019. https://www.theguardian.com/environment/2019/oct/09/

revealed-20-firms-third-carbon-emissions.
[15] "New global analysis: At current rates, oil and gas companies will prevent world from hitting 1.5°C warming goal." World Benchmarking Alliance. July 22, 2021. https://www.worldbenchmarkingalliance.org/news/wba-launches-oil-and-gas-benchmark/.
[16] Sam Meredith. "Just 20 companies are responsible for over half of 'throwaway' plastic waste, study says." *CNBC*. May 18, 2021. https://www.cnbc.com/2021/05/18/20-companies-responsible-for-55percent-of-single-use-plastic-waste-study.html.
[17] Maddie Stone. "Bowing to investors, Microsoft will make its devices easier to fix." *Grist*. Oct 7, 2021. https://grist.org/accountability/bowing-to-investors-microsoft-will-make-its-devices-easier-to-fix/.
[18] "Mondelez International, PepsiCo Agree to Cut Use of Virgin Plastic, After dialogue with As You Sow." As You Sow. March 9, 2021. https://www.asyousow.org/press-releases/2021/3/9/mondelez-pepsico-cut-virgin-plastic.
[19] David Chandler. "Leaving our mark." *MIT News*. April 16, 2008. https://news.mit.edu/2008/footprint-tt0416.
[20] Mark Kaufman. "The carbon footprint sham." *Mashable*. 2021. https://mashable.com/feature/carbon-footprint-pr-campaign-sham.
[21] Mark Kaufman. "The deceiving thing about the big, historic drop in CO2 emissions." *Mashable*. May 1, 2020. https://mashable.com/article/carbon-emissions-drop-2020-coronavirus.
[22] "Crown JEWEL Conversation with Rabbi Jennie Rosenn." *Jewish Women's Foundation of New York*. February 2, 2023. https://www.youtube.com/watch?v=M9yDQtoyDaM.
[23] Shelley Rivkin, speaking in Jakir Manela, et al. "Jewish Federations Leading on Climate." Panel: Big Bold Jewish Climate Fest. January 20, 2022. https://www.youtube.com/watch?v=JOI9YNc-KS4.
[24] Jakir Manela, Nigel Savage, Mariana Bergovoy, and Noga Levtzion-Nadan. "COP26: Sound the Call Podcast Interview." Adamah. https://www.youtube.com/watch?v=XzfQdNjBZFo.
[25] See *Magen Avraham* and others on *Orakh Chayim* 514. Remarkably, Rabbi Yaakov Yehoshua Falk (1680-1756, Poland) in his work *P'nei Yehoshua* permitted smoking even on a holiday, when lighting fires is normally prohibited, because of its positive health benefits for digestion.
[26] Rabbi Moshe Sternbuch explicitly suggests that the tobacco being used hundreds of years ago is a categorically different issue than modern cigarettes. *Teshuvos VeHanhagos* 3:354.
[27] "Tobacco-Related Mortality." Centers for Disease Control and Prevention. https://www.cdc.gov/tobacco/data_statistics/fact_sheets/health_effects/tobacco_related_mortality/index.htm.
[28] Surgeon General's 1964 report: making smoking history." *Harvard Health Blog*. January 10, 2014. https://www.health.harvard.edu/blog/surgeon-generals-1964-report-making-smoking-history-201401106970.
[29] Oreskes and Conway, 15.
[30] *Igrot Moshe Yoreh De'ah* 2:49.
[31] Talmud *Bava Batra* 60b.
[32] Talmud *Gittin* 58a.
[33] Ibid.
[34] This is poetically rendered in the Yom Kippur Machzor in the prayer *Eleh Ezkera*.
[35] *Mishneh Torah Hilchot Mamrim* 2:6.
[36] Rabbi Moshe Sternbuch said this explicitly in *Teshuvos VeHanhagos* 3:354. Regarding Rabbi Feinstein: Rabbi Aharon Adler, student of Rabbi Moshe Tendler, Rabbi Feinstein's son-in-law, reported this in the name of Rabbi Tendler. Rabbi Aharon Adler. "Smoking and Halacha." *YUTorah Online*. June 13, 2018. https://www.yutorah.org/lectures/lecture.cfm/902576/rabbi-aharon-adler/smoking-and-halacha/.
[37] *Tzitz Eliezer* 15:39.
[38] Letter from Rabbi Moshe Feinstein to Rabbi Reuven Sofer, September 1980. Quoted in Rabbi Chaim Steinmetz. "Is Smoking Kosher?" Jewish Law Commentary. http://jlaw.com/Commentary/smoking.html.
[39] See *Igrot Moshe Choshen Mishpat* 2:76, written five years before his death.
[40] Actually, the first modern Jewish legal authority to caution against smoking, the *Chafetz Chayim*, did so in the 1920s, but it

is clear from his concerns that he did not understand smoking to be lethal to one's health the way modern science understands it to be. His concern was for behavioral addiction, a physical weakening of one's body (but not illness per say), waste of money, and distraction from learning Torah.

[41] *Aseh Lecha Rav,* 2:1. Rabbi HaLevi points out in the beginning of his responsum that the number of smokers had fallen since Rabbi Feinstein's original responsum permitting smoking and argues that the science has become so clear that if the rabbis of the Talmud were alive today they surely would have prohibited smoking explicitly.

[42] *Tzitz Eliezer* 17:22 (dated 1985).

[43] "Smoking." *Union for Reform Judaism.* 1987. https://urj.org/what-we-believe/resolutions/smoking.

[44] Rabbi Seymour Siegel. "Smoking: A Jewish Perspective." *Proceedings of the Committee of Jewish Law and Standards.* 1986-1990. https://www.rabbinicalassembly.org/sites/default/files/public/halakhah/teshuvot/19861990/siegel_smoking.pdf.

[45] Rabbi Asher Bush, Chairman. "The Prohibition of Smoking in Halacha: A Ruling by the Va'ad Halacha." Rabbinical Council of America. June 30, 2006. https://www.rabbis.org/pdfs/Prohibition_Smoking.pdf. To be fair, even this position is not universal in the Jewish world (what ever is?). See, for example, Kushner, writing from a Hareidi perspective, who in 2018 notes that smoking is unhealthy and people are urged not to do so, but carefully avoids using the word "prohibited." A separate direction where Jewish law might have additional compassion (though not permission) is when smoking might be considered "self-medication" for those dealing with trauma or stress who do not have access to affordable healthcare.

[46] *Aseh Lecha Rav* 6:58.

[47] *Tzitz Eliezer* 21:14.

[48] Levine, *Case Studies in Jewish Business Ethics,* 367. Note that Dr. Levine says "rabbis dispute" whether tobacco is clearly prohibited. Although the book was published in 2000, he draws his sources from the late 1970s through 1982, another indication of how a change in public perception over a relatively short period of two decades can drastically alter a discussion. See also Rabbi Chaggai Resnikoff's writing on climate change quoted later in the chapter. Rabbi Resnikoff articulates a nuance that even for those who might not have held that smoking is prohibited, they may have held that avoiding smoking and protecting one's health is required.

[49] For a fairly comprehensive list numbering in the dozens, see Rabbi Yehuda Spitz, "Smoking and Halacha." Ohr Someyach blog. August 17, 2019. https://ohr.edu/this_week/insights_into_halacha/5717.

[50] For one Jewish approach to climate change and the addiction analogy, see Rabbi Natan Margalit. "Addiction, Hasidic Spirituality and Climate Change." Presentation: Big Bold Jewish Climate Fest. January 27, 2021. https://www.youtube.com/watch?v=I91RX44fMp0.

[51] Shannon Hall. "Exxon Knew about Climate Change almost 40 years ago." *Scientific American.* October 26, 2015. https://www.scientificamerican.com/article/exxon-knew-about-climate-change-almost-40-years-ago/.

[52] Benjamin Hulac. "Tobacco and Oil Industries Used Same Researchers to Sway Public." *Scientific American.* July 20, 2016. https://www.scientificamerican.com/article/tobacco-and-oil-industries-used-same-researchers-to-sway-public1/.

[53] Klein, 36-7.

[54] "The Overton Window." Mackinac Center for Public Policy. https://www.mackinac.org/OvertonWindow.

[55] "Climate Change 2022: Impacts, Adaptation and Vulnerability." Intergovernmental Panel on Climate Change. February 2022. https://www.ipcc.ch/report/ar6/wg2/.

[56] "Oil and Gas Benchmark: Measuring the 100 most influential companies on their progress to 1.5°C." World Benchmarking Alliance. July 2021. https://www.worldbenchmarkingalliance.org/publication/oil-and-gas/.

[57] "Affirmation of Climate Finance Moral Standards for Asset Managers." GreenFaith. February 2022. https://actionnetwork.org/

58 "Shell to pay $111m over decades-old oil spills in Nigeria." *The Guardian.* August 11, 2021. https://www.theguardian.com/business/2021/aug/12/shell-to-pay-111m-over-decades-old-oil-spills-in-nigeria.
59 Bill McKibben. "The Case for Fossil-Fuel Divestment." *Rolling Stone Magazine.* February 22, 2013. https://www.rollingstone.com/politics/politics-news/the-case-for-fossil-fuel-divestment-100243/.
60 Global Fossil Fuel Divestment Commitments Database. https://divestmentdatabase.org/.
61 Louise Boyle. "Senior citizens lead climate protest in rocking chairs at major US banks." *Yahoo! News.* March 22, 2023. https://news.yahoo.com/senior-citizens-lead-climate-protest-162756025.html.
62 "With All Our Might: How the Jewish Community Can Invest in a Just, Livable Future." Dayenu. December 2022. https://dayenu.org/wp-content/uploads/2022/12/DAYENU_Report_FINAL.pdf. See also Zach Stein. "Chapter 3: Why Sustainable Investing Will Likely Outperform." *Carbon Collective.* https://www.carboncollective.co/sustainable-investing/performance.
63 "Dayenu: A Jewish Call to Climate Action." Dayenu. https://dayenu.org
64 Alexander Gelfand. "Why Divestment Doesn't Hurt "Dirty" Companies." *Stanford Business.* Oct 27, 2021. https://www.gsb.stanford.edu/insights/why-divestment-doesnt-hurt-dirty-companies.
65 "Fossil fuel groups hit extra hard by divestment pledges that go viral." *Financial Times.* April 10, 2023. https://www.ft.com/content/a446f9a7-2fcb-4d48-bdd8-2ff1dcbe1bb3.
66 Hirschman, *Exit, Voice, and Loyalty.*
67 Jennifer Goodman, et al. "Social Shareholder Engagement: The Dynamics of Voice and Exit." *Journal of Business Ethics.* Vol. 125(2), pages 193-210, December 2014. https://ideas.repec.org/a/kap/jbuset/v125y2014i2p193-210.html.
68 Michael J. de la Merced. "How Exxon Lost a Board Battle With a Small Hedge Fund." *New York Times.* May 28, 2021. https://www.nytimes.com/2021/05/28/business/energy-environment/exxon-engine-board.html.
69 Dominic Webb, "Updated: Exxon divestments stopped fourth Engine No.1 board nominee being elected, says CalPERS' Simpson." Responsible Investor. August 3, 2021. https://www.responsible-investor.com/articles/exxon-divestments-stopped-fourth-engine-no-1-nominee-from-being-elected-to-oil-giant-s-board-says-calpers-s-simpson.
70 Personal conversation with the author, 8/11/2021.
71 Amy Cortese. "Engine No. 1 opts for accommodation over confrontation with Big Oil and big banks." ImpactAlpha. May 26, 2022. https://impactalpha.com/engine-no-1-opts-for-accommodation-over-confrontation-with-big-oil-and-big-banks/. See also Andrew Ross Sorkin, et al. "Reassessing the Board Fight That Was Meant to Transform Exxon." *The New York Times.* May 31, 2023. https://www.nytimes.com/2023/05/31/business/dealbook/engine-no-1-exxon-mobil.html.
72 "Church Commissioners to vote against directors of Exxon, Occidental, Shell, Total over lack of progress on climate change." Church of England. May 9, 2023. https://www.churchofengland.org/media-and-news/press-releases/church-commissioners-vote-against-directors-exxon-occidental-shell.
73 "Countdown to COP26: An analysis of the climate and biodiversity practices of Europe's largest banks." ShareAction. June 9, 2021. https://shareaction.org/reports/countdown-to-cop26-an-analysis-of-the-climate-and-biodiversity-practices-of-europes-largest-banks.
74 "Commerzbank, Citi and Bank of America among banks issuing new deal for Russian coal giant SUEK just two months before COP26." BankTrack. Email. September 9, 2021. https://mailchi.mp/banktrack/commerzbank-citi-and-bank-of-america-among-banks-issuing-new-deal-for-russian-coal-giant-suek-just-two-months-before-cop26.
75 "Shareholder Resolutions: BlackRock." *Mercy Investment Services.* https://www.mercyinvestmentservices.org/shareholder-resolutions-detail.aspx?bid=347840.

76 Ron Bousso and Simon Jessop "BlackRock goes against BP board in climate resolution vote." *Reuters.* May 28, 2021. https://www.reuters.com/business/sustainable-business/blackrock-goes-against-bp-board-climate-resolution-vote-2021-05-28/.

77 "Practicing Responsible Policy Engagement: How large U.S. companies lobby on climate change." Ceres. 2021. https://www.ceres.org/practicingRPE.

78 "50 Years of Impact: ICCR Member Advocacy on Governance." ICCR. January 2022. https://my.visme.co/view/pv6pk9d4-ok32rz6kvm0z5w8d.

79 Fiona Reynolds. "Time must be called on negative climate lobbying." UNPRI. August 12, 2021. https://www.unpri.org/pri-blog/time-must-be-called-on-negative-climate-lobbying/8259.article.

80 "Investors See Momentum Building as Companies Agree to Support Paris-Aligned Climate Policy." Interfaith Center on Corporate Responsibility. April 8, 2021. https://www.iccr.org/investors-see-momentum-building-companies-agree-support-paris-aligned-climate-policy.

81 "50 Years of Impact: ICCR Member Advocacy on Governance." https://www.iccr.org/50-years-member-advocacy.

82 "Food Loss and Waste." USDA. https://www.usda.gov/foodlossandwaste.

83 Mireya Villarreal. "More than 50 million Americans facing hunger in 2020, projections show." *CBS News.* November 24, 2020. https://www.cbsnews.com/news/hunger-50-million-americans-2020-projections-show/.

84 "2020 Impact Report." JLens. April 2021. https://www.jlensnetwork.org/

85 Frances Seymour. "2021 Must Be a Turning Point for Forests. 2020 Data Shows Us Why." World Resources Institute. March 31, 2021. https://www.wri.org/insights/2021-must-be-turning-point-forests-2020-data-shows-us-why.

86 "Bunge Shareholders Resoundingly Support Green Century Proposal on Deforestation." Green Century Funds. May 7, 2021. https://www.greencentury.com/bunge-shareholders-resoundingly-support-green-century-proposal-on-deforestation/.

87 "Fossil Free Funds." Fossil Free Funds—A Project of As You Sow. https://fossilfreefunds.org/.

88 "Green Century Funds: Shareholder Advocacy." Green Century Funds. February 2022. https://www.greencentury.com/wp-content/uploads/2022/02/Shareholder-Advocacy-2-Pager.pdf.

89 *DivestInvest.* https://www.divestinvest.org/.

90 "With All Our Might: How the Jewish Community Can Invest in a Just, Livable Future." Dayenu. https://dayenu.org/climateinvest/.

91 As defined by the United Nations. See Jag Bhalla. "What's your 'fair share' of carbon emissions? You're probably blowing way past it." *Vox.* February 24, 2021. https://www.vox.com/22291568/climate-change-carbon-footprint-greta-thunberg-un-emissions-gap-report.

92 "Goal 7: Ensure access to affordable, reliable, sustainable and modern energy for all." United Nations. https://sdgs.un.org/goals/goal7.

93 "7: Affordable and Clean Energy." United Nations. https://www.un.org/sustainabledevelopment/wp-content/uploads/2016/08/7_Why-It-Matters-2020.pdf.

94 Deuteronomy 4:9.

95 Deuteronomy 22:8.

96 *Mishneh Torah Hilchot Rotzeach U-Shmirat Nefesh* 11:4.

97 Yerucham Fishel Perlow, *Commentary on Sefer HaMitzvot: Negative Mitzvot* 53-55, page 54b.

98 Jakir Manela, et al. "Jewish Federations Leading on Climate." Panel: Big Bold Jewish Climate Fest. January 20, 2022. https://www.youtube.com/watch?v=JOI9YNc-KS4.

99 Arno Rosenfeld. "Roadblocks ahead as activists push for Jewish fossil fuel divestment." *Forward.* January 12, 2022. https://forward.com/news/480708/roadblocks-ahead-as-activists-push-for-jewish-fossil-fuel-divestment/.

100 "Jewish Climate Leadership Coalition." Adamah. https://adamah.org/for-educators-organizations/jewish-climate-leadership-coalition/.

101 Personal conversation with the author, December 5, 2021.

102 "Daily CO2." CO2 Earth. https://www.co2.earth/daily-co2.

103 Talmud *Yoma* 87a.
104 Rabbi Rachel Kahn-Troster, Beth Sirull, Amanda Joseph, and Jeff Perkins. "Fossil Freedom: Greening Endowments and Investments." Panel: Big Bold Jewish Climate Fest. January 19, 2022. https://www.youtube.com/watch?v=K2HMPFicGdE.

Chapter 11

1 Eillie Anzilotti. "This Startup Lets You Use Your Extra Cash To Invest In Community Development." *Fast Company*. September 28, 2017. https://www.fastcompany.com/40470833/this-startup-lets-you-use-your-extra-cash-to-invest-in-community-development.
2 Afdhel Aziz. "How Fintech Platform CNote Gives Socially Conscious Investors New Ways To Battle Inequality: An Interview With Catherine Berman." *Forbes*. August 4, 2020. https://www.forbes.com/sites/afdhelaziz/2020/08/04/how-fintech-platform-cnote-gives-socially-conscious-investors-new-ways-to-battle-inequality-an-interview-with-catherine-berman/.
3 Interview with the author, December 3, 2021.
4 Anzilotti. "This Startup Lets You Use Your Extra Cash."
5 "CNote: Individual Investors." CNote. Accessed 12/1/2022. https://www.mycnote.com/individuals/.
6 Michele Weldon. "Karma is Good: 2 FinTech Entrepreneurs Invest in Women." *Take the Lead*. January 22, 2018. https://www.taketheleadwomen.com/blog/karma-is-good-2-fintech-entrepreneurs-invest-in-women/.
7 "CNote's Flagship Fund." CNote. https://www.mycnote.com/solutions/flagship-fund-1/.
8 Neil Bhutta, et al. "Disparities in Wealth by Race and Ethnicity in the 2019 Survey of Consumer Finances." Board of Governors of the Federal Reserve System. September 28, 2020. https://www.federalreserve.gov/econres/notes/feds-notes/disparities-in-wealth-by-race-and-ethnicity-in-the-2019-survey-of-consumer-finances-20200928.html.
9 CNote. Accessed 12/1/2021. https://www.mycnote.com/.
10 "Getting Money off the Sidelines: A Starting List to Invest for Racial Equity." *Bridgespan Social Impact et al.* November 8, 2021. https://bridgespan-social-impact.com/starting-list-to-invest-for-racial-equity/.
11 Sacks, 59.
12 Mishnah *Sanhedrin* 4:5.
13 Rabbi Yitz Greenberg notes that while the version in the Babylonian Talmud includes the word *mi'yisrael*, the version in the Jerusalem Talmud (*Sanhedrin* 4:9) does not.
14 Wilkerson, 141.
15 See Chapter 1 and its endnotes for references to Baptist and others who make this case eloquently.
16 Christian E. Weller and Lily Roberts. "Eliminating the Black-White Wealth Gap Is a Generational Challenge." Center for American Progress. March 19, 2021. https://www.americanprogress.org/article/eliminating-black-white-wealth-gap-generational-challenge/.
17 Carlos Moreno. "Decades After the Tulsa Race Massacre, Urban 'Renewal' Sparked Black Wall Street's Second Destruction." *Smithsonian Magazine*. June 2, 2021. https://www.smithsonianmag.com/history/black-wall-streets-second-destruction-180977871/.
18 Terry Gross. "A 'Forgotten History' Of How The U.S. Government Segregated America." *National Public Radio*. May 3, 2017. https://www.npr.org/2017/05/03/526655831/a-forgotten-history-of-how-the-u-s-government-segregated-america.
19 For just a snippet of the systemic campaigns of violence and intimidation, see: Farrell Evans. "The 1868 Louisiana Massacre That Reversed Reconstruction-Era Gains." *HISTORY*. September 29, 2020. https://www.history.com/news/voter-suppression-history-opelousas-massacre; "GEORGIA.; The Camilla Riot---An Unprovoked Massacre--Dangers of Civil War in Case of Seymour's Election." *New York Times*. October 6, 1868. https://www.nytimes.com/1868/10/06/archives/georgia-the-camilla-riotan-unprovoked-massacredangers-of-civil-war.html.
20 Jean Folger. "The History of Lending Discrimination." Investopedia. March 3, 2022.

https://www.investopedia.com/the-history-of-lending-discrimination-5076948.
21 "Mapping Inequality: Redlining in New Deal America." *University of Richmond.* https://dsl.richmond.edu/panorama/redlining/#loc=5/39.1/-94.58&text=intro.
22 Gross.
23 Andre M. Perry, Jonathan Rothwell, and David Harshbarger. "The devaluation of assets in Black neighborhoods: The case of residential property." Brookings Institution. November 27, 2018. https://www.brookings.edu/research/devaluation-of-assets-in-black-neighborhoods/.
24 Brown, 13.
25 "A CLOSER LOOK: Juneteenth and the Racial Wealth Gap." Email. Patriotic Millionaires. June 15, 2021. https://mailchi.mp/a087c2f9c726/a-closer-look-juneteenth-and-the-racial-wealth-gap.
26 Bonnie Kristian. "Ahmaud Arbery and the racist history of loitering laws." *The Week.* May 7, 2020. https://theweek.com/articles/912977/ahmaud-arbery-racist-history-loitering-laws.
27 Alexander, *The New Jim Crow.*
28 "Prison Labor in the United States: An Investor Perspective." Mission Investors Exchange. April 2018. https://missioninvestors.org/resources/prison-labor-united-states-investor-perspective-0.
29 "The Prison Industry: Mapping Private Sector Players." *Worth Rises.* May 2020. https://worthrises.org/theprisonindustry2020.
30 Bulbul Gupta. "How CDFIs are rethinking lending risks to build BIPOC-led businesses and wealth." ImpactAlpha. August 18, 2021. https://impactalpha.com/how-cdfis-are-rethinking-lending-risks-to-build-bipoc-led-businesses-and-wealth/.
31 Villanueva, 4.
32 Price, Anne. "Anne Price on centering Blackness in the economic liberation of all Americans." *The Reconstruction* (podcast). Accessed 7/12/2021. https://open.spotify.com/episode/404PnFR5IPDBoCZFwr1rWb.
33 Shahanna McKinney-Baldon. "Speak Torah to Power: An Accounting of the Soul for the Jewish New Year." Speak Truth to Power online series. *Avodah.* https://www.youtube.com/watch?v=FjZczpk4zkM.

34 Leviticus 5:23; see also *Mishneh Torah Hilchot Gneivah Chapter 1.*
35 Ta-Nehisi Coates. "The Case for Reparations." *The Atlantic.* June 2014. https://www.theatlantic.com/magazine/archive/2014/06/the-case-for-reparations/361631/.
36 Rabbi Aryeh Bernstein. "The Torah Case for Reparations." *Medium.* March 29, 2018. https://aryehbernstein.medium.com/the-torah-case-for-reparations-bbe41e7763c0.
37 Exodus 12:35. The Israelites themselves were commanded later in the Torah that when setting an indentured servant free, they should not be set free empty-handed, but given abundant resources, because, "remember—you were slaves in Egypt." Deuteronomy 15:15.
38 See Bernstein's article as well as that of Rabbi Brous (next note).
39 See also Coates' book, *We Were Eight Years in Power,* for additional commentary and defense of his choice to include the example of German reparations to Israel.
40 Rabbi Sharon Brous. "Why Jews should support reparations for slavery." *Los Angeles Times.* March 7, 2018. https://www.latimes.com/opinion/op-ed/la-oe-brous-reparations-slavery-jews-holocaust-20180307-story.html.
41 Christian E. Weller and Lily Roberts. "Eliminating the Black-White Wealth Gap Is a Generational Challenge." Center for American Progress. March 19, 2021. https://www.americanprogress.org/article/eliminating-black-white-wealth-gap-generational-challenge/.
42 "Transformative Investment Principles." Resource Generation. 2021. https://resourcegeneration.org/transformative-investment-principles/. Emphasis in original.
43 Cathy Cheney. "One system, (un)equal access." *Washington Business Journal.* October 1, 2020. https://www.bizjournals.com/washington/news/2020/10/15/how-the-financial-system-has-failed-black-business.html.
44 Andrea Armeni and Curt Lyon. "Grassroots Community-Engaged Investment: Redistributing power over investment processes as the key to fostering equitable outcomes." Transform Finance. April 2021. https://www.transformfinance.org/blog/participatory-investment-report.

45 Mishnah *Shevi'it* 10:3.
46 Monique Aiken and Lisa Mensah. "Impact Briefing June 18: CDFI's and Juneteenth hit the big time." ImpactAlpha. June 18, 2021. https://impactalpha.com/impact-briefing-week-of-june-18/.
47 Baradaran, 10.
48 Monique Aiken and Lisa Mensah, "Impact Briefing June 18th: CDFI's and Juneteenth hit the big time."
49 Ibid.
50 See, for example, comments from Roy Swan, Head of Mission Investments at the Ford Foundation, in "The Next Move: How Business Can Close Racial Economic Gaps in 2021." The Aspen Institute. January 29, 2021. https://www.aspeninstitute.org/blog-posts/the-next-move-how-business-can-close-racial-economic-gaps-in-2021/.
51 Price, Anne. "Anne Price on centering Blackness in the economic liberation of all Americans." *The Reconstruction* podcast. May 2021. https://open.spotify.com/episode/404PnFR5IPDBoCZFwr1rWb.
52 "Turning pledges into policies to invest in Black Americans and multi-racial prosperity." ImpactAlpha. June 24, 2021. https://impactalpha.com/turning-pledges-into-policies-to-invest-in-black-americans-and-multi-racial-prosperity/.
53 "Racial Equity Governing Agenda." PolicyLink. Accessed 2/3/2022. https://www.policylink.org/federal-policy/racial-equity-governing-agenda.
54 Catherine Berman. "Women of Color–The Investment of this Century." *Green Money Magazine*. April 2021. https://greenmoney.com/women-of-color-the-investment-of-this-century/.
55 Villanueva, 80.
56 Amazon (@Amazon). "The inequitable and brutal treatment of Black people in our country must stop. Together we stand in solidarity with..." Tweet. May 31, 2020, 1:05pm. https://twitter.com/amazon/status/1267140211861073927.
57 Jason Del Rey. " Amazon's Black employees say the company's HR department is failing them." *Vox/Recode*. June 15, 2021. https://www.vox.com/recode/22524538/amazon-diversity-black-employees-human-resources-department.
58 Tejal Patel, et al. "Racial Equity Audits: A Critical Tool for Shareholders." Webinar. SOC Investment Group. April 13, 2021. https://www.socinvestmentgroup.com/critical-tool-for-shareholders.
59 Dana Peterson and Katherine Mann. "Closing the Racial Inequality Gaps: The Economic Cost of Black Inequality in the US." Citi Global Perspectives and Solutions. September 2020. https://www.citivelocity.com/citigps/closing-the-racial-inequality-gaps/. The four key areas identified by the Citi report are lack of access to education, inequitable lending or lack of lending to entrepreneurs of color, lack of access to housing credit, and wage discrimination depressing consumption and investment.
60 Ibid.
61 Alex Gorsky. "A Message from Johnson & Johnson Chairman and CEO Alex Gorsky About Recent Events in the United States." Johnson & Johnson. June 2, 2020. https://www.jnj.com/latest-news/a-message-from-johnson-johnson-ceo-alex-gorsky-about-recent-events-in-the-united-states.
62 Patel, et al.
63 Jasper Jolly. "Johnson & Johnson faces push to force global ban on talc baby powder sales." *The Guardian*. February 6, 2022. https://www.theguardian.com/business/2022/feb/06/johnson-johnson-faces-push-to-force-global-ban-on-talc-baby-powder-sales.
64 Patel, et al.
65 Ron S. Berenblat and Elizabeth R. Gonzalez-Sussman, et al. "Racial Equity Audits: A New ESG Initiative." Harvard Law School Forum on Corporate Governance. October 30, 2021. https://corpgov.law.harvard.edu/2021/10/30/racial-equity-audits-a-new-esg-initiative/.
66 Ben Maiden. "Citi to conduct racial equity audit." Corporate Secretary. October 25, 2021. https://www.corporatesecretary.com/articles/esg/32765/citi-conduct-racial-equity-audit.
67 Robert A. Pape. "What an analysis of 377 Americans arrested or charged in the Capitol insurrection tells us." *Washington Post*. April 6, 2021. https://www.washingtonpost.com/opinions/2021/04/06/

capitol-insurrection-arrests-cpost-analysis/.

68. Alan Feuer. "Fears of White People Losing Out Permeate Capitol Rioters' Towns, Study Finds." *New York Times*. April 6, 2021. https://www.nytimes.com/2021/04/06/us/politics/capitol-riot-study.html.

69. For example, see: Kevin Morris. "Georgia's Proposed Voting Restrictions Will Harm Black Voters Most." Brennan Center for Justice. March 6, 2021, https://www.brennancenter.org/our-work/research-reports/georgias-proposed-voting-restrictions-will-harm-black-voters-most. See also Alexa Ura. "Texas Republicans say their proposed voting restrictions are color blind. But many see 'Jim Crow in a tuxedo.'" *Texas Tribune*. April 9, 2021. https://www.texastribune.org/2021/04/09/Texas-voting-GOP-suppression/.

70. Andrew Ross Sorkin and David Gelles. "Black Executives Call on Corporations to Fight Restrictive Voting Laws." *New York Times*. March 31, 2021. https://www.nytimes.com/2021/03/31/business/voting-rights-georgia-corporations.html.

71. "Equity in the Boardroom: How Asset Manager Voting Shaped Corporate Action on Racial Justice in 2021." Majority Action. https://www.majorityaction.us/equity-in-the-boardroom-2021.

72. "Robert Maguire and Caitlin Moniz. "Insurrectionist members have received $2.6 million from corporate interests since January 6th." Citizens for Responsibility and Ethics in Washington. May 19, 2021. https://www.citizensforethics.org/reports-investigations/crew-reports/insurrectionist-members-have-received-2-6-million-from-corporate-interests-since-january-6th/.

73. Talmud *Berakhot* 55a; see also "Rabbis Endorse Freedom to Vote Act, Condemn State Attempts of Voter Suppression." T'ruah. October 20, 2021. https://truah.org/press/rabbis-freedom-to-vote-act-voter-suppression/.

74. Emile Hallez. "Record proxy season stars are climate and human rights." *InvestmentNews*. March 21, 2022. https://www.investmentnews.com/shareholder-resolutions-climate-human-rights-report-218823.

75. "Equity in the Boardroom: How Asset Manager Voting Shaped Corporate Action on Racial Justice in 2021." Majority Action. https://www.majorityaction.us/equity-in-the-boardroom-2021

76. Ibid.

77. "An Open Letter to the Companies that Advertise on Facebook." Anti-Defamation League. June 25, 2020. https://www.adl.org/news/letters/an-open-letter-to-the-companies-that-advertise-on-facebook.

78. "Equity in the Boardroom: How Asset Manager Voting Shaped Corporate Action on Racial Justice in 2021." Majority Action. https://www.majorityaction.us/equity-in-the-boardroom-2021#:~:text=Instead%2C%20as%20Equity%20in%20the,and%20inequitable%20practices%20and%20governance.

79. Gina Gambetta. "Financial giants under review for 'fossil fuel boycotts' among sponsors of US anti-ESG group." *Responsible Investor*. June 21, 2022. https://www.responsible-investor.com/financial-giants-under-review-for-fossil-fuel-boycotts-among-sponsors-of-us-anti-esg-group/. Also Fidelity. https://www.fidelity.com/mutual-funds/investing-ideas/sustainable-investing

80. Jariel Arvin. "The Keystone XL pipeline is dead. But the fight against similar projects is far from over." *Vox*. June 10, 2021. https://www.vox.com/2021/6/10/22526803/keystone-xl-oil-gas-biden-climate-change.

81. "Standing Rock Sioux Tribe Takes #NODAPL to the United Nations." Indian Law Resource Center. September 20, 2016. https://indianlaw.org/undrip/Standing-Rock-Sioux-Tribe-Takes-NODAPL-to-the-United-Nations.

82. "White Earth files Rights of Nature lawsuit against Minnesota DNR." Wisconsin Citizens Media Cooperative. August 5, 2021. https://wcmcoop.org/2021/08/05/white-earth-files-rights-of-nature-lawsuit-against-minnesota-dnr/.

83. "Honouring the Truth, Reconciling for the Future: Summary of the Final Report of the Truth and Reconciliation Commission of Canada." Truth and Reconciliation Commission. 2015. https://ehprnh2mwo3.exactdn.com/wp-content/uploads/2021/01/Executive_Summary_English_Web.pdf.

84. Shannon Rohan. "Advancing Reconciliation in

Canada: A Guide for Investors." Reconciliation and Responsible Investment Initiative. April 2019. https://reconciliationandinvestment.ca/wp-content/uploads/2019/04/RRII-Guide-FINAL-2.pdf.

[85] Nick Pelosi and Rebecca Adamson. "Managing the "S" in ESG: The Case of Indigenous Peoples and Extractive Industries." *Journal of Applied Corporate Finance.* 2016 28(2), Pages 87–95. https://www.colorado.edu/program/fpw/sites/default/files/attached-files/managing_the_s_in_esg.pdf.

[86] Yessenia Funes. "A Pipeline of Abuse." *The Frontline* by Atmos. August 2, 2021. https://atmos.earth/line-3-sexual-violence-mmiw-climate-justice/.

[87] "Report reveals criminalization and killings of Indigenous Peoples defending their lands against mining, agri-business and energy companies; incl. co. responses." Business and Human Rights Resource Centre. May 4, 2021. https://www.business-humanrights.org/en/latest-news/report-reveals-criminalization-and-killings-of-indigenous-peoples-defending-their-lands-against-mining-agri-business-and-energy-companies-incl-co-responses/.

[88] "Investors & Indigenous Peoples Working Group: About IIWPG." First Peoples Worldwide, University of Colorado. https://www.colorado.edu/program/fpw/investors-indigenous-peoples-working-group.

[89] "DAPL & Beyond." Investors and Indigenous Peoples Working Group. https://www.colorado.edu/program/fpw/iipwg/ensuring-fpic-advocacy-extractive-industry-projects.

[90] Emil Sirén Gualinga. "Respecting Indigenous Rights: An Actionable Toolkit for Institutional Investors." *Amazon Watch.* April 18, 2023. https://respectingindigenousrights.org/.

[91] Debra Rubin. "Rabbis give support to Fla. tomato pickers." *New Jersey Jewish News.* March 10, 2015. https://njjewishnews.timesofisrael.com/rabbis-give-support-to-fla-tomato-pickers/#.VQBO1o54q0c.

[92] Holly Burkhalter. "Fair Food Program helps end the use of slavery in the tomato fields." *Washington Post.* September 2, 2012. https://www.washingtonpost.com/opinions/fair-food-program-helps-end-the-use-of-slavery-in-the-tomato-fields/2012/09/02/788f1a1a-f39c-11e1-892d-bc92fee603a7_story.html.

[93] Ira Flatow, et al. "The Unsavory Story Of Industrially-Grown Tomatoes." *Talk of the Nation*—National Public Radio. August 26, 2011. https://www.npr.org/2011/08/26/139972669/the-unsavory-story-of-industrially-grown-tomatoes.

[94] Ibid.

[95] Florida tomato pickers are disproportionately immigrants from South and Central America. Mireya Navarro. "Florida Tomato Pickers Take On Growers." *New York Times.* February 1, 1998. https://www.nytimes.com/1998/02/01/us/florida-tomato-pickers-take-on-growers.html. The Coalition of Immokalee Workers is predominantly Hispanic as well. "Florida Tomato Pickers, Taco Bell Reach Agreement." *Vegetable Growers News.* March 10, 2005. https://vegetablegrowersnews.com/news/florida-tomato-pickers-taco-bell-reach-agreement/.

[96] "Fair Food Program: Partners." Fair Food Program. Accessed February 8, 2022. https://fairfoodprogram.org/partners/.

[97] "Wendy's Shareholder Resolution News, Part One: Resolution calling for documentation of Wendy's claims of social responsibility gaining real momentum ahead annual meeting..." Coalition of Immokalee Workers. March 31, 2021. https://ciw-online.org/blog/2021/03/wendys-shareholder-resolution-news-part-one-resolution-calling-for-documentation-of-wendys-claims-of-social-responsibility-gaining-real-momentum-ahead-annual-meeting/.

[98] Mishnah *Pesachim* 10:4; see also the Pesach Haggadah.

[99] Talmud *Bava Metzia* 77a and *Rashi* s.v. *yad poel al ha'elyona*

[100] Leviticus 19:13; Deuteronomy 24:14.

[101] *Sefer HaChinukh* 482. This is used as a source in discussions by modern Israeli rabbis Ben Zion Meir Hai Uziel and Eliezer Waldenburg.

[102] "Apparel brands pressed to act as end of Bangladesh Accord looms." Business and Human Rights Resource Centre. Email. May 26, 2021.

[103] "Fired, Then Robbed: Fashion Brands' Complicity in Wage Theft During COVID-19." Worker Rights Consortium. April 2021.

https://www.workersrights.org/wp-content/uploads/2021/04/Fired-Then-Robbed.pdf.

[104] Anita Dorett. "Support for resolutions at H&M AGM on Thursday, 6 May 2021." Email. April 8, 2021.

[105] Zeynep Ton. "Equality in the U.S. Starts with Better Jobs." *Harvard Business Review.* August 17, 2020. https://hbr.org/2020/08/equality-in-the-u-s-starts-with-better-jobs.

[106] "Call No. 29: Capitalism reimagined for fair gainsharing and equitable prosperity." ImpactAlpha. July 9, 2021. https://impactalpha.com/agents-of-impact-call-no-29-capitalism-reimagined-for-fair-gainsharing-and-equitable-prosperity-video/.

[107] Nitin Nohria, Thomas R. Piper and Bridget Gurtler. "Malden Mills (A)." Harvard Business School Case Collection. December 2003. https://www.hbs.edu/faculty/Pages/item.aspx?num=30633.

[108] David B. Green. "This Day in Jewish History, 1995: Malden Mills Burns Down, Shows What an Employer With a Heart Looks Like." *Haaretz.* December 11, 2015. https://www.haaretz.com/jewish/.premium-1995-malden-mills-burns-down-1.5435757.

Chapter 12

[1] Hadarim Urban Renewal Impact Fund." *Hadarim.* https://www.hadarimfund.com/impact.

[2] Ibid.

[3] Rabbi Jacob Siegel, Dalia Black, and Louise Jacobs. "A Jewish Institution's Journey to Impact Investing in Israel." Panel: Jewish Impact Investing Summit. JLens. May 19, 2020. https://www.youtube.com/watch?v=X_f8tWjSi1U.

[4] Ibid.

[5] Dalia Black, personal conversation with the author, February 25, 2020.

[6] "Hadarim." *Si3 by UJIA.* https://si3.ujia.org/portfolio/hadarim/.

[7] Talmud *Bava Kamma* 80b.

[8] Talmud *Yoma* 54b; *Mishneh Torah Beit HaBechira* 2:1-2.

[9] *Esther Rabbah* 1:17.

[10] Talmud *Ketubot* 111a.

[11] Talmud *Bava Kamma* 80b. The list goes on; for example, the rabbis noted that if one rents a house, normally one has 30 days to attach a *mezuzah*, a small scroll, to the doorpost. In Israel, however, one needs to affix a *mezuzah* immediately, because of the principle of *yishuv Eretz Yisrael.*

[12] Talmud *Ketubot* 110b. Note there is a debate in later rabbis whether the *mitzvah* of moving to Israel dates all the way back to the Torah or was merely instated later by the Sages. *Hasagot HaRamban on Sefer Hamitzvot, Positive Commandments Omitted by Rambam* 4.

[13] Talmud *Bava Batra* 91a; *Shulkhan Arukh Yoreh De'ah* 286:22.

[14] For example, the historic Shearith Israel community in Brazil and in New York was regularly sending funds or entertaining emissaries from Israel in the 17th century. Rabbi David De Sola Pool. *An Old Faith in the New World.* Columbia University Press: New York, 1955. 396-397.

[15] Author's personal communication with Rabbi Dr. Yehudah Mirsky and Rabbi Dr. Alan Brill, December 28, 2021.

[16] Corwin Berman, 95.

[17] Lustig, *Greenbook.*

[18] Corwin Berman, 95 and 64.

[19] Helen Chernikoff. "The Leichtag Foundation aims to make 100% of its portfolio 'mission-aligned.'" *Forward.* Aug 20, 2021. https://ejewishphilanthropy.com/the-leichtag-foundation-aims-to-make-100-of-its-portfolio-mission-aligned/.

[20] Carrie Rubenstein. "Stand By: MSCI Is About To Welcome A New Member That May Tilt The Scales." *Forbes.* January 25, 2022. https://www.forbes.com/sites/carrierubinstein/2022/01/25/stand-by-msci-is-about-to-welcome-a-new-member-that-may-tilt-the-scales/.

[21] *Tzitz Eliezer* 7:48.

[22] Lustig .

[23] "Announcing a New $1M Impact Investing Matching Grants Initiative." Jewish Funders Network. July 15, 2020. https://www.jfunders.org/new_impact_investing_matching_grants.

[24] "OGEN Israel Social Loan Fund Raises

$30 m. for Coronavirus Relief in Israel." *eJewishPhilanthropy*. June 1, 2020. https://ejewishphilanthropy.com/ogen-israel-social-loan-fund-raises-30-m-for-coronavirus-relief-in-israel/.

[25] David Angel, personal communication with author, March 3, 2022. The author has reviewed the text of the actual *heter iska*.

[26] Ari Jaffe. "Ogen: The New Way to Invest in Israel." *eJewishPhilanthropy*. November 26, 2020. https://ejewishphilanthropy.com/ogen-the-new-way-to-invest-in-israel/.

[27] "Ogen: Israel Social Loan Fund." Ogen. August 2020. https://www.ogen.org/wp-content/uploads/2020/09/Ogen-Social-Loan-Fund_A4_Aug.2020.pdf.

[28] Ben Sales. "Israel's nonprofit loan fund hopes a $15 million bond will change Israeli philanthropy." *eJewish Philanthropy*. March 2, 2022. https://ejewishphilanthropy.com/israels-free-loan-association-hopes-a-15-million-bond-will-change-israeli-philanthropy/.

[29] Betsy Corcoran. "CodeMonkey Acquired by TAL Education Group." *EdSurge*. December 5, 2018. https://www.edsurge.com/news/2018-12-05-codemonkey-acquired-by-tal-education-group.

[30] Rachel Cohen, et al. "The Impact Investing Ecosystem in Israel." Panel: Jewish Impact Investing Summit. JLens. December 5, 2017. https://www.youtube.com/watch?v=iLcTGbai3lw.

[31] Energiya Global. https://energiyaglobal.com/investors/.

[32] Brendan Pierson. "Teva to pay Nevada $193 million over role in opioid epidemic." *Reuters*. June 7, 2023. https://www.reuters.com/business/healthcare-pharmaceuticals/teva-pay-nevada-193-million-over-role-opioid-epidemic-2023-06-07/.

[33] Ari Feldman. "'Jewish Values' Investors Are Targeting An Israeli Company—For The First Time." *Forward*. July 25, 2019. https://forward.com/news/428215/teva-pharma-opioid-impact-investing-jewish/.

[34] "Impact Investing in Israel: Status of the Market." *OurCrowd and Social Finance Israel*. March 2019. https://www.social-finance.org.il/userfiles/banners/Status%20of%20the%20Market%20Report%20_Print.pdf.

[35] Lustig.

Chapter 13

[1] "Heroes of the Environment 2008: Gidon Bromberg, Nader Al-Khateeb And Munqeth Mehyar." *Time*. September 24, 2008. http://content.time.com/time/specials/packages/article/0,28804,1841778_1841781_1841807,00.html.

[2] Personal interview with the author, October 17, 2019.

[3] Thomas Friedman. "Climate Change Will Destroy Arabs and Israelis Before They Destroy Each Other." *New York Times*. December 6, 2022. https://www.nytimes.com/2022/12/06/opinion/how-biden-can-help-save-the-middle-east.html.

[4] Ibid.

[5] Nigel Savage. "6 of 7: Why does shmita matter?" Hazon. August 20, 2021. https://hazon.org/why-does-shmita-matter-6-of-7/.

[6] Micah 4:3-4.

[7] Psalms 34:15.

[8] Midrash *Rabbah Bamidbar* 11:7.

[9] Talmud *Sanhedrin* 6b.

[10] Talmud Yerushalmi *Pe'ah* 1:1 [4a].

[11] Mishnah *Sanhedrin* 4:5 as quoted in the Talmud Yerushalmi.

[12] For example, see "Open Road's bridge loans enable essential service providers to carry on in conflict areas." ImpactAlpha. March 24, 2022. https://impactalpha.com/open-roads-bridge-loans-enable-essential-service-providers-to-carry-on-in-conflict-areas/.

[13] For an example, see Eric Rice and Sir Ronald Cohen. "How impact can enhance the risk-return equation." BlackRock. July 2021. https://www.blackrock.com/ch/individual/en/insights/impact-investing.

[14] "Commissions and Task Forces." Sir Ronald Cohen. https://sirronaldcohen.org/commissions-task-forces.

[15] "The Portland Trust." The Portland Trust.

Accessed 1/5/2022. https://portlandtrust.org/.

[16] Ibid.

[17] "The Role of Business in Peacemaking: Lessons from Cyprus, Northern Ireland, South Africa and the South Caucasus." The Portland Trust. August 2013. https://portlandtrust.org/wp-content/uploads/2019/12/role_of_business_2.pdf.

[18] Jenna White, Jason Saul and Cheryl Davenport. "Cisco Pioneers Market Development Approach in Palestine." *Mission Measurement*. June 11, 2012. https://missionmeasurement.com/wp-content/uploads/Cisco-pioneers-Market-Development-Approach.pdf.

[19] Julie Hammerman, et al. "Business & Investment to Further Peacebuilding and Coexistence." Panel: Jewish Impact Investing Summit. JLens. May 19, 2020. https://www.youtube.com/watch?v=f9KyPml3fa0.

[20] Jenna White, Jason Saul, and Cheryl Davenport.

[21] Ibid.

[22] Ibid.

[23] Ibid.

[24] Julie Hammerman, et al.

[25] "Palestinian Economic Bulletin 175." *Portland Trust*. April 2021. https://portlandtrust.org/wp-content/uploads/2021/12/Bulletin-175-English-A4.pdf.

[26] "Palestinian Economic Bulletin 179." *Portland Trust*. August 2021. https://portlandtrust.org/wp-content/uploads/2021/08/bulletin_179_-_august_-_english_a4.pdf.

[27] Doug Krikler in Julie Hammerman, et al.

[28] Catherine Clifford. "Why billionaire Mark Cuban invested in an Afghan saffron start-up run by veterans on 'Shark Tank.'" *CNBC*. May 6, 2017. https://www.cnbc.com/2017/05/06/why-billionaire-mark-cuban-invested-in-an-afghan-saffron-start-up-run-by-veterans-on-shark-tank.html.

[29] *Rumi Spice*. https://www.rumispice.com/.

[30] Ibid.

[31] Clifford.

[32] Esha Chhabra. "Spice Company In Afghanistan Stays Committed To Its Farmers." *Forbes*. September 30, 2021. https://www.forbes.com/sites/eshachhabra/2021/09/30/spice-company-in-afghanistan-stays-committed-to-its-farmers/.

[33] "Twenty-Year Timeline." *Media Development Investment Fund*. September 8, 2015. https://www.mdif.org/20th-timeline/.

[34] Ibid.

[35] David Bank. "How Media Development Investment Fund calculates political risk to back press freedom (Q&A)." ImpactAlpha. March 9, 2022. https://impactalpha.com/how-media-development-investment-fund-calculates-political-risk-to-back-press-freedom-qa/.

[36] Julie Hammerman et al.

[37] "USAID—Economic Growth and Trade." US Agency for International Development. https://www.usaid.gov/economic-growth-and-trade.

[38] Julie Hammerman, et al.

[39] For Himelfarb's heritage, see Anthony Lewis. "Abroad at Home: 'It Is So Simple.'" *New York Times*. September 10, 1984. https://www.nytimes.com/1984/09/10/opinion/abroad-at-home-it-is-so-simple.html.

[40] "Investments With Impact." Open Road Alliance. https://openroadalliance.org/investors/.

[41] "Open Road's bridge loans enable essential service providers to carry on in conflict areas." ImpactAlpha. March 24, 2022. https://impactalpha.com/open-roads-bridge-loans-enable-essential-service-providers-to-carry-on-in-conflict-areas/.

[42] David Smith. "Shell accused of fuelling violence in Nigeria by paying rival militant gangs." *The Guardian*. October 2, 2011. https://www.theguardian.com/world/2011/oct/03/shell-accused-of-fuelling-nigeria-conflict.

[43] Ibid.

[44] "The Role of Business in Peacemaking." Portland Trust.

[45] Proverbs 3:18.

Epilogue

[1] Michael McAfee and Monique Aiken. "Impact Briefing: Week of July 2." ImpactAlpha. July 2, 2021. https://impactalpha.com/impact-briefing-week-of-july-2/.

Index

Abergel, Rabbi Eliyahu, 29, 266n332
abortion, 82, 265n305
Abraham and Sarah, 216
Abramowitz, Yosi, 220
Abu Dhabi, 223
Abzuk, Zika, 226–27
access to capital, 105, 148, 149–50, 158, 166, 193–95. *See also* Community Development Financial Institutions (CDFIs)
access to voting, 206
accountability, 78, 204–5, 207, 225
accredited investors, 121, 162–64, 188, 221
action tanks, 225–26
active participation of government policy, 197–98
Activest, 149–50, 152–53
activists/activism, 24–25, 34, 70, 172, 178–79, 183, 202, 207, 228, 231. *See also* Indigenous rights; workers' rights
Adamah, 188–89
Adasina Social Capital, 150, 152–53
advocacy, investor on climate, 184–86
advocacy, own-and-advocate approach, 182–83
advocacy for racial justice, 201–2, 205
AES, 130
affordable housing, 163, 215, 226
Afghanistan, 228–30
Africa, 150–51, 187, 205
African National Congress, 232
agrarian society, 21, 140–41
agricultural commodity traders, 186
agricultural law, 98
agricultural practices, 218
agricultural slavery rings, 210
Agudath Israel of America, 147
aiding and abetting, 81, 83–84, 85, 88, 91, 98. *See also* stumbling blocks before the blind
AIG, 185
Aiken, Monique, 203
Airbnb, 205
alcohol, 81
All Our Might report, 181
Amalgamated Bank, 70
Amazon, 10, 33, 42, 59, 117, 185–86, 204–5
Amazon Watch, 210
American Electric Power, 190
American Express, 206
American Jewish World Service, 188
American Jews, 217–18
American Petroleum Institute, 35
Amnesty International, 94
Anan, Rav, 62, 64
ancient Israel, 31
Ancselovits, Rabbi Elisha, 43
Angola, 230
annual ballots, 124–25, 127–28
anonymous giving, 161
Antarctica, 174
anti-apartheid efforts, 232
antibiotic overuse, 50–51, 80, 125
anti-climate corporate lobbying, 185
anti-ESG sentiment, 125–26, 128, 184
antimicrobial resistance, 50–51
anti-union practices, 230
apartheid South Africa, 7–8, 14, 70, 124, 232
Apple, 69
appropriation, 172
arms trade, 91, 92–95
artificial person, 114
ascetic poverty, 20
Asher ben Yechiel, Rabbi, 65
asset classes, 103–12, 118, 136, 158, 163, 166, 195, 220
asset managers, 108, 125, 128, 130, 179, 184–85, 206, 207–8, 210
assets, 2–3, 12, 49, 69, 70, 71–73, 103, 107, 114, 117, 125, 156, 158, 163, 165, 179–80, 188–89
assets under management (AUM), 108, 252n23, 252n25
assimilation, 36, 72, 79
The Associated: Jewish Federation of Baltimore, 189
As You Sow, 173, 186, 189–90
The Atlantic, 200
AT&T, 207
AUM (assets under management), 108, 252n23, 252n25
Auschwitz Memorial and Museum, 59
Austin, Duncan, 109
auto loans, 136, 151
avodah zarah (Idol Worship), 78, 80–81, 84–85, 88, 90
awareness, 34–35, 179–80
Azaria Figo, Rabbi, 65

Babylon (present-day Iraq), 142
Badatz of Jerusalem, 120–21
Baird, Donnel, 152
Bais HaVaad Rabbinical Court, Lakewood, New Jersey, 96, 273–74n464
Baker McKenzie, 26–27
balance, 17, 23–26, 231, 233
Bank for Good, 105
bank.green, 105
Bank of America, 104, 181, 184, 205, 284n683
banks, 70, 103–5, 116, 117,

119, 131, 141, 147, 164–65, 179, 181, 184–85, 197, 198, 209
BankTrack, 70
Baptist, Edward, 11–12
Baradaran, Mehrsa, 203
barriers, 35–36, 72–73, 94–95, 108, 193–94, 232, 252n17
Bartenura, Ovadiah, 43
Bay Area, 53, 163–64
B Corporations, 228
Beer Sheva, 219
behavior, 5, 9, 27–28, 30, 36, 45, 48–49, 69, 79, 80, 82, 83, 88, 108, 126–28, 131, 175, 182, 201, 205
Ben and Jerry's, 164
benchmark, 41–42, 50, 228
benefit, items prohibited from. See *issurei hana'ah* (items prohibited from benefit)
benefit(s), 13–14, 26–28, 34, 41, 44, 45, 148, 158–59
Ben-Gurion, David, 217–18
Benstein, Jeremy, 22
Bergovoy, Mariana, 174
Berk, Jonathan, 182
Berman, Catherine, 55, 193–94, 204
Bernstein, Rabbi Aryeh, 200
Besadno, 120–21
Bezalel, 206
Bezos, Jeff, 59
biases, 72, 107, 197
Biden administration, 35, 94
Big Oil, 35, 180
Bill & Melinda Gates Foundation, 71
bipartisan infrastructure bill in 2021, 152
BIPOC (Black, Indigenous, and people of color), 164, 203
B Lab, 228
Black, Dalia, 216
Black, Indigenous, and people of color (BIPOC), 164, 203
Black Americans, 12, 54, 107, 142, 149, 193–213
Blackness, 204

Black-owned businesses, 150–51, 204
BlackRock, 51, 52, 56, 74, 109, 128, 149, 184–85, 207–8, 219
Black Vision Fund, 55
Black voters, 206
Black Wall Street, 196–97
Black women, 3, 151, 204
Bleich, Rabbi J. David, 277n524
BlocPower, 152–53
Bloomberg, 184, 252n23
blue sky laws, 161
Blum, Karin, 157
boards, 27, 34, 39, 59, 109, 114, 124–28, 183
bonds, 70, 113, 148, 149, 150, 162, 184, 219. *See also* benchmark
Book of Education, 78, 129–30, 139, 211
Book of Psalms, 224
Book of the Pious, 129
borrowing, 63, 104, 118, 136–37, 141–43
Bosnia, 230
Boston, Massachusetts, 152, 155–57
Boston Jewish community, 156
Boston Trust Walden, 125
Boston Ujima Fund, 70
Bowers, Ryan, 149
BP, 129, 172, 184, 189
Brahmins, 61
Brandeis, Louis, 28
Brandeis University, 181
Brazil, 205, 292n836
Bressler, Rabbi Dr. Barry, 127
bridge loans, Open Road Alliance, 230
Britain, 10–12, 96
Britain's Joint Stock Company Act of 1862, 117
British East India Trading Company, 10–11, 115, 117
British monarchy, 116
Bromberg, Gidon, 223
Brookings Institution, 197

Brooklyn, New York, 70
Brous, Rabbi Sharon, 200–201
Brown, Dorothy, 197–98
Brown, Erica, 24
Brown, Michael, 150
Brown, Sharlene, 104
Broyde, Rabbi Michael, 269n386
Bruck, Ophir, 73–74
Brussels, 182
budgets, 149–50
Buffett, Warren, 33–34
building wealth, 136, 147, 148, 194, 197–99
Burger King, 96
Burundi, 230–31
Business and Human Rights Resource Centre, 211
business and investment capital, challenges of, 231–32. *See also* peacebuilding
business as usual, 9–14, 23, 35, 37, 71, 73, 126, 127, 174, 180, 233. *See also* Capitalism 1.0; disaster capitalism
business loans, 145, 147, 202
business models, 89, 128, 180, 183, 268n373
business owners, 8, 46, 150–51, 194
business partnerships, 114, 118–19
business risk, 141–42
business ventures, 63–64, 65, 141–43
buying local, 158, 161, 166
buying objects that were likely stolen, 88

Cain and Abel, 216
California, 68, 198
Call to Action, 209
CalPERS, 183
Calvert Impact Capital's Impact Notes, 153, 194
Canadian government, 209
cannibalization of philanthropy, 157
capital accumulation, 65, 117,

Index

136–37
capital gains, 34, 198
capitalism, 4, 9–11, 13, 14, 17, 22, 25, 26, 27–28, 32, 33, 36, 43, 73, 104, 158, 255n84
Capitalism 1.0, 4, 9, 11, 17, 28, 158, 233
Capitalism 2.0, 9, 14
Capitol insurrection, 206–7
carbon emissions, 173–74, 179
carbon footprint, 172–73, 181, 189
carbon tax, 34
Carbon Underground 200, 189
carciofi alla giudìa, 233
caring for our bodies, 86
carve-out, 218
"The Case for Reparations" (Coates), 200
cash, 98, 103–6
Caste (Wilkerson), 12, 196
caste ladder, 198
catalytic capital, 46, 49, 53–54
Catholic Church, 1, 61
CDFIs (Community Development Financial Institutions), 46, 55, 105, 163–65, 193–94, 198, 202, 203, 253n29
Cellebrite, 94
Ceniarth, 53, 56, 121
Center for American Progress, 12, 196, 201
Center for Inclusive Capitalism, 9
centering racial justice, 193–213
CEOs, 41, 50, 124, 205, 206, 268n372
Ceres, 109, 185
Chafetz Chayim, 282n649
challah portion, 273n456
challenges of business and peacebuilding, 231–32
challenges of local investing, 161–62
character of Sodom, 42–44, 45
charging interest. *See* usury (charging interest to

someone in need)
charity, 41, 49, 60–67, 70, 71, 79, 114, 139, 159–61, 163, 202, 217–18, 263n254
Charlottesville, Virginia, 206
chartered corporations, 10, 116–17
Chase, 181
Chicago, Illinois, 142
Children of Israel, 30, 139, 206
China, 94, 181, 229
Chinese Buddhist monasteries, 61
Chinese *hui* system, 140
Chisda, Rav, 44
Christianity, 10, 136, 140, 145
Christian religious fund, 7
Christian sin stocks, 81–82, 89
churches, 115
cigarettes, 86–87, 174–79, 266n315
Cisco, 226–28, 231
cistern example, 259n177
Citi, 104, 181, 184
Citigroup, 205, 206
Citizens for Responsibility and Ethics, 206
civil rights, 93
Civil Rights movement of the 1960s, 46
civil society organizations, 94, 164, 267n347
Civil War, 12, 196
CJP (Combined Jewish Philanthropies) of Greater Boston, 156–57
class or economic privilege, 79–80
Clean Clothes Campaign, 27
clean energy investments, 186–87
climate change/crisis, 2, 22, 171–90, 233; arguments for divestment, 182–83; BlackRock, 51–52; climate action plan, 189; climate catastrophe, 1, 3–4, 180; climate science, 34–35; climate technology, 166, 187; end of the fossil fuel

era, 180–81; Exxon Knew, 34–35; field leaders, 69–71; *gneivat daat* (stealing awareness), 35; investing in climate solutions, 186–89; investor advocacy on climate, 184–86; Jewish Youth Climate Movement (JYCM), 74; market-rate returns, 51–52; shareholder advocacy, 125–26, 130
CMOs (collateralized mortgage obligations), 29
CNote, 55, 165, 193–95
CNote Flagship Fund, 55, 194
Coalition of Immokalee Workers, 210
Coates, Ta-Nehisi, 12, 200
Coca-Cola, 186
CodeMonkey, 220
coerced labor, 210
coexistence, 160, 221, 224–25, 228, 232
coffee, 229–30
Cohen, Ronald, 225–26
collateralized mortgage obligations (CMOs), 29
collective action, 172, 174
collective and individual, 189
Colombia, 229
colonization, 10–11, 115–17, 271n425
The Color of Law (Rothstein), 197
Columbia University, 114
Combined Jewish Philanthropies (CJP) of Greater Boston, 156–57
commandments, 25, 137, 139, 224
commentaries, 18–19, 265n305
Commerce Department, 94
commitments, 73, 184
commodities, 11–12, 29, 88, 186, 277n524
communal authorities/ leadership, 19, 30, 32, 64, 66, 67–71, 175, 188
communal behavior, 30, 131,

139, 175–76
communal endowments, 60–67, 71–72
communal religion, Judaism as, 172–73, 178
communal standard. *See* modesty
communal tax, 173
communism, 36, 43, 255n84
communities of color, 8, 104, 193, 195, 198, 204, 206
community, 45, 48, 49–50, 53–55, 60, 66, 72–73, 138–39, 140, 141–43, 150; ethical framework for debt, 153–54; grassroots community engaged investment, 152–53; obligation to care, 159–61; *shmita* (Sabbatical) year, 30–32
Community Capital Management, 149
community development agency bonds, 70
community development finance, 8, 46, 153, 195, 203
Community Development Financial Institutions (CDFIs), 46, 55, 105, 163–65, 193–94, 198, 202, 203, 253n29
Community-Engaged Investing, 150
Community Reinvestment Act of 1977, 149, 202
Companies Acts, 117
company-community conflict, 208–9
company law *versus* corporate law, 270n415
complex products, 30
compounding interest, 139
concessionary returns, 36, 42, 45–49, 52, 53–55, 56
conflicts and peacebuilding, 223–32. *See also* Israeli-Palestinian conflict
Congress, 28, 116, 206
consent, 208–10. *See also* Free, Prior, and Informed Consent (FPIC)
Conservative movement, 19, 177
conservatives, 125–26, 128
Consolidated Foods, 68
Constitutional Convention, 116
constructive rebuke, 83, 87, 129–31
consumers, 35, 37, 60, 82, 88, 122, 171, 178, 230, 277n524; consumer boycott, 11; consumer goods, 186; consumerist society, 30; consumer loans, 145, 147
consumption, 4, 14, 17, 30, 171
contemporary investors, 12–13
contemporary racism, 195–96
control and ownership, 114
convict leasing system, 198
cooperatives, 8, 54–55, 104–5, 164–65
Corporate Affairs, Cisco, 227
Corporate Social Responsibility (CSR), 108–9, 125
corporations, 10–11, 113–14, 147–48, 279n412; business partnerships, 118–19; climate change/crisis, 171–73; and conflicts, 231; corporate behavior, 10–11, 69, 108, 126, 220; corporate boards, 34, 59; corporate bonds, 136; corporate charters, 116, 131; corporate lobbying, 185; corporate management, 27, 117, 123, 126, 127, 131, 268n372; financial performance, 40–41; Jewish approaches in practice, 121; Jewish legal approaches to, 119–20; letter of the law, 26–28; moral responsibility to the actions of, 122–23; owning stock in other corporations, 273n456; partnerships, 272–73n456; prison labor, 198; public benefit corporations, 3, 122, 228; public equities, 131–32; publicly traded corporations, 115–18; shareholder advocacy, 108–9, 124–26, 129–30; shareholder campaigns, 182; shareholder resolutions, 59; tax breaks, 158; trading in prohibited foods, 95–96; universal standards, 127; values-based investors, 185; and wages, 212; workers' rights, 210. *See also* B Corporations
Cortese, Amy, 161–62, 165
cost-benefit analysis, 126
costs of conflict, 231–32
cotton industry, 11–12
courts, 61–62
COVID-19 pandemic, 2, 4, 54, 71, 140, 172, 173–74, 198, 211, 219
crash of the stock market in 1929, 161–62
creation narrative, 24, 195
credit, 141, 203; credit cards, 105, 136, 147, 151; credit unions, 103–5, 119, 269n386
Croatan Institute, 104
crowdfunding, 121, 221
Crown Family Foundation, 218
Crying Indian Ad, 171–73
CSR (Corporate Social Responsibility), 108–9, 125
CSX, 185
Cummings, James, 69
Cummings, Nathan, 68
curb-cut effect, 204
cybersecurity, 93–94

DAF (donor-advised fund), 54–55, 162–64
Dakota Access Pipeline, 70,

Index

208–9
Danone Corporation, 2–3, 228
David, King, 216
Dayenu, 181, 186
day trading, 29
Debt (Graeber), 11, 31
debt(s), 61, 135–54, 157, 203; debt allocation, 148, 149, 154; debt cancellation, 31–32, 61, 66; debt contracts, 136, 143, 146–47, 151; ethical framework for in Judaism, 153–54; re-centering impact, 148–49; sharing decision-making power, 151–53
deceptive marketing, 35
decision-making power, 151–53
Decolonizing Wealth (Villanueva), 72
decree(s), 122, 142, 176
default, 142
defense budget, 148
defense companies, 89–92
deforestation, 186
dehumanization, 195–96, 199, 211
DEI (diversity, equity, and inclusion) initiatives, 125–26
Delaware, 212
Delta, 207
democracy, 206–7, 229
Democratic Republic of Congo, 229
Denmark, 115
Department of Labor, 3
depositing money at a bank, 119
desalination plants, 223
destabilization, 231
destruction of the Second Temple, 175–76
destructiveness of Sodom, 136
dialectics, 25
Diaspora Jewish communities, 217
Dick's Sporting Goods, 92
dietary laws, 97. *See also*

kosher food
dignity, 4–5, 23, 40, 72, 77–78, 159, 161, 196, 198, 210–12
The Dignity of Difference (Sacks), 196
DiNapoli, Thomas, 205
direct and indirect lobbying, 185
direct donations, 157
directing money, 107
direct investments, 8, 69
Direct Public Offering, 164
dirty dozen, 104
disaster capitalism, 4, 9
discrimination, 12, 72, 195–99, 201, 202, 205, 225
discriminatory mortgage lending, 147
disinformation, 11, 179, 207
disinvestment, 215
diversity, 107–9, 205
diversity, equity, and inclusion (DEI) initiatives, 125–26
DivestInvest, 186
divestment, 82, 89, 131–32; from fossil fuels, 180–84, 186–87;
divestment of capital, 228
Divine image, 195–96, 224
Dodd-Frank Act, 69
Dodson, Daryn, 107, 152
doing good while doing well, 40–42
Domini, Amy, 60
donations, 54, 157, 217, 270n413
donor-advised fund (DAF), 54–55, 162–64
Dow Jones Sustainability Index, 129
drug prices, 34, 257n131
Due Diligence 2.0 Commitment, 108
Duke Energy, 185, 190
Dutch East India Company, 10–11, 271n425
Dutch government, 115

early capitalism, 11–13, 36
early corporations, 10–11, 115–18, 271n426
early-stage startups, 68, 106, 121
Earways Medical, 121
East Bay Permanent Real Estate Cooperative, 54
East India trading companies, 10–11, 115–16, 271n425
Ecclesiastes, 20–21, 41
economy, 24, 43; centering racial justice, 204; climate change/crisis, 185; context that makes ethical violations profitable, 88–89; economically distressed communities, 198; economic cycles, 31; economic development, 9–14, 116, 225–28, 230 (*See also* monopolies); economic impact, 158; economic opportunity, 150; economics of enough, 17, 20–23, 24, 37, 56; economic suffering, 1–2; economic systems, 9–10, 28, 255n84; racial inequities, 205; workers' rights, 211–12
EcoPeace Middle East, 223
ecosystem, 226–27
Edmond de Rothschild Foundation, 219
Egypt, 18, 190, 200, 210–11
Eida HaChareidit, 32
electricity from fossil fuel sources, 190
Electronic Frontier Foundation, 94
Elevate/Elevar Capital fund, 151
Ely, Alyssa, 151
emergency loans, 54
emissions, 173–74, 179, 181, 185
employment, 89, 155
Enbridge's Line 3 pipeline, 104, 208–9
Encyclopedia Talmudit, 259n179
endowed foundations, 55

293

endowments, 46–47, 59–60, 61, 74, 180–81, 188, 215; communal, 60, 62, 64–67, 71–72; and difficult choices, 71–72; field leaders, 67–70
Energiya Global, 220
energy investments, 186–87
energy supply, 190
Engine No. 1, 183
England, 115–16
English language education, 155
Enron, 10–11
Entergy, 185
enterprises, 226–27
entity list, 94
entrepreneurs, 93, 105, 107, 137, 149, 150–51, 161, 226, 228
entrepreneurs of color, 46, 194, 195, 198, 202–3, 204
environment: environmental impact, 149, 190; environmental issues, 14, 47, 109, 125, 130, 172–74; environmental justice, 187; environmental organizations, 130, 188; environmental sustainability, 180; Indigenous rights, 208–9. *See also* climate change/crisis
Environmental, Social, and Governance investing (ESG), 3, 40–41, 50–51, 81, 109, 125, 126, 128–29, 184, 207
Episcopal Church, 7–8, 14, 124
equitable and just access to land and other resources, 25
equitably shared risk, 63–64, 67, 142–44, 146–48, 153–54
equity, 59, 108, 118, 152, 157, 158, 216, 218, 229
Erech Shai, 263n254
ESG (Environmental, Social, and Governance investing),
3, 40–41, 50–51, 81, 109, 125, 126, 128–29, 184, 207
essential items, 33
ETFs, 113, 128, 207
ethics: and concessionary returns, 56; core principles of, 79; of early corporations, 117; and endowment capital, 66–67; ethical approach to corporations, 122–23; ethical banking and finance, 105; ethical custom, 28; ethical investing, 17, 41, 128–29, 142, 150 (*See also* values-based investing); ethical motive, 144; ethical questions, 79–80; ethical standards, 9, 17–37; ethical violations, 88–89, 91; expectation of financial return, 40; expectations for corporate behavior, 126; framework for debt in Judaism, 148, 153–54; grounds for charging interest to strangers, 140; importance of de-centering the investor, 148; and negative screens, 82, 98–99; purchasing of fair trade and organic goods, 8
Ethiopian *ekub* system, 140
ethnicity, 195
etrogs, 224
Europe, 10, 19, 115–16, 126
European Jews, 141
European Protestants, 81
evil, 42–43
executives, 28, 34, 107, 114, 220, 228
exile, 18, 81, 217
Exit, Voice, and Loyalty (Hirschman), 69, 182–83
Exodus narrative, 200, 211
expectations of human behavior, 126–28
exploitation, 10, 12, 14, 15, 17, 37, 142, 149, 198

exploitative prices, 32
extractive capitalism, 4, 9, 29, 208–10
extreme weather, 179
extremist regimes, 92
extremists, 228
Exxon Knew, 34
ExxonMobil, 34–35, 127, 129, 180, 183, 189, 279n407
Ezekiel, 137

Facebook (now Meta), 11, 207
Fair Food Program, Coalition of Immokalee Workers, 210
Fair Housing Act, 197
fair wages, 212
faith-based investors, 47–48, 56, 106, 183
faith-based shareholder advocates, 124
faith groups/institutions, 1, 4, 5, 7, 9, 56, 82, 118, 179, 251n1
families of color, 202
Fancy, Tariq, 51–52, 56, 109
far from profit, near to loss, 157
farmers/farmworkers, 8, 29, 210, 228–30
federal bonds, 148
federal civil service, 198
federal government, 162
Federal Housing Authority, 197
Federal Reserve, 194
feedback, 87, 129–30, 172, 180
Feinstein, Rabbi Dovid, 275n477
Feinstein, Rabbi Moshe, 49, 123–24, 131, 175–76, 178, 269n386, 270n415, 272n456, 275n477, 283n650
Feinstein, Rabbi Reuven, 275n477
Ferguson, Missouri, 150
Feuerstein, Aaron, 212
FFI Solutions, 189
Fidelity, 207–8

Index

fiduciary duty, 27, 39, 45–47, 52, 53
fiduciary rule, 110
Filene, Edward, 104
filing requirements, 162, 164
financial advisors, 8, 109–10
financial concessions. *See* concessionary returns
financial cooperatives, 104–5
financial crisis of 2008, 12, 29, 30, 31, 33, 69, 122, 136
financial institutions, 104–5, 149, 198, 205
financial loss, 45, 48, 96, 209, 256n122, 267n354
financial performance, 2–3, 40–41
financial return, 7, 8, 24, 37, 39–57, 60, 67, 68, 73, 107, 230; character of Sodom, 42–45; concessionary returns, 45–49; doing good while doing well, 40–42; expectations around, 55–56; fiduciary duty, 45–47; limited financial return and high social impact, 54; market-rate problems, 49–52; private foundations, 52–55
Financial Times, 182
FirstEnergy, 185
fiscal justice, 149–50
Fischer, Norman, 144–45
fixed incomes, 47, 136, 149, 166
fixed-interest loan, 145
fixed price, 29
Flagship Fund, CNote, 55, 194
flexible debt contract, 146–47, 151
Florida, 210
Floyd, George, 204
foods, 9, 95–97, 99, 256n122
food waste, 185–86
forced labor, 210–11
Ford foundation, 181
foreign governments, 92–95
Forward, 163
Fossil Free Funds, 189

fossil-fuel-free bonds, 149
fossil-fuel-free investing, 182–83, 189–90
fossil-fuel-intensive utilities, 190
fossil fuels, 2, 34–35, 68, 70, 74, 172–75, 177–90; and cash, 103–4; divestment from, 180–84, 186–87; end of the fossil fuel era, 180–81; ESG funds, 128–29; Indigenous rights, 208; infrastructure, 70, 184, 186; investing in climate solutions, 188; investor advocacy on climate, 184–86
foundations, 53–55, 66–69, 71–72
401(k) retirement account, 165
Foxworth, Rodney, 51
FPIC (Free, Prior, and Informed Consent), 208–10
France, 115, 145–46
Francis (pope), 1, 4, 208
Free, Prior, and Informed Consent (FPIC), 208–10
free and fair elections, 125
Freedman, Rabbi Avidan, 93–95
free labor, 143
free loans, 46, 48, 54–55, 65, 219
Friedman, Milton, 8, 13, 27–28, 123
frontline communities, 3–4
funding for climate solutions, 181
funding of fossil fuel infrastructure, 186
fund managers, 108, 128
fundraising, 156, 263n250
funds, donor-advised, 162–63
futures contracts, 29

gambling, 29, 81–82
Gamliel, Rabban, 32, 256n117
Ganzfried, Rabbi Shlomo, 119
garment industry, 211

Gaza War, 227
Gemara, 18, 19, 90–91, 143–44
gender bias, 107
gender pay gap, 73, 130
General Electric, 190
General Mills, 96, 119, 273n456
General Motors, 8, 14, 124
generational wealth, 56, 147
Genesis, 79
genocide, 196, 200
geopolitical issues, 174
ger, 140
Germany, 145–46, 200
Get A Better Bank website, 105
Gidulei Terumah, 65
Gilbert, Dan, 147
giving practice (*ma'aser kesafim*), 264n274
global carbon, 173
Global Coffee Sustainability, 230
Global Impact Investing Network, 47, 118
global partnerships, 225
global poverty, 51–52, 53, 55, 121, 187
Global South, 55
global sustainable development, 218
Global Sustainable Investment Alliance (GSIA) report, 252n23
global warming, 34, 173, 178, 185, 190
gneivat daat (stealing awareness), 35
goals. *See* Sustainable Development Goals (SDGs)
God, 18, 21–23, 43–44, 78–79, 137, 138–39, 196, 199
Goldman Sachs, 205
Goldsmiths, University of London, 94
Gonzalez, Richard, 33
Goodejohn, Kelly, 230

295

governance issues, 40–41, 109. *See also* Environmental, Social, and Governance investing (ESG)
governmental decision-making, 206
government and monopolies, 34
government and publicly traded corporations, 115–16
government and redlining, 197, 202
government and usury, 148
government funding, 202, 230
government lobbying, 185
governments and peacebuilding, 230–31
grading companies, 109
Graeber, David, 11, 31, 43, 104
grasshopper farm, 223
grassroots movements, 125–26, 152–53, 178, 181
gratitude, 21–23, 187, 202, 233
Great Depression, 135, 155, 162
Great Recession, 135–36
Great Replacement conspiracy theory, 206
Great Synagogue of Rome, 233
Green America, 105, 130–31
Greenberg, Rabbi Yitz, 23, 25–26, 29, 143–44, 286n727
green bond funds, 149
Greenbook (Lustig), 221
green building investments, 188
Green Century Funds, 125, 186
Greenfaith, 179
greenhouse gas emissions, 174, 189
Greenpeace, 34, 130
grocery stores, 95
Gross Domestic Product, 158, 226
growth, 4, 8, 10–14, 17, 37, 226–27
GSIA (Global Sustainable Investment Alliance) report, 252n23
Gualinga, Emil Sirén, 209
The Guardian, 27, 231
Guide to the Perplexed (Rambam), 265n293
gun reform, 122

Habitat for Humanity, 163
Hadarim Fund, 215–16
Hadar neighborhood, 215
Hafetz Hayim, 78
Haifa, Israel, 215
halakha, 18, 272n456. *See also* Jewish law
Hala Systems, 230
HaLevi, Rabbi Chaim David, 176–77, 282–83n650
The Half Has Never Been Told (Baptist), 11–12
hametz (leavened products), 97, 118–19, 120–21
Hanina, Rabbi, 81
Hareidi Orthodox population, 96
Harper, Fletcher, 47–48
Harris, Kamala, 203
Harvard University, 181, 182
hate speech, 59, 207
Hayani, Abdulkader, 155
Hayes, Rutherford B., 113
Hearn, Denise, 151
Hebrew Bible, 18
Hebrew Free Loan Society (HFLS), 54
hedge funds, 3, 29–30, 127, 183
Heinemann, Rabbi Moshe, 269n386
helping others while costing nothing, 45
Herat, Afghanistan, 229
Herman, Jake, 41–42
Hershey Chocolate Corporation, 96
heshbon hanefesh (soul accounting), 205
heter iska, 145–48, 153, 219, 269n386, 278n543
HFLS (Hebrew Free Loan Society), 54
high-frequency trading, 30
high-impact investments, 49, 55
High Middle Ages, 115
High Priest, 23
Hillel the Elder, 61–62, 142, 149, 203
hillul Hashem, 122
Himelfarb, Sheldon, 230–31
Hinduism, 136
Hirsch, Rabbi Samson Raphael, 139
Hirschman, Albert O., 69, 182–83
Hispanic Americans, 210–12
Hispanic-owned businesses, 151
H&M, 211
HOLC (Home Owners' Loan Corporation), 197
Holocaust, 200
Holy Temple in Jerusalem, 23, 60–61, 81, 97–98, 216, 217
home appraisals, 197
Homebuilding Investment Fund, 163
Home Depot, 207
home equity, 142
homeownership, 135, 147, 164, 197
Home Owners' Loan Corporation (HOLC), 197
homeowners of color, 202
household debt, 135
House of Debt (Mian and Sufi), 136, 151
housing stock, 158
hovel be'atzmo assur li'vnei noach principle, 266n315
How the Other Half Banks (Baradaran), 203
human dignity, 4–5, 23, 40, 78, 87, 196, 198, 211
humanity, 160
human life, 79, 89, 91–92, 99, 224
human psychology, 43, 122

Index

human rights, 93–94
Human Rights Resource Centre, 211
human service agencies, 157, 161
human society, 39
Humira, 33

ICT (information and communications technology) sector, 226–27
idolatry, 56, 77–81, 84–85, 90–91, 97–98, 139
illiquid investments, 68–69
Illumen Capital, 107
image of the Divine, 224
immigrants, 22, 140, 155–56, 206, 210
Immokalee region of Florida, 210
immoral behavior, 80–81
immunity, 117
impact alpha, 41
impact bond funds, 149
Impact-First Capital Preservation strategy, 53
impact/impact investing, 7–15, 40–41, 53–55, 103, 230; balance, 24–25; and cash, 104; climate solutions, 186–89; communal authorities/leadership, 67–71; concessionary returns, 45–49; doing good while doing well, 40–42; endowments, 67; expectations around financial return, 55–56; fiduciary duty, 45–47; financial return, 39–40; *heter iska,* 147–48; impact-first investment, 230; impact investing pools, 162–63; investment advisors, 106–10; in Israel, 215–22; market-rate returns, 49–52; problems with market-rate, 51–52; publicly traded corporations, 118; shared risk, 150–51; sharing decision-making power, 151–53; Si3 impact investing initiative, 70. *See also* CNote
imperialism, 10–11
incarceration system, 88–89, 198
incentive packages, 33
income disparities, 197
incorporated entities, 270–71n415
independent free press, 229
index funds, 36, 45, 87, 108
India, 10–11, 61, 117
Indian Country, 209
Indigenous communities, 54, 179
Indigenous people of color, 194
Indigenous Peoples Rights International, 209
Indigenous rights, 104, 196, 198–99, 208–10
Indigenous women, 209
individualist extremes, 44
individuals, 1–2, 26, 31, 45, 47, 52, 71–72, 92, 162–63; individual actions, 172–74; individual and collective, 189; individual investors, 117–18, 165, 193–94; individual shareholders, 114, 120
Industrial Revolution, 19
Inexhaustible Treasuries, 61
infinite return, 48
Inflation Reduction Act of 2022, 181
inflexible debt contracts, 135–36, 143, 146, 151, 153–54, 277n527
influence, 69, 117, 122–24, 131, 207
information and communications technology (ICT) sector, 226–27
in-group lending, 140
inheritance, 64, 72, 198. *See also* Resource Generation
innovative technology startups, 121
Institute for Policy Studies, 2
institutional capital, 59–75; barriers, 72–73; communal authorities/leadership, 67–71; communal endowments, 60–67; early forms of capital, 60–62; endowments and difficult choices, 71–72; orphan trust funds, 62–64
institutional endowments, 71–72, 180–81
institutional investors, 54, 59–60
institutions deserving preferred treatment, 65
insurance companies, 116
insurrection, January 6, 2021, 206–7
interest, 118–19, 219; charging interest to a fellow community member, 138–39; communal endowments, 65; different sets of rules for Jews and non-Jews, 139–40; early forms of capital, 61; *heter iska,* 145–48; interest-bearing loans, 48, 136, 138, 143, 145; interest-free capital, 165; interest-free loans, 54–56, 68, 164, 189, 277n522; interest rates, 139; orphan trust funds, 62–64; prohibition on charging interest, 136, 137–40; shared risk, 140–45. *See also* usury (charging interest to someone in need)
Interfaith Center on Corporate Responsibility, 70, 109, 124, 130
intergenerational wealth, 197
internal migration, 215
international banks, 104
international companies, 104–5

International Consortium of Investigative Journalists, 26–27
international development work, 227
internationalism, 217
international markets, 228
international warfare, 93
internet, 152, 164
investees, 104, 142–43, 148, 151–54
Investination, 121, 220
investing in Israel, 215–22
investing in peacebuilding, 223–32; around the world, 228–31; challenges of, 231–32; Palestinian economy, 225–28
investing in small businesses, 164–65
investing locally. *See* local investing
investment advisors and Indigenous rights, 210
investment allocation, 218
investment bankers, 30
investment capital/arena, 1–3, 7–15, 37, 60, 202–3; advocacy on climate, 184–86; catalytic capital, 53–54; centering racial justice, 193–95; challenges of local investing, 161–62; and chase, 103–6; concessionary returns, 47; environmental issues, 174; ESG funds, 128–29; field leaders, 68–71; *heter iska*, 146–48; and Israel, 217–18; Jewish wisdom, 166; near to profit and far from loss, 62–65; negative screens, 81–82; racism, 198–99; re-centering impact, 148–49; renewable energy, 187; shared risk, 64, 141–44, 150–51; sharing access, 149–50; spyware as a weapon, 94. *See also* monopolies

investment committees, 46, 69–70, 73, 120
investment decisions, 3, 8, 24, 40, 49, 128–29
investment funds and renewable energy, 187
investment funds and shareholder advocacy, 130–31
investment managers, 107–9, 143, 149
Investment Policy Statement, 216
investment portfolios, 1, 8, 11–12, 80, 113; advocacy on climate, 184–86; asset allocation, 103; barriers to change, 73; centering racial justice, 203–4; charitable funds maintaining, 65; field leaders, 68–69; fossil fuels, 186; Israel, 221; Israeli bonds, 218; negative screens, 81, 99; private prisons, 89; racial injustice, 198; universal standards, 128
investment returns, 47, 68, 107
investment screens. *See* negative screens
Investors and Indigenous People's Working Group, 209–10
investors' portfolios, 117–18
involuntary servitude, 198
Iraq, 230
iron, 91
Isaac, 216
Isaac Aaron Ettinger, R., 273n461
Isaiah, 89
Isenberg, Diane, 53, 56, 121
iska (investment partnership), 142
Islam, 81, 136, 146
Islamic banking, 151
Israel, 31, 61, 68, 92–95, 98, 103, 147, 153, 164, 174, 200, 215–22, 223–28, 292n833

Israel bonds, 147, 217–18
Israel Free Loan Association, 219
Israeli companies, 120–21
Israeli-Jordanian agricultural venture, 224
Israeli Ministry of Defense, 93
Israel Impact Fund, 220
Israeli-Palestinian conflict, 225–32
Israeli spyware, 93–94
Israelites, 18, 31, 77–78, 137, 190, 200
Israel's Start-Up Nation, 94
Isserlein, Rabbi Israel, 146
issurei hana'ah (items prohibited from benefit), 97–98, 268n372, 268n373
Italy, 61, 145

Jacob ben Asher, Rabbi, 48
Jacobs, Louise, 215–16
Jafta, Luyanda, 150
James I, King, 116
January 6 insurrection, 206–7
JCFSD (Jewish Community Foundation of San Diego), 162–63
Jerusalem, 18, 81, 216, 223
Jerusalem Talmud, 260n194
Jerusalem Venture Partners, 68, 106–7, 220
Jewish Advocacy Strategy, 41–42, 130
Jewish Alliance of Greater Rhode Island, 188
Jewish approach to communal charitable funds. *See* communal endowments
Jewish approach to investing in public equities, 119–21
Jewish approach to negative screens, 81–82
Jewish approach to reparations, 200–202
Jewish approach to shareholder advocacy, 129–31
Jewish calendar, 23, 205
Jewish Climate Leadership

Index

Coalition, 188–89
Jewish Community Center, 188
Jewish Community Foundation of San Diego (JCFSD), 162–63
Jewish Community Relations Council, 188
Jewish ethics, 17–37, 45, 51–52, 56, 67, 179, 187–88, 202
Jewish Federations, 54–55, 60, 163–64, 174, 188–89
Jewish Funds for Justice, 153
Jewish immigrants, 155
Jewish Impact Investing Summit, 25, 96
Jewish institutions, 1, 60, 65, 67, 70–71, 72–74, 92, 130, 148, 163–64
Jewish investors, 45, 47–48, 87, 92, 96, 98, 113, 118–20, 122–23, 131, 163, 174, 268n373, 270n412
Jewish landholding, 216
Jewish law, 9, 26–28, 274n464; and abortion, 82, 265n305; arguments regarding divestment, 182; business partnerships, 118–19; communal behavior, 175; communal endowments, 65–67; concessionary returns, 48–49; corporation as own entity, 122; corporations, 131; corporations and partnerships, 272–73n456; dietary laws, 97; giving practice *(ma'aser kesafim)*, 264n274; hazard in the public domain, 187–88; helping others while costing nothing, 45; interest, 138–39; *issurei hana'ah* (items prohibited from benefit), 97–98; Jewish approaches in practice, 120–21; Jewish sources, 18–19; limited liability, 114, 117, 118–19, 121, 270n415; Noachide laws, 126, 127, 131; shared risk, 63–64, 143; smoking, 176–77; tobacco, 174–75; usury, 136–40, 147–48
Jewish legal approaches to a corporation, 119–20
Jewish mystical tradition, 216
Jewish prayer, 217
Jewish sources, 18–20
Jewish tradition and values: balance, 23–26, 231, 233; business partnerships, 118–19; charity, 159–61; climate change/crisis, 190; coexistence, 160, 221, 224–25, 228, 232; communal endowments, 65–67; communal norms, 30, 79, 139, 176; concessionary returns, 48–49; re-centering impact, 148–49; economics of enough, 20–23; endowments, 71–72; ESG funds, 128–29; expectations around financial return, 55–56; feedback, 180; free loans, 54–55; helping others while costing nothing, 45; investing locally, 105, 155–67; investment advisors, 110; investment capital, 203; and Israel, 218; Jewish sources, 18–20; living with gratitude, 187; loan capital, 141; modesty, 30; and monopolies, 34; moral responsibility to the actions of corporations, 122–23; negative screens, 81–82; obligations to care, 210–11, 218; prayers, 172; prohibition against interest, 137, 138–39; rebuke, 129–30; reparations, 200–202; restrictions on profit for essential items, 33; shared risk, 63–64, 135–54; *shmita* (Sabbatical) year, 30–32; sustainable development, 216–21; sustainable global development, 28–30; Temple treasury, 115; theft of freedom, 89; tobacco, 174–75; trading in prohibited foods, 95–97; universal standards, 126–28; weapons and self-defense, 89–90; weapons trade, 93–95
Jewish values investment strategies. *See* values-based investing
Jewish Vocational Service of Greater Boston (JVS), 155–56
Jewish wisdom, 3, 23, 225, 233–34; capitalism, 26; centering racial justice, 212; doing good while doing well, 41; how we make money, 39; investment opportunities, 166; re-centering impact, 148
Jewish Youth Climate Movement (JYCM), 74, 184–85
JLens, 41–42, 107, 130, 185–86, 220
Johnson & Johnson, 205
joint and several liability, 114
Joint Stock Company Act of 1862, 117
joint-stock corporations, 11, 113, 115–17, 270n412, 271n425, 275n476
Jonah, 129
Jordan, 223–24
Joseph, Amanda, 153
Journal of Halacha, 96
JPMorgan Chase, 70, 103–4, 181
Judaism, 2, 9, 10, 233–34; and alcohol, 81; amount of time available to spend on making money, 21; ancient approach, 37; ancient approach to economics and social justice, 18; anonymous giving, 161;

299

arguments regarding divestment, 182; balance, 23–25; climate change/crisis, 190; coexistence, 160; as communal religion, 178; concessionary returns, 56; concessionary returns in Jewish law, 48; economic systems, 28, 255n84; engagement, 180; ethical expectation of financial return, 40; ethical framework for debt, 153–54; fiduciary duty, 27; giving practice (*ma'aser kesafim*), 264n274; *gneivat daat* (stealing awareness), 35; governmental decision-making, 206; *heshbon hanefesh*, 205; *hillul Hashem*, 122; individual actions, 172; interest, 138–39; Jewish sources, 18–20; *kol yisrael arevin zeh bazeh* (all members of the Jewish community are bound up with one another), 172; learning, 19–20; living with gratitude, 187; market rate of return, 40, 49; modesty, 30; moral conscience, 87; non-kosher meat, 95; personal sacrifice, 52; price-gouging, 32; property rights, 44; public equities, 131–32; racial injustice, 195–99; as religion of protest, 14–15; selling weapons, 99; shareholder advocacy, 129–31; sharing access, 149; sharing decision-making power, 151–53; sustainability, 4–5; theft, 88–89; transformational change, 80; unethical acts, 28, 79, 82–83, 85–86, 91, 121; universal standards, 126–28; usury, 136–37, 148; and wealth, 66–67; weapons and self-defense, 89; weapons trade, 91–92; workers' rights, 210–11. *See also* money ethics

Justice Department, 175
Justice For Myanmar, 104
JVS (Jewish Vocational Service of Greater Boston), 155–56
JYCM (Jewish Youth Climate Movement), 74, 184–85

A Kaddish for Bernie Madoff (film), 144–45
Kagan, Rabbi Yisrael Meir, 32, 78
Kahan, Dan, 178
Kansas, 161
kashrut, 14–15
Kataly Foundation, 53–54
Keefe, Joe, 81
Keep America Beautiful, 171. *See also* Crying Indian Ad
Keystone XL pipeline, 104, 208
Khashoggi, Jamal, 93
Killip, Rabbi Avi, 80
King David, 137
The Kitchen, 157
Klapper, Rabbi Aryeh, 83–84
Klein, Naomi, 4
Klein, Rabbi Menashe, 120
Kolot Chayeinu, Brooklyn, New York, 70
kol yisrael arevin zeh bazeh (all members of the community are bound up with one another), 172
Korean *kye* system, 140
kosher food, 9, 82, 95–97, 99, 120–21, 127, 139
Krikler, Doug, 226, 228
Kroc, Ray, 96
Kushner, Rabbi Yosef Y., 267n356, 268n373, 283n654

labor issues, 230
labor market, 155, 204
landowners, 31

large-cap companies, 113
large companies, 117, 158, 279n415
Latinx entrepreneurs, 107
Lauder, Laura, 54–55
Laura and Gary Lauder Philanthropic Fund, 54–55
Lavi, Aharon Ariel, 31
lawsuits, 35, 130
Le, Vu, 71, 73
leaders of color, 71, 203
learning, 19–20
leaving Israel, 217
legal codes, 18–19, 33, 45, 65, 88, 138–39, 187, 260n194
legislation, 94–95, 171, 173, 176
Leibowitz, Nechama, 87–88
Leichtag, Lee and Toni, 67
Leichtag Commons, 68
Leichtag Foundation, 67–68, 106–7, 220
lending, 31, 48, 61, 62–64, 118, 119–20, 140, 141–42, 145–48, 203, 253n29
lending at interest, 61, 64, 136, 137–38, 140, 141, 145, 148
lending circles, 151
Leon of Modena, 277n521
letter of the law, 26–28, 43
Levine, Rabbi Dr. Aaron, 28, 45, 177, 283n657
Leviticus Fund, 165
Levy, John, 69
liberation, 203
Liberia, 230–31
Libra Foundation, 53
life insurance, 162
lifnei iver (stumbling block). *See* stumbling blocks before the blind
lifnim mishurat hadin (beyond the letter of the law), 28
limited liability, 114–15, 117, 118–19, 121, 270n415
limited-life, 68
limits on profits, 32–34
Line 3 tar sands pipeline, Minnesota, 74, 104, 208–9
Lintz, Rabbi George, 96

Index

Linzer, Rabbi Dov, 264n274, 269n386
living with gratitude, 187
loans, 8, 103–6, 119, 131, 159–61, 197, 202–3, 219; access to capital, 158; Black-owned firms, 204; bridge loans, 230; concessionary returns, 48; early forms of capital, 61–62; *heter iska,* 145–48; interest-free green, 189; interest-free loans, 68, 164, 189, 277n522; loan capital, 54, 141, 148, 219; loan loss rate, 198; to local businesses, 163–64; prohibition against interest, 137–38; shared risk, 140–43; without interest, 142
lobbying, 28, 34, 125, 126, 127, 177, 179, 185, 220
local businesses, 157–58, 164–66
local charity, 159–61
local communities, 141, 158–61
Local Dollars, Local Sense (Shuman), 162, 165
local housing, 158
local investing, 55, 155–67; as an accredited investor, 162–64; benefits of, 158–59; challenges of, 161–62; charity, 159–61; finding investment opportunities, 167; for nonaccredited investors, 164–65
local markets, 145
Locavesting (Cortese), 161–62, 165
locavesting movement, 166
locavore movement, 158, 166
long-term investment, 29
loopholes, 27, 34, 146, 198
Love, Rabbi Yaakov, 269n386
low- and moderate-income communities, 149, 152
low-cost capital, 46
lower financial return, 42, 48
low-income borrowers, 104

low-income women, 203
low-interest loans, 54, 229
Lustig, Michael, 218–19, 221
Luther, Martin, 145

MacArthur Foundation, 46, 181, 202
Macedonia, 230
Madison, James, 116
Madjsberg, Saadia, 108–9
Maharam Shick, 267n351, 275n476
main street, 165, 166
Main Street Journal, 165
major holidays, 21, 84
Majority Action, 207
Malden Mills textile factory, 212
managing partners, 63, 142–43, 146
Mandela, Nelson, 232
manufacturers, 171, 173
Mapping Inequality Project, 197
marginalized communities, 3–4, 55, 78–79, 105, 152, 202, 203
marijuana, 81–82
market capitalizations, 33, 113, 117
market rate of return, 39–40, 41, 45, 47–53, 56, 163, 165
Martinez, Jerry and Marcie, 135–36, 141, 149, 151
Mar Ukba, 62, 160–61
Marx, Karl, 36
Maryland, 189
Massachusetts, 116, 155
mass incarceration, 88–89, 198
Maung, Yadanar, 104
"May a Jew Invest in McDonald's?" (Lintz), 96
McAfee, Michael, 1–2, 233
McDonald's, 50, 96, 210
McKibben, Bill, 174, 180–81, 182, 187
McKinney-Baldon, Shahanna, 199
Media Development Investment Fund (MDIF), 229

Medicaid, 148
medicine, 32–34
medieval Italy, 145
Mensah, Lisa, 46, 203, 204
merchants, 10, 32, 141, 277n524
Merck, 206
mesayea (not aiding), 86
Meta (formerly Facebook), 11, 207
methane emissions, 173
Mexican *tandas* system, 140
mezuzah, 292n833
Mian, Atif, 135–36, 141–42, 146, 147, 151
Micah, 224
Micklethwait, John, 10, 115
microcap companies, 113
Microsoft, 173
Middle Ages, 61, 86, 141, 145–46
Middle East, 174, 223–24
Mighty Deposits, 105
mi ika midi principle, 265n305
millennial investors, 8–9
Minchat Yitzchak, 272n456, 275n476
Minderoo Foundation, 173
mindset, 17, 33–34, 35, 37, 47, 50
Minnesota, 74, 104, 208–9
minorities, 79, 206
minority affinity groups, 140
minority borrowers, 50, 104
minority entrepreneurs, 105
minority-owned firms, 107–8
minyan, 172
Mishnah, 18, 42–43, 49, 88, 90–91, 95–96, 196, 199, 267n354
Mishneh Halakhot, 272n456
misinformation, 34–35, 178
mission alignment, 68–69. *See also* values-based investing
MIT, 173
mitzvah of *orlah,* 265n293
mitzvot (commandments), 18, 172
Moadim Uzmanim, 273n461,

275n476
modern banking, 148
modern energy sources, 187
modern responsible investing movement, 7–8, 81
modern slavery, 210–11
modern tobacco industry, 175
modesty, 30
monasteries, 61, 115
money ethics, 17–37
moneylending, 140, 146
monopolies, 11, 32–34, 116–17
Moody's, 33
morality, 3, 10–11, 83, 87, 90–91, 121–23, 138–39, 142–43, 177, 182, 199
Morgan Stanley, 51, 104, 153
mortgages, 12, 29, 135–36, 141–42, 147, 151, 197, 202
Moses, 18–19, 44, 82–83, 137, 224, 254n77
mourning, 21, 176
MSCI, 129
multinational corporations, 165, 231
municipal bonds, 136, 148
municipalities, 148
Murphy, Sara, 50–51
mutual aid societies, 140
mutual funds, 87, 96, 108, 113, 128, 148, 153, 162, 186, 207, 267n354
mutualism, 104
mutual social contracts, 140
Myanmar, 94, 104

Nachman, Rav, 62, 64, 90
Nathan Cummings Foundation, 59, 68–69, 125, 188
Nathansohn, Rabbi Joseph Saul, 119
The Nation, 33
National Coalition for Community Capital, 165
Native American tribes, 208
natural disasters, 178
natural gas, 35, 189
Nature Communications, 22

near market-rate, 48–49
near to profit and far from loss, 62–65, 143, 262n247
negative screens, 69, 81–82, 89, 95, 97, 98–99, 129, 180
Nehardea, 142
Neichin, Greg, 53, 56
neshech, 138, 139
networking, 164
New Jersey, 165
newsletters, 165
New York, 2, 12, 292n836
New York City, 35, 165
The New Yorker, 35
New York Stock Exchange, 94
New York Times, 8, 27, 52, 93, 123, 135, 182
The Next Egg, 165
NGOs (non-governmental organizations), 231
Nigeria, 180, 231
Nike, 26–27
Noachide laws, 79, 126, 127, 131
Noah, 79, 126–27, 216
nochri, 140
nonaccredited investors, 162, 164–65
non-Christians, 140
non-financial impacts, 41, 109
non-governmental organizations (NGOs), 226, 231
non-Jewish Arabs, 218–19
non-Jewish corporate ownership, 121
non-Jewish entities, 148
non-Jewish person, 85, 138, 139, 145
non-kosher food, 95–96, 99
Nonprofit Futures Lab, 105
nonprofits, 46–47, 162–64
non-recourse mortgages, 141
norms, 30, 79, 139, 176
Northern Ireland, 231–32
NSO Group, 93–94
Nyack, New York, 165

Obama administration, 164
obligations, 40, 45, 179, 187–88, 256n122; to care, 210–11, 218; coexistence, 160; concessionary returns, 48–49; to help other people stop smoking, 177; local investing, 160, 166; to offer support to community members in need, 139
Occidental Petroleum, 69
Ogen, 219, 221
oil and gas companies, 69, 173, 180, 183, 189
Ojibwe nations, 74
Open Road Alliance, 230
opioid epidemic, 35, 130, 220
Opportunity Finance Network, 46, 203, 253n29
oral law, 146
Oregon Clean Power Cooperative, 55
organizational funds, 163
organizational stakeholders, 71
orphan trust funds, 62–65, 143
Orthodox community, 81, 174–75
Orthodox rabbinic authority, 176–77
Orthodox Union, 82
Ottoman Jewry, 217
OurCrowd, 221
out-group rules, 139–40
Overton window, 179
overuse of antibiotics on livestock, 50–51, 80, 125
own-and-advocate approach, 182–83
ownership, 30–31, 63, 66, 96, 114, 119–20, 121, 123, 152
Oxfam, 2, 51, 55, 56
Ozelius, Carol, 156–57

Pacific Community Ventures, 163, 198
Pacific Northwest, 179
paid sick leave, 125
Pakistan, 230

Palestine Growth Capital Fund, 227

Index

Palestinian Economic Bulletin, 225
Palestinian economy, 225–28
Palestinian IT Association (PITA), 227
Palestinian Social Impact Bond, 226
Palmer, Martin, 56
Pandora Papers, 26–27
Panel on Climate Change, 179
Paris Climate Accords, 70, 125, 127, 185, 190
partnerships, 113–14, 115, 118–19, 120, 122, 137, 142, 145–46, 163, 272–73n456
Passover, 32, 97
Patriotic Millionaires, 198
Pava, Moses, 28
Pax, 81
Pax World Fund, 8
pay-for-success investment, 155
peacebuilding, 223–32; around the world, 228–31; challenges of business and, 231–32; Palestinian economy, 225–28
PeaceTech Accelerator, 230
Pearlstone campus, Maryland, 189
Pegasus, 94
pension funds, 3, 46–47, 158, 162
people of color, 12, 46, 50, 89, 107–8, 147, 152, 194, 196, 198
The People's Fund, 150–51
Perisha, 260n194
Perkins, Ebony, 104–5, 152
Perlow, Rabbi Yerucham Fishel, 187–88
permanent endowments (*keren kayemet*), 65, 262n247
permitting interest, 140
Perry, Andre, 202
Persians, 91, 92, 94
Persson family, 211
Pesach, 118–19, 120, 121, 210–11, 268n373, 275n476

pharmaceutical industry, 32–35
philanthropy, 60, 71–72, 156–57, 181. *See also* communal endowments
Phillip Morris, 129
PITA (Palestinian IT Association), 227
Platform, 231
pledges, 66, 182
PolicyLink, 204, 233
policymakers, 185
political advocacy, 188
political donations, 206–7, 270n413
political influence, 117, 122
political resolutions, 228
political risk, 229
political spending, 117, 127
politicians, 3, 174, 185, 231–32
politics, 226
pollution, 171, 173, 186, 190
poor and vulnerable, 4, 44, 53–54, 61, 64, 65–67, 72, 142, 159–61, 187, 203, 218
Portland Trust, 225–28, 231
positive externalities, 204
positive impact, 7, 8, 41–42, 45, 49, 51–52, 55–56, 67, 81, 99, 106–10, 166, 199, 203–4, 216, 219, 230
possessions, 66, 138
post-conflict regions, 229–30
post-war consumption, 171
poverty, 1–2, 20, 25, 51–52, 53, 55, 66–67, 71, 141, 165, 203, 225. *See also* poor and vulnerable
power, 17, 33–34, 59–60, 63–64, 72, 78, 142–43, 172–73, 231
practical prohibition on interest, 138–39
prayers, 65, 172
pre-capitalist societal institutions, 11
predatory subprime loans, 104
preferential risk-based treatment, 65–67

preservation of capital, 48
pressure, 14–15, 34, 59, 70–71, 73, 108–9, 185–86
Price, Anne, 3–4, 14, 199, 204
price gouging, 32–34
principal, 63–65, 146
prison labor, 198
Pritzker, Nick and Susan, 53
Pritzker, Regan, 53–54
private banks, 117
private capital, 157, 215
private companies, 8, 148
private debt, 106, 148, 157, 166
private equity, 46, 106, 155–67
private foundations, 52–55, 66–67, 162–63, 264n274
private individual capital, 67
private investors, 3, 155, 215
private prisons, 50, 70, 88–89
private property, 21, 25–26
private shareholders, 125
privilege, 53, 72, 79–80
Procter and Gamble, 186
productive use, 30
productive work, 25
profit, 2–3, 4, 9–15, 20–21, 37, 39; balance, 24–25; and capitalism, 26–28; concessionary returns, 42, 48, 56; economics of enough, 22–23; endowments, 71–72; extractive capitalism, 4, 9, 29, 208–10; far from profit, near to loss, 157; fiduciary duty, 46; *gneivat daat* (stealing awareness), 35; *heter iska*, 145–48; and idolatry, 78; limits on, 32–34; near to profit and far from loss, 62–65; private prisons, 88–89; problems with market-rate, 49–52; profit motive, 143–44, 233; public benefit corporations, 228; re-centering impact, 148–49; restrictions on profit for essential items, 33; shared risk, 142–44;

stumbling blocks before the blind, 84–87; trading in prohibited foods, 95–97
profit at all costs, 9–15, 17, 132
progressives, 125–26, 128–29
prohibition, 33, 83–88, 90–92, 95–99, 110, 118–19, 127, 136, 137–40, 145–48
property, 25–26, 43–44, 45, 259n176
prophets, 18, 216, 224
American and European,

protests, 5, 14–15, 70, 94–95, 234
Proverbs, 232
proxy voting, 69–70, 127–28, 130–31, 184, 207–8, 275n477
prozbul, 61, 203
Psalms, 23, 175, 224
psychological challenges, 201
public, 34–35, 175
public benefit corporations, 3, 122, 228
public companies, 69, 120, 123, 156, 162, 185, 187, 220, 270–71n415, 272n456
public corporations, 11, 108, 113–14, 118, 120, 121, 122, 123, 131–32, 147
public equities, 113–33; business partnerships, 118–19; and cash, 106; Environmental, Social, and Governance investing (ESG), 128–29; influence of a shareholder, 123–24; investing in Israel, 218; investing locally, 163; investment advisors, 108; Jewish approach in practice, 120–21; Jewish legal approaches to a corporation, 119–20; moral responsibility to the actions of corporations, 122–23; prohibition on trading in prohibited foods, 96; publicly traded

corporations, 115–18; rabbinic consensus that the prohibitions on usury, 121, 148; racial equity audits, 204–6; shareholder advocacy, 124–26, 129–31; universal standards, 126–28
public hazard, 187–88
publicly traded corporations, 94, 115–18, 274n471
publicly traded joint-stock corporations, 113, 115–17
publicly traded stocks, 120, 162
public relations, 179
public stock exchanges, 157
public thoroughfare, 172, 187–88, 259n176
public welfare, 28, 44, 116, 131
purchasing cigarettes, 177
purchasing shares from another investor on the secondary market, 127, 274n471

Quakers, 7
quality of life, 48–49, 223
Quicken Loans, 147

rabbinic Sages. *See* Sages of the Talmud
rabbis/rabbinic authorities, 65–66, 91, 136–37, 176–77; approaches to public corporations, 123; commandment to pursue peace, 224; communal endowments, 65–67; covenant with Noah, 126; decrees, 122; economic systems, 255n84; gambling, 29; *issurei hana'ah* (items prohibited from benefit), 97–98; *lifnei iver*, 85; and marijuana, 82; *mezuzah*, 292n833; modesty, 30; opinions on the status of a corporation, 119–20; permanent endowments (*keren kayemet*), 262n247;

rabbinical courts, 45;
rabbinic consensus, 44, 96, 121, 131, 148, 274n471;
rabbinic rule on *mesayea* ("not aiding"), 86; *shmita* (Sabbatical) year, 31; temptation to loan at interest, 137–38; tobacco, 174–75; trading in non-kosher meat, 99; trading in prohibited foods, 95–96; *tzelem elohim*, 196; usury, 148; window of public opinion, 179; workers' rights, 210–11. *See also* Sages of the Talmud
Rabins, Alicia Jo, 144–45
racial bias, 107, 197
racial discrimination, 12, 19, 202, 205
racial equity audits, 204–6, 207
racial injustice, 151, 152, 195–99, 204–5, 206, 212, 233
racial justice, 46, 125–26, 193–213
racial wealth gap, 12, 55, 130, 194, 197, 202
racism, 12, 71, 80, 195–99, 202, 204–5
radical economic justice, 30–31
Raise Green, 153
Rambam, 21, 33, 41, 71, 172, 187, 218, 259n179, 265n293
Rami bar Chami, 44
Rashi, 139
rate of return, 55, 56, 165, 195
Rava, 17
Reagan, Ronald, 27
real estate assets, 188–89
rebuke, 87, 129–30, 131, 180
Reconciliation and Responsible Investment Initiative, 209
Reconstructionist movement, 19
recreational weapons, 92

Index

redemptive vision, 25
redistribute the land, 31–32
redlining, 197, 202
reform, 122
Reform movement, 19, 69–70, 177
Reform Pension Board (RPB), 69–70
refugees, 155–56
regenerative capitalism, 9
Regulation Crowdfunding, 164
regulations, 117
regulations/regulators, 129, 153, 164–65, 185
religious institutions, 115
religious investors, 8
renewable energy, 180, 187–88
renewables, 190
renouncing ownership, 30–31
reparations, 200–202, 212
repayment, 146, 150–51
repression of voting rights, 206
reputational risk, 59–60, 125, 156
research consultants, 178
researching candidates, 128
resilience, 31, 105, 233–34
resistance, 14–15, 104
Resnikoff, Rabbi Chaggai, 283n657
Resnikoff, Rabbi Haggai, 179
resolution of conflict, 231
resolutions of the Reform movement, 70, 177
Resource Generation, 72, 109, 121, 202
resources, 25, 42–43, 161, 187, 225
responsa, 19, 275n476
responsibility, 22–23, 53, 83, 86–88, 122–23, 159–60, 171–72, 273n464. *See also* fiduciary duty
responsible investment initiative. *See* UN Principles for Responsible Investment
restrictions on profit, 33
retirement, 46–47, 49, 113, 163, 165

return to right relationship, 190, 199
revenues, 151
Reynolds, Fiona, 185
righteous monetary behavior, 49
right relationship, 77, 190, 199
right-sizing, 22, 187
right-to-repair movement, 173
risk and Indigenous rights, 208–9
risk and racial justice, 205
Rockefeller Asset Management, 40
Rockefeller foundation, 8, 181
Rodin, Judith, 108–9
Roman rule, 78, 81, 176
Rome, Italy, 233
rooftop solar farm, 189
Root Capital, 51, 56
Rosenn, Rabbi David, 54
Rosenn, Rabbi Jennie, 174, 181, 187
Rosh, 65
Rothstein, Richard, 197
rotzeh bekiyumo, 268n371, 268n373
royal charters, 10
RPB (Reform Pension Board), 69–70
Rumi Spice, 228–29
Russia, 94, 184, 229

Sackler family, 35
Sacks, Rabbi Lord Jonathan, 14, 78, 196, 234
Sadara, 227
saffron, 228–29
Sages of the Mishnah, 48
Sages of the Talmud, 18, 39; buying objects that were likely stolen, 88; character of Sodom, 42–44; commandment to pursue peace, 224; Divine image, 196; doing good while doing well, 41; far from profit, near to loss, 157; helping others while costing nothing, 45; idolatry,

78–79; interest-bearing loans to non-Jews, 145; investment focused on wealth creation, 141; *issurei hana'ah* (items prohibited from benefit), 97; *kol yisrael arevin zeh bazeh* (all members of the community are bound up with one another), 172; *lifnei iver* prohibition, 83, 84–86; local charity, 159–60; locations of manufacturing processes, 173; *mitzvah* of moving to Israel, 292n834; orphan trust funds, 63–64; relying on interest for one's income long-term, 140; right relationship motivated by love, 190; Roman rule, 81; self-serving advice, 110; selling arms to the Persians, 92, 94; shared risk, 142–43; social change, 178; squatters, 258–59n170; trading in prohibited foods, 95; weapons and self-defense, 89–91; *yetzer hara* (self-centered urge), 24; *yishuv Eretz Yisrael*, 216, 217; *yishuvo shel olam* (settling of the world), 29–30
Salanter, Rabbi Yisrael, 273n461
sale of cigarettes, 177
sales of securities, 162
sanctions, 229
San Diego Habitat for Humanity, 163
San Francisco Community Land Trust's BIPOC Homeownership project, 164
San Francisco Jewish Community Federation and Endowment Fund, 54, 163–64
Sara Lee Corporation, 68
Saudi Arabia, 93–94

305

Savage, Nigel, 96
say-on-pay provisions, 69
Schwartz, Debra, 51, 166, 201–2
Science Advisory Committee, 35
scientists, 2, 175, 178
SDGs. *See* Sustainable Development Goals (SDGs)
SEC (Securities and Exchange Commission), 107–8, 124–25, 129, 162, 164, 194
secondary market, 127, 274n471
Second Temple, 18, 103, 175–76
secular investors, 89
secular law, 114, 120, 122, 279n413
secular nonprofits, 163
securities, 12, 29; securities laws, 157, 162, 164, 166
Securities and Exchange Commission (SEC), 107–8, 124–25, 129, 162, 164, 194
security, 162, 225–26
segregation, 197–98, 202
Seidle, Charlene, 67–68
self-defense, 89–92
self-directed 401(k), 165
Self-Help Credit Union, 105
selfishness of Sodom, 43, 45, 49, 56
Service Employees International Union, 207
Severance Guarantee Fund, 211
severance pay, 211
severance theft from garment workers, 211
sex trafficking, 209
Shabbat, 14, 21, 32, 89, 118–19, 120, 121, 272n456
shared risk, 63–64, 67, 135–54
The Shareholder Commons, 50–51, 56
shareholders, 27, 41, 114, 270–71n415, 270n415, 273n461, 275n477; in a food or restaurant corporation, 95; influence of, 123–24; Jewish legal approaches to a corporation, 120; moral challenges, 122–23; public traded corporations, 116–17; responsibility for unethical acts of corporations, 121; shareholder advocacy, 34, 36, 42, 69, 87, 108–9, 124–26, 129–31, 173, 180, 187–89, 220, 230; shareholder campaigns, 131, 182–83, 207; shareholder resolutions, 34, 50, 59, 69, 124–26, 130, 173, 184–86, 190, 207, 210–11; shareholder value, 50
shares, 59, 114, 115–17, 119, 120, 127, 184
shares being sold on the open market, 271n424
shekel investment, 216
Shell, 180, 231
sheva mitzvot b'nei Noach (the seven practices of the children of Noah), 127
Shick, Rabbi Moshe, 119, 148
shields, 90–91
Shimon ben Shetach, 17
Shkreli, Martin, 32
shmita (Sabbatical) year, 21, 22, 25, 30–32, 61, 66, 95, 137, 142, 203, 231; and agriculture, 224
Shmuel, 32–33, 62, 256n122
Shoel U'Meishiv, 119
short-term gains, 3, 78, 275n477
Shulkhan Arukh, 88, 119, 256n122
Shuman, Michael, 162, 165
Si3, 70, 216
significantly below market rate, 48–49
Simpson, Anne, 183
single-use plastic waste, 171, 173
Sirull, Beth, 163
Six-Day War, 92
Skoll, Jeff, 50
SLAPP (Strategic Lawsuits Against Public Participation), 130
slavery, 7, 10–14, 89, 196, 198, 200–202, 210–11
small banks, 105
Small Business Administration, 158
small businesses, 8, 113, 150–51, 158, 164–65, 194, 203, 204, 219
Small Change, 164
Smith, Adam, 24, 117
smoking, 86, 174–78, 282–83n650, 282n649, 283n654, 283n657
social change, 39, 42, 59–60, 109, 128–29, 178, 185
social contracts, 138, 139, 140
Social Finance Israel, 220, 221
social impact, 48, 52, 54
Social Impact Bonds, 155–57, 161, 220
social issues, 41, 47, 51, 125, 130, 216
social justice, 18, 22, 109, 202, 204–5
socially responsible investing (SRI), 8, 40; arguments against divestment, 182; asset management firms, 128; ESG investment, 41, 50; fixed-income funds, 149; fossil fuels, 186; investment advisors, 108–9; mainstream investment community, 52; negative screens, 81; public equities, 118; workers' rights, 210
Socially Responsible Investing Heart Rating, 130
social media, 182
social responsibility, 27–28, 187–88
"The Social Responsibility of Business Is to Increase Its Profits" (Friedman), 8, 27–28, 123

Social Security, 148
societal approach to debt, 150–51
societal injustice, 80–81
society, 13–14, 23–26, 29–30, 31, 37, 41, 45, 52, 77–80, 87–88, 124, 136, 139, 148, 178, 210–11, 218
Sodom, 42–44, 45, 49, 56, 136
solar projects, 55, 188–89, 220, 223
sole proprietorship, 113, 118
soliciting investments, 219
SolidBlock, 121
Solnit, Rebecca, 22
Solomon, King, 216
solutions privilege, 73
Soros, George, 229
South Africa, 150, 231
South African apartheid, 7–8, 14, 70, 124, 232
South Sea Bubble, 116
Spain, 145–46
special treatment, 61, 64–66, 72
spend-down, 72
spiritual ideals, 48–49
spiritual limit on accumulation and growth, 37
spiritual practice around food, 95–97
spiritual prohibition on interest, 138–39
sponsor organizations, 162
spyware, 93–94
squatters, 44, 258–59n170
SRI. *See* socially responsible investing (SRI)
stability, 225, 232
stakeholders, 60, 69, 157, 188, 228
standards of behavior, 30, 45, 126–28
standards of living, 14, 22
Standing Rock Sioux Tribe, 70, 208
Stanford Social Innovation Review, 129, 151
Stanford University, 47
Starbucks, 205, 229–31

Starting List to Invest for Racial Equity, 195
startup capital, 194, 204, 229
startups, 106, 121, 143
state legislatures, 128, 206
State of Israel, 68, 92, 263n250
state pension funds, 3
State Street, 207–8
state treasurers, 3
stealing, 79, 127, 137
stealing awareness (*gneivat daat*), 35
Sterbuch, Rabbi Moshe, 273n461
Stern Center for Sustainable Business, New York University, 40
St. Louis, Missouri, 151
Stockholm, 182
stock in fossil fuel companies, 182–83
stock market, 2, 8, 29, 50, 86–87, 113, 118, 120–21, 122–23, 131, 158
stock market crash of 1929, 161–62
stock ownership, 87, 122, 124
stocks, 29, 40, 96, 108, 116–17, 120, 143, 148, 162, 189, 272n456. *See also* benchmark; Christian sin stocks
stolen goods, 98, 196, 199, 200–202
stolen labor, 196
stolen objects, 88–89
Stora Enso, 115
Strategic Lawsuits Against Public Participation (SLAPP), 130
strategic plans, 188
Strine, Leo, 212
structural racism, 80
structure of corporations, 11, 121
student loans, 136, 147
stumbling blocks before the blind, 82–87, 91, 98, 110, 122, 127, 131, 177
suffering, 1–2, 3, 14, 24,

71–72, 160
Sufi, Amir, 135–36, 141–42, 146, 147, 151
Sukkot, 32, 224
supply chains, 27, 89, 122, 131, 184, 211, 230
support, obligation to offer, 139
support for Israel, 215–22
surveillance technology, 93–94
sustainability, 1, 3, 4–5, 34, 180, 223–25, 233; sustainable capitalism, 9; sustainable development, 28–30, 37, 216–21; sustainable economy, 158; sustainable energy solutions, 187; sustainable global development, 28–30
Sustainable Development Goals (SDGs), 1, 28–29, 187, 221, 224–25
synagogues, 55, 65, 109, 114, 156, 163, 188
Syria, 230
systemic issues, 36, 51, 71, 185

Tabernacle, 206
Tahboub, Murad, 227
Talmud, 77–80, 206; buying objects that were likely stolen, 88; and cash, 103; character of Sodom, 42–44; commandment to pursue peace, 224; concessionary returns, 48; idolatry, 80–81; Jewish sources, 18–20; *kol yisrael arevin zeh bazeh* (all members of the community are bound up with one another), 172; leaving Israel, 217; loan dollars, 159–61; non-kosher meat, 95; orphan trust funds, 62–64; ownership of work, 123; profit motive, 143–44; restrictions on profit for essential items, 33; stumbling blocks before

the blind, 84–87; *tzedakah* collections, 66; and wealth, 23; weapons in, 90–92; woman's deeds, 160–61; *yetzer hara* (self-centered urge), 24
Tam, Rabbeinu, 145
Tamari, Meir, 9, 19, 20–22, 24, 28, 255n84
Tanakh (the Jewish Bible), 18, 77–78
Taparia, Hans, 50
Tarasava, Yuliya, 194
tax breaks, 158
tax code, 197–98, 213
tax havens, 26–27
tax loopholes, 34
tax system, 198
technologies, 93–94, 160, 164, 187, 217
TechSoup, 164
telecommunications, 152
Temple. *See* Holy Temple in Jerusalem
Temple Israel of Boston, 70, 152
Temple treasury, 60–61, 115
tenant-owned cooperative, 165
teshuvah (repentance and right return), 199, 205, 267n356
Teva, 219–20
Thatcher, Margaret, 13, 27
theft, 88–89, 199
13th Amendment, 89, 198, 210
"This Movement Is Taking Money Away From Fossil Fuels, and It's Working" (McKibben), 182
350.org, 180–81, 190
TIAA, 206
tiered return, 47
timely pay of workers, 211
TJ Maxx, 130
tobacco, 7, 67, 68–70, 86–87, 129, 174–80, 283n657
Toledano, Rabbi Yaakov, 92
tomato rabbis, 210
Ton, Zeynep, 211–12
Torah, 9, 18, 195, 199, 216,
232; aiding and abetting, 83–84, 85, 91, 98; balance, 25; "beware for yourself, and guard your life," 187; business partnerships, 118; character of Sodom, 43–44; and debt, 203; Exodus narrative, 200; idolatry, 77–78; inflexible debt contracts, 143; interest-free loans, 54; investment advisors, 110; Jewish dietary laws, 97; kosher, 95–96; lending at interest, 64, 141; not stand idly by the blood of your neighbor, 67; obligations to care, 139, 210–11, 218; precept can be violated for the sake of saving a life, 89; prohibition on charging interest, 137–38; rebuke, 129; rhythm of Jewish life, 21; *shmita* (Sabbatical) year, 30–31, 61; smoking, 177; stumbling blocks before the blind, 82–86, 98; universal standards, 126–28; usury, 136–40, 148
Tosafot, 48–49
trade associations, 185
trade in arms, 92–95
trademarks, 33
trading in prohibited foods, 95–97, 99
trading with idolaters, 84–85
traditional investing, 8, 9, 129
Transform Finance, 49–50, 150, 152, 202
transgressions, 83–87, 98, 139, 199
transparency, 32, 207, 225
trauma, 36, 72, 283n654
trayf (non-kosher), 95
Treasury bonds, 148
Treasury Department, 105, 202
treasury of the Temple, 60–61
treating workers well, 2–3
trees, 186, 265n293
Trek to Lusaka, 232
Trillium Asset Management, 125, 205
Trump, Donald, 156
trustees, 69
trust funds of orphans, 62–64, 143
Truth and Reconciliation Commission, 209
Tucker, Rabbi Ethan, 96, 267n354
Tulsa, Oklahoma, 196–97
Turei Zahav, 138
Twitter, 35, 73, 204
tzedakah collections, 66
tzelem elohim, 195–96

UJIA (United Jewish Israel Appeal), 70, 215–16, 218, 220, 226
Ujima Fund, 70, 152–53
UK Jewry, 215–16
Ukraine, 229–30
UK Task Force on Arab Citizens of Israel, 226
uncompensated labor, 12
under-invested communities, 202
unemployment, 4, 155
unethical acts, 28, 79, 82–83, 85–86, 91, 121
United Health Group, 69
United Jewish Israel Appeal (UJIA), 70, 215–16, 218, 220, 226
United Methodist Church, 8
United Nations, 1, 173, 187, 208, 224–25. *See also* Sustainable Development Goals (SDGs)
United Nations Declaration on the Rights of Indigenous Peoples, 208
United States, 1–2, 11–12, 14; barriers, 36, 72; carbon footprints, 173; centering racial justice, 193–213; challenges of local investing, 161–62; credit unions, 104–5; discriminatory mortgage lending, 147; Hebrew

Index

Free Loan Societies, 54; individualist extremes, 44; in-group lending, 140; investment advisors, 110; Jewish identity, 79; monopolies, 33–34; private prisons, 88–89; public corporations, 131; public equities, 113; publicly traded corporations, 116–17; shareholder advocacy, 124–26; tobacco, 175, 178; victory gardens, 172; wildfires, 179
United States Capitol, 206–7
United States Institute of Peace, 230
United States Surgeon General, 175
universal standards, 126–28
universities, 115, 180
University of California, 73–74
University of Richmond, 197
University of Zurich, 47, 106–7
UN Principles for Responsible Investment, 74, 109, 118, 252n25
upfront capital, 155
US Agency for International Development (USAID), 230
USAID (US Agency for International Development), 230
US Centers for Disease Control, 35
US college freshmen, 13
US exports, 12
US House and Senate, 3
US Institute for Peace, 230
US South, 11–12
usury (charging interest to someone in need), 81, 119, 121, 136–40, 147–48, 269n386, 270n415
utility companies, 189–90

vagrancy laws, 198

valence, 136
value of human life, 224
value of peacebuilding, 228, 231–32
values and social impact, 48, 52
values-based investing, 1–3; advocacy on climate, 184–86; arguments regarding divestment, 182–83; balance, 24–25; barriers, 35–36; barriers to change, 72–73; charitable causes, 163; concessionary returns, 42, 47; expectations around financial return, 55–56; fiduciary duty, 45–47; helping others while costing nothing, 45; investment advisors, 106–10; Israel bonds, 218; limited-life, 68; negative screens, 82, 99; sacrificing returns, 39–40; shareholder advocacy, 124–26, 180–81; stumbling blocks before the blind, 88; sustainable development goals, 28–30; universal standards, 126–28; voting proxies, 127–28, 130–31, 184, 207–8. *See also* socially responsible investing (SRI)
Vancouver Jewish Federation, 174
Van Eck, 149
Vanguard, 36, 128, 207–8
Vatican, 1, 3, 9, 18, 208, 233
venture capital, 68–69, 106, 107, 220
Vermont, 171
Veterans Administration, 197
victory gardens, 172
Villanueva, Edgar, 10, 19, 72, 79, 149, 151–52, 199
violence, 31, 36, 78, 79, 91, 94, 196–97, 207, 209, 231
Virginia, 116, 206
Virginia Company, 116
voices, 4, 69, 183
volunteer service, 188

voter fraud, 206
voter suppression laws, 207
voting proxies, 69–70, 127–28, 130–31, 184, 207–8, 275n477
voting record, 128, 184
voting rights, 206–7

wages, 27, 211–12
Waldenburg, Rabbi Eliezer, 176–77
Walgreens, 87
Walgreens Boots Alliance, 87
Walken, Rabbi Aharon, 267n354
Wall Street Journal, 109
Walmart, 92, 210, 270n407
Washington Post, 210
waste industry, 171–73
water access, 223
wealth, 2, 8, 12, 17, 20–22, 23, 25, 30, 41–42, 49, 52–55, 66–67, 72, 121, 141; building of, 136, 147, 148, 194, 197–99; caste ladder, 198–99; pay gap, 12, 55, 73, 130, 194, 197–98, 202; redistribution, 109, 203; reparations, 201–2. *See also* extractive capitalism
weapons, 68–69, 89–95, 99, 266n332
weather, 2, 4, 174, 177
welfare, 139
Wells Fargo, 104, 127, 181, 205
Wendy's, 210
Western models, 19
West Indian *susu* system, 140
West Indies, 11
what's mine is mine, 42–44, 136
Wheeler, Tarah, 73
White Earth Band of the Ojibwe, 209
white homeowners, 142
The Whiteness of Wealth (Brown), 197–98
Whitfield, Ed, 13, 196, 199, 202
wildfires, 2, 68, 179

Wilkerson, Isabel, 12, 196, 198–99
window of public opinion, 179
witnesses, 146
woman's deeds, 160–61
women, 3, 8–9, 107–8, 140, 194, 198, 203, 229
women of color, 204, 205, 209, 211
Wooldridge, Adrian, 10, 115
worker-driven social responsibility, 210
Worker Rights Consortium, 211
workers' rights, 2–3, 10, 27, 118, 210–12
workforce preparedness, 155–56
World Bank, 51, 227
WorldCom, 10–11
world governments, 92–94
"The World May Be Better Off Without ESG Investing" (Taparia), 129
World Resources Institute, 186
World War II, 171–72
Wurzburger, Walter, 28

Yadigaroglu, Ion, 50
Yanshoof, 95
Yao, Shu Dar, 157
Yehuda Halevi, 20
Yeshivat Hadar, 96
yetzer hara (self-centered urge), 23–24, 26, 39
yetzer tov (selfless, noble urge), 23–24
Yishmael, Rabbi, 176
yishuv Eretz Yisrael, 216–18, 292n833
yishuv ha'olam, 218
yishuvo shel olam (settling of the world), 29–30
Yitzchak, Rabbi, 103, 106
Yochanan, Rabbi, 217
Yom Kippur, 23, 119, 199, 205
younger generations, 8–9, 47, 56, 71, 216. *See also* Resource Generation
YUM! Brands, 50

Zambia, 232
zeh neheneh ve'zeh lo haser (this one benefits while that one suffers no loss), 67
zero-percent return, 46
Zevin Asset Management, 125
ZORA Ventures, 220, 221

About the Author

Rabbi Jacob Siegel has spent years working with individuals and institutions across North America to bring Jewish values and wisdom to bear on investment decisions and to invest in a climate-smart future. He received rabbinic ordination from Yeshivat Chovevei Torah and earned his undergraduate in mathematics from Washington University in St. Louis. He lives in Eugene, Oregon with his family, where he serves on the board of his local Jewish Federation and his local credit union.

Reflections on the weekly Torah portion from *Ben Yehuda Press*

An Angel Called Truth and Other Tales from the Torah by Rabbi Jeremy Gordon and Emma Parlons. Funny, engaging micro-tales for each of the portions of the Torah and one for each of the Jewish festivals as well. These tales are told from the perspective of young people who feature in the Biblical narrative, young people who feature in classic Rabbinic commentary on our Biblical narratives and young people just made up for this book.

Torah & Company: The weekly portion of Torah, accompanied by generous helpings of Mishnah and Gemara, served with discussion questions to spice up your Sabbath Table by Rabbi Judith Z. Abrams. Serve up a rich feast of spiritual discussion from an age-old recipe: One part Torah. Two parts classic Jewish texts. Add conversation. Stir... and enjoy! "A valuable guide for the Shabbat table of every Jew." —Rabbi Burton L. Visotzky, author *Reading the Book*

Torah Journeys: The Inner Path to the Promised Land by Rabbi Shefa Gold. Rabbi Gold shows us how to find blessing, challenge and the opportunity for spiritual transformation in each portion of Torah. An inspiring guide to exploring the landscape of Scripture... and recognizing that landscape as the story of your life. "Deep study and contemplation went into the writing of this work. Reading her Torah teachings one becomes attuned to the voice of the Shekhinah, the feminine aspect of God which brings needed healing to our wounded world." —Rabbi Zalman Schachter-Shalomi

American Torah Toons 2: Fifty-Four Illustrated Commentaries by Lawrence Bush. Deeply personal and provocative artworks responding to each weekly Torah portion. Each two-page spread includes a Torah passage, a paragraph of commentary from both traditional and modern Jewish sources, and a photo-collage that responds to the text with humor, ethical conscience, and both social and self awareness. "What a vexing, funny, offensive, insightful, infuriating, thought-provoking book." —Rabbi David Saperstein

The Comic Torah: Reimagining the Very Good Book. Stand-up comic Aaron Freeman and artist Sharon Rosenzweig reimagine the Torah with provocative humor and irreverent reverence in this hilarious, gorgeous, off-beat graphic version of the Bible's first five books! Each weekly portion gets a two-page spread. Like the original, the Comic Torah is not always suitable for children.

we who desire: poems and Torah riffs by Sue Swartz. From Genesis to Deuteronomy, from Bereshit to Zot Haberacha, from Eden to Gaza, from Eve to Emma Goldman, *we who desire* interweaves the mythic and the mundane as it follows the arc of the Torah with carefully chosen words, astute observations, and deep emotion. "Sue Swartz has used a brilliant, fortified, playful, serious, humanely furious moral imagination, and a poet's love of the music of language, to re-tell the saga of the Bible you thought you knew." —Alicia Ostriker, author, *For the Love of God: The Bible as an Open Book*

Eternal Questions by Rabbi Josh Feigelson. These essays on the weekly Torah portion guide readers on a journey that weaves together Torah, Talmud, Hasidic masters, and a diverse array of writers, poets, musicians, and thinkers. Each essay includes questions for reflection and suggestions for practices to help turn study into more mindful, intentional living. "This is the wisdom that we always need—but maybe particularly now, more than ever, during these turbulent times." —Rabbi Danya Ruttenberg, author, *On Repentance and Repair*

Jewish spirituality and thought from *Ben Yehuda Press*

The Essential Writings of Abraham Isaac Kook. Translated and edited by Rabbi Ben Zion Bokser. This volume of letters, aphorisms and excerpts from essays and other writings provide a wide-ranging perspective on the thought and writing of Rav Kook. With most selections running two or three pages, readers gain a gentle introduction to one of the great Jewish thinkers of the modern era.

Ahron's Heart: Essential Prayers, Teachings and Letters of Ahrele Roth, a Hasidic Reformer. Translated and edited by Rabbi Zalman Schachter-Shalomi and Rabbi Yair Hillel Goelman. For the first time, the writings of one of the 20th century's most important Hasidic thinkers are made available to a non-Hasidic English audience. Rabbi Ahron "Ahrele" Roth (1894-1944) has a great deal to say to sincere spiritual seekers far beyond his own community.

A Passionate Pacifist: Essential Writings of Aaron Samuel Tamares. Translated and edited by Rabbi Everett Gendler. Rabbi Aaron Samuel Tamares (1869-1931) addresses the timeless issues of ethics, morality, communal morale, and Judaism in relation to the world at large in these essays and sermons, written in Hebrew between 1904 and 1931. "For those who seek a Torah of compassion and pacifism, a Judaism not tied to 19th century political nationalism, and a vision of Jewish spirituality outside of political thinking this book will be essential." —Rabbi Dr. Alan Brill, author, *Thinking God: The Mysticism of Rabbi Zadok of Lublin*

Return to the Place: The Magic, Meditation, and Mystery of Sefer Yetzirah by Rabbi Jill Hammer. A translation of and commentary to an ancient Jewish mystical text that transforms it into a contemporary guide for meditative practice. "A tour de force—at once scholarly, whimsical, deeply poetic, and eminently accessible." —Rabbi Tirzah Firestone, author of *The Receiving: Reclaiming Jewish Women's Wisdom*

Enlightenment by Trial and Error: Ten Years on the Slippery Slopes of Jewish Mysticism, Postmodern Buddhist Meditation, and Heretical Flexidox Spirituality by Rabbi Jay Michaelson. A unique record of the 21st century spiritual search, from the perspective of someone who made plenty of mistakes along the way.

The Tao of Solomon: Finding Joy and Contentment in the Wisdom of Ecclesiastes by Rabbi Rami Shapiro. Rabbi Rami Shapiro unravels the golden philosophical threads of wisdom in the book of Ecclesiastes, reweaving the vibrant book of the Bible into a 21st century tapestry. Shapiro honors the roots of the ancient writing, explores the timeless truth that we are merely a drop in the endless river of time, and reveals a path to finding personal and spiritual fulfillment even as we embrace our impermanent place in the universe.

Embracing Auschwitz: Forging a Vibrant, Life-Affirming Judaism that Takes the Holocaust Seriously by Rabbi Joshua Hammerman. The Judaism of Sinai and the Judaism of Auschwitz are merging, resulting in new visions of Judaism that are only beginning to take shape. "Should be read by every Jew who cares about Judaism." —Rabbi Dr. Irving "Yitz" Greenberg

Recent books from *Ben Yehuda Press*

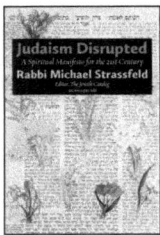

Judaism Disrupted: A Spiritual Manifesto for the 21st Century by Rabbi Michael Strassfeld. "I can't remember the last time I felt pulled to underline a book constantly as I was reading it, but *Judaism Disrupted* is exactly that intellectual, spiritual and personal adventure. You will find yourself nodding, wrestling, and hoping to hold on to so many of its ideas and challenges. Rabbi Strassfeld reframes a Torah that demands breakage, reimagination, and ownership." —Abigail Pogrebin, author, *My Jewish Year: 18 Holidays, One Wondering Jew*

The Way of Torah and the Path of Dharma: Intersections between Judaism and the Religions of India by Rabbi Daniel Polish. "A whirlwind religious tourist visit to the diversity of Indian religions: Sikh, Jain, Buddhist, and Hindu, led by an experienced congregational rabbi with much experience in interfaith and in teaching world religions." —Rabbi Alan Brill, author of *Rabbi on the Ganges: A Jewish Hindu-Encounter*

Liberating Your Passover Seder: An Anthology Beyond The Freedom Seder. Edited by Rabbi Arthur O. Waskow and Rabbi Phyllis O. Berman. This volume tells the history of the Freedom Seder and retells the origin of subsequent new haggadahs, including those focusing on Jewish-Palestinian reconciliation, environmental concerns, feminist and LGBT struggles, and the Covid-19 pandemic of 2020.

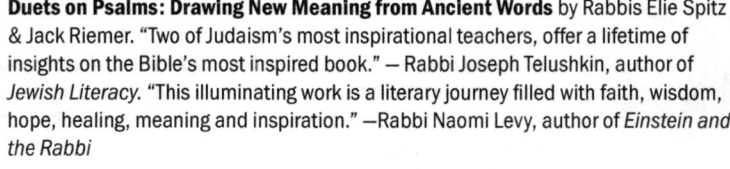

Duets on Psalms: Drawing New Meaning from Ancient Words by Rabbis Elie Spitz & Jack Riemer. "Two of Judaism's most inspirational teachers, offer a lifetime of insights on the Bible's most inspired book." — Rabbi Joseph Telushkin, author of *Jewish Literacy*. "This illuminating work is a literary journey filled with faith, wisdom, hope, healing, meaning and inspiration." —Rabbi Naomi Levy, author of *Einstein and the Rabbi*

Weaving Prayer: An Analytical and Spiritual Commentary on the Jewish Prayer Book by Rabbi Jeffrey Hoffman. "This engaging and erudite volume transforms the prayer experience. Not only is it of considerable intellectual interest to learn the history of prayers—how, when, and why they were composed—but this new knowledge will significantly help a person pray with intention (*kavvanah*). I plan to keep this volume right next to my siddur." —Rabbi Judith Hauptman, author of *Rereading the Rabbis: A Woman's Voice*

Renew Our Hearts: A Siddur for Shabbat Day edited by Rabbi Rachel Barenblat. From the creator of *The Velveteen Rabbi's Haggadah*, a new siddur for the day of Shabbat. *Renew Our Hearts* balances tradition with innovation, featuring liturgy for morning (*Shacharit* and a renewing approach to *Musaf*), the afternoon (*Mincha*), and evening (*Ma'ariv* and *Havdalah*), along with curated works of poetry, art and new liturgies from across the breadth of Jewish spiritual life. Every word of Hebrew is paired with transliteration and with clear, pray-able English translation.

Forty Arguments for the Sake of Heaven: Why the Most Vital Controversies in Jewish Intellectual History Still Matter by Rabbi Shmuly Yanklowitz. Hillel vs. Shammai, Ayn Rand vs. Karl Marx, Tamar Ross vs. Judith Plaskow... but also Abraham vs. God, and God vs. the angels! Movements debate each other: Reform versus Orthodoxy, one- two- and zero-state solutions to the Israeli-Palestinian conflict, gun rights versus gun control in the United States. Rabbi Yanklowitz presents difficult and often heated disagreements with fairness and empathy, helping us consider our own truths in a pluralistic Jewish landscape.

Recent books from *Ben Yehuda Press*

Reaching for Comfort: What I Saw, What I Learned, and How I Blew it Training as a Pastoral Counselor by Sherri Mandell. In 2004, Sherri Mandell won the National Jewish Book award for *The Blessing of the Broken Heart*, which told of her grief and initial mourning after her 13-year-old son Koby was brutally murdered. Years later, with her pain still undiminished, Sherri trains to help others as a pioneering pastoral counselor in Israeli hospitals. "What a blessing to witness Mandell's and her patients' resilience!" —Rabbi Dayle Friedman, editor, *Jewish Pastoral Care: A Practical Guide from Traditional and Contemporary Sources*

Heroes with Chutzpah: 101 True Tales of Jewish Trailblazers, Changemakers & Rebels by Rabbi Deborah Bodin Cohen and Rabbi Kerry Olitzky. Readers ages 8 to 14 will meet Jewish changemakers from the recent past and present, who challenged the status quo in the arts, sciences, social justice, sports and politics, from David Ben-Gurion and Jonas Salk to Sarah Silverman and Douglas Emhoff. "Simply stunning. You would want this book on your coffee table, though the stories will take the express lane to your soul." —Rabbi Jeff Salkin

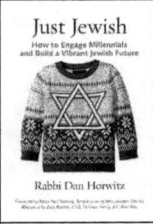

Just Jewish: How to Engage Millennials and Build a Vibrant Jewish Future by Rabbi Dan Horwitz. Drawing on his experience launching The Well, an inclusive Jewish community for young adults in Metro Detroit, Rabbi Horwitz shares proven techniques ready to be adopted by the Jewish world's myriad organizations, touching on everything from branding to fundraising to programmatic approaches to relationship development, and more. "This book will shape the conversation as to how we think about the Jewish future." —Rabbi Elliot Cosgrove, editor, *Jewish Theology in Our Time*.

Put Your Money Where Your Soul Is: Jewish Wisdom to Transform Your Investments for Good by Rabbi Jacob Siegel. "An intellectual delight. It offers a cornucopia of good ideas, institutions, and advisers. These can ease the transition for institutions and individuals from pure profit nature investing to deploying one's capital to repair the world, lift up the poor, and aid the needy and vulnerable. The sources alone—ranging from the Bible, Talmud, and codes to contemporary economics and sophisticated financial reporting—are worth the price of admission." —Rabbi Irving "Yitz" Greenberg

Why Israel (and its Future) Matters: Letters of a Liberal Rabbi to the Next Generation by Rabbi John Rosove. Presented in the form of a series of letters to his children, Rabbi Rosove makes the case for Israel — and for liberal American Jewish engagement with the Jewish state. "A must-read!" —Isaac Herzog, President of Israel. "This thoughtful and passionate book reminds us that commitment to Israel and to social justice are essential components of a healthy Jewish identity." —Yossi Klein Halevi, author, *Letters to My Palestinian Neighbor*

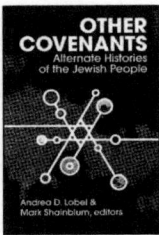

Other Covenants: Alternate Histories of the Jewish People by Rabbi Andrea D. Lobel & Mark Shainblum. In *Other Covenants*, you'll meet Israeli astronauts trying to save a doomed space shuttle, a Jewish community's faith challenged by the unstoppable return of their own undead, a Jewish science fiction writer in a world of Zeppelins and magic, an adult Anne Frank, an entire genre of Jewish martial arts movies, a Nazi dystopia where Judaism refuses to die, and many more. Nominated for two Sidewise Awards for Alternate History.

www.ingramcontent.com/pod-product-compliance
Lightning Source LLC
Chambersburg PA
CBHW050548160426
43199CB00015B/2576